Defining Chu

Defining Chu

Image and Reality in Ancient China

EDITED BY

CONSTANCE A. COOK AND

JOHN S. MAJOR

UNIVERSITY OF HAWAI'I PRESS

HONOLULU

04 03 02 01 00 99   5 4 3 2 1

Library of Congress Cataloging-in-Publication Data
Defining chu : image and reality in ancient China /
    edited by Constance A. Cook and John S. Major ;
    contributions by Barry B. Blakeley . . . [et al.].
        p.   cm.
    Includes bibliographical references and index.
    ISBN 0-8248-1885-7 (cloth : alk. paper)
        1. China—Civilization—To 221 B.C.   2. China—Civilization—
To 221 B.C.—Historiography.   3. Historiography—China.
I. Major, John S.   II. Cook, Constance A.   III. Blakeley, Barry B.
IV. Title: Image and reality in ancient China.
DS741.65.D44   1999
931—dc21   99–27952
                                               CIP

Frontispiece: Detail of a bronze figure at the base of the Zheng Hou
Yi bell stand [after Hubeisheng bowuguan 1991]

University of Hawai'i Press books are printed on acid-free paper
and meet the guidelines for permanence and durability
of the Council on Library Resources.

Designed by Diane Gleba Hall
Printed by The Maple-Vail Book Manufacturing Group

Contents

Color plates follow page 126

Preface

What Does "Defining Chu" Mean?

Constance A. Cook

and John S. Major

Exhausted and corrupt, a state called Chu collapsed in 223 BCE[1] under military pressure from a northwestern state called Qin. Chu had been pushed out of its homeland in central China by the expanding state of Qin over the course of the Warring States period, 481–221 BCE. By the time of its defeat in 223 BCE, Chu existed only in the newly conquered eastern and southern fringes of its formerly massive territory. The military thrust of northern and western peoples to the resource-rich lands of the south and east began with the Zhou over a millennium earlier. By the time China's first empire was established by Qin, the different peoples from all corners of the ancient Chinese world would have experienced a long history of interaction and mutual influence. Chu peoples, originally located just southeast of the Zhou homeland in modern Shaanxi Province, had likewise been both the subject and object of military and diplomatic intercourse for hundreds of years before their self-proclaimed status as a legitimate kingdom.

After the disintegration of Zhou lineage domination in the eighth century BCE, the Chu polity grew in strength and began its own campaigns for military domination of the east and south. In the process Chu became a conduit for intercourse between peoples of all regions. Before Chu was crushed by the Qin it had, at its military peak, threatened to dominate all of early China. Despite its political defeat, the intense cultural mix that had become identified with the Chu polity over the course of history was reinvented by the Han emperors after the short-lived Qin rule. In order to provide a spiritual and romantic antidote to the harsh laws of the Qin, Han period writers were encouraged to preserve the images and songs of what they remembered as Chu, an exotic shamanistic culture of southern and southeastern barbarians. The Han established a subkingdom named Chu near the ancestral burial ground of its first emperor; its capital, Pengcheng (modern Xuzhou, Jiangsu), became a center of Daoist and early Buddhist cult activity. This eastern kingdom, along with the southern kingdom of Changsha, established around the mythic Dongting Lake region in modern Hunan, represented for the Han the spirit of Chu. It is the image of this spirit that has persisted up to modern times and what we will use as a foil against which to compare the image of a real Chu, one currently emerging from the material remains—texts, tombs, and cities—excavated from the original territory of the Chu state in the Han River valley in modern Hubei and Henan.[2]

Much of our book is devoted to describing and analyzing the Warring States period construction of the Chu polity as it moved farther and farther from its original homeland, absorbing as it went the customs and culture of the peoples it dominated. Eventually, over the course of the book, we see the emergence of the constructed Chu *image* from historical *reality*—a reality argued according to each author's interpretation of archaeological or historical materials that they accept as *defining Chu*.

Chu culture—a complexity of institutions and beliefs that evolved over time—has fascinated the Chinese since the Han period. This book is simply an attempt to present for the Western reader a glimpse of the twentieth-century image of Chu, as presented in a recent flurry of articles and books by archaeologists and scholars.[3] It is impossible for one book adequately to represent the entire field of Chu studies—our debt is too great. We leave the analysis of the post-Han images of Chu as a topic for specialists in those periods. We shall simply express here our gratitude to those interpreters of pre-Qin data who came before us and paved the road to this book. Noel Barnard and K. C. Chang in particular have produced studies critical to our emerging understanding of Chu. As early as 1959, long before the discovery of the Mawangdui tomb complex in 1972, Barnard called for "a complete re-appraisal of the culture of this 'barbarian' state."[4] In that same year, K. C. Chang published a study of Neolithic archaeological material that connected the early cultural history of south China to the larger archaeological context of Pacific Basin cultures.[5] Barnard added to this effort in 1974 with an unsurpassed edited volume of scholarly research on the links between the arts of these cultures.[6] His 1973 work on the Chu Silk Manuscript influenced a number of chapters in this volume;[7] we are proud to include in our own book Li Ling's masterful translation of that very difficult and recalcitrant document.

The discovery of southern texts from tombs during this century, such as the Chu Silk Manuscript and the Mawangdui Han tomb materials, revealed the sophistication of the south but at the same time reinforced the traditional image of a literate Chu culture centered in the Changsha region; archaeological materials discovered in recent decades have radically altered that view, and our review of the present state of the field reflects the influence of this new material. It is in answer to Barnard's original call for a reappraisal of the evidence, and in response to K. C. Chang's plea for the integrated study of cultures past and present,[8] that we dedicate the effort of this book.

The editors also owe many people and institutions credit for their help and inspiration. We are grateful to Martha Avery of Avery Press, Inc., for her encouragement in the early stages of the book and for allowing us to use slides from her collection. For their work on the maps and figures, we thank the following Lehigh University staff and students: Zhong Yin and

Tan Xiaodong of the Earth and Environmental Sciences Department, Patrick Sheridan and Johanna Brams of the International Media Resource Center, and the staff of Media Production at Linderman Library. Anne Holmes, Rob Rudnick, and Sabrina Starnaman worked on the bibliography. We thank Jessica Rawson and Carol Michaelson of the British Museum for their help on short notice. Financial support for production of the book came from the editors, especially John Major; from the individual authors, especially Barry Blakeley; and from Lehigh University. Constance Cook's research was supported by the Center for Scholarly Communication with the Peoples Republic of China (National Academy of Sciences) and Lehigh University.

Introduction

CONSTANCE A. COOK

AND BARRY B. BLAKELEY

THE state of Chu occupied the southern fringe of ancient China's heartland. From a small base in the west, it expanded in all directions. At one point, in the sixth century BCE, it came within a political hair of dominating all of China. Three centuries later the state was crushed, but the image of "Chu" has survived in the Chinese consciousness as a poetic symbol of an alternative, slightly barbarous culture—one that existed outside the mainstream of proper Confucian society and civilization. Archaeological evidence confirms the evolution of a distinctive southern culture, but it also reveals a level of sophistication that challenged and surpassed that of its northern neighbors with the advent of the Han. Evidence also reveals that in both areas the high culture was deeply rooted in recognizable earlier Zhou and Shang cultural foundations, so that the south and the north, far from being strangers to each other, were in fact blood relations. Chu culture was a synthesis of transmitted high culture and the numerous regional cultures absorbed during its expansion. It was a force so strong that when rebels first rose up against the oppressive, unifying Qin dynasty at the end of the third century BCE, their cry was "Great Chu shall rise again!"—and so it did, revived first in name by the rebel leader Xiang Yu and later in spirit by Liu Bang, the first emperor of the Han.[1]

The Northern Bias

THE historical and archaeological records of the Eastern Zhou Chu state give a conflicting view of southern culture from the eighth through the third centuries BCE. A typical modern survey of Chinese history gives the impression that all Chinese culture diffused from northern China, the lands surrounding the middle and lower valleys of the Yellow River and its tributaries. The fruits of the archaeological efforts of the past half century or so, however, have made it increasingly evident that this conventional view is only partly correct. It is clear now that in fact Chinese civilization is a synthesis of cultural elements drawn from various areas, including the south. Unfortunately, what is evident from archaeological research has not yet affected the mainstream of historical writing about China. Sinologists still cherish the traditional text-based view of the south, a view that we term the "Northern Bias."

The Northern Bias derives both from the Chinese reverence for the written words of antiquity and from the fact that the most ancient of surviving historical texts were written by court scholars with northern roots. As Confucianism was established as state orthodoxy (during the Han period, in the first century BCE), these early texts were adopted as classics and became the foundation for Chinese historical consciousness. Since these texts framed the past in terms of three northern dynasties—the Xia, the Shang, and the Zhou—southern contributions were ignored. The tendency to equate civilization with the Confucian culture of the court is apparent even in the great book of the famous Han historian, Sima Qian: the *Shiji* (Records of the Archivist), of about 100 BCE. Although he traveled to the south and expressed sympathy with Daoism, a religion he associated with Chu, Sima Qian still described Chu in the imperialist terms of a northerner.[2]

Questions of Origin

SIMA Qian described the Han region of Chu-Yue (a general term for the south by then) as vast, fertile, and relatively unpopulated. The people, he claimed, were lazy and poor, living hand-to-mouth off the plentiful rice, fish, and fruit. Free from the fear of freezing to death or going hungry, they made no effort to store up for hard times.[3] In his chapter on the royal house of the Eastern Zhou period Chu state, he quoted an ancestral ruler of Chu as saying, "We are southern barbarians" (*manyi*, literally, fringe Yi-peoples).[4]

The conception of the Chu as barbarians appeared earlier in the *Guoyu* (Conversations of the states), written late in the Warring States period (481–221 BCE). There is a record of a conversation between northern military men contemplating the material bounty of Chu in a manner similar to the later Sima Qian: "since the Chu are *manyi*, they are unable to treasure it."[5] The *manyi* heritage is given historicity when the *Shiji* records that an early Chu lord, Xiong Yi, served King Cheng of Zhou (late eleventh century BCE) and was awarded the land of the Chu *man*,

Ancient Chinese graph "Chu" from the Zhongzi Hua *pan* [after Zhang Yu et al. *Jinshi dazidian.* Taipei, 1973 reprint, 304]

"the barbarians of Chu." One of Xiong Yi's descendants, Xiong Qu, after pacifying the peoples between the Jiang and Han Rivers, claimed independence from the Zhou, called himself a *manyi*, and set his sons up as kings of various southern regions. This independence lasted until the Zhou King Li's reign (mid-ninth century BCE), when Xiong Qu, fearing Li's belligerence, backed down.[6]

Constance A. Cook and Barry B. Blakeley

The northern association of an ancient Chu-Jing region with "barbarians" can be traced to the Western Zhou period (1056–771 BCE). In Western Zhou bronze inscriptions, southerners, referred to both as *manyi* and *nanyi* (southern Yi-peoples), were the objects of repressive military campaigns. Zhou warriors were rewarded for capturing people and booty, most particularly in the form of metal.[7] Inscriptions proclaimed the "taming" of the Chu and Jing peoples, noting that the leaders of the *man* came to the Zhou court, no doubt bearing gifts.[8] The word *chu* at that time did not refer to a specific state, but to a region coterminous with the Jing region. A Han etymological dictionary defines the words *chu* and *jing* as clusters of prickly bushes, "barbs," connoting wild lands. The early graph representing the word *chu* shows a foot surrounded by vegetation. While this graph represents a place name as early as 1200 BCE, during the Shang period, there is currently no material culture that can be unequivocally identified as Chu until after the end of the Western Zhou period in the eighth century BCE.[9]

Ancestors

THE Chinese scholarly obsession with tracing the ancestral and tribal roots of the Chu has necessarily begun with Sima Qian's account of the Chu lineage. There we see the Han scholars' own obsession with tracing all peoples back to astral deities. While late Warring States and Han texts are inconsistent in their naming of the high gods of Chu, all associate them with the sun, fire, or heat: the gods Gao Yang (High Sun-essence), Yan Di (Flame God), and Zhu Rong (Invoking Melter; also known as *huozheng,* Fire Corrector). Of these, only Zhu Rong is attested in pre-Han texts, such as the *Zuozhuan*. Recent bamboo divination texts from fourth-century BCE tombs in the Jiangling region list three divine ancestors: Lao Tong (Old Boy), Zhu Rong, and a mysterious female by the name of Yu Yin, a loan for Yu Xiong, traditionally believed to be an early tribal leader of the Chu people. Yu Xiong may have been a Chu manifestation of Nügua and Zhu Rong of Fuxi, anthropomorphized deities of Yin and Yang, thus providing a pre-Han locus for Yin-Yang thought in Chu.[10]

Shamans and Lewd Rites

BAN Gu, author of the *Han Shu* (Book of Han), added to Sima Qian's already negative view of the south. Ban Gu claimed that in the Jiangnan region, the region he understood to be Chu, the people employed shamans in the worship of "ghosts and spirits" *(guishen)* and placed great weight on *yinsi* (excessive, or lewd, rites)—a term used by Han and later writers to describe the religious practices of other peoples. These regional practices involved great expenditures, dancing and singing, animal sacrifices, and the use of shamans, exorcism, or prayers to local gods.[11] They were the practices, in fact, that the Han emperors were obsessed with, much to the distress of their Confucian ministers.[12]

The kingdom of Chu most familiar to Han historians was actually a new state of Chu that rose in rebellion against the harsh Qin rule. This Chu and another, both in northern Jiangsu, later resurrected by the Han for the worship of their ancestral spirits, represented just a northeastern fraction of the territory left over from the late Warring States stronghold of Chu power in the Huai River valley.[13] The original population of that region was known in the Zhou period texts as Yi peoples of the Huai River valley (the *huaiyi*) and were distinguished from the Eastern Yi *(dongyi)* and Southern Yi *(nanyi)*.[14]

Eastern Zhou period archaeological records directly contradict the Zhou and Han historical accounts of the Chu. Recent archaeological discoveries reveal an affluent Chu elite with a strong Zhou bias that was gradually modified as the state pushed east and south in its quest for resources and power. Although archaeology at present does not reveal much about the ethnic identities or lives of commoners, it does suggest that the Chu state absorbed many communities of different peoples—peoples that at an earlier stage might be classified by Chinese archaeologists as Yue and by Han dynasty Chinese as Yi-barbarians; peoples whose worship of *gui* (spirits) had also been deplored in Han historical sources.[15]

The religious practices and beliefs associated with Chu and Yue—use of shamans in the worship of ghosts and spirits—most likely referred to local variations of ancient practices that can be attested at least back to the Spring and Autumn period (770–481 BCE) and probably as far back as the Shang. The fact that the Han historians label them "excessive" reveals not only their own lack of historical perspective, but also that, by the Han period, these rites had become associated with classes of people or cultural elements the court elite wished to repress. In an attempt to reorient the imperial identity away from Chu culture and to demote the literati of Chu regions, such as those at the court of Huainan, the term "Chu" became associated with local *man* traditions, and thus all of Chu—past, present, and future—was demoted to barbarian status.[16]

Changsha

POPULAR imagination (including elements handed down from Han times), reinforced by the discovery in the twentieth century of late Warring States period and Han period tomb treasures in Changsha, led to the conventional view that Chu culture was centered in the middle Yangtze valley. While there is no question that this valley, a cradle of cultural interaction among many different peoples, contributed immeasurably to what would by Han times be thought of as Chu culture, it was not the center of Chu activity during its military peak, from the sixth to the third centuries BCE. During that period, the attention of the Chu rulers was focused on the Huai River valley and the Nanchang Basin.[17] Changsha for the Chu was a military outpost called Linxiang (Overlooking the Xiang River), maintained most likely to facilitate trade.[18] The strategic importance of this region was recognized by the Han.[19] Shortly after 202 BCE Han Gaozu, the first emperor of Han, sent Wu Rui, a native of the southeastern lake region—the former territory of Yue—to turn the Qin garrison into the kingdom of Changsha.[20]

Jia Yi (ca. 200–168 BCE), a northerner from Luoyang, made the kingdom resonate with the spirit of Qu Yuan (ca. 340–278 BCE), a Chu minister popularly thought of as the author of the *Chuci,* the only collection of poetry traditionally associated with Chu culture.[21] Qu Yuan, like Jia Yi, had been exiled from court to this "low and wet" land of no return. Qu Yuan committed suicide by jumping into the Milo River, but Jia Yi, after contemplation of Qu Yuan's watery grave, went on to Changsha as tutor to the Wu family.[22] Despite the horror both men apparently felt for the Changsha region, the shamanistic songs of the *Chuci,* rich with imagery of the Dongting Lake region, evoke in the Chinese mind a romantic image of Chu, the land of poetic tristesse and divine trysts.[23]

The Real Chu

IN what follows, the coauthors of this book join forces in an attempt to define Chu. But it will become obvious to readers as they move through each author's contribution that a culture that might be defined as Chu at one point in time would not necessarily fit the Chu of another point in time. One is forced to conclude, in fact, that there was no single real Chu; rather, we should say that there were many Chu, with the Han-period image merely representing one layer in a long history of how that elusive entity has been defined.

PART I

Perspectives in Defining Chu Culture

I

The Geography of Chu

BARRY B. BLAKELEY

FROM a very meager territorial base at the outset, Chu eventually absorbed over sixty states and a number of tribal peoples.[1] The result was a virtual empire, covering about one-half of the Chinese world of the time. Within this empire were various regional cultural traditions, and this raises fundamental questions concerning the nature and evolution of Chu culture: what elements were native to the Chu people? How much was a legacy from the Shang and Zhou? What was derived from the peoples Chu conquered? When did the various elements enter the matrix? Answering these questions is complicated by two critical issues. The first is that the locations of two critical capital cities have yet to be determined archaeologically. This means that we do not as yet have a clear picture of the metropolitan culture through most of the history of the state. Second, and as a result, the bulk of archaeological evidence generally taken to relate to Chu culture derives from peripheral areas. And the fact that these materials also are from relatively late phases of Chu history raises the question as to what extent "Chu culture" as currently understood is a late, peripheral phenomenon. Obviously, then, an understanding of the geography of Chu history is fundamental to any consideration of Chu culture.

Relations with the Western Zhou Court

THE history of the Chu state was played out entirely during the tenure of the Zhou dynasty.[2] In late Shang times Zhou was centered in the Wei valley (Shaanxi Province). Its relations with the Shang (centered to the east, in the North China Plain) were mixed, and it eventually resisted Shang domination under kings Wen (d. 1050) and Wu (r. 1049–1043). In 1046 or 1045 it succeeded in overthrowing the Shang.[3] For nearly three centuries thereafter the Zhou capital remained in the western homeland,[4] but in 770 the court was forced to move eastward to Luoyang (northwest Henan, near the Yellow River), the event that demarcates the Western and Eastern Zhou periods.

According to the *Shiji,* the Chu leader Yu Xiong served King Wen as a ritualist,[5] and this hint that there were relations between Chu and Zhou before the conquest of the Shang may be confirmed by a recently discovered inscription.[6] After the conquest, during the reign of King Cheng (r. 1043–1006), it is recorded that the Chu leader Xiong Yi, who served at the Zhou court, was enfeoffed among the Chu *man,* at Danyang, and sent tribute to the Zhou king.[7] Also during these years, the famous Duke of Zhou (a regent for the young King Cheng) reportedly sojourned in Chu at a troublesome point in his career.[8] Amicable relations between the two parties seem to have continued until the middle of the tenth century, when King Zhao (r. 977–957) launched campaigns against Chu (in 960 and 956), at least in part in quest of ores.[9] During the second campaign the king and some of his troops were drowned, although whether this was due to any action on the part of Chu is difficult to say.[10] In any case, before long Chu resumed dispatching tribute to the Zhou court. Thereafter, the Chu attitude toward their Zhou overlords seems to have wavered,[11] and Zhou attacked it again in 823.[12] The outcome of this final record of Chu-Zhou relations in the Western Zhou period is not clear, but Chu probably went its own way as Zhou power went into decline in the early eighth century.

When Chu reappears on the historical stage, at the end of the eighth century, it was beginning to expand along the southern fringe of the Zhou ecumene. Before turning to that story, however, we need to examine the question of the geographical locus of Chu down to that point.

The Locations of Danyang and Ying

THERE is no question that through most of its history (early seventh to late third centuries) the core of the Chu state was in western Hubei and southwestern Henan. The Han-period *Shiji* tells us (as seen above) that Chu was centered at Danyang[13] in early Zhou times and that Ying became the capital in about 690 and remained so until 278.[14] If we accept the *Shiji* record, the location of Danyang is clearly an essential key to finding the roots of Chu culture. On the other hand, the location of Ying is important in discerning the evolution of Chu culture during the long phase (some four centuries) in which the state expanded into ever-widening geographical and cultural spheres.[15]

Three types of evidence come into play in the debates over the locations of these capitals: clues buried in early geographical sources, analyses of Chu foreign relations, and archaeological evidence.[16] Opinions on the locations of Danyang and Ying fall into two general camps, the Southern School and the Northern School.[17] The Southern School (which has a long tradition behind it) places both capitals in southwest Hubei, along the Yangtze River: Danyang in Zigui and/or Dangyang Counties,[18] and Ying at Jinancheng, a settlement just north of the seat of Jiangling County (Jingzhou) (fig. 1.1). The Northern School (of more recent vintage) argues that both capitals were situated considerably further north: Danyang in the Dan valley (Shaanxi / Henan) and Ying at a site known as Chu Huangcheng, in Hubei's Yicheng County (not far south of the Bend of the Han River at modern Xiangfan) (fig. 1.2).

In locating Danyang the name itself is a clue, since it signifies either south of a Dan mountain or hill or north of a Dan river. Arguments for the former (employed only within the Southern School) are extremely forced and rely on relatively late evidence. On the other hand, the river known even today as the Dan bore this name from quite early times (at least by the third century BCE). It is, therefore, the best clue to the location of Danyang and is an important point in favor of the Northern School view. On the archaeological front, recent surveys and excavations along the Yangtze have eliminated the Southern School's Zigui suggestion and, for all intents and purposes, its Dangyang one (at Jijiahu, slightly northwest of Jinancheng) as well. On the other hand, recent finds in the Dan valley (the Xiasi tombs[19]) lend some support to the Northern School suggestion. Until more concrete evidence emerges from the ground, however, the strongest evidence in favor of this view is its proximity to the Western Zhou royal domain: the intimate ties between Chu and Zhou in Western Zhou times outlined above are more easily understood from the perspective of Chu being situated in the nearby Dan valley than along the quite distant Yangtze.[20]

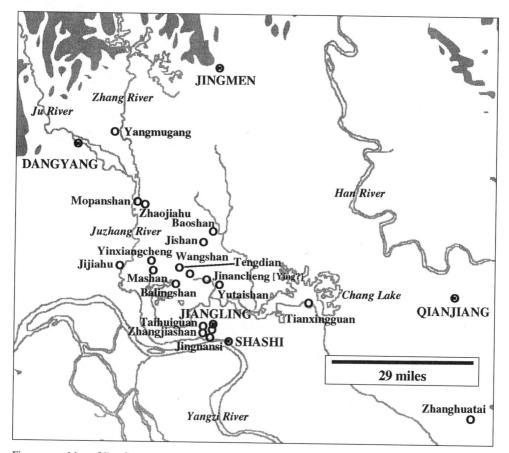

Figure 1.1 Map of Jiangling region [by Zhong Yin, Tan Xiaodong, Barry Blakeley]

The Geography of Chu

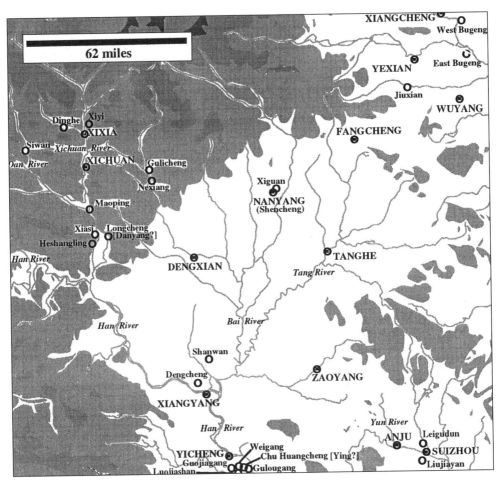

Figure 1.2 Map of Upper Hanxi, Nanyang Basin, and Dan River valley regions [by Zhong Yin, Tan Xiaodong, Barry Blakeley]

The name "Ying" provides no clue to its location. A thorough evaluation of centuries of geographical commentary, however, seriously deflates the Jinancheng (Southern School) view and provides considerable support for the Chu Huangcheng (Northern School) hypothesis.[21] Archaeologically, while Jinancheng was a city of impressive size and one with clear-cut Chu cultural connections, the remains there are generally of Warring States time and thus are too late to represent the Ying of Spring and Autumn times.[22] Consequently, some Southern School scholars have nominated Jijiahu (not far northwest of Jinancheng). Some of the tombs in the vicinity are early enough to support this contention, but none are elite burials and the date of settlement itself is too late.[23] In any case, historical geography offers nothing in favor of this proposal. At Chu Huangcheng (the Northern School candidate) only preliminary archaeological surveys have so far been made, with as yet inconclusive results.[24] This site, however, is far closer to the geographical nexus of foreign relations and expansion (discussed below) than is either Jinancheng or Jijiahu.

Barry B. Blakeley

In sum, the best evidence currently available places Danyang in the Dan valley, and Ying just south of the Bend of the Han.

The Move to Hubei

IF Danyang was in fact north of the Han River, two further questions arise. First, since the move to Ying did not take place until around 690, there must have been another capital in the interim. We have no name, however, for such a capital (usually also referred to, confusingly, as Danyang), and suggestions for a location are either illogical or purely conjectural.[25] The second question— when Chu moved southward—is based on the view that Danyang was in the Dan valley (north of the Han River) and that Ying was in Hubei (south of the Han). Recent studies have provided a definite terminal date; a military campaign in 699 clearly began somewhere south of the Han River in Hubei's Yicheng County;[26] and Chu military activities in the years preceding that seem to indicate that campaigns were launched from a Hubei base as early as 706.[27] Moving backward in time, an episode in the mid- to late ninth century is equivocal,[28] but much has been made of the 956 attack on Chu launched by King Zhao alluded to earlier. Some claim that the Zhou king and his troops drowned in the Han River. If so, the Zhou army must have attempted to cross the river from north to south, and this has been taken to mean that Chu was situated below the Han (in Hubei) by that time. This reference to the Han River, however, is somewhat suspicious,[29] as none of the bronze inscriptions dealing with the episode mention it.[30] Moreover, even if the Zhou troops did cross the Han River, this does not necessarily mean that Chu was situated south of it.[31] The most that can be said at present, then, is that Chu was in Hubei by 706 and that there is a possibility (but no irrefutable evidence) it was there by the mid-tenth century.

From all of the above, it should be clear that the locations of Danyang and Ying remain uncertain on both historical and archaeological grounds. Not until this is rectified will we have an adequate basis on which to determine either the eleventh-century roots of Chu culture or its metropolitan form in the long Ying phase (ca. 690–278). Fortunately, tracing Chu expansion in Eastern Zhou times faces far fewer difficulties.

Territorial Expansion (710–ca. 400)

The Setting

THE authority of the Zhou royal house after its move eastward to Luoyang in 770 was merely symbolic. Real power was in the hands of the lords of territorial states, who competed fiercely to fill the political void and become *ba* (Hegemon) and to force their smaller, weaker neighbors into submission. In this, Chu was a major player.[32] The strongest and most long-term counterweight to Chu ambitions was the state of Jin, centered just north of the Yellow River. Jin and Chu fought over the allegiance of the smaller states located in the plain south of the Yellow River: from west to east, Zheng, Xu,[33] Cai, Chen,[34] and Song (all in Henan), Lu and

Qi (both in Shandong). Chu's major competitors outside the Yellow River Plain were Wu and Yue, in the extreme southeast,[35] and Qin (which had taken over the original Zhou homeland in the Wei valley), in the west. Qin would eventually sweep east during the Warring States period and, in 221, unify the entire land into a single state. Chu was the most stubborn obstacle to this, and its fall was one of the very last steps in the process of Qin unification.

We turn now to a survey of the regions that were eventually encompassed within the Chu realm, each of which was to a greater or lesser extent a distinct cultural sphere.

The Chu heartland through most of its history, in western Hubei and southwestern Henan, can be subdivided as follows: Hanxi (West of the Han), the broad area of Hubei south and west of the Han River; Handong (East of the Han), the lands bordering the Dahong mountains; the Dan valley; and the Nanyang Basin of southwestern Henan. Areas added to this core were concentrated north and east of the Nanyang Basin, the northern rim of which is defined by a string of steep hills known in ancient times as Fangcheng.[36] On this basis, the area north and east of the basin was known as Fangcheng Wai (Outside Fangcheng[37]). Farther east lay the Huai valley, which may be divided into the Upper Huai (west of its conjunction with the Ru River, in Henan), the Middle Huai (between the Ru and the course of the ancient Sha River,[38] in Anhui), and the Lower Huai (eastward from the Sha, in Anhui and Jiangsu). Huaibei (North of the Huai) is an ancient term referring to the area north of the Middle and Lower Huai (in Anhui, Jiangsu, and southern Shandong, including the Si valley). Below this and north of the Yangtze lay Huainan (South of the Huai, in Anhui and Jiangsu), the eastern portion of which became the realm of Wu and, later, Yue. To the south of Huainan (below the Yangtze River) was the area known as Jiangdong (East of the Yangtze River), in southern Anhui and Jiangsu, as well as northern Jiangxi and Zhejiang. Finally, below the Chu heartland was Jiangnan (South of the Yangtze).

With this picture in mind, we may turn to an examination of the course of Chu expansion and contraction.[39]

Creation of a Hubei Sphere of Influence (710–689)

The onset of Chu expansion was undoubtedly influenced by the weakened power of the Zhou court after 770, but what internal factors may have been at play are lost in the mists of history. The first allusion to Chu in the Spring and Autumn period, dating to 710, relates that the lords of the states of Cai and Zheng (along the outer edges of Fangcheng Wai) met out of "fear of Chu."[40] We are not informed what prompted this, but Chu pressures on Handong, the Dan valley, or both could have been involved. A more reasonable explanation is that Chu was beginning to cast a covetous eye on the Nanyang Basin, which lay in the direction of both Cai and Zheng.[41] In any case, their concern was a bit premature, as Chu attention remained focused on targets farther south for some time.

Between 706 and 690 Chu launched a series of assaults on various Hubei states—in Handong (against Sui and Yun[42]), in Hanxi (against Luo, LuRong, and Jiao[43]), and along the southern edge of the Nanyang Basin (Deng[44]). A glance at the map in fig. 1.2 is sufficient to show that all of these lay in the area around the Bend of the Han, so it is clear that Chu was trying to carve a sphere of influence in that area.[45]

Barry B. Blakeley

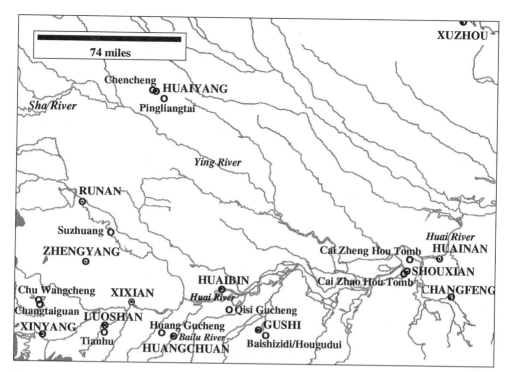

Figure 1.3 Map of Huai valley region [by Zhong Yin, Tan Xiaodong, Barry Blakeley]

At this point Chu may have been content with expressions of loyalty from most of its neighbors, but it did incorporate one or two Hanxi states (Quan and, perhaps, Ran[46]). And if (as the Northern School would have it) Chu was centered just south of the Bend of the Han at this time, it would stand to reason that the same fate befell any other states below the Bend,[47] some just west of the Bend,[48] and several in Handong.[49]

Expansion Northward: Formation of the Fangcheng Perimeter (688–656)

Having extended its sway over its immediate environs, Chu set out on a new mission: during the next three decades it pushed into the Nanyang Basin and carved out a zone beyond it in Fangcheng Wai.[50] Shen (at the heart of the basin) was attacked in 688, and this was soon followed by marches against states on the edges of Fangcheng Wai (Cai, Zheng, and Xi[51]). As for territorial acquisitions, in the basin itself, Shen and its neighbor, Lü,[52] must have fallen early in this phase, and Deng succumbed in 678. It stands to reason that Liao, to the east, fell as well. (Within the basin, only Tang is known to have survived to later times.[53]) Beyond the basin the western portion of Fangcheng Wai (below the Ru River) was swallowed up; and (eastward) Xi became the first acquisition in the Upper Huai valley.

Chu experienced not a single defeat in these years. Nevertheless, its attacks on Zheng and Cai portended a thrust into the heart of the Yellow River Plain and prompted an array of states there to unite under the leadership of Qi (at the time fulfilling the role of Hegemon), since this presented the unwelcome prospect of a thrust into Fangcheng Wai. Chu concluded a pact with the coalition and turned its attention to the Huai valley.

The early years of this phase coincided with the decline of the leadership role of Qi and a failed attempt by Song to replace it as Hegemon. Chu was involved in all of this but focused its territorial aims on the Huai region. In rather quick succession (655–645) it incorporated the Upper Huai states of Xuan and Huang and the northwest Huainan state of Ying (or Ying-shi). After the famous defeat of Chu at Chengpu in 632 Jin rose to the position of Hegemon, forcing Chu to redirect its attention to the Fangcheng Perimeter. The result was a long, see-saw struggle between the two (632–546),[54] in which the small states along the fringe of Fangcheng Wai were pulled first one way and then another. All of this, however, did not deter Chu in its *drang nach Osten*. It absorbed Jiang (on the north bank of the Huai) in 623, and Fan the following year.[55]

The thrust into Huainan also intensified. Lyao was taken in 622, so Jyang (to the west) probably had fallen before that.[56] Zhoulai (eventually the most strategic spot in the Middle Huai valley) must have been taken over before the end of this era, and the absorption of Liu (just south of Zhoulai) opened an uncontested route into eastern Huainan. There, the remaining polities (the Shu states[57]) pledged allegiance to Chu, but an independent spirit (encouraged by Wu) persisted, prompting Chu to incorporate Chao (the most northerly of the group[58]) and (in 601) ShuLiao (farther south). In that year Chu also concluded a pact with Wu and Yue, which kept them from wooing the Shu states for a quarter century. This also allowed Chu to direct its attention to Fangcheng Wai, leading to a major defeat of Jin and its allies in 597, at the Battle of Bi.

Meanwhile, Chu gained a foothold in western Huaibei in 637. This opened a route through the northern tier of the area and made possible the incorporation of Xiao (in eastern Huaibei) in 597. The Chu push in that direction, however, was soon cut off by a major new threat.

The Struggle with Wu over the Middle Huai (584–508)

Wu began to impinge on Chu hegemony in the Huai valley and Huainan in 584 with strikes at Zhoulai and the small state of Tan (eastern Huaibei). Within a decade, Wu had achieved a temporary foothold at Chu expense along the Middle Huai.[59] It was during this time (575) that Chu experienced a serious defeat at the hands of Jin and its allies, at the well-known Battle of Yanling. Perhaps because of this, Chu went on the offensive elsewhere—in Huainan, absorbing another Shu state (574) and soon launching its first foray into Wu territory.[60] Periods of peace and war alternated thereafter, during which Wu involved itself directly in the affairs of western Huainan in 549–548, resulting in Chu's incorporation of yet another of the Shu states.[61] The northern frontier (Fangcheng Wai) achieved stability soon thereafter (546–545), when Jin and Chu reached an accommodation (amounting to an unofficial joint hegemony).

The confrontation with Wu heated up in the 530s.[62] For about two decades the struggle was centered in the Huai valley proper, with some Wu excursions into western Huainan. Wu began to get the upper hand in 519, when it incorporated Xyu (just above the Lower Huai) and occupied Zhoulai. The latter was the key to the Upper Huai, and in 511 the first Wu push into that region (an attack on Xuan) occurred. In 508, Wu brought the Shu states of western Huainan under its banner and occupied Chao. By that point Wu was in control of the Middle and Lower Huai and had a protective cushion to the south. The scene was set for a dramatic turn of events.

Invasion, Recovery, and Renewed Expansion (507–ca. 400)

The route through the Upper Huai region toward the Chu heartland now was open to Wu. Seeing this, Chu's erstwhile client states and most of the major states of the plain joined the Wu cause, leading to the greatest humiliation Chu had ever experienced. In 506–505, Wu pushed into the Chu heartland and occupied its previously inviolate capital, prompting the king to flee for sanctuary to Handong. Chu recovery from this crisis was facilitated by a succession dispute in Wu and by aid from Yue (in the east) and Qin (in the west). Consequently, the Wu forces were pushed back down the Huai.[63] In the meantime, Chu destroyed Tang (in the Nanyang Basin) for having defected.

The historical record is frustratingly (and curiously) blank thereafter until 496,[64] so the details of the Chu reoccupation of the Upper and Middle Huai are unknown. When the curtain reopens, we find Chu avenging itself by destroying two of the Fangcheng Wai states— Dun and Hu—that had deserted it during the crisis.[65] Then, in response to Wu pressures on Chen to defect, Chu incorporated the territory of Chen in 478.[66] In the meantime, Chu had attacked Wu's staunchest ally, Cai (at the time situated in the Lower Ru valley, near the Huai). This prompted Cai to move once again (493), this time eastward to Zhoulai, becoming a Wu client.[67] Much to the relief of Chu, Yue then became involved in a struggle with Wu and destroyed it in 473. Chu then retook Zhoulai from Cai (447), and, having inherited Wu's Huaibei lands along the Si River from Yue (445), went on to absorb the small state of Ju.

For the Warring States period the sources are far more sketchy and less reliable. It is clear, however, that by about 400 Chu's four centuries of almost uninterrupted expansion had come to an end.

Contraction and Fall (ca. 400–223)

CHU's long-time arch rival Jin broke up into three successor states (Han, Zhao, and Wei) in the middle of the fifth century. Han and Wei were the principal problems for Chu, as they expanded into the plain below the Yellow River. By about 400, Wei had taken over lands of two second-rate powers (Wey and Cao), and it soon (365) moved its capital to Kaifeng. In the meantime (375), Han had incorporated Zheng and then moved its capital there. These developments radically changed the military dynamics along Chu's northern frontier. After the accommodation with Jin in 546, Chu had for the most part been able to keep the states in and bordering the Fangcheng Wai area under its control. With Han and Wei now centered below the Yellow River (Huanghe), this was no longer the case.

Chu's focus on the east after the Wu invasion may have weakened its stance along the northern frontier. Encounters with Han (to the north) and Wei (to the northeast), especially the latter, led to a seesaw exchange of territories, with Wei even occupying parts of Fangcheng Wai at times.

Meanwhile, there were problems far to the west, in Sichuan, where Ba[68] launched an attack in 377. Chu then built up a defensive line along the upper Han River (the Hanzhong region[69]), but by the end of this phase an even more serious threat appeared in that quarter as Qin pushed southward into Sichuan.[70] Chu, however, continued to devote considerable effort to expansion in the east, taking the Huaibei area around Xuzhou from Qi in 333.[71]

316–278

There is no doubt that the single most significant event in the balance of power in Warring States times was the Qin conquest of Sichuan (Ba and Shu) in 316.[72] This creation of a Qin base on Chu's western flank could only portend a major struggle between the two. This struggle began in earnest in 312, when the two traded blows in the Dan and Han valleys, resulting in losses of Chu territory. Qin soon returned some of what it had taken (in Hanzhong), but a decade later it colluded with Chu's enemies in the plain, resulting in Chu's loss of portions of Fangcheng Wai. Within a few years the entire Dan valley was in Qin hands. The Nanyang Basin was thus exposed, and much of it was soon taken from Chu. Before long, however, Chu and Qin became allies for a time (311–282), and Chu took advantage of this respite (in 286) to reappropriate Huaibei lands earlier taken by Song. Southward, Yue lands in Jiangdong were evidently in Chu hands by the end of the third century.[73]

Chu's fate was sealed in 281, when hostilities with Qin resumed. Within three years what remained to Chu of Hanzhong, the region south of it (Qianzhong[74]), and the remainder of the Nanyang Basin had been lost. This thoroughly exposed the Chu core, and Qin pressed on and occupied it (including Ying) in 278.[75] The Chu court then fled northward to Henan, where it set itself up at the former seat of Chen.[76] From there, Chu launched a counter-offensive, but to little avail.

With the entire western realm lost, there was little option but to solidify and expand the eastern one. Chu experienced some minor setbacks there, but one of its major additions was the lands of Yue.[77]

277–223

Expansion in eastern Huaibei continued between about 264 and 256, as Chu took over a string of small states (Pi, Zhu, Xiao [small] Zhu, Fei). The ultimate target was the ancient and proud state of Lu, which Chu erased from the map in 256.[78] With virtually the entire east now under its control, Chu shortly thereafter (253) moved its capital from Chen slightly southward to Juyang.[79] After a failed attempt to mobilize the surviving states of the plain against the Qin juggernaut, Chu shifted its capital once again (in 241) to a still more secure location (Shouchun), on the southern bank of the Huai, near Zhoulai.[80] In the meantime, Qin had put an end to the Zhou royal house in 256 and then in a few short years (230–225) conquered the principal powers of the plain (Han, Zhao, and Wei). This provided Qin with a base from which to begin an assault on Chu's haven in the east, the approaches to which had been left exposed by the move to Shouchun. Qin defeated a Chu force in western Huaibei (225). Chu managed one final victory the following year and even launched a counteroffensive into Hubei, but Qin responded with a march into Huaibei and then on to Shouchun, which fell in 223. A last-ditch Chu stand was made in Huainan, but to no avail, and the Chu state (but by no means its memory) came to an end.

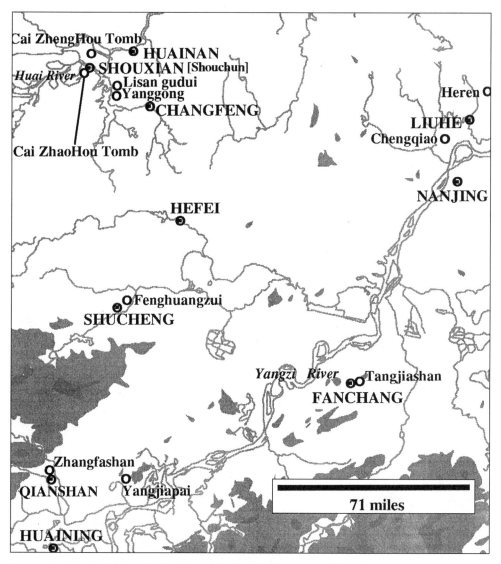

Figure 1.4 Map of Anhui region [by Zhong Yin, Tan Xiaodong, Barry Blakeley]

The Geography of Chu

· 19 ·

Chu in Jiangnan

ANALYSTS in much later times offered rather confident assessments concerning the geography of Chu expansion below the Yangtze, ones that have heavily influenced modern archaeological analysis.[81] Nevertheless, various factors complicate the issue.[82]

There are chronologically widely spaced references to Chu control over Yue groups presumed to have been situated in Hunan, one from the seventh century (Spring and Autumn period)[83] and two from the early fourth century (Warring States period).[84] However, the seventh-century account smacks heavily of postfacto hagiography, is historiographically suspect, and is improbable from a chronological standpoint;[85] and with respect to all allusions to Yue groups there are serious problems in locating them and related place-name clues.[86] Two other allusions to Chu activity in Jiangnan (dating to the sixth century) are no more helpful.[87]

In sum, there is precious little textual evidence to go on in tracing Chu activity in Jiangnan, and most of what is available is of questionable help. The most that can be said is that it is reasonable to assume Chu activity below the Yangtze intensified after the crisis of the Wu invasion at the end of the sixth century.[88]

Conclusion

IN general terms, the territorial history of Chu was as follows: just before the turn of the seventh century Chu set out on what was to be a three-century campaign of expansion. There were setbacks, but when opposition stiffened in one quarter, Chu simply shifted its attention to others. The first objective was to create a sphere of influence around the Bend of the Han, a task that was completed by the early seventh century. Chu then immediately set out to gain control of the Nanyang Basin and the approaches to it (Fangcheng Wai). The next targets were the Upper Huai region and western Huainan. This brought on an inevitable conflict with Wu, resulting in the most serious crisis for Chu in Spring and Autumn times. Basic recovery was relatively quick, however, and Chu set out to solidify its control over Fangcheng Wai, to regain its eastern territories, and to expand upon them.

The age of expansion faltered in the early fourth century, eventually leading to the loss of Fangcheng Wai, thereby focusing Chu attention on the east. The penultimate struggle (with Qin) began in the late fourth century, leading to the losses of Hanzhong, the Nanyang Basin, Fangcheng Wai, and eventually (in 278) the heartland as well. Shifting its base to the northeast, there followed intense efforts to expand in Huaibei in order to create a defensible haven. Within decades, however, the capital had to be moved still farther east, and Qin then nibbled away at what territory remained to Chu and swallowed the last morsel in 223.

2

Chu Culture

An Archaeological Overview

XU SHAOHUA

Emergence of a Distinctive Chu Culture

THERE is little archaeological evidence of a distinctive Chu culture during the Western Zhou times.[1] The earliest inscribed Chu ritual bronzes—bells and vessels—most likely date to the end of the Western Zhou period or the beginning of the Spring and Autumn period, and in shape and style are virtually identical to northern examples.[2] Only in the excavated materials from tombs located in the southern Hanxi region of Hubei, such as those of Zhaojiahu in Dangyang, can we detect the incipient rise of a distinct culture.[3]

Zhaojiahu: Early Chu Culture

THE earlier of the Zhaojiahu burials date from the early to the beginning of the middle Spring and Autumn period. The structure of the tombs, the shapes of the bronze and ceramic burial items, and the composition of the ritual vessel sets all reflect Central Plains patterns— a fact that has led archaeologists to understand Chu elite culture as originating in the north. Only the shapes of some bronze vessels and the actual composition of the sets deviate slightly from Central Plains influence in ways that are later to be considered characteristic of Chu. By the late Spring and Autumn period, for example, the contents of Zhaojiahu tombs clearly represent different cultural concerns than those in the north. The distinctive traits evident in the ritual bronze sets, their vessel shapes, decor, and calligraphic styles all point to the emergence of a divergent cultural pattern.[4]

Emergence of a Chu Culture

MIDDLE and late Spring and Autumn period burials provide the clearest evidence for the beginning of a distinct Chu culture, although the interpretation of this evidence—tomb structure and the sets, shapes, decor, and technology of ritual bronzes—by archaeologists continues to be a subject of debate.

Chu tombs, like those of the north, generally consisted of vertical pits without mounds or ramps (entrance passageways). Bodies were placed in double (inner and outer) wooden coffins. Unlike the tombs of the north, Chu tombs—at least large elite tombs—were oriented to the east.[5] The majority of the smaller tombs, on the other hand, were oriented to the south.[6] In northern tombs, the heads of the bodies were generally oriented to the north, with the exception of Qin tombs, in which heads were oriented to the west.

Early Spring and Autumn period ritual vessels were arranged in typical Zhou-style sets consisting of a *ding* (a cauldron with legs for cooked meats and stews) and a *gui* (a round, lidded vessel on a square base for cooked grains). By the middle Spring and Autumn period the *gui* vessel had been replaced by a *fu* (a flat, rectangular-shaped grain vessel). The number of *ding* vessels, considered a status symbol, also varied. In the north, *ding* usually came in odd-numbered sets, whereas in the Chu region most of them are found in even-numbered sets.[7] Besides the *ding* and *fu,* the Chu ritual set included, as in the north, a *pan* (large round bowl for liquids) and *yi* (a tureen-style vessel for liquids), as well as a *zhan* (a squat, lidded bowl) and *yufou* (a squat urn), both unlike northern types. By the late Spring and Autumn period a *dui* (a bowl and lid forming a sphere with legs above and below) frequently replaced the use of a *zhan* in Chu tombs. This also occurred in the north, but with less frequency.[8]

As the vessel sets changed in composition, so, too, did their shape and decor, resulting in the emergence of a distinct Chu style of vessel. We see, for example, in the Xiasi tombs of Xichuan, Henan, a number of unique vessels. Most outstanding was a set of *ding* vessels with flat bottoms, concave sides, high, outward-curving "ear"-style handles, and numerous ornate flanges. This type of *ding* was called *shengding*. Another unique Chu *ding* is called a *shiding*—characterized by its three legs and deep, round belly, a lid, and vertical "ear"-style handles. Other unusual vessels include a round-bellied, small-mouthed *guanyuding* with upright handles (with an upper section resembling a *gui* but the lower section consisting of three short feet like a *zhan* vessel); a spherical *dui* vessel with three feet on the lower half and round or

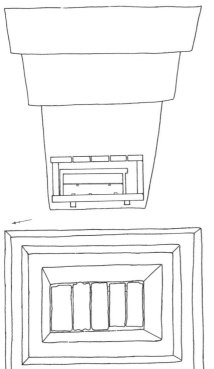

Figure 2.1 Classic Chu tomb [courtesy of Xu Shaohua]

Xu Shaohua

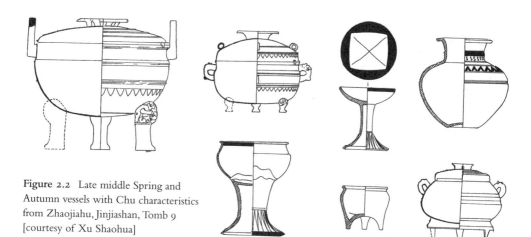

Figure 2.2 Late middle Spring and Autumn vessels with Chu characteristics from Zhaojiahu, Jinjiashan, Tomb 9 [courtesy of Xu Shaohua]

animal knobs on the upper half; a round-bodied, flat-bottomed *yufou* with flanges, handles, and whorl patterns on the shoulders; and a *he* vessel (similar to a teapot) with a handle, three feet, and an animal-shaped spout.

Before the middle Spring and Autumn period, Chu bronzes were largely of utilitarian character with little surface decoration. Over time the decor became increasingly sophisticated so that by the time of the Xiasi burial, bronzes were covered with elaborate designs: we see strange beasts climbing the sides, zoomorphic designs on the knobs, feet, and handles, as well as highly ornate flanges. Later tombs in Chu client states such as Cai in Shouxian, Anhui, and Zeng in Suixian, Hubei, reveal vessels clearly influenced by this ornate style.[9]

Also prior to the middle Spring and Autumn period, the bronze decor was typical of the north, with patterns Chinese archaeologists describe as the "ragged curve" pattern, the "descending fish-scale" pattern, and the coarse "interlaced hydra" pattern. Later the decor became more detailed and unique. We find on Chu vessels an intricate interlaced hydra pattern,

a coiled serpent pattern, and "cloud-in-triangle" patterns joined by "twisted rope" and "banana leaf" patterns.

During the late Spring and Autumn period we see an increasing tendency toward even greater intricacy and complexity in such designs as the "dragon-phoenix" and "beast-bird" patterns, which can be found in sites in Zhaojiahu, Xiasi, or Shanwan in Xiangyang, Hubei.

Figure 2.3 Bronze base for a pole-drum, Tomb of Zeng Hou Yi, Suixian [courtesy of Avery Press]

Chu bronze vessels, like earlier Zhou bronzes and contemporary northern vessels, were at first cast in combined or section molds. In the Xiasi burials we find the use of lost-wax and soldering techniques evident in the open-work interlaced coiled dragon decor. The Chu Xiong Shen *zhan* of the Freer Gallery is a result of these new techniques.

By the end of the Spring and Autumn period Chu artisans began to inlay bronzes with copper, turquoise, and lacquer. A *yufou* from Xiasi, for example, is covered with inlaid copper animals.

Sources of Distinctive Chu Features

SOME features accepted as diagnostic of a Chu culture (which emerged during the Spring and Autumn period in southwestern Henan and in northern Hubei) existed earlier in the north. One example is the *ding* and *fu* ritual set.[10] Chu artisans also incorporated features developed from earlier models in the east.[11] The flat-bottomed *shengding* is typical of Chu tombs of this period and is clearly derived from earlier models (such as the Western Zhou period Ke *ding*) and the *ding* from the more easterly sites of Jiaxian and Liujiayan.[12]

Borrowing from even farther east, from the Huai River valley, legendary home of the Eastern Yi peoples, the Chu developed a penchant for even, rather than odd, numbers of vessels in their mortuary ritual sets.[13] Another loan from this region includes the small-mouthed *yuding*, a vessel unknown in the north.[14]

Another source of artistic inspiration for Chu artisans was the Jiang-Han plain (the regions of Hanxi and Handong in Hubei). A ceramic *li* vessel (a shallow bowl supported on three tapering triangular legs) from this region with no direct stylistic northern precedent is commonly referred to as the "Chu-style *li*." It seems to derive from proto-Shang and Shang-period *li* vessels that have been discovered both in the Jiang-Han region and in more northerly Shang sites.[15] Also borrowed from the Jiang-Han region was the Chu practice of surrounding the outer coffin with sticky greenish gray and white clays as a method of preservation. The tendency to orient burials toward the east may also have come from this region, as no other source for this practice is yet known.

Chinese archaeologists understand the Chu region during the Spring and Autumn period to be centered in southwestern Henan and the northern and central Han River valley. The material culture represented a northern base with an overlay of features seen earlier at sites in eastern regions and the Jiang-Han plains.

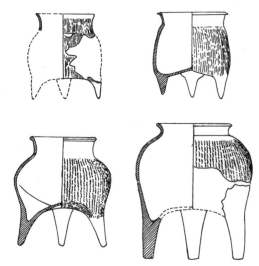

Figure 2.4 Evolution of Chu-style pottery *li* vessel. Upper vessels from Panlongcheng, Hubei (Shang period), lower vessels from Zhaojiahu, Dangyang, Hubei (Spring and Autumn period) [courtesy of Xu Shaohua]

Xu Shaohua

Warring States Period Developments

As the territory under Chu political dominance expanded to the south and east, so, too, did the repertoire of distinctive features employed by Chu artisans. These features are evident in the structures of tombs believed to be occupied by members of the Chu elite, the ritual sets and other burial goods found in the tombs, and the decor and technology exhibited in the burial goods.

Tombs in the north did not typically include mounds and ramps, although this tendency changed during the Warring States period. Tombs associated with Chu elite, however, often included large mounds, possibly signifying social rank, and pronounced ramps. Chu burial chambers tended to be larger and deeper, with the sides of the pit terraced and sloping downward—and with the number of terraces or steps increasing with the social rank of the occupant. The outer coffin was divided into sections along the sides, head, and feet, for the placement of mortuary offerings. There could be as many as nine compartments as in Chu King You's tomb (Shouxian, Anhui).[16]

The greatest change in burial goods was the decreasing emphasis placed on bronze and the increased use of iron, lacquer, and wooden objects.[17] The standard ritual sets of bronze vessels were replaced with lacquerware or imitation bronze vessels made out of pottery painted in red and black designs typical of bronzes: cloud, lozenge, interlaced hydra, bow, and thunder patterns. Sets of these vessels included the *ding, dui,* and *hu* (tall curvilinear, small-mouthed vase for liquids) combination or the *ding, fu,* and *hu* combination. Either might be paired with a *pan* or *yi*. By the late Warring States period the *fanghu* and *he* replaced the standard *dui* and *fu* set. Also during this period we see the appropriation by the lower elite of ritual sets formerly limited to the upper elite. These sets not only increased in number, but in the variety of vessel types included as well.[18]

The inner coffins were brightly painted with lacquer and the compartments were filled with painted lacquer earcups, *he, zun* (cylindrical vases with bulbous midsections and flared mouths), *dou* (round, lidded

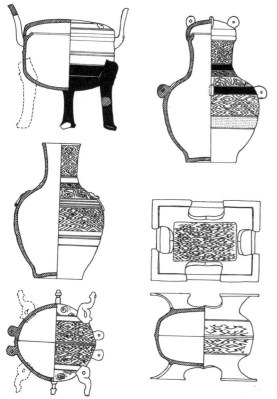

Figure 2.5 Classic Chu painted pottery, late middle Warring States period, Jiangling, Jiudian, Tomb 296. Clockwise from upper left: *ding, hu, fu* (2 views), *dui, hu* [courtesy of Xu Shaohua]

bowls on a pedestal), *zu* (altar tables), *zhenmushou* (tomb guardians), and bird-and-tiger drum-stands. As the bronzes that remained became plainer in decor, the lacquers exhibited a fusion of red, yellow, and gold geometric designs, animal or phoenix patterns, or whorl patterns against a black background. Lacquer was applied in repeated layers over cores of wood, bamboo, leather, and hemp cloth. Artisans might add appliques of gold or bronze (features found both in Jiangling and Anhui sites) or prick designs through the surface.[19] Other colors, such as blue, green, and white, were used more sparingly but can be seen on a zither found in Xinyang (pl. 1) and a round box found in Baoshan (pl. 2) (both sites are in the Jiangling region). A multicolored lacquer screen, discovered in Wangshan, Jiangling, consists of fifty-one finely carved and painted animals (pl. 3).

In a strip around the Baoshan lacquer box are painted five scenes depicting men in chariots, trees, flying birds, and standing human figures.[20] The execution of these figures suggests artisan links with the silk paintings of men with dragons and phoenixes found in Chu tombs of the Chen Jia Dashan site in Changsha.[21] The design and weave of colorful silk fabrics found both in Jiangling and Changsha area tombs also reinforces the suggestion of links between the artisans of the two regions.

The number and quality of iron objects discovered in the Chu-dominated region has led scholars to suggest that China's earliest center for smelted iron may have been a Chu operation. Artisans in northern Hunan not only worked with iron but were capable of making carbonized steel.[22]

The material culture of the Chu-occupied territory during the Warring States period reflected great social change—a departure from Zhou-dominated patterns of ritual usage to the development of its own style, itself a clever amalgam of borrowed decor and technology. Although the political elite of Chu might be credited with bringing these characteristics together into something Chinese archaeologists can identify as Chu culture, the fact remains that Chu culture was a combination of many mini-regional patterns of use and fashion (cultures). We see that while Chu artisans homogenized their manipulation of regional features into a Chu style, regional variations continued to persist.

Regional Variations in Chu Culture

THE expansion of the Chu state did not eradicate regional differences within the state. Here I will discuss the most important Chu regions; for sites referred to in this section and other important sites as well, see the following list.

Important Chu Archaeological Sites

Hanxi Region	Zhangjiashan [25]	Mopanshan [28]
Settlement Sites	Jingnansi [26]	Yangmugang [29]
Jiangling County		
Jinancheng [23]	*Dangyang County*	*Qianjiang County*
Yinxiangcheng [24]	Jijiahu [27]	Zhanghuatai [30]

Yicheng County
Chu Huangcheng [31]
Guojiagang [32]
Gulougang [33]

Tomb Sites
Jingmen County
Jishan [34]
Guodian [35]
Baoshan [36]

Jiangling County
Yutaishan [37]
Balingshan [38]
Taihuiguan [39]
Tianxingguan [40]
Wangshan [41]
Tengdian [42]
Mashan[42]

Dangyang County
Zhaojiahu [43]

Yicheng County
Luojiashan [44]
Luogang [45]
Weigang [46]

The Nanyang Basin
Settlement Sites
Xichuan County
Longcheng [47]
Siwan [47]

Xixia County
Xiyi [48]
Dinghe [48]

Neixiang County
Gulicheng [48]

Nanyang County
Shencheng [48]

Xiangyang County
Dengcheng [49]

Tomb Sites
Xichuan County
Xiasi [50]
Maoping [51]
Heshangling [52]

Nanyang County
Xiguan [53]

Xiangyang County
Shanwan [54]

———

Handong
Settlement Sites
Sui County
Anju [55]

Yunmeng County
Chu Wangcheng [56]

Tomb Sites
Leigudun [57]

———

Eastern Hubei
Settlement Sites
Echeng County
E Wangcheng [58]

Daye County
Caowang Zuicheng [59]

Tomb Sites
Echeng County
Baizifan [60]

———

Fangcheng Wai
Settlement Sites
Wuyang County
East Bugeng [61]

Xiangcheng County
West Bugeng [61]

Huaiyang County
Chencheng [62]

Shang Cai County
Cai Gucheng [63]

Tomb Sites
Ye County [64]

Huaiyang County
Pingliangtai [65]

Shang Cai County [66]

———

The Upper Huai
Settlement Sites
Xinyang County
Chu Wangcheng [67]

Huangchuan County
Huang Gucheng [68]

Gushi County
Liao Gucheng [69]

Huaibin County
Qisi Gucheng [70]

Tomb Sites
Xinyang County
Changtaiguan [71]

Luoshan County
Tianhu [72]

Zhenyang County
Suzhuang [73]

Gushi County
Baishizidi [74]

———

Huaibei and Huainan
Tomb Sites
Shucheng County [75]

Huailin County [76]

Fanchang County [77]

Shou County
Cai Zhao Hou mu [78]
Chu Yu Wang mu [79]

Huainan County
Cai Sheng Hou mu [80]

Liuhe County [81]

Changfeng County
Yanggong tomb complex [82]

Qianshan County [83]

Qingjiang County (Jiangsu)
Gaozhuang mu [84]

———

Jiangdong
Tomb Sites
Suzhou City (Jiangsu)
Huqiu [85]

Wuxi City (Jiangsu)
Eling Jun, Wuxi [86]

Wu County
Heshan [87]

Wujin County
Menghe [88]

Shaoxing County (Zhejiang)
Fenghuangshan [89]

Shanghai City
Jiading [90]

———

Jiangnan
Settlement Sites
Northern Hunan sites
Shimen [91]
Xiangyin [92]
Linli [93]

Pingjiang [93]
Mayang [93]
Taoyuan [93]
Cili [93]

Tomb Sites
Hunan sites
Yueyang [94]
Changde [94]
Chenzhou [95]
Zixing [96]
Mayang [97]
Guzhang [98]
Changsha [99]
Liuchengguo [100]
Niuxingshan [101]

Jiangxi sites
Pingxiang [102]
Xinjian [102]

Hanxi

There are numerous settlements and tombs in the Hanxi region dating from the early Spring and Autumn period to the late Warring States period. The more important settlement sites include those in Jiangling, Dangyang, Qianjiang, and Yicheng Counties. Thousands of tombs are distributed in the vicinity of these settlements, of which over one thousand have been excavated. The most important tomb complexes are listed in the table. For the Spring and Autumn period the settlements and accompanying tombs are concentrated in Dangyang and Yicheng, and for the Warring States period, in the Jiangling area.

Before mid-Spring and Autumn times the cultural features in this area are rather varied. For instance, while the hilly, western portion shows a strong Ba/Shu cultural influence (cultures centered in Sichuan), the lower hill areas and riverine plains exhibit more Central Plains features. It was only from the middle Spring and Autumn period on that the distinctive Chu features described above become more apparent and extended throughout the region.

The Nanyang Basin and Its Environs

The material cultural pattern here before middle Spring and Autumn times was entirely consistent with that of the Central Plains; but (as in Hanxi) from middle Spring and Autumn on, Chu cultural features become evident. The principal Chu-related settlement sites in the region are found in Xichuan, Xixia, Neixiang, Nanyang, and Xiangyang Counties. Collectively, these constitute the greatest concentration of walled settlements in the entire Chu realm. This was undoubtedly a result of the early (Western Zhou) development of the area, but it was also related to the strategic importance of the area in terms of Chu military actions to the north (Fangcheng Wai) and east (Huai valley). The major tombs excavated to date in this area (over two hundred) are distributed mainly in relation to the Longcheng, Dengcheng, and Shencheng settlements. These tombs are among the earlier and most elaborate of the over five thousand Chu tombs excavated to date. In fact, the Xiasi complex is the single most important tomb group so far found, a function of both its largely undisturbed state and the quality and diagnostic importance of the contents.[103] This seems to have been the cemetery of the notable Wei lineage (its most important tomb being that of the Lingyin Wei Zipeng).

Handong

The archaeological record for the northern segment of Handong extends from the Western Zhou period up through the Warring States period. Until the middle Spring and Autumn period the material remains in this area clearly follow the Central Plains cultural pattern. But from the middle Spring and Autumn period, some characteristics similar to Chu culture appear there, albeit with some distinctive features.[104] This can be seen in the tomb structure and the composition and shapes of ritual vessel sets in tombs 1 and 2 of Leigudun. Known settlement sites here include Anju in Suixian, which was probably the capital of Sui. Farther

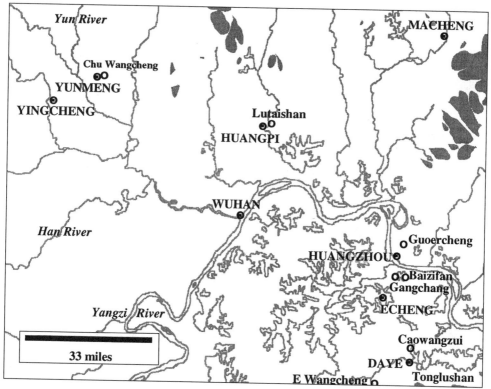

Figure 2.6 Map of Lower Hanxi and Middle Yangtze valley regions [by Zhong Yin, Tan Xiaodong, Barry Blakeley]

south, Chu Wangcheng, in Yunmeng, appears to have been an important Chu outpost during the Eastern Zhou period.

Eastern Hubei

Before late Spring and Autumn times eastern Hubei fell within what is generally considered to be the Yue cultural pattern, but thereafter Chu characteristics become apparent. The principal Chu-related settlement sites, all of Eastern Zhou date, are E Wangcheng in Echeng, and Caowang Zuicheng in Daye. Particularly notable is the mining complex at Tonglushan in Daye, which must have been a major source of copper for the Chu smelters.[105] Some Chu-style tombs here may date to as early as late Spring and Autumn times, but most are of Warring States date.[106] That some of these are from the late Warring States period suggests continued Chu presence in this area after the fall of the Hanxi heartland to Qin in 278. However, few of the Warring States tombs contained complete ritual bronze sets, and thus the majority of the tombs in these areas, with the exception of Baizifan tomb 5, at Echeng, belonged to commoners. In these tombs we find ceramic sets (composed of *ding, dui,* and *hu* or *ding, he,* and *hu*) mimicking bronze forms, and lacquered wood *zhenmushou* sculptures and tiger-and-bird sculpted drumstands. The frequency of the ceramic and lacquer ware suggests a cultural similarity with the Hanxi heartland.

Fangcheng Wai

Before Chu penetration into this region, the material culture, including that of the states of Chen, Cai, and Ying, was the same as that of the Central Plains. See the list of important archaeological sites for the numerous important settlement and tomb sites with Chu characteristics in this region. Some scholars believe that the size, structure, and date of the tomb at Yexian may indicate that it is a royal tomb. The area became part of the Chu cultural sphere rather more slowly than it entered the Chu political realm.[107] Politically, even though Chu power penetrated into the region in middle Spring and Autumn times, intensive Chu influences in material culture are observable only during the mid- to late Warring States period.

The Upper Huai

Material cultural evidence of the Chu occupation of this westernmost outpost of the Eastern Yi peoples during the middle Spring and Autumn times is not evident until late in that period. Of the settlement and tomb sites listed on page 27, the Changtaiguan tomb was likely that of a high official, as it was large and contained many Chu materials of high quality.

Huaibei and Huainan

Characteristic Chu materials do not appear in the middle and lower Huai region until mid- to late Warring States times,[108] although Chu military power had penetrated this segment of the Eastern Yi cultural sphere in middle Spring and Autumn times also. Several groups of early to middle Spring and Autumn bronzes showing markedly local (presumably Eastern Yi) characteristics have been found in various Anhui locations. After the middle Spring and Autumn period, however, these local features are little in evidence.

Xu Shaohua

Since Cai moved to the middle Huai (Zhoulai) area in the early fifth century, a considerable number of its remains have been unearthed there. Representative of these are the Cai Zhao Hou tomb in Shouxian and the Cai Sheng Hou tomb in Huainan. Some analysts have considered these tombs to be representative of Chu culture, but while they do exhibit some Chu features, the Central Plains tradition is even more evident, as are some Wu cultural elements. Farther south, in Liuhe on the northern banks of the Yangtze, are several late Spring and Autumn to early Warring States tombs that, judging from both the vessel shapes and their inscriptions, probably belong to Wu.

Artifacts from this region that clearly belong to the Chu culture include the E Jun tallies[109] and the Ying Dafu weigh-scale.[110] There are over twenty important Chu-related tombs in the area. From a diagnostic standpoint the royal tomb of Chu King You in Shouxian is understandably the most important. It is also significant that the bronze and ceramic ritual sets found in this region are quite similar to those found in the areas of earlier Chu capitals in Hanxi and at Chencheng.[111] There are, however, some marked distinctions that suggest cultural differences. Certain materials prevalent in the Hanxi area, such as the long-necked ceramic *hu* and the lacquer *zhenmushou* and drumstands, for example, are not found here.

As for the Huaibei region, the Si and Yi valleys originally were within the political and cultural spheres of Lu and a number of small Eastern Yi states. Chu cultural influences only appear in middle to late Warring States times, and specifically Chu materials such as the "high" *fou* and Chu coins have been found in southern Shandong at Taian and in Fei County.[112]

Jiangdong

Originally this region was within the Wu/Yue cultural sphere.[113] The archaeological remains of the area support a late fourth century infiltration of the area by Chu. There may even have been earlier Chu influence, as evidenced by bronzes found in the early Warring States (late fifth century) tomb at Huqiu in Suzhou, Jiangsu (see the list), which bear some Chu characteristics, although generally they are of Wu/Yue style. However, fully Chu materials do not appear until late Warring States times, as clearly exhibited in the Eling *Jun* bronzes found in Wuxi at Qianzhou, Jiangsu. Other tombs containing characteristic Chu materials generally date to after the conquest of Yue. Two of these are particularly noteworthy: the Heshan tomb contained thirty-three Chu-style bronze vessels; the inscription on one of them showed that it was the possession of a Chu personage, Chu Shuzhisun Tu Wei. The late Warring States Fenghuangshan tomb produced a ceramic ritual vessel set (consisting of *ding, dui,* and *hu*), bronze weapons, and lacquer and wooden ware, all characteristically Chu. These tombs also yielded Wu/Yue-style materials (such as ceramic geometric-patterned *guan* and proto-porcelain vessels). Possibly because Chu did not enter the Jiangdong region until long after its political peak, its culture did not fully replace local tendencies here.[114]

Jiangnan

Before Chu features began to infiltrate the Jiangnan region in late Spring and Autumn times, most of the region south of the Yangtze River belonged to the Yue cultural sphere except for the material culture of northwestern Hunan, which had Ba cultural features. Chu features did not become extensive until the early Warring States era.[115] Approximately 70 percent of the three thousand Chu tombs of the Jiangnan region excavated to date are located in Hunan. Not many date to Spring and Autumn times, and few of these are elite burials, but from the middle Warring States period on, there is a heavy concentration of both Chu tombs and settlement sites, especially in northern Hunan. Significant tombs, some of considerable size,[116] are distributed across a broad area—from Yueyang and Changde in northern Hunan, as far south as the foot of the Nanling range, west to Mayang and Guzhang, and, beyond Hunan, east to Pingxiang and Xinjian in Jiangxi. The heaviest concentration, however, is in the centrally located Changsha area, which contains about as many tombs as the Chu heartland in Hubei.

These apparently Chu sites had a number of features unique to the Hunan region. For example, the Jiangnan ceramic ritual sets are generally composed either of *ding, dui,* and *hu* or of *ding, he,* and *hu,* with the *fu* form, so prevalent in Hubei and Henan, little in evidence. Utilitarian ceramic sets consist largely of *li, guan, dou,* and *yu,* with a total absence of the long-necked *hu* so typical of the Hubei heartland region. Moreover, in Hunan Chu tombs we find many balance weights of a type seldom found elsewhere in the Chu sphere. Probably the most famous Chu artifacts emerging from Hunan are the texts and banners on silk found at Changsha.

Despite the many Chu settlements and tombs, Chu, Yue, and Ba traits coexisted in the same locales for quite some time. For instance, tombs of both Chu and Yue types are found in the same mortuary complexes, in Xiangxiang[117] and Zixing,[118] for example, in both late Spring and Autumn and Warring States times. We even find artifacts of both cultures in the same tomb. A similar case is found for Chu and Ba tombs: in the northwest (west of the Xiang River), the Xupu burial ground has both Ba and Chu tombs,[119] and tombs at Guzhang[120] have Ba and Chu goods mixed together.

As a final note, the large volume of late Warring States Chu materials in the Jiangnan region suggests that it remained under Chu control even after the loss of the northern heartland to Qin in 278.[121]

Conclusion

THE above survey has shown that the material culture of Chu underwent a transformation —from one closely tied to the Central Plains to one with distinctive traits derived largely from the various neighboring regions with which Chu interacted and/or incorporated. The label "Chu culture" can, with justification, be applied to a complex of distinctive traits widely found within the Chu political realm. We must keep in mind, however, that within the different regions of the Chu state, local cultural characteristics survived.

Xu Shaohua

3

Chu Art

Link between the Old and New

JENNY F. SO

LIKE their peers in the states of the North China Plain, Chu aristocrats surrounded themselves with articles befitting their power and rank. The best of these were often buried with them in death. Spectacular discoveries through controlled excavations of some of these Chu tombs in the last ten to twenty years have begun to paint a fascinating picture of Chu art and culture during the three or four centuries when the state was at the height of its power. Beginning with monumental bronzes (fig. 3.1), followed by colorful painted lacquers (pls. 1, 2, 3, 4, 5) and deli-

Figure 3.1 Wangzi Wu bronze *sheng-ding* from Xiasi, Xichuan, Henan [courtesy of Avery Press]

cately embroidered silks (fig. 3.2), these artifacts present a picture of a sophisticated society in the south rivaling the grandest principalities in the north. The study of these artifacts reveals Chu's pivotal role at an important point in the history of China's artistic development: providing an inspired transition from the arts of an

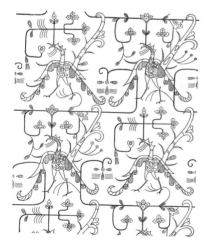

Figure 3.2 Drawing of embroidered silk textile from Mashan [after Beijing 1985, fig. 54]

entrenched Bronze-Age tradition to the liberating variety of the Han and subsequent periods. Heir to the ritual legacies of the Shang and Zhou kings in the north and rooted in the native customs of the south, Chu art served as a geographical and temporal link between the ancient Shang-Zhou traditions and the subsequent Han regimes, as well as a herald for later Chinese artistic trends.

From Bronzes to Lacquers and Silks

THE sixth to third centuries BCE, when Chu was at the height of its power, also marked the last flowering of China's Bronze-Age culture,[1] when the emerging prominence of other materials like iron, steel, glazed high-fired ceramics, lacquered wood, and woven textiles began to challenge the supremacy of bronze as the material of choice and prestige. By the time of Chu's demise at the end of the third century, ritual bronze artifacts—which had been the symbols of social and political status since their first production in the early second millennium—had been all but superseded by artistic creations in other media. This dramatic change is vividly illustrated by artifacts recovered from Chu tombs that spanned these three hundred years.

At the beginning of Chu's rise to power, ritual bronzes in the ancient Shang and Zhou traditions still ruled the Chu court as symbols of power and status. The earliest Chu burials excavated, datable to the sixth century and located along the Dan and Xi Rivers, tributaries of the Han River in the Henan-Hubei border, clearly demonstrate this phenomenon. In the latest series of excavations between 1990 and 1992, over fifty Chu burials were opened at Xichuan in southern Henan. Several large tombs yielded sets of ritual bronze tripods and bells, many of which were inscribed and attributable to Chu nobles active at the end of the seventh century BCE.[2] From the mid-sixth century comes a second group of graves excavated between 1978 and 1979, at Xiasi, also in Xichuan.[3] The richest grave, Tomb 2, contained fifty-two ritual bronzes, including a set of seven monumental *ding* vessels ranging in size from 68 to 61.3 centimeters high and 66 to 58 centimeters wide, inscribed with the name of the Chu noble Wu, who died in 552;[4] a set of twenty-six bronze bells, the largest of which stands 1.22

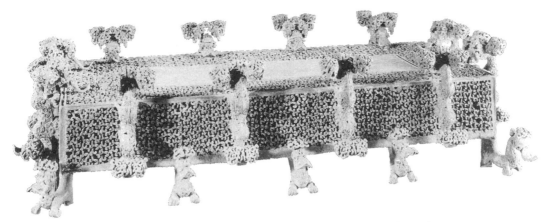

Figure 3.3 Bronze altar table from Xiasi [courtesy of Hamilton Photography and Film Co.]

Jenny F. So

meters tall, weighs 160.5 kilograms, and is also inscribed with 108 characters;[5] a rectangular bronze altar table measuring 103 by 46 by 28.8 centimeters and weighing 94.2 kilograms (fig. 3.3); and probably two large wine containers like the pair recovered from an adjacent tomb. In providing large numbers of bronze ritual vessels and musical instruments in burials, sixth-century Chu nobles were following a venerable tradition spanning over a thousand years during the Shang and Zhou periods.

Figure 3.4 Bronze *zun-pan* from Zeng Hou Yi tomb, Suixian, Hubei [after Hubeisheng bowuguan 1991, color plate 83]

Chu's contribution to this tradition emerges in the distinctive ornamental style of these vessels, most obviously the intertwined serpentine configurations and the addition of animals on the walls or bases of vessels.[6] Although animal accents on vessels may be traced back to the Western Zhou period, turning them into the complex openwork and intertwined ornaments on the Xiasi bronzes seems to be a Chu trait. These creatures clamber up the sides of the large tripods, the altar table, and the wine containers, where they also serve as supports below. On the top and sides of the altar table, a dense and wormy openwork of serpentine creatures forms the sole decoration. The production of this intricate openwork probably inspired the development of a new casting technique—the lost-wax method—to supplement the traditional section-mold casting technique used since ca. 1500 BCE. To date, the bronzes from Xiasi are the earliest undisputed examples of Chinese bronzes that applied the lost-wax technique in their production, and later examples using the same technique are mostly associated with Chu.[7]

Chu continued to follow this tradition for another hundred years. A richly furnished tomb opened in 1978 near Leigudun in Suixian, Hubei Province, contained hundreds of bronze vessels, a set of sixty-five bronze bells, weapons, and decorative accessories, weighing a total of almost ten tons.[8] The tomb belonged to a Marquis Yi of Zeng, a minor vassal of Chu, who was interred around 433. The size of the bronze industry that would have been required to produce all of the marquis' bronzes—the manpower to handle the mining, smelting, mold-making, and pouring of bronze in such staggering quantities—reflects the high status and priority placed on ritual bronzes in Chu circles during the sixth and early fifth centuries BCE. If a politically insignificant vassal of Chu could have all this buried with him, the contents of a contemporaneous Chu ruler's tomb would be formidable indeed.

Lost-wax casting, already evident a hundred years earlier at Xiasi, reached spectacular heights on a bronze *zunpan* buried with Zeng Hou Yi at Suixian (fig. 3.4). The elaborate ser-

pentine clusters from the crown of the *zun* to its shoulders and around the rim of the matching *pan* are the flamboyant descendants of the more restrained creatures on the Xiasi table and *ding* vessels. The premier status of ritual bronzes is assured when lacquered wood vessels, like the pair of large stemmed *dou* from the marquis' tomb, were made to imitate bronze shapes and decoration (pl. 4).[9]

A second tomb (number 2), most likely that of the marquis' consort, was excavated in 1981 about one hundred meters west of his grave. Compared with the marquis', the bronzes from this tomb are far fewer and greatly inferior in workmanship. However, the burial still contained a set of thirty-six bronze bells and over fifty large bronze vessels.[10] The diminished quantity and quality of the ritual bronzes from this tomb, dating near the end of the fifth century, serve as a prelude to a steady decline in the status of ritual bronzes in Chu territory over the next two hundred years.

Throughout the fourth century richly furnished Chu tombs reveal that lacquered wooden vessels and decorated silks were the preferred status goods. In a series of Chu tombs dating from ca. 400–300 BCE, the number and quality of ritual bronzes appear to diminish steadily in relation to articles in other materials. The most significant burials include Tomb 1 at Changtaiguan in Xinyang, southern Henan Province,[11] Tomb 1 at Wangshan,[12] burials at Yutaishan,[13] Tomb 1 at Tianxingguan,[14] Tomb 1 at Mashan,[15] and Tomb 2 at Baoshan[16]—the latter five in the Jiangling region of Hubei Province. These are all large and richly furnished tombs comparable to those excavated at Xiasi and Suixian, but instead of ritual bronzes, lacquered wooden vessels and decorated silks predominate.

Changtaiguan Tomb 1, datable around the beginning of the fourth century, yielded 150 lacquered wooden vessels in comparison to less than 30 in bronze. Furthermore, the bronze vessels are mostly plain, and the few that were decorated used colored inlays or lacquer as ornamental materials.[17] At Wangshan Tomb 1 bronze and lacquers occupy similar proportions of the tomb inventory, lacquer again surpassing bronze in quantity and quality. From over five hundred tombs excavated at Yutaishan, only fifty-two bronze vessels—in contrast to more than nine hundred lacquered articles—were recovered.

Tomb 1 at Mashan is distinguished by its astonishing wealth of over thirty embroidered and woven silk robes and textiles (fig. 3.2), twenty-five woven bamboo articles, and thirty lacquered wooden objects. By contrast, it contained only eighteen bronze vessels that are mostly undecorated or copies of lacquered ones.[18] Tomb 2 at Baoshan, the latest in this group, dating to the last decade of the fourth century, belongs to an important Chu noble. It contained fifty-nine ritual bronzes and a single bronze handbell, but eighty-one vessels and thirteen musical instruments in lacquered wood. Compared to the fashionable designs and colorful palette of the lacquers, the bronzes from Baoshan, with few exceptions, appear routine and dull.[19]

Not even the royal furnishings from the tomb of one of the last Chu kings at Lisan'gudui in Shouxian, Anhui Province, can counter the trend established during the fourth century. The grave, opened in 1933, was severely plundered.[20] Inscriptions on the bronzes indicate that they belonged to the last Chu kings who resided at Shouxian, their capital until it was captured by Qin troops in 223 BCE. In contrast to Chu tombs of the preceding century, bronze ritual vessels again dominated the inventory of this third-century royal burial. Like the vessels from Xiasi and Suixian, the Shouxian bronzes are also monumental in scale, but unlike their earlier counterparts, they are all crudely cast, thin, and light. They seemed to strive only for the appearance of status, but nothing of its substance. Just like the kings who commissioned and owned them, the Shouxian bronzes are mere shadows of their former magnificence, and they remain poor cousins of the richly decorated lacquers and silks that came to replace them. By the beginning of the early second century it was clearly acceptable for a Chu noblewoman like the Lady of Dai to go to her grave with only a single bronze mirror among hundreds of lacquered wooden vessels and accessories.[21]

The greatly diminished role of ritual bronzes in Chu burials signals a shift in Chu loyalties. In their quest for power and peer recognition, the early Chu rulers subscribed to traditional Zhou values and rituals as signs of their power and status. Confident in their political and territorial success, later Chu rulers returned to native customs as symbols of their unique tradition and achievements. Local products of the Chu domain—the multicolored lacquers and luxurious silks—flourished under royal patronage as they came to replace bronze as prized items in burials. Chu's extensive experience with wood-working in making coffins, tables, beds, vessels, and other tomb furnishings encouraged the development of joinery techniques that became the foundations of China's furniture industry in subsequent dynasties.[22]

From Court Ceremony to Personal Pleasures

THE movement away from massive bronze vessels associated with somber rituals to colorful painted lacquers reflects yet another trend that developed in Chu society during the sixth to third centuries BCE. In abandoning bronze in favor of other materials, the Chu princes departed from the traditional preoccupation with, and worship of, the dead and gone, and focused on enjoying the pleasures of the here and now. This shift reveals itself in the layout of the tombs, which began to resemble more and more the deceased's earthly dwelling rather than a temple for offering and worship. The ardent quest for immortality during the following Qin and Han periods may be seen as a natural consequence of this attempt to maximize life's potential.

Like Tomb 2 at Xiasi, Chu burials from the mid-sixth century were constructed in the Shang-Zhou tradition—a rectangular pit with a large tomb chamber, lined with ritual paraphernalia (bronze vessels, altar tables, and bells) along the sides. By the late fifth century the burial chamber of Zeng Hou Yi at Suixian was subdivided into four separate chambers to denote different aspects of the marquis' daily life: servants/attendants in one side chamber, weapons and battle regalia in another, the marquis himself with more attendants or consorts in the third, and an impressive array of wine and food vessels and musical instruments for state and religious ceremonies in the largest central chamber, where the marquis would have held court.[23] Tomb I at Changtaiguan, dating to the early fourth century, is organized in a similar way, divided into six separate chambers, with the deceased occupying the central chamber and musical instruments and vessels in the antechamber. These are the modest beginnings of a trend that eventually led to the construction of Qin Shihuangdi's mausoleum at Lishan, outside Xi'an, and the brick tombs of the Han dynasty, all of which were virtual underground structures that duplicated the deceased's earthly palaces or living quarters.

The sixth- and fifth-century burials at Xiasi and Suixian were all accompanied by human victims, a custom Chu had retained from late Shang times.[24] Twenty-one women accompanied Zeng Hou Yi to his grave at Suixian, perhaps his favorite consorts, musicians, and dancers, to ensure that he would be well entertained and attended to in his new life. By the fourth century wooden figures—not humans—were buried with Chu nobles (pl. 6). These wooden figures are the immediate predecessors of the magnificent terra-cotta army of the first emperor of Qin, as well as the painted earthenware dancers, soldiers, and entertainers of Han, all of which were placed in their masters' tombs to duplicate the circumstances of their earthly existence.

Although Zeng Hou Yi's bronze vessels and musical instruments in the central chamber may have been appropriate for grand, courtly occasions, entertainment of a more intimate nature was apparently enjoyed in his private chambers, because a second and smaller group of musical instruments, together with eight attendants, were buried with him in the adjacent chamber.[25] The marquis apparently preferred more intimate chamber music over the Wagnerian sound of the full orchestra in the ceremonial hall.

Two incense burners, not grand ritual bronzes, amused the marquis in his private chambers. One of them is an openwork cylinder composed of intertwined serpents, a recurring article in later Chu burials at Changtaiguan, Wangshan, Yutaishan, and Baoshan.[26] The incense burner is characteristic of fifth- to fourth-century Chu burials, suggesting that burning fragrant scents was a popular Chu custom. As a type, Chu incense burners are the ancestors of the hill-censers found frequently in Han tombs in the north,[27] and Chu custom may be held partly responsible for this diagnostic Han artifact. Both the incense burners and smaller musical ensembles are evidence that daily pleasures and native delights were important aspects of Chu life by the end of the fifth century. The rising prestige of Chu lacquers and silks is further evidence of a preoccupation with self-indulgence. If following pompous Zhou customs was necessary political protocol, more relaxed native pleasures were a personal Chu choice.

The preference for colorful objects was apparent even in early Chu art. Chu was among the first Eastern Zhou states to exploit in a major way the potential of color in precious metals or semiprecious stones in the decoration of ritual and luxury paraphernalia. Almost two hundred thin sheets of gold foil with repoussé designs were recovered from the mid-sixth century

Figure 3.6 Painted coffin,
Baoshan [after Beijing 1991b,
vol. 2, pl. 4]

Chu tomb at Xiasi.[28] They were affixed to wooden shields, chariot fittings, and armor for decoration. Beside nearly a thousand pieces of gold foil and several cast gold garment hooks, Zeng Hou Yi even had vessels cast in solid gold, one of them weighing over 2,100 grams (pl. 7).[29]

Although few could afford the extravagance of solid gold vessels, many were able to enjoy the luxury of colorfully inlaid bronzes. Chu seemed to be at the forefront of this development as well, because the earliest groups of bronze vessels that consistently exploited the contrasting colors of different metals and materials have also been recovered from Chu tombs. Tomb 2 at Xiasi contained several vessels decorated with feline figures inlaid in red copper;[30] crushed malachite, turquoise, and copper accented similar designs on the Suixian bronzes.[31] By the fourth century multicolored lacquers were painted directly on bronze surfaces while lacquered wooden articles, like the coffin from Tomb 2 at Baoshan, began to resemble inlaid bronze (fig. 3.6). On a covered container from the same tomb, gold and silver inlays form the patterns on the lid, while red lacquer coats the interior.[32] Lavishly inlaid bronze vessels, weapons, fittings, and personal accessories dominated tomb inventories from the fourth century on, not just among burials in Chu territory, but throughout most of China.[33] The multicolors of copper, gold, silver, turquoise, and malachite on bronze were probably the only effective means to rival the alluring palette used on painted lacquers and embroidered silks, and the three art forms became inextricably entwined in each other's developments.[34] Seduced by glittering inlaid bronzes, luxuriously embroidered silks, and colorfully painted lacquers, the Warring States elite in the north and south surrounded themselves with every possible trapping of their worldly success. Ritual worship, the foundation of political power for the Shang and early Zhou kings, became mere excuses for excessive display; courtly ceremony, which reinforced that power, became the occasion for personal entertainment.

From Patterns to Pictures

TOGETHER with this shift from religious ritual to urbane pleasures came an intensified interest in the natural world. Neolithic and Shang inhabitants of the Yangtze River valley showed
a special leaning toward portraying naturalistic images. Crudely modeled earthenware sculptures of animals—elephants, birds, turtles, dogs—and human beings were among the artifacts
recovered from a late Neolithic context in Hubei Province.[35] Ritual bronze vessels in the
shape of animals dating from the Shang period have been repeatedly found in the same
region, and three-dimensional animals were often used as ornamental appendages on vessels
from the south.[36] At the same time, the fantastic imagery that dominated Shang and early
Zhou bronze decoration continued in all art forms.

By the sixth century BCE Chu art displayed a curious blend of the fantastic with the real.
The fabulous creatures on the monumental bronze *hu* or the altar table from Tomb 2 at Xiasi
demonstrate the art's links with the older Shang and early Zhou traditions (fig. 3.3).[37] By the
mid-fifth century more realistic figures emerged. In addition to bronze vessels with fantastic
animal handles and fabulous creatures supporting chimestones,[38] the marquis' tomb at Suixian

also included human figures supporting the bell chime, their facial
features, clothing, and weapons described in painted lacquer (fig. 3.7).
During the fourth century, wooden
figures, representing attendants for
the deceased, became common
items in Chu tombs. The majority
were carved in simple blocky masses
with details of the garments and
accessories painted on;[39] the more
elaborate ones were given real hair-
pieces and dressed in real silks to
resemble real people (pl. 6).[40]

Chu's blending of the fabulous
and real is also evident in animal
sculpture: a bronze crane-like bird
with majestically branching antlers
(fig. 3.8), or a reclining deer in lacquered wood, both from Zeng Hou
Yi's tomb (fig. 3.9). The Yutaishan
excavations yielded a phoenix-like

Figure 3.7 Bronze support for bell
rack from Zeng Hou Yi tomb [after
Hubeisheng bowuguan 1991, pl. 39]

Jenny F. So

· *40* ·

Figure 3.8 Bronze antlered bird from Zeng Hou Yi tomb [courtesy of Avery Press]

Figure 3.9 Lacquered wooden deer from Zeng Hou Yi tomb [after Hubeisheng bowuguan 1991, pl. 192]

bird, made into a stemmed food container. Red, yellow, and gold colors on black described the bird's plumage and scaled body in detail; but an abstract pattern of diagonals and curls decorate the stem and base. A close contemporary from Wangshan Tomb 1 is a small openwork screen composed of birds, leaping deer, and intertwined snakes (pl. 3).

This mixing of realism and fantasy also occurs on two-dimensional designs. Chu painted lacquer designs of the sixth and fifth centuries often copy contemporaneous bronze patterns (pl. 4). During the fourth century, they took on a calligraphic character directly linked to the use of brush and paint. A wine cup in the Nelson Gallery of Art shows a spotted deer in flying gallop in the center (fig. 3.10). Its ear and hind leg extend in long abstract filaments to echo those sweeping across the rest of the surface in strictly ornamental patterns. The broad elements and scallops that punctuate the filaments are natural results of the viscous nature of thick lacquer applied with a brush. The strokes of the lacquer-loaded brush produced delicate filaments with fluctuating widths and tenuous volutes, another characteristic trait of calligraphy. Similar designs appear in the silk industry. A piece of embroidered silk from Tomb 1 at Mashan shows long-necked birds and dragons whose tails and crests also form long filaments punctuated by broad elements and flourishes (fig. 3.2).

By the end of the fourth century BCE abstract design and descriptive elements were so intricately enmeshed that one was virtually indistinguishable from the other. On the cover of a lacquered box from Tomb 2 at Baoshan, birds are all but lost among a complex scaffolding of sweeping diagonals and curls (fig. 3.11). In contrast, a simple descriptive scene fills the side walls (pl. 2). Figures wearing long robes stand in profile or with their backs to the viewer, as others run or ride in horse-drawn carriages. Separating each group of figures are windblown trees interspersed with flying birds above and running animals below. Although they are

Chu Art

Figure 3.10 Lacquered wooden cup [courtesy of Nelson-Atkins Museum of Art, Kansas City, Missouri. Purchase: Nelson Trust]

placed on an empty space, the trees, birds, and animals suggest a landscape setting, and the overlapping horses and riders in the carriages imply a recession in three-dimensional space. Banners trailing from the carriages, the figures' backward-sweeping garments, and the trees' curved branches indicate motion.

The scene on the walls of the Baoshan box is an outstanding example of early painting in China. In subsequent centuries similar images depicting ritual or mythological scenes came to be painted on silk, a small number of examples of which were preserved in airtight, third- and second-century BCE Chu tombs in Changsha. One third-century BCE silk painting shows a male figure riding a dragon-drawn chariot, and another shows a woman behind a fancy bird, both figures rendered in profile, as were those on the Baoshan box, with the bottoms of their robes extended in billowing profile (fig. 9.1). The burial banners of the Lady of Dai and her son at Mawangdui in Changsha, dating from the beginning of the second century BCE (pl. 8, fig. 8.2), depict, in hierarchical order, the deceased among real and mythological creatures of the Chu universe. Some of China's earliest surviving paintings, the Baoshan and Changsha images are the immediate ancestors of the figure paintings of Gu Kaizhi (ca. 344–406), who lived six hundred years later.[41] These images also stand at the head of a long tradition in China's history of representational art.

Eventually, the vitality of the swirling scrolls, like those on the Baoshan box, take on a life of their own. A cosmetic box in the collection of the Museum of Fine Arts, Boston, dating from the last decades of the third century BCE, illustrates this transformation beautifully. A single dragon, in black reserve against red, fills the central

Figure 3.11 Drawing of design on lacquer box lid, Baoshan [after Beijing 1991b, fig. 89b]

Jenny F. So

roundel on the cover. Its mouth is wide open, as if in broad laughter, revealing a trim row of teeth. One of its neatly manicured, clawed forelimbs extends in front of its chest as the other wraps around its neck with double-jointed dexterity. The dragon's thin body swings back in a curve that echoes the round shape of the box, its two hind limbs and tail sweeping dramatically upward to end in scrolls. Similar scrolls issuing from the back of its head and under its belly fill the remaining ground.

This painted dragon presents an image that is at once a masterful design and an extraordinarily real image. In this near-magical leap from abstract design to lively image, as well as in the straightforward painting of figures in landscape, Chu art becomes the true link between the past and the future. Between the ancient Shang and Zhou traditions that excelled in elaborate ornaments of undefinable character, and the Han and later periods' profound involvement with nature and its representation in two and three dimensions, spans the bridge that is Warring States Chu sculpture and painting.

From Nebulous Tales to Concrete Images

THE proliferation of both fantastic and real images in Chu art expresses Chu's urge to depict, in concrete visual form, earthly events as well as supernatural phenomena. Chu customs and beliefs survive today in poetry (the *Chuci,* or *Songs of the South*)[42] as well as artifacts, revealing a culture populated by an imaginative pantheon of demons and deities that inspired complex rituals with the requisite regalia. Unlike that of the Shang and Zhou periods, Chu religious paraphernalia consistently attempts to portray, in graphic terms, religious ideas and the gods associated with them.[43] The systematic portrayal of abstract beliefs and fantastic deities in art paves the way for the canonical representations in Buddhist and Daoist art of the ensuing Han through Tang dynasties.

Early surviving examples of these beliefs and deities are the images painted on two lacquered garment boxes from the late fifth century tomb of Zeng Hou Yi at Suixian. On the lid of one box are written the names of the twenty-eight lunar lodges, surrounding a large central depiction of the Northern Dipper constellation and flanked by a dragon and tiger, the animals of the east and west (fig. 3.12). The cover of the second box shows, along one edge,

intertwined serpents with human heads, a motif that, by the Han period, became the standard image for the gods Fuxi and Nügua, the progenitors of the universe in Chinese myth.[44] The remaining decoration includes two pairs of trees.

Figure 3.12 Zeng Hou yi lacquer clothes box showing the lunar lodges [after Hubeisheng bowuguan 1991, pl. 186]

The branches terminate in multiarmed circles—the tall tree has eleven, the shorter tree nine. Between the trees is a bird pierced by an arrow from an archer on the ground. The birds, archer, trees, and radiating circles together suggest that the scene depicts the myth of the archer Yi who saved the universe by shooting down the nine suns that appeared simultaneously in the sky one day.[45]

Another important document, dating from the third century, is an illustrated silk manuscript in the Arthur M. Sackler collections.[46] The text of this document is divided into two sections. The first describes the natural order and Chu's beliefs on the origins of the universe and of their ancestors. The second focuses on the human order and the consequences of man's behavior in relation to Nature. Surrounding the text are twelve images depicting the gods of the twelve months, each identified by the short caption next to it. At the corners of the manuscript are plant motifs symbolic of the four seasons, rendered in green, red, white, and black, the colors of the four cardinal points. The layout of the text with its images is conceptually similar to that of the *shi,* or cosmograph.[47] This manuscript is the earliest surviving document where ancient Chu beliefs are recorded in writing, and illustrated systematically by a set of deities associated with the cosmic scheme.

Although the identity and nature of some of the figures remain elusive, a few relate directly to images in other media. One of them, the deity for the twelfth month, combines a human head with antlered projections and a bird's body (fig. 3.13). A dark squiggly line between his teeth suggests a snake. The deity of the twelfth month is a standing figure with a square head, clawed hands, and bird-like legs; he, too, sports antler-like projections on his head and a long squiggly creature between his teeth.

These images are reminiscent of bronze and lacquered wooden sculptures associated with Chu. A sixth-century bronze animal with large round eyes squats with serpents coiled at its feet and gripped between its teeth and front paws (fig. 3.14).[48] A similar creature comes from Tomb I at Changtaiguan, a kneeling feline with enormous blood-red eyes, long tongue, antlers on its head, and clawed limbs clutching a black snake firmly between its teeth

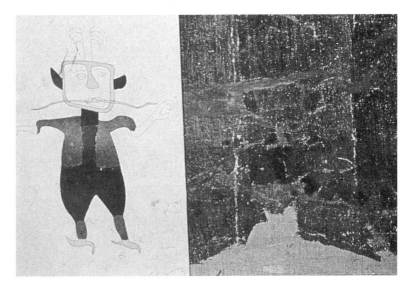

Figure 3.13
Deity for the twelfth month, Chu Silk Manuscript [courtesy of Arthur M. Sackler Foundation]

Jenny F. So

Figure 3.14 Bronze tomb figure from Xinzheng, Henan [courtesy of the National History Museum, Taipei, Taiwan]

(fig. 3.15).[49] Less graphic and more commonplace are statues on a square pedestal, depicting just the torso of a creature with large eyes, protruding tongue, and long antlers. Imposing versions, like the torsos from Tomb 1 at Tianxingguan, can reach 170 centimeters tall. Their prominent placement at the head of the coffin points to apotropaeic functions.[50]

Figures resembling the deities on the Sackler manuscript appear in other contexts, such as the lacquered inner coffin of Zeng Hou Yi (fig. 3.16). Flanking portal-like openings on the sides of the coffin are two rows of bird-man figures, armed with menacing weapons, presumably to ward off unwanted intruders to the marquis' sanctuary. They could be protective deities or shamans in professional gear. The complex maze of bird, snake, and human-headed configurations that fill the remaining panels of the coffin cannot have been random decoration; they must signify various good and bad forces or deities relating to death and the afterlife.

Birds, snakes, and deer (often symbolized by just their antlers), together with quasi-human or feline figures, are the main protagonists in these Chu representations. Crane-like birds often join with felines to form drumstands; some of them display fancy antlers on their heads (fig. 3.8).[51] A lacquered wooden drumstand in the Cleveland Museum of Art shows these birds with entwined serpents at their feet. The small lacquered wooden screen from Tomb 1 at Wangshan combines bird, snake, and deer in an ornamental composition (pl. 3). Intertwining snakes form the walls of an egg-shaped box from Yutaishan. The similarity of these images with those on the marquis' coffin and the Sackler manuscript suggests that their popularity was deeply rooted in Chu mythology.

Snakes and other serpentine creatures also interact with shaman-like figures, portrayed as wearing long robes and fancy headdresses. On a painted *se* stringed instrument from Tomb 1 at Changtaiguan, one of these figures grasps a serpent in each of his bird-like claws (fig. 8.5), another subdues a defiant dragon with his staff (pl. 1), while a third is seen between two entwined serpents.[52] On the large bottom panel of the largest bells from Tomb 2 at Suixian, a bare-

Figure 3.15 Reconstruction of lacquered tomb guardian from Xinyang, Changtaiguan [after Beijing 1962, pl. 66]

Chu Art

Figure 3.16 Detail of lacquered wooden coffin from Zeng Hou Yi [after Hubeisheng bowuguan n.d. (1985?), 22]

chested, athletic figure stands astride a fantastic creature while he clutches a snake in each hand. These bird-snake, feline-snake, and shaman-snake combinations have often been read as identifying traits of Chu art, although their occurrence was not confined to Chu art alone.[53] More important for this discussion is their systematic and persistent portrayal in all aspects of Chu art, so that they acquire a formulaic character and instant recognition essential to religious art. It is with this unrelenting urge to portray, in concrete or pictorial images, the abstract ideas of the universe or the fantastic tales and deities in ancient myths that Chu art sets the course for the rapid development of both secular and religious sculpture and painting in the Han and subsequent periods.

Defining Chu Art

THE picture of Chu art from the sixth to third centuries BCE that emerges from the above discussions is complex and multifaceted. In the gradual decline of bronze and the corresponding rise of lacquers and silks as prestige materials, and in the movement away from pompous ritual toward personal pleasures, the Chu artistic world is a close reflection of trends that were sweeping the rest of the country. Chu art thus closely parallels and reflects developments in the rest of China.

Within the framework of this broader picture, however, Chu art at the height of its power was also a catalyst for and herald of things to come. Chu's predilection for intertwined serpentine decoration may have inspired the exploitation of lost-wax casting—a major technical innovation in China's traditional section-mold bronze-casting method. The enhanced political status of Chu encouraged the rise of its native customs and pastimes, among which was the burning of fragrance and incense. This facilitated the production of incense burners during the Qin and Han periods, when they became key instruments for the Daoist pursuit of immortality. Secure political status also encouraged the growth of native Chu industries—

decorated lacquers and silks. Their increased production challenged the bronze industry to produce equally striking surfaces by inlaying with gold, silver, and semiprecious stones, with the result that the fifth to third centuries gave us some of the most beautiful and colorful designs in all of China's Bronze Age.

In China's early history of representational art, Chu was a leader in its unwavering commitment toward portraying real and mythical images in two and three dimensions. Inspired by the fabulous images in Chu art, China's ancient myths and their gods began to appear increasingly as subjects of reliefs and paintings. As Buddhism penetrated China during the Han dynasty, this existing tradition provided a ready foundation for the depiction, in two and three dimensions, of Buddhist stories and deities. Finally, as Chu tombs yielded some of the earliest surviving writing instruments in China[54] and, in its surviving lacquers and silk, provided evidence for artistic exploitation of the calligraphic properties of the brush, Chu may be considered the nurturing ground for calligraphy and painting, the twin arts that were to dominate China for the subsequent two thousand years.

PART II
State and
Society

4

Chu Society and State

Image versus Reality

BARRY B. BLAKELEY

A thorough understanding of historical institutions requires insight not only into their structures but also into the actors who bring them to life. Accomplishing this for Chu is impeded by several factors. Some of these relate to the study of early China, generally. Others are peculiar to the investigation of Chu.

Most information concerning ancient Chinese social and political matters appears in piecemeal fashion. Thus the researcher encounters hundreds of discrete pieces of data and must then construct a general framework from them. Even on the relatively rare occasions when one encounters a generalized statement, certain characteristics of ancient China's historical writing are cause for caution. The most crucial of these derive from the fact that describing the past was viewed less as an exercise in presenting objective historical "truth" than as an opportunity to instruct or entertain. This prompted the presentation of history in a narrative form, including a heavy dose of oral discourse.[1] All of this was accepted as reliable historical fact in the traditional Chinese historiographical tradition (and, in most quarters, still is today), but the critical scholar must always consider the issue of how much is embroidery supplied by later hands. Another problem is that misconceptions had emerged by Han times.[2] Overcoming these roadblocks requires a thorough reevaluation of all ancient Chinese texts—a daunting task, and one that (despite some two millennia of effort) still has a long way to go.[3] It should be noted also that we are hampered in tracing developments in Warring States times by the meager and scattered nature of the available data (much of which was destroyed under the Qin dynasty). As for the study of Chu, problems arise from the fact that while it lay in the south, the compilers of the texts on which we rely (as well as later commentators) were largely northerners.[4] This resulted in a "Northern Bias" vis-à-vis the historical role and cultural achievements of Chu, but at a more specific level it also meant that some distinctive aspects of Chu culture simply were incomprehensible to many later writers.

The effect of these historiographical obstacles—along with the fact that critical study of Chu is in its infancy—is that, below, we can offer only tentative conclusions on many points and must concentrate on the Spring and Autumn period.[5] The obvious place to start is with the question of the extent to which Chu society and state conformed to the general pattern of the time. In order to do so, we first take a short look at the essentials of that pattern.

The Nature of Pre-Imperial Politics in China

THE political tradition of pre-Imperial China might best be characterized as a "kinship state,"[6] because government and elite society were inextricably intertwined. The dominant social stratum was a hereditary warrior aristocracy organized into clans and lineages.[7] The power of this class derived (in an objective sense) from control of economic resources, the governing apparatus, and bronze weaponry. It was justified and reinforced (in a more subjective way) through appeal to the achievements and personal qualities of ancestors. These achievements and qualities were honored in elaborate rituals and extolled in inscriptions on the exquisite bronze ceremonial vessels employed in those ceremonies.[8] Understandably, it is this stratum of society that constitutes the principal subject of state chronicles, as well of various stories and tales. Moreover, the tombs of these aristocrats have supplied most of the evidence on material culture. Understanding, then, the life of the elite is a central occupation of both historians and archaeologists.

After the Zhou confederation conquered Shang (in the mid-1040s BCE[9]), only a fraction of the total territory was governed directly by the Zhou kings. Much of the rest was parceled out to their kinsmen.[10] In time, a similar pattern developed within most of the regional states thereby created: government posts and landed estates were distributed, with preference given to kinsmen of the lords. Kinship, then, was the essential mortar cementing the political structure.[11] This prompts a closer look at kinship structure and its political ramifications.

At the apex of each clan and lineage was a hereditary head or chief who was responsible for the rites dedicated to the ancestors of the group.[12] These heads also presided over the core unit of the clan, the main lineage (*dazong*, "great temple" group), including the siblings and progeny of the head (and, generally, those of his two immediate predecessors). After two generations or so, the descendants of male siblings or sons of a clan chief tended to establish subunits (segmented or collateral lineages), known as "small temple" (*xiaozong*) groups (also *shi*).

The polity (whether the Zhou empire as a whole or a territorial state) was essentially the communal property of its leading clan. Given this corporate tradition, members of the proprietary clan had a constitutional claim to share political power and its fruits. Subdivision into lineages, however, fostered competition among them, often intense. This can be seen most clearly in competition for court offices. Close kinship to the lord meant that members of the main lineage could claim priority in this respect over those of collateral lineages. (The main lineage also had an advantage in heading regencies, although the collateral lineages were unlikely to sit idly by in such times.) There was, however, one factor that could offset the inherent advantages of the main lineage: hereditary office tenure. By virtue of this, an office originally held by a member of the main lineage might, when lineage segmentation occurred, become the preserve of a collateral lineage.

Despite its importance, the kinship that formed the cement of the political order was prone to decay over time. The major factor behind this was the communal nature of kinship, by virtue of which the "assets" (ancestors, status, reputation, and wealth) of a lineage were the common heritage of the entire membership. As a result, the particularistic interests of immediate kinship groups (lineages) came to take precedence over more remote ties (to the clan as a whole, remote ancestors, and the main lineage). In fact, these groups often sought to overshadow the lord (clan chief).

An important ramification was that both the corporate tradition of the clan as a whole and the special interests of lineages within it tended to limit the authority of rulers.[13] Concretely, it could be difficult—at a minimum—for a ruler to determine who was to serve under him and in what capacity; at the maximum, there was always the danger of domination by kinsmen. Thus only a truly capable and strong-willed ruler had much chance of ruling and not merely reigning. As a result, the personal qualities of rulers were an important ingredient in the dynamics of state power.

With this general pattern in mind, we may now turn to a consideration of the degree to which conditions in Chu matched it. We first consider some of the basic features of Chu state and society.

Basic Features

IN ancient Chinese society, *xing* were mega-kinship units tying together broad segments of the elite, generally across the political boundaries of the territorial states.[14] (For instance, the granting of areas to kinsmen of the Zhou kings meant that a number of the local ruling houses were branches of the Ji *xing*.) The question of the *xing* affiliation of the Chu royal house has become enmeshed in debates over the nomenclature of rulership there.

According to both the *Shiji* and bronze inscriptions, the Chu ruling house belonged to the Mi *xing*.[15] The matter has been complicated, however, by the fact that "Xiong" appears in the initial position in the names of Chu rulers, both in the *Shiji* and (according to most analysts) in bronze inscriptions.[16] It has been suggested that Xiong was the lineage *(shi)* name of the main branch of the Chu ruling house.[17] There are, however, no known examples of the main lineage of a territorial state having a *shi* name.[18] Some other explanation of Xiong, therefore, must be sought. The most reasonable one is that it was an early Chu leadership title (for the head of state, clan, or both), perhaps deriving from a sacrificial role involving wine.[19] If this were the case, however, for most of Chu history its kings had at least two titles, because the northern title "king" *(wang)* was adopted, temporarily in Western Zhou times and permanently from the late eighth century on.[20] This is not inconceivable, because "Xiong" always appears with a personal name *(ming)* and "Wang" with a posthumous name *(shi)*. We may have here, then, parallel usage of indigenous and northern titles, but with different functions. There is, however, a further complication. Another title, *ao* (encountered first in connection with Ruo Ao, mentioned below), existed. Originally this title may have alluded to the managing of certain rituals (i.e., in ancestral rites[21]), but after the adoption of the northern *wang* it seems to have been reserved for those who ascended the throne but who (for various reasons) were not considered legitimate rulers (and to whom no posthumous name was given).[22] In sum, the most that can be said at this point is that the *xing* of the Chu ruling house was Mi, that Chu leaders may originally have borne titles arising from two distinct ritual roles, and that one of these *(xiong)* persisted after the adoption of the northern *wang,* while the other *(ao)* was set aside for use in specific circumstances.

The Chu succession system also has been the subject of much discussion.[23] Two statements in the *Zuozhuan* have been taken to indicate that the throne did not pass to the eldest son: "Elevation [of an heir] in Chu ordinarily involves the youngest"[24] and "That it must be the youngest son who achieves the throne is the constant practice of Chu."[25] The problem is that when we examine historical realities, there were no unambiguous cases of succession by a younger son. In other words, succession was normally through the eldest son. How, then, are the *Zuozhuan* statements to be understood? The answer is rather simple: they must be considered in context, because both are preceded by qualifying statements (respectively, "When the legitimate heir is set aside, causing dissension" and "When there is dissension in the Mi *xing*"[26]). Thus these passages in fact do not allude to normal successions, but rather to unusual circumstances.[27] In this light, it is worthwhile recounting the following well-known incident:[28]

> King Gong had no consort[29] and, although he had five beloved sons [by other women], had designated none of them as his successor. He therefore held a great sacrifice to the *qun wang* (hills and rivers, collectively) and prayed, saying: "I beg that the spirits choose among these five one who will take charge of the rites of the grains and soil [become ruler]." He then exhibited a jade disc (*bi,* symbol of high rank) to the *qun wang* and said: "The one who worships directly before the *bi* shall be the one chosen by the spirits. Who would dare to oppose this [judgement]?" When the ceremony was over, he and his Ji-*xing* concubine from Ba secretly buried the *bi* in the courtyard of the great hall [of the ancestral temple]. He had the five sons fast and then enter to worship in order of age, beginning with the eldest. [The future] King Kang stepped over [the spot where the *bi* was buried], and [the future] King Ling (inadvertently) touched it with his arm, while Zigan[30] and Zizhe[31] both missed it by a wide mark. [The future] King Ping, who was very young, was carried in and [after being set down?] worshiped twice, both times crushing the rope [of the *bi*]. Dou Weigui[32] entrusted the boy to [his son] Dou Chengran,[33] saying, "This flouts propriety, and [in any case] the decree [of the spirits] will be ignored.[34] [From both angles,] Chu is surely in danger!"

Here, then, we see exactly what the statements alluded to above really suggest: that a son by the primary wife would normally succeed and that only when one was not available did the possibility of choosing a younger son arise. Despite this, it has been suggested that Dou Weigui's complaint about the ignoring of "propriety" (i.e., accepted practice) means that, even in the absence of a conventional heir, the eldest candidate should have been chosen. This is probably based on the general assumption that the northern tradition emphasized seniority.[35] We have seen, however, that this contradicts the passages cited above. It is more probable, therefore, that the speaker is complaining about the *means* employed on this occasion (a form of divination), rather than the result. If so, the implication would be that the king should have designated an heir (regardless of relative age) on the basis of his own best judgment, rather than relying on an appeal to the spirits.[36]

The Chu succession tradition, then, can probably be summarized as follows: the throne normally went to a son of the primary wife (whether to the eldest being unknown); when this was not possible or when there was social discord within the ruling house, there was a proclivity to choose a younger son (even if by a concubine).

Turning to the lineages of Chu, they seem to have exhibited some peculiarities in their internal dynamics. This is suggested by the absence of a northern practice—lineage heads being alluded to by a formula (lineage=name+*shi*) implying that they represented or personified the lineage as a whole.[37] Second, it appears that lineage heads in Chu exerted less authority over their kinsmen than was the case elsewhere.[38] These characteristics of the Chu lineage tradition may well relate to two other unusual circumstances. One is that Chu lineages did not control large landed estates.[39] The other is that major court offices were rarely (if ever) held on a hereditary basis,[40] perhaps in part due to an unusual tendency toward promotion through the ranks.[41] Thus Chu lineages had comparatively little in the way of common economic and political heritage, and this probably reduced the authority of lineage heads. Lineages in Chu, then, were less intensely "corporate" than those elsewhere, but the difference is only one of degree, because they clearly functioned as political interest groups (as will be seen below).[42]

Compared to some (but not all) northern states, lineage segmentation was not highly developed in Chu.[43] Still, it did occur within the ruling house. The earliest collateral lineages to emerge within it were the Dou and Cheng,[44] conventionally labeled as the "Ruo Ao lineages," in light of their descent from the ruler of that name (r. 790–764).[45] Two other collateral lines appeared soon after, the Qu and Wei.[46] The Qu lineage emanated from a son or brother of King Wu (r. 741–690).[47] The standard view has been that the Wei lineage descended from the ruler Fen Mao[48] (r. 758–741), but it may have had more ancient roots.[49] Considerable time passed before further collateral lines emerged: the Yang, descending from a son of King Mu (r. 626–614), and the Nang and Shenyin,[50] emerging from descendants of King Zhuang (r. 614–591). Still later (in Warring States times) we encounter the Zhao lineage, stemming from King Zhao (r. 515–489) of the late Spring and Autumn period.[51]

Kinship groups unaffiliated with the royal house played only a very minor role in Chu politics in Spring and Autumn times.[52] (In this respect Chu was quite similar to Lu and Song but quite at variance with states such as Jin.[53]) It is interesting, too, that there were few independent lineages that were clearly indigenous to Chu.[54] This is probably a function of the meager geographical proportions of Chu in its formative days (see Blakeley, chapter 1). Quite the contrary, the majority of nonroyal clan kindreds had alien roots, undoubtedly drawn to the Chu court as its influence and conquests expanded.[55] Already in Spring and Autumn times there were examples from Chu's major competitor states (Qi,[56] Song,[57] and Jin[58]), although most had roots in states that Chu either had conquered or had reduced to clientage: Ruo,[59] Shen,[60] Xu,[61] Chen,[62] Zheng,[63] Deng,[64] Cai,[65] Dao,[66] and perhaps Fan.[67] This phenomenon persisted in Warring States times, as reflected in the late fourth century Baoshan materials. There we encounter individuals from not only Ruo, Deng, Cai, Song, Chen, and Wu, but especially (in terms of numbers) from Zhou and Huang.[68] Despite their numbers, few members of these lineages achieved high office in Chu. (This is the case also with men who themselves immigrated, the most noteworthy exception being Wu Qi, discussed below.[69])

Turning to the political system, the apparatus of Chu governance was in most ways similar to that found elsewhere, but with variations—mostly minor, but in one respect significant.[70] With respect to nomenclature, a unique Chu title was *moao*. This has always been taken as a state post (with unknown responsibilities[71]), but it has been suggested recently that the title adhered to the person in charge of the ancestral rites of the Qu lineage.[72] In any case, it has long been noted that the suffix *yin*, reminiscent of Shang terminology (and equivalent to *ao*[73]), was common in Chu office titles. Most *yin* offices were of relatively minor significance,[74] with the exceptions of *lingyin* (a title unique to Chu) and its lieutenant posts (of the Left, *zuoyin*, and Right, *youyin*).[75] The *lingyin* originally may have been the field commander,[76] but by the seventh century it had assumed the function of prime minister, in charge of both civil and military administration.[77] The roles of the adjunct posts are not clear for the Spring and Autumn period, but the *zuoyin* was an important office by the fourth century, with broad responsiblities in the administration of justice.[78] In contrast, the prefix *si*, characteristic of the Zhou tradition, was somewhat less in evidence in Chu. In the textual sources we find it only in the title *sima* (Master of the Horse or Minister of War) and related posts. At least by the fourth century, however, there were also central offices such as *sifeng* (or *sili*[79]), in charge of ritual vessels and/or rites), and *siyi* (handling the royal wardrobe?),[80] as well as local posts responsible for punishments (*sibai*[81]), city walls (*sicheng*[82]), and military matters (*sima*[83]).

There probably was at least some distinction between state and royal household administration (a rather advanced practice, as far as the development of bureaucracy is concerned). It stands to reason, for instance, that offices such as the chamberlain *(qinyin),* various types of tutors for royal heirs, and the Administrator of the Palace Stables *(gongjiuyin)* were part of the household. The latter had a counterpart in state administration—the Administrator of the Central Stables *(zhongjiuyin)*—and the Chief Remonstrator *(zhenyin)* was presumably a state post. In some cases the category is not readily apparent (e.g., *taizai*, Chief of Protocol; *gongyin*,[84] Administrator of Works), but it would not be surprising if precise separation of public and private was not always made.

The distinctive features of the Chu sociopolitical scene indicated above were of only superficial significance, as they had little if any impact on functional processes. In one respect, however, governance in Chu was unique (at least among the larger states): in its relatively high degree of centralization. Fundamental to this must have been the absence of large lineage estates in the countryside (which so often served as local power bases elsewhere). This seems to have been the case from the beginning, and as Chu expanded territorially (from the early or mid-seventh century on), newly incorporated states were organized into *xian* (counties).[85] These *xian* were border garrisons overseen by administrators (titled *gong* or *yin*), over whom a considerable degree of central control was exercised. In fact, it is quite probable that credit for the creation of this institution (which was to become central to the administrative structure of imperial times) belongs to Chu. In any case, it placed the Chu political system far in advance of any other state (by some three centuries, even in the case of Qin) and must have been a major factor in its rise to power and its success in territorial expansion. From the fifth century, the practice of enfeoffment *(feng)* did appear,[86] and there was a late (third century) case of the granting of massive territories to Prime Minister Huang Xie (known as Chun-shen Jun). However, before those late days the terminology probably masked a quite different reality, as the late fourth century Baoshan materials suggest a considerable degree of central authority by that time.[87] It should be mentioned, too, that there is a strong possibility the *jun* (prefecture) also originated in Chu (in Warring States times). In a nutshell, Chu governance —in the critical respect of centralization of power—lay on the cutting edge of developments throughout much of Eastern Zhou times but perhaps experienced a setback in the final half century (when centered in the east).

So far we have examined the Chu state and society on a fairly abstract level. A look at some of the groups and personalities involved can serve to bring things more to life. In doing so, it might be expected that we would begin at the top of the hierarchy, with the kings. But while it is commonly held that the Chu kings (at least of Spring and Autumn times[88]) were unusually powerful individuals (in comparison to their peers in other states), the tradition of lineage participation in the exercise of power placed serious limits on royal authority in Chu.

Figure 4.1 Drawing of wooden figurines with facial tattooing from Changsha, Hunan [after Barnard 1972 vol. 1, p. 32]

Before examining the kings, therefore, we begin with the role of lineages, turn to some of the leading personalities they produced, and only then take up the kings.

Lineages in Court Politics

THE history of Chu politics is essentially one of the rise and fall of various lineages of the royal house, struggles among them, and competition with the throne (when it was occupied by a forceful enough figure).[89] These matters can be traced in considerable detail from the mid-seventh to the mid-fifth centuries.

From 664 to 605, the Ruo Ao lineages (the Dou and Cheng) were the leading group at court, their members holding most of the important offices. Their rise began (in 664, under King Cheng) with the murder of a main lineage prime minister[90] and the replacement of him by Dou Ziwen. In 637, after having served for thirty years, Ziwen voluntarily stepped aside in favor of a scion of the Cheng lineage, Dechen. Dechen clearly was a strong figure, but the staff under him was largely drawn from the Dou lineage, and when he was pushed aside (in 632), the Dou returned to the forefront.

The next king (Mu, r. 625–613) appointed two successive Cheng lineage prime ministers, possibly as a counterweight to the Dou (who, nevertheless, were not shut out of lesser posts). Mu, then, did not impinge on the dominance of the Ruo Ao group as a whole, and circumstances remained unchanged during the first few years of his young successor (Zhuang); but the Dou returned to prominence in about 611 and remained there down to 605. In sum, the preeminence of the two Ruo Ao lineages was maintained over some six decades, despite competition between them and regardless of the qualities of individual kings.

After 605, for the remainder of Zhuang's reign, there was rather a balance of lineages represented at court. After Zhuang's death, however, circumstances changed dramatically; and throughout the rest of the Spring and Autumn period the main lineage predominated for the most part, especially in the name of young and/or weak kings. The few activist kings had to look in other directions for counterbalances. Both King Kang (in his mature years, 551–545) and the usurper King Ling made considerable use of the Wei and Qu collateral lineages. King Ping, on the other hand, introduced a new element into the court equation by elevating for the first time the more recently founded Yang and Nang collateral lines. These lines continued to dominate under the immature King Zhao, but the main lineage returned to the fore in 505 and remained the leading group at least until the close of the Spring and Autumn period.

A Han source mentions three collateral lineages of Warring States times: the Qu, Zhao, and Jing.[91] We know little if anything of the Jing group.[92] Members of the (by then) hoary Qu lineage, however, do appear in the Warring States sources in various guises; but except for scattered references to them as *moao* and in the poorly understood post of *sanlü daifu*,[93] we know only (from the Baoshan materials) that they were not above serving in relatively low-level (local) offices by the late fourth century.[94] (The most famous man of this line was, of course, the third-century BCE poet Qu Yuan, discussed by Sukhu in chapter 9.) As for the Zhao lineage, the Baoshan bamboo strips are rich in information about it, as they emanate from the tomb of one of its members (see Weld, chapter 6).[95]

Barry B. Blakeley

Implicit in this overview of the role of lineages is the fact that leading figures in them often dominated the court scene. Some of them—virtually all of whom held the post of prime minister—should be introduced in greater detail.

Prime Ministers

ALL but two of Chu's prime ministers came from the royal clan.[96] Needless to say, some are worthy of praise; others are not. On the negative side, we may mention two men in particular. An example of an egotistical king maker is Gongzi Yuan. When King Wen (r. 690–675) died, he left behind two young sons (Zhuang [or Du] Ao and the future King Cheng) who succeeded each other in short order. Presumably it was Gongzi Yuan (Wen's brother) who maneuvered the assassination of Zhuang Ao and the enthronement of Cheng. In any case, he surely was the power behind the throne and evidently even harbored royal ambitions, as he took up residence in the palace and was infatuated with a royal consort. His domination of the court extended over the span of a decade and was brought to an end (in 664) only when he was assassinated by a scion of the Dou lineage (thereby initiating the era of the Ruo Ao lineages).

Wa, of the Yang collateral lineage, was another prime minister whose record was less than laudable. From the time he rose to the supreme post under King Ping, and through the early years of King Zhao, he proved to be corrupt and easily swayed by gossip. It was during his tenure, also, that the Chu heartland was invaded by Wu, and this debacle can at least in part be attributed to his ignoring warnings about the impending problem. Although eventually he began to listen to the advice of more responsible officials (albeit only when the crisis had reached a critical stage) and finally went on campaign against the enemy, as soon as the tide turned decisively against Chu, he took the easy way out and fled into exile.

On the other side of the ledger, Dou Ziwen (mentioned above) undoubtedly deserves to be listed among the more competent prime ministers. After all, he served for nearly three decades, during all but the final few years of the long period of King Cheng's inactivity (664–632), precisely in the phase when Chu first rose to prominence on the interstate scene. Despite this, we have very few details on his career.[97] One episode in which he figures, however, is widely known. It runs as follows:

> Ruo Ao married a woman of the state of Yun, by whom he sired Dou Bobi. When Ruo Ao died, Bobi accompanied his mother, who returned to her native state, where he was raised. Having an affair with a daughter of the Lord of Yun, he sired Ziwen. The wife of the Lord of Yun had the child abandoned in the marsh of Meng, where he was suckled by a tiger. The Lord of Yun, on a hunt, observed this, and was so frightened that he returned home forthwith. His wife then informed him of the daughter's indiscretion [thus that the child was his grandson], whereupon he had the child retrieved . . . and conferred his daughter on [Bobi] as wife.[98]

This obviously legendary tale may well be designed to enhance the status of Ziwen, who not only served as *lingyin* longer than any other individual, but who (at least in later times) was lauded for not being power hungry.[99] It also may have a more subtle point: the account accords not only Ziwen, but all of Bobi's descendants (at least one line of descent within the Dou group[100]), with a maternal ancestry at least as prominent as that of the descendants of Ruo Ao in the main lineage (i.e., subsequent rulers).[101] This could help explain the dominant role played by the Dou lineage from Ziwen onward (outlined above).[102]

Unlike the case of Dou Ziwen, we encounter frequent allusions in the literature to another prime minister, Wei Ao (more widely known as Sunshu Ao), who served under King Zhuang. He is easily the most famous of Chu's prime ministers and (other than Qu Yuan) is probably the most celebrated figure from Chu history. It is instructive, however, that this is so despite the fact that (compared to many a lesser figure) he is almost a passing shadow in the *Zuozhuan*. He is mentioned therein at only three points, over a span of but two years (598–597), so that we cannot even discern the dates of his tenure in office. One of the allusions (the only one of any substance), however, has played a major role in establishing his reputation. It describes circumstances in Chu in his time (albeit in words attributed to an official of Jin). These circumstances may be summarized as follows:

> He first put in order the statutes and records and then prescribed in detail the responsibilities of units within the military when on campaign. In the area of personnel, "[W]hen the ruler makes appointments, in the case of [candidates] of the same *xing* (clan) [as the Chu royal house], he chooses those closest in kinship; when they are of different *xing*, he chooses those whose ancestors have served in the past." The speaker goes on to claim that *de* (virtue?) was taken into account in making appointments, that rewards were conferred according to accomplishments, that particular favor was accorded to the aged, and that those from abroad were provided for. Regulations were extensive: dress was distinguished between the aristocracy and the commoners, the highborn were to be properly respected, lower levels of society were to behave in a manner proper to their station, etiquette was emphasized, the standards of virtue were fixed, and punishments were carried out properly. Government functions were carried out in accordance with both the task and the time.[103]

Obviously, if all of this were historically reliable, Chu at the time would have been a veritable utopia, which is highly improbable. There may be some basis to the description of Sunshu Ao's personnel policies,[104] but that the rest need not be taken literally is suggested by the fact that an equally laudatory *Shiji* version is rather different in its specifics.[105] Thus it seems that over time differing accounts of Sunshu Ao's career and achievements emerged. He also is the subject of a series of tales preserved in a considerable number of works (none of which is echoed in the comparatively sober *Zuozhuan*). Some of these tales overlap elements of the *Shiji* account of the man; some do not. A number of them are clearly variants of the same tale, but sometimes with significant differences. Others have no counterpart in other sources. The significant point is that they all exhibit an ideological perspective of some sort (but not necessarily the same one, even when treating the same incident). One trope in these, for instance, is Sunshu Ao as the almost Daoistic "reluctant official": having lived as some sort of a recluse (at least, far from court), he supposedly refused office three times. Suspicion is thrown on this, however, when other versions are taken into account, because in these he was *dismissed* on two occasions (resulting in three tenures in office).[106] In sum, Sunshu Ao clearly is one of those figures frequently encountered in early Chinese literature (such as Wu Zixu, discussed below) who in later times simply served as a peg on which a historical lesson or philosophical stance could conveniently be hung.[107] The unfortunate result for the historian is that it is unreasonable to expect the historical Sunshu Ao to "please stand up."

Chu's prime ministers, then, included a full array of arrogant manipulators, cowards, and capable administrators. Given the nature of the sources, however, we often know rather little about them and—in the case of Sunshu Ao—encounter considerable difficulty in assessing their actual achievements. From our examination of the roles of lineages and prime ministers, it should be clear that they represented serious challenges to royal power. We now examine a few kings to see how they coped with the situation—and how the sources can mislead us.

Kings

CHU's kings were a mixed lot, running from would-be autocrats to political ciphers. Discerning where an individual lay along this continuum, however, is often impeded by misleading impressions given in the sources.[108]

Of the eleven kings who reigned during the period when circumstances can be judged adequately (ca. 675–464), only three (Mu, Ling, and Ping) were in full charge of state affairs throughout their reigns.[109] Each usurped the throne and thus was necessarily a strong personality. The remaining eight kings during this span of time, however, either came to the throne at a tender age or experienced ill health. These circumstances resulted in regencies or domination by strong-willed kinsmen. And, of the kings whose reigns began with regencies, only half (Cheng, Zhuang, Gong, and Kang) succeeded in gaining a semblance of personal power. Even with their achievements, however, in absolute terms the kings dominated the court less than one-half of the time during those two centuries.

Among the unarguably powerful kings, the most interesting was Ling (r. 540–529), a notoriously unsavory character and Chu's greatest despot. The power behind the throne during the reign of his nephew, Jia Ao (544–541), he killed the ruler and took the throne for himself. He then set out to cow the Chu nobility into total submission. He confiscated their wealth in order to fund the construction of an elaborate palace and a pleasure retreat, and executed several of them. He also treated Chu's allied states with utter contempt and may have harbored grandiose dreams of dominating the entire Chinese world.[110] Given his behavior and ambitions, it is hardly surprising that he was left without a single source of support, either at home or abroad. And when the limits of tolerance had been reached, the first and only general rebellion against an occupant of the Chu throne broke out. Both court and countryside rose up against Ling, his sons were murdered, and when rebel armies approached the capital, the tyrant committed suicide.

Kings Cheng and Zhuang are examples of kings for whom great authority has been claimed but whose roles diminish greatly upon close examination. Contributing to the image of King Cheng (672–626) has been the following *Shiji* account of his rise and early career:

> When King Wen died, his son Zhuang Ao succeeded him. In his fifth year, Zhuang Ao decided to kill his brother [the future] King Cheng, who thereupon fled to the state of Sui and with its aid murdered Zhuang Ao and took the throne. Immediately upon ascending the throne, King Cheng exhibited virtue *(de)*, displayed compassion, renewed good relations previously enjoyed with the territorial lords, and dispatched an envoy to present tribute to the Son of Heaven [Zhou king]. The Son of Heaven conferred on him [the honor of] sacrificial meat, saying: "Protect your southern borders, and should the YiYue rebel, do not allow them to invade the Central States."[111]

There are reasons to be suspicious about several aspects this passage. One of the most damaging is that the *Zuozhuan* renders Cheng (as well as Zhuang Ao) too young to have played the roles assigned to him here, either before or after ascending the throne. Nor does the *Zuozhuan* record anything about a commission from the Zhou king to defend the southern realms.[112] It is probable, in fact, that this "strongman" image of King Cheng after his time may have been based in part on Chu achievements during his reign, as they were considerable— both in terms of territorial expansion and competition with the other superpower (Jin). In fact, Chu reached an early height at that time (see Blakeley, chapter 1). However, there is no particular reason to give credit to the king for these successes. In fact, the most serious defeat Chu had yet experienced (at the famous Battle of Chengpu in 632) can be attributed directly to poor decisions on Cheng's part. Nor does Cheng's performance at home prompt us to view him as a strong personality. His reign fell within the era in which the court was dominated by the Ruo Ao lineages, and there is no indication that he was active in any guise until 654. Even then, he did not become openly involved in court affairs until 632, when he forced the prime minister (Cheng Dechen) to commit suicide. He then cast his lot with the Dou lineage, but they were not docile servants. Nor, it might be noted, was Cheng very astute, even when it came to his own family. He miscalculated in trying to disenfranchise his designated heir, who rallied the palace guard, killed his father, and ascended the throne in his stead (as King Mu).

Even greater personal achievements have been claimed for King Zhuang (r. 613–591).[113] In one respect, there is no doubt that the reputation is deserved, based on the following episode:

> Ziyue, a Dou lineage prime minister, gathered the forces of the Ruo Ao lineages, intending to assault the king. In response, King Zhuang offered princes as

hostages. These having been declined, an open confrontation took place. During the battle, the king's soldiers lost heart and began to retreat; but the king emboldened them, ordered the attack drums sounded, and advanced. The result was a royal victory, and King Zhuang thereupon decimated the Ruo Ao lineages.[114]

Zhuang's victory ranks as the single most successful political maneuver ever achieved by a Chu king. It put an end to the sixty years of Ruo Ao lineage domination and set the stage for the rise of the main lineage. Beyond this, however, other stimuli to his image, such as the following story (dated to 606), are suspect.

> The lord of Chu [King Zhuang] attacked the Rong of Lunhun and then proceeded to the Luo River, where he inspected his troops on the border of Zhou. King Ding of Zhou dispatched Wangsun Man to greet the lord of Chu, who inquired of him concerning the size and weight of the tripods *(ding)*. He replied, "[Universal rulership] is a matter of virtue *(de)*, not of [possession of] the [nine[115]] tripods. Of old, when virtue was present in Xia's quarter, distant regions made depictions of their unusual creatures and offered metal [bronze] to the overseers of the nine districts, who cast those creatures in the designs on tripods. . . . When the virtue of [the Xia ruler] Jie became obscure, the tripods passed to Shang, with whom they remained for six hundred years. When King Zhou of Shang became depraved, the tripods were shifted to Zhou. . . . [Its] King Cheng [of Zhou] . . . divined that Heaven had ordained that Zhou rule would persist for thirty generations and seven hundred years. Even though the authority *(de)* of Zhou has declined, the decree of Heaven has not changed [i.e., Zhou's tenure is not complete]. Therefore, the weight of the tripods [i.e., whether they can be transferred] is not yet a matter for inquiry."[116]

There can be little doubt that this story is a post-facto embroidering of historical fact. Particularly damaging is the fact that there is no solid independent evidence that there ever was a set of tripods (of whatever number) that symbolized rulership in ancient China (as, for instance, with the English crown, scepter, and orb). The idea appears only in relatively late texts and smacks of being a Warring States period invention (particularly in the numerological implications of the number nine). Thus it is improbable that King Zhuang ever inquired about the tripods, and there are other reasons to question the historicity of the incident as a whole.[117]

That King Zhuang gave rise to apocryphal stories also is clearly indicated by this well-known passage in the *Shiji:*

> After ascending the throne, the king issued no commands for three years, attending instead to his own pleasures and threatening death to anyone who should criticize him on this account. A brave official, however, decided to take his chances. Upon entering the palace, finding the king seated amid his musicians

with a female companion on either side, he said: "I should like to put forth a riddle. What kind of bird perches on a mound and for three years neither flies nor sings?" Replied the king: "One which does not fly because it would crash into the skies and which does not sing out for fear of scaring people. You may retire. I get your point." The king nevertheless persisted in his lascivious ways for another three months, whereupon another official came forth to complain. Upon seeing him enter, the king said: "Have you not heard of my threat against criticism?" The officer replied: "My hope is that my death would enlighten my Lord." The king then ceased his lewd pleasures, attended to state affairs, executed several hundred bad officials, promoted a like number of good ones, and placed the government in the hands of the two critics—all of which was a great relief to the people.[118]

There is strong evidence from other sources that all of this is pure fiction.[119] Zhuang was probably rather young when he ascended the throne and, in any case, was for some time thereafter no more than a pawn in the hands of the Cheng lineage. In other words, no one at the time would have expected him to issue any decrees in his early years. And, in fact, Zhuang did not become openly involved in state affairs until the suppression of the Ruo Ao lineage in 605 or shortly before.[120] Finally, over the centuries Zhuang's image as a strongman was virtually insured by the fact that the third-century BCE philosopher Xunzi (who, incidentally, spent time in Chu) listed him as one of the five Hegemons (ba) who dominated during Spring and Autumn times. However, in a technical sense this surely was not the case;[121] and while it may be that Zhuang dreamed of achieving the hegemony, Chu was by no means the dominant power of his time (facing, as it did, intense competition from Jin).[122] With King Zhuang, then, we have a figure who (on the one hand) was by no means a total figurehead (at least late in life), but whose role was eventually blown all out of proportion.

In sum, the record compiled by Chu's kings was a very mixed one, and only a few of them can safely be said to have been the dominant figures of their times. Having now treated the main players—from the upper rungs of society—something should be said of men from less prominent backgrounds.

Nonroyal Clan Figures

WHILE rarely the major power brokers or holders of high office, men from relatively low social background and aliens occasionally came to some degree of prominence. The prime example was Wu Qi, an immigrant and the most celebrated Chu official of Warring States times. A native of Wey who had previously served in both Lu and Wei, Wu Qi arrived in Chu in about 390. After being assigned to a local post for a time by King Dao, he was elevated to the prime ministership. His most famous measure was to address what he saw as Chu's greatest weaknesses—excessively powerful officials and an overabundance of enfeoffed lords (fengjun). His solution was a series of policies designed to favor the capable (regardless of social background) and to terminate all hereditary privileges after three generations. However, upon the death of the king, the aristocracy rose up and killed Wu Qi (in 381), and his measures were reversed. This restoration of aristocratic privileges is often cited as the principal reason that Chu was unable to compete in the long run with Qin (which set out on a thorough reform not long after, in 350). Still, even presuming that at least the central thrust of the Wu Qi episode is historically reliable,[123] the revival of aristocratic prerogatives must have been either partial or short-lived (in light of the considerable degree of centralization suggested by the Baoshan materials, noted above).

Another nonroyal clan figure (also an immigrant) was Fei Wuji. Originally from the state of Cai, he was appointed by King Ping as junior tutor to his heir apparent (Taizi Jian). Fei Wuji, ambitious from the outset, soon began a slur campaign against a rival for the ear of the king, who then fled into exile. Although not pleased, King Ping took no action. Fei Wuji soon targeted another potential rival, the principal tutor (thus his immediate superior) and a member of a prominent nonroyal clan kindred, Wu She.[124] Accusing Wu She of dereliction of duty in not finding a wife for the heir, Fei Wuji convinced the king to turn this task over to him. Once a suitable woman had been found, however, he prevailed upon the king to take her for himself. Fei Wuji then set out to get rid of Wu She. He proposed that Taizi Jian be posted to the northern frontier, where Wu She would naturally accompany him. The king agreed, but the location Fei Wuji suggested was such that he could accuse the heir and his tutor of plotting rebellion. The king, taken in by this subterfuge, issued an order for the seizure of Wu She and the execution of the heir. (By the time the king realized his mistake, his son had fled to safety abroad.) Once again, Ping made no move to punish Fei Wuji for his machinations.

Now it happened that Wu She had two sons who were living abroad. Fei Wuji convinced the king to offer a pardon for the father if the sons would return to Chu. Only one did so, leaving the condition for a pardon unfulfilled. Consequently, Wu She and the repatriated son were executed on the king's orders. Emboldened by his success and confident of his relationship with the king, Fei Wuji then began to accept bribes. When this came into the open, the king, despite some displeasure, still made no move against him and died without doing so.

Fei Wuji's plots continued into the following reign, that of King Zhao. He accused one Xi Wan of plotting to assassinate his patron, Prime Minister Nang Wa. This action drove Xi Wan to commit suicide, and despite strong complaints about Fei Wuji's behavior from courtiers, Nang Wa executed Xi Wan's family and associates. The latter included men of the Yang collateral lineage, and its surviving members therefore launched an intense campaign against Fei Wuji. In the face of this, the prime minister finally gave in and executed Fei Wuji.

We have this degree of detail on no other Chu figure of comparable social background. Suspicions that it is not entirely reliable as historical fact, however, arise from several angles. The account of Fei Wuji's career has qualities suggesting that it was originally an integrated story, one concocted after the fact, that has been cut up and placed at appropriate points in the *Zuozhuan*'s chronology.[125] A major reason for caution is that the story does not really end where we have left it. Fei Wuji's manipulations, we eventually learn, had long-range effects. One was a rebellion raised by a son of the disenfranchised Taizi Jian.[126] The other is that the son of Wu She who remained abroad, Wu Zixu, avenged his father's death by giving military advice to his adopted home—Chu's archival at the time, the state of Wu. This led to the most serious military crisis Chu had experienced to date: the invasion and occupation of the Chu heartland by Wu in 506–505 (see Blakeley, chapter 1). We have here, then, a theme common in the quasi-historical literature of early China—tracing the source of crises back to some unsavory, inept, or immoral character. It may be, too, that the tale was an element in a broader story cycle containing another didactic theme: one of its central figures—Wu Zixu—is the protagonist of the most extensive body of lore concerning any figure of Spring and Autumn times.[127] Since most of the tale concerns his career in Wu, we will not delve into it here, but it should be noted that its leitmotif is a popular one in the quasi-historical literature: maltreatment by a ruler of a righteous and/or capable official.[128] A final source of suspicion is the rather evenhanded treatment of Fei Wuji and his social superiors. While Fei Wuji is clearly the villain, neither King Ping nor Nang Wa is without fault, and there is almost a sense of satisfaction over Fei Wuji's ability to manipulate the nominal wielders of power. The story, then, reflects less the aristocratic conditions of Spring and Autumn times than the growing social leveling of Warring States times.

Conclusion

WE have seen in this chapter that the nature of the sources poses major obstacles to comprehending state and society in Chu. The available data permit insights into a good many aspects, but at the same time leave a number of issues clouded (especially with respect to the roles played by individuals). Nevertheless, it can safely be said that the characteristics of Chu society and state fell largely within the general framework of the time (and ultimately derived from the north) but exhibited certain distinctive characteristics. Most of the latter lay at the level of details and therefore are not particularly significant. One unique feature, however, stands out—a degree of political centralization unknown elsewhere in ancient China until the mid-fourth century.[129] This must have been critical to Chu's ability to create and administer a virtual empire, one unequaled in extent and sophistication before the rise of Qin. And it seems likely that Qin's creation of a truly centralized, bureaucratic empire owed a deep debt to innovations first made in Chu.

5

The Ideology of the Chu Ruling Class

Ritual Rhetoric and Bronze Inscriptions

CONSTANCE A. COOK

THE quest of Chu kings for power was a popular subject for ancient storytellers. Beginning as early as the *Zuozhuan,* we see, for example, the famous tales of two arrogant but successful seventh-century Chu rulers, Kings Zhuang and Ling, who suggested that the time had come for Zhou to pass the sacred "Nine Caldrons" on to Chu.[1] The Nine Caldrons represented the Heavenly Mandate *(tianming),* the right to rule the empire; they also symbolized the Zhou lineage authority to cast sacred bronze vessels for communication with heaven.[2] In each case, the Chu kings were outmaneuvered by artful ministers who guarded the spiritual rights of the Zhou ruler, subtly hinting at the moral inferiority of the Chu rulers. The caldrons, it was explained, moved of their own will. They were heavy or light depending on the accumulation of power *(de)* by the ruler. Although the story describes this power as an almost magical control over evil forces, we know from the Zhou inscriptions on bronze ritual vessels that this special power was tied to the accretion of symbolic Zhou treasures or wealth associated with a lineage member's merit *(gong).* Merit was gained through active roles in ritual sacrifice to the Zhou royal ancestors or in military expansion of the sacred Zhou empire. What the ministers were hinting, then, was that the Chu kings did not have the power because they were not connected to the Zhou legacy. However, analysis of the Chu bronze inscriptions reveals a loyalty to Zhou ritual that contradicts these early tales.

Zhou ritual was perpetuated in Chu by ritualists who often held official positions as advisors to the king. These advisors, the brains behind Chu success (and failure),[3] were considered a Chu treasure by envious northern states.[4] By the end of the Warring States period the Chu ritualists had become so powerful that sacred bronzes were no longer cast for use by the royal Chu descendants, but for the ritual officers instead. In this chapter we will see how the ritualists manipulated Zhou ideology to fit the Chu quest for power and simultaneously enhanced their own power.

The Treasure of Chu

ONE of the famous treasures of Chu was Guan Shefu, an advisor to King Zhao (r. 515–489). He explained the importance of using ritualists in terms that clearly show his knowledge of Zhou liturgy and that can be confirmed by an examination of Zhou bronze inscriptions. According to him, the proper relations between rulers, spirits, and the people are maintained by ritualists (*xian,* male shamans; or *wu,* female shamans). Shamans, he said, knew the "rules of 'awe-inspiring decorum' *(weiyi)*" and how to "respect and revere the luminous spirits" *(jinggong mingshen).* They were experts in choosing the proper sacrificial animals, jades, silks, clothing, and vessels; they knew how to possess "luminous power" *(mingde)* through the spirits. Guan Shefu, most likely a ritualist himself, then proceeded to explain to the king how the kings of antiquity sacrificed to spirits unceasingly—daily, they sacrificed *(ji);* monthly, they "made offerings [in a lineage mortuary feast]" *(xiang);* and yearly, they "sacrificed to ancestral spirits" *(si)* in order to glorify *(zhao,* literally, make shine) their filial piety and quiet the peoples. In order to "perform the shining sacrifice" *(zhaosi)* to his ancestors, he said, one must gather together for a feast all male relations and relations by marriage from neighboring districts. In presenting the sacrifices, one's luminous power makes the spirits shine, and "harmonious sounds" make them heard.[5]

Although the Western Zhou ritualists were originally called governing officials *(yin)* or archivists *(shi)*[6] and not shamans, the ritual language used by Guan Shefu, like that in the Chu bronze inscriptions, has a clear Zhou precedent, one that can be traced back to the tenth century and earlier. The ideology of their presentation, however, reflects the political-religious changes of the late Western Zhou period. This is particularly evident in the changing ritual role of the inscriptions' narrators.

The Power of Words

THE Zhou king, like the Shang king, acted as the conduit for communication with the spirits. In the early inscriptions the king's spoken words (what he *yue,* said) were recorded by scribes in a solemn gift-giving ceremony that took place in the presence of the king's ancestor in his ancestral temple.[7] The content of the king's speech was his charge, or mandate *(ming).* The charge—as well as brief notes choreographing the ceremony—was then cast by the gift recipient as an inscription inside a sacrificial vessel. The text was then read by the recipient's own patron spirit during the presentation of sacrificial offerings. The king's word was the spiritual conduit that connected man with heaven.[8] The ritualist transcribed his speech, and the recipient bowed and extolled the king's "greatly manifested" *(pixian)* grace. The grace was the gift of legitimation to participate in the Zhou order. It was symbolized by the gift of precious metal (and other ritual implements) and the inscribed charge.

Virtue and Conquest

BOTH the giver and the recipient of a command had to be legitimate—that is, had to have "power"—in the eyes of the overseeing ancestral spirits; this was achieved through the ritual reenactment of the Zhou conquest, the primal Zhou act that caused heaven to shift its mandate from the earlier Shang ruler to the Zhou (and, according to legend, caused the movement of the Nine Caldrons.) The giver was linked to heaven through his ancestors and the recipient through the giver.[9] Both had to grasp *(bing)*, as one would a sword, the luminous power[10] inherited from the first Zhou kings, Wen and Wu (whose names symbolize ritual and military accomplishment). With the power in hand, the descendent had to display his "awe-inspiring decorum," the ritual or military subjugation of border peoples (and eternal expansion of the Zhou state). This proved to the manifested ancestral spirits that they had faithfully followed the ancestral model *(xing,* a metaphor of the mold used to cast bronzes) and did not let the mandate fall. Only then did they have the power to give or receive a command.

Revelry in the Temple

BY the end of the Western Zhou period the role of the king as intermediary between the recipient and the spirits vanished from the paleographical record. The recipients—descendants of those with connections to the Zhou—cast their own bronzes and recorded their own speeches detailing how they modeled themselves upon their greatly manifested ancestors' luminous power and awe-inspiring decorum. They described how—in sacrificing to the deities "from dawn to dusk"—they, like their spiritual predecessors, made their hearts luminous *(ming),* wise *(zhe),* or intelligent *(cong,* literally, all-hearing); they described how they pacified the peoples *(min)* with their primal, luminous, harmonious, or governing power and made the glory of their military deeds (i.e., the suppression of border peoples) heard throughout the four regions of the world.

The late Western Zhou lords did not proclaim the merits of their ancestors in private temple ceremonies but at large feasts, much like those described by Guan Shefu.[11] Ritual instructions inscribed on the inside of sacrificial food and wine vessels and, increasingly, on the outside of bells[12] explained that the vessels or bells were to be used for the feasting and musical entertainment of the ritual participants (the spirits, the lords, colleagues, and attendant ritualists).[13] While presenting the sacrifices or ringing the bells, the lords prayed for long life and good fortune. Everyone was to be made happy and tranquil with specially prepared foods and wines.[14] The ritual instructions were often followed by words representing musical sounds—the sounds of the gods who delivered the desired blessing in exchange for a promise that the sacrifices would be continued generation after generation.[15]

By acting as their own intermediaries to the spirits, these lords opened the door for the later complete usurpation of the ritual role of the king. By the Eastern Zhou period the Zhou king, or "Son of Heaven," was given but passing reference in inscriptions.[16] Vessels or bells were all commissioned by the lords themselves who, in essence, commanded and legitimized themselves in inscriptions cast for the eyes of spirits and mortals during celebration of the annual sacrificial rites and covenant feasts.

Southern Arrogance in the Eastern Zhou Period: Ritual Rhetoric and Military Motives

THE Chu elites, representing a border people themselves, not only jettisoned all reference to the mandate of the Zhou king, but redirected the power of the Zhou ancestral spirits. Unlike the Qin and Jin in the northwest or the Cai in the east, the Chu never referred to the Heavenly Mandate and never felt the need to model themselves upon the Zhou ancestors. Nevertheless, they used the rhetoric of the Zhou conquest and performed a "luminous sacrificial rite" *(mingsi)* to their own "brilliant and accomplished" *(huangwen)* ancestors. They adopted terminology originally preserved to describe the virtues of the Zhou kings and applied it to themselves, spreading their own power *(de)* "throughout the four regions."

The manipulation of Zhou rhetoric in Chu reached its height during the sixth century. The most informative inscribed texts were commissioned by royal descendants of the main lineage but were found in a Wei lineage tomb (Tomb 2 in the Xiasi section of the Xichuan burial ground).[17] This tomb belonged to Weizi Ping, who died in 548. The long inscriptions, however, belonged to Prince Wu (Wangzi Wu), also known as Commanding Governor Zigeng (Lingyin Zigeng). Wu had died in 552, four years earlier, the same year that Weizi Ping succeeded to the position of commanding governor *(lingyin)* under King Kang (Wu's nephew).

Figure 5.1 Rubbing of Wangzi Wu *sheng-ding* inscription [after Ma Chengyuan et al, vol. 2, 410–411]. The graph *de* is the first graph in the fourth line from the left. The inscription reads right to left.

Constance A. Cook

The seven intricately decorated high-legged caldrons of Wu placed in Weizi Ping's tomb all had the word "Ping" scratched into their surfaces. Whether Weizi Ping received Wu's bronzes as an emblem of merit during his lifetime or as a lineage debt paid at his death remains a mystery.[18]

Prince Wu became commanding governor in 558. Two years earlier, in 560, Wu's brother, King Gong, died, and Gong's son (Wu's nephew), Kang, ascended the throne.[19] The vessels were probably cast around that time. According to the inscription, Wu made the caldrons to present meat offerings [20] to "express filial piety to 'our' Brilliant Ancestors and Accomplished Dead-father" (Wu's father was King Zhuang, who died in 591). In exchange for the sacrifice, he prayed for long life.

To legitimize his right to cast the bronzes and be commanding governor, he described his ritual and military merit (his *wen* and *wu*) to the spirits. In ritual, he behaved "with deep reverence and extensive fairness, expressing awe and care when paying his respects [to the spirits] in their luminous sacrificial rite." In return, he expected "to eternally receive good fortune from them." In military affairs, he claimed: "I am neither fierce nor flawed, but am beneficent with my power and am skilled with my awe-inspiring decorum." Words representing music followed—sounding something like *"glan glan djog djog"* (Clang! Clang! Ding! Dong!)—indicating perhaps the acceptance of Wu's merit speech by the spirits and the commencement of the feast. Prince Wu proclaimed: "It is me, Commanding Minister Zigeng, wherein lies the respect of the people."

The humane influence of the Wei family was extolled by Chu's enemy to the north, the state of Jin, in 598.[21] When Chu wiped out the Jin army at Bi in 597, Prince Wu's father, King Zhuang, declined to express his triumph in the barbaric manner suggested by one of his less humane advisors, namely, by piling up the bodies of the conquered as a display of his martial merit *(wugong)* to his descendants. Rather, he chose to model himself upon the legendary behavior of the Zhou king Wu. He explained that the true meaning of the word *"wu"* could not refer to a vulgar display of defeated enemies; instead, the word must be understood as a sum of the meaning of its graphical parts: *zhi*, "to stop"; and *ge*, "dagger-axe." In other words, he explained (showing off his knowledge of the Zhou eulogies to their former kings):

> Then put away your shields and axes,
> Encase your arrows and bows;
> I have stored enough good power,
> to spread over all the lands of Xia.[22]

To show off his power, he did not display barbarian brutality but built a temple instead. There, he sacrificed to his ancestral spirits to report his *wu* and how he (like the Zhou king) had brought harmony to the land.[23]

When King Kang came to the throne, his uncle, Prince Wu, still was most likely the real power behind the throne; thus it is not surprising that he would express himself in terms fit for a king. He had led military campaigns, but, just as he claimed in the inscription, he was not bellicose by nature. In fact, in 555, three years after Wu had been promoted to commanding governor, the young King Kang complained that he had been king for five years and had yet to go out on a military campaign. The people would think him lazy. How could he live up to the former kings? Prince Wu agreed to the king's proposed campaigns only with reluctance, noting that Chu and Jin had been at peace for some time now. Indeed, according to the *Zuozhuan,* the inauspicious expeditions—which the young king insisted upon—were unsuccessful, and many of the troops died from illness.[24]

The ritual language on Prince Wu's sacrificial vessels was copied—almost to the word—in two bell inscriptions commissioned by two royal grandsons, Gao (Wangsun Gao) and Yizhe (Wangsun Yizhe). Their exact relationship to Prince Wu is unclear, but the similarity of the inscribed texts points to a "common archival source."[25] With the sound of the bells, they made their inscribed merits, their power, heard throughout the world. Like Prince Wu, they governed the people with "diligent plans" and displays of awe-inspiring decorum; they were "martial *(wu)* in putting into effect their military merit *(ronggong).*"

The terminology of these sixth-century Chu inscriptions can be traced, phrase by phrase, to earlier Western Zhou inscriptions; it is also echoed throughout the ritual rhetoric of contemporary inscriptions of other states.[26] This clearly suggests that Chu participated in a continuous scribal tradition, one inherited from the Zhou and disseminated throughout early China. A study of the fragments of ritual rhetoric used in the inscriptions of Chu and its neighbors reveals that the most archaic versions of the rhetoric in early Spring and Autumn period inscriptions come from the states of Qin and Jin in the northwest, confirming a northwestern origin or, at least, preservation of the tradition. The rulers of Qin and Jin, unlike those of Chu, carried on the rhetoric of modeling themselves upon their own ancestral rulers, but, like the Chu, they "paid their respects to their [ancestors'] rites in order to receive much good fortune." The Qin rulers made their luminous power heard through the world, and the Jin rulers extolled their ancestors through their diligence and their plans.[27] These rulers were concerned that the spirits protect their states and admire their efforts to expand. Expansion, in the case of Jin particularly, was at the expense of Chu. The Jin, like the Zhou kings, wanted access to southern metals, in particular the bronze of Fanyang.[28]

Politics and the Feast

THE Chu ritual food vessels and bells were made to be used in grand feasts in order to glorify the living as well as the dead. The Chu inscriptions, while dedicated to their ancestral spirits, do not specifically mention spirits among the guests at the feast, although it is very likely that their presence was assumed, as the vessels used in the feast were made on their behalf. The Chu feast included the Chu king, the many archer-lords *(zhuhou),* celebrated guests *(jiabin),* associates—possibly relatives by marriage *(pengyou)*—and patrilineal relatives *(fuxiong).* This secularized version of the ecstatic cultivation of power is further reflected in the sixth-century writing of the term "luminous sacrificial rite" *(mingsi).* The graph read *ming,* composed of sun and moon elements, was often confused with the graph read *meng,* composed of the phonetic *ming* over a vessel element. This latter graph represented the term "covenant rite" *(meng),* a rite where lords of various contending states met to arrange peace contracts. We find this curious loan of *meng* for *ming* in the inscriptions of states at battle with, or in the process of being absorbed by, Chu: the Jin, Zhu, Xu, and Cai.[29]

The ritual feast, used in the Western Zhou as a forum for gift-giving and the adjustment of social status, had become by the late Spring and Autumn period—the time when Chu was at the peak of its power—the ultimate scene of political machination. Indeed, contemporary records show that the feasting of visiting emissaries from other states was a common arena in which to show off one's awe-inspiring demeanor, often to the embarrassment of the visitor (who would then report the excess to his own government and subsequently be assured by a ritualist that such arrogance was in fact inauspicious for the host).[30]

We see, for example, that when Chu and Jin were negotiating peace in 578, the Chu and Jin sent envoys to each other's states. Going first to Chu, a Jin envoy heard the sounds of music coming from an underground room and became frightened that the ritual of presenting sacrificial offerings and hosting feasts (*xiang yan zhi li*) would be used for a simple envoy and not the head of state.[31] Before entering the room, he lectured Zifan, the Chu minister in charge of the ceremony: "[O]ne presents offerings (*xiang*) in order to give [participants] a lesson in modesty. One hosts a feast (*yan*) in order to show [participants] one's beneficence. Use modesty to practice ritual and beneficence to spread government. Government is accomplished through ritual." Only then, he continued, would the people be at rest (not rebellious) and the officers get their proper orders. Thus proving himself the moral superior (and rationalizing himself in a sticky situation), he partook of the Chu ceremony. Later, however, a Jin minister, upon hearing of the Chu audacity, interpreted it as a bad omen. Indeed, the peace did not last.

The feast was a place where the host also observed the awe-inspiring demeanor of the guests and determined from it the inauspicious or auspicious fortunes in store for his state.[32] Wine was passed around in rhinoceros horn cups, strategically selected odes were sung back and forth, games were played, and specially prepared dishes were consumed.[33] The true nature of the represented states' relations were divined from the ability of the guest to select an appropriate song, from his response to the food service—whether he enjoyed the roast meat that was sliced (for envoys) or served whole (for lords), or whether he lost at a game of tossing arrows into a wine vessel. The guest's demeanor, or political savvy, was a measure of his knowledge of Zhou etiquette and rites.

On occasion, the feasts that followed covenants were less than joyful. Once when the high lord of Cai was being entertained in Chu, the Chu king Ling (r. 540–529) soldiers captured and murdered him.[34] One ruler, a victim of a coup d'état in Wei, was pursued by a contending prince and his men (dressed as women) into his privy, where they caught him and forced him to feast on roast pig and drink wine, thus sealing a covenant that effectively forced him out of power.[35]

Out with the Old, In with the Ancient: The Warring States Period

IN 489, Zizhang (the Chu king Hui), a child of the Chu king Zhao (r. 516–489) and his wife from Yue, came to the throne. In the fifty-sixth year of his reign, a year before his death in 432, he commissioned a set of bells to be used while sacrificial offerings were presented in the temple of Archer Lord Yi of Zeng (Zeng Hou Yi), the deceased ruler of an eastern neighbor and affiliate of Chu. Two of these bells were found near Suixian, Hubei, during the Song dynasty, and another one was found recently in Zeng Hou Yi's elaborate tomb (fig. 3.5).[36] The inscriptions on these bells are essentially the same except that those found during the Song period contain some additional musical terms;[37] they may have represented above- and below-ground copies of the text signifying the use of the dead as a conduit for conveying a contract between the living and their ancestors. This contract was like the covenant feasts aboveground, sealed with a feast below ground, the remains of which have been preserved for us in the tomb.[38] Both the inscribed bronzes and the feast functioned to fix Zeng Hou Yi's rank (in heaven and on earth) as a high lord in the Chu government.

Zizhang's scribe employed a combination of archaic and new rhetorical forms. The inscription begins with a dating formula going back to the late Shang–early Western Zhou period. At that time the word si, "sacrificial rite," also meant "year" of a living king's reign, an event no doubt marked by the revolving ritual calendar of sacrifices to patron ancestral spirits.[39] By the time of Zizhang, however, the term si clearly referred to sacrificial rites to all spirits, ancestral as well as those of nature.[40] The use of a Shang-style dating formula either represents a purposeful archaism or ignorance on the part of the scribe. It also suggests that this scribe did belong to the Zhou tradition and symbolizes the beginning of an era when, the Zhou mandate having clearly slipped, kings began to rely on other, perhaps local, traditions to preserve their legitimacy. These local traditions may have preserved conventions dating back to the Shang and early Western Zhou periods. We see, for example, that after stating the year, the scribe noted that the Chu king was "returning from Xiyang."[41] Noting the king's movements goes back to the era when the state was maintained through traveling and gift-giving feasts performed in situ for chiefs initiated into the early Zhou order.[42]

The remaining text of the inscription is rather simple, describing the manufacture of a sacrificial object for the temple of Zeng Hou Yi and its placement in Xiyang. The inscription ends with a graphically skewed version of a blessing typical of the time and region: "[E]ternally treasure it and use it to present sacrifices." This and other similar variants common to Zeng, Cai, and this "Chu" bell suggest their manufacture in the same foundry operated by a single school of scribes or ritualists, or at least scribes that shared an oral tradition.[43]

Two weapon inscriptions, also commissioned by Zizhang, confirm the piecemeal nature of the language of Warring States period inscriptions: a sword, found in the tomb of the Chu king You (r. 237–229) in Shouxian, Anhui, and a dagger-axe, found somewhere around Luoyang, Henan.[44] The sword inscription uses typical Warring States rhetoric: "Chu king Yin[45] Zhang cast a sword for Cong X Shi. Use it on travels; use it on military expeditions."[46] The dagger-axe inscription, on the other hand, is unprecedented. The text is inscribed with bird-script of inlaid gold, typical of the state of Yue and the Huai River valley.[47] Whereas weapon inscriptions are normally perfunctory statements of manufacture, the Chu inscription borrows from the rhetoric of legitimation seen earlier in the inscriptions of sixth-century ritual bells and food vessels: "Chu king Yin Zhang, stern, reverent, and respectful, made a chariot lance dagger-axe, a dagger to be used in order to glorify and extol Wen and Wu." The concept of extolling one's ancestors *(zhaoyang)* through the military expansion of the empire preserved the spirit of the Zhou conquest. However, actually to inscribe this sacred message onto a weapon instead of onto a sacrificial vessel was a bold, even crude, step—one that combines a lapse of understanding of the old rites with a curious memory of the rhetoric. Most interesting is the ambiguous, perhaps metaphorical, reference to Wen and Wu. Was the scribe alluding to the early Chu kings Wu (r. 740–690) and Wen (r. 689–676), to the founders of the Zhou empire, Wen and Wu, or simply to the concepts of *wen* and *wu,* the ritual and martial behavior imitated by and extolled in Zizhang himself? Quite possibly it was all three.

One aspect of the old rites was certainly not lost in Warring States period Chu: the use of ritual vessels in feasts. Earlier this century, looters discovered the royal Chu mausoleum at the last capital of Chu, Shouchun in Shouxian, Anhui. One tomb most likely belonged to the Chu king You (d. 229), but as with the Wei mausoleum in Xichuan, it included earlier vessels. King You's tomb included vessels commissioned by his father, King Kaolie (r. 263–238).[48] The high-footed caldrons, food service vessels, and basins of both kings were cast "in order to present the annual autumnal sacrifice" *(yi gong suichang).* The calligraphy and rhetoric of the inscriptions are similar to that found on Warring States bamboo texts and reaffirm earlier evidence of the use of scribes trained in a non-Zhou tradition.

Many of the vessels were specifically made for the ritualists in charge of the administration and service of grains, meats, and wines at the grand feast. The master ritualists included a number of officials, aligned to the right or left of the High Temple Elder, who was in charge of setting up the sacrificial feast. Inscribed on certain sacrificial implements were the names of different subordinate groups of officials in charge of various aspects of the food and wine service.[49] Other inscribed vessels plundered from this tomb or neighboring sites[50] were made for the dining halls, chambers, and repositories of the queen *(hou)* or the royal heirs *(taizi).* Ritualists were in charge of their food service as well.

When King Kaolie came to the throne in 263, he set his tutor (and his father's faithful minister) up as lord of Chunshen in the former territory of the Wu state. Sometime between this date and 223, when Chu fell to the invading Qin, this local lord (or a later replacement) cast a set of oversized sacrificial wine vessels *(yi* and *jian)* and food vessels *(dou).*[51] Scratched into the surfaces of the basin and food serving vessels is the following inscription: "Prince Shen, Lord of Eling (Chunshen), used these [metals] to create a metal basin (or food vessel). Use it to prepare the annual autumnal sacrifice in order to perform the sacrificial rite to the Brilliant Ancestors and to bring together the fathers and older brothers. Forever using it, may the officials use it without limit."[52]

On the eve of the extinction of the Chu state, we see that a Chu prince no longer cast his vessels for the eternal use of his descendants as in days of old. Instead, as with the Shouxian vessels above, these vessels were made for the use of ritualists who controlled the great feast and brought together members of the patriarchy to celebrate and perform the annual sacrificial rite *(si)* to their ancestral gods. After the Chu moved east, fleeing from western invaders just like the Zhou before them, they lost their connection to heaven. The king and his descendants no longer mediated communications between the spirits and the people. Instead, as with the later Han emperors, their spiritual matters were managed by a bureaucracy of officials.

The Ideology of the Chu Ruling Class

Royal Rhetoric versus Local Practices:
Questions of Tradition, Text, and Culture

THE Chu debt to the Zhou ritual tradition is evident from the inscriptions cast by its kings and princes. Throughout the history of the Chu state, its rulers emulated the Zhou virtues of *wen* and *wu* and hosted grand religious feasts to perform the *si* sacrificial ritual to the ancestral spirits. Long after the inscribed rhetoric of other states was limited to brief statements on weapons, pieces of the Zhou legacy were still preserved by the Chu royal family.[53]

The decline of the Zhou rhetorical legacy followed the disintegration of the Zhou Heavenly Mandate. By the beginning of the Warring States period society could no longer function along the old rules. A rapidly rising urban elite elevated local customs to replace or isolate the stilted Zhou rituals no longer so well understood (or obeyed) in the royal courts. Literacy, once limited to a small caste of scribes and ritualists, had spread to the point where local officials had libraries of bamboo and silk texts. A number of these texts recently have been excavated from southern tombs that belong to Chu, Qin, or Han period elites. The Chu books, particularly, show a concern with divination and a literary style that resonates back to the Shang period, suggesting that no matter how much the royalty were instructed in the use of a Zhou-style liturgy, the local literati maintained even older traditions.[54]

As the Zhou mystique faded and local liturgical traditions thrived, the power of the inscribed text was transferred from the hands of the royalty to those of the ritualists. Eventually, inscriptions became simple lists of ritual measurements and designations of function, and the sacred bronze vessels, once the ultimate sign of prestige, were replaced by shiny lacquerware.

6

Chu Law in Action

Legal Documents from Tomb 2 at Baoshan

SUSAN WELD

T HE books transmitted to modern readers from early China, whether histories, philosophical works, or anthologies, do not tell us much about the practical operation of
legal institutions. In this respect, Chu differs little from other states in having a decidedly low
"legal profile" in the best-known classical works. In the last few decades archaeologists have
opened graves containing thousands of strips of legal and ritual texts that begin to fill the gaps
in our understanding of law in early China. Students of Chu are fortunate in that several of
the great "law graves" have been found in the heartland of cultural Chu, and that one such
grave dates to the Warring States period.

In April 1986 a team of salvage archaeologists working on the construction of the new
Jingmen-Shashi railroad line investigated a small group of Chu tombs on a hill called Baoshan
in the village of Wangchangcun, Hubei Province.[1] Wangchangcun is located in hilly country,
on the northern edge of the Jiang-Han plain.[2] Since 1956 the Chu cemeteries in this area
have been recognized as important cultural sites, and the thirteen burial areas found so far
within ten kilometers of Baoshan include at least forty-one large tombs marked with sizable
tumuli. Baoshan itself is only sixteen kilometers north of the ancient Chu city site of Jinancheng, and its remains form part of an extensive system of Eastern Zhou cemeteries centered
on this city, famous in historical sources as the Chu capital of Ying.[3]

Tomb 2, the largest in the group of five Baoshan graves, yielded 278 well-preserved
inscribed bamboo strips, containing altogether 12,472 graphs. These strips tell us that the
master of the tomb was a high official in the Chu government, the *zuoyin* Shao Tuo. A literal
translation of *zuoyin* would be "Director of [or on] the Left,"[4] but the documents in Shao

Tuo's grave suggest that in his case, at least, *zuoyin* should be understood more specifically as the Chu equivalent of the Zhou position of *sikou,* sometimes translated as "minister of justice."[5] It is because Shao Tuo held this key position in the Chu judicial system that the documents carefully laid in his tomb—to guide him in his bureaucratic activities in the beyond, symbolize his prestige among the spirits, or perhaps just fend off boredom in the afterlife—offer legal historians an irreplaceable glimpse of the actual operation of Chu law and justice in the Warring States period.

Other Sources of Information about the Chu Legal System

BEFORE 1987 evidence on Chu law was limited to tantalizing scraps and oblique references tucked in transmitted texts such as the *Analects,* the *Zuozhuan,* the *Guoyu,* the *Zhanguoce,* and the *Shiji.* Perhaps the best-known reference to Chu ideas about law is the boast of a Chu lord in the *Analects:*

> The Duke of She said to Confucius: In our village, we have a true example of an upright person. When the father stole a sheep, the son gave evidence against him. Confucius answered: Among us, the upright are quite different. Fathers cover up for sons and sons cover up for fathers. Such is truly upright behavior.[6]

Chu's image in this passage is legalistic to a fault; however, the conversation has more the feeling of a moral parable than a depiction of reality. Another example is the admiring speech of the Jin commander Shi Hui before Jin's disastrous defeat by Chu at the battle of Bi in 597 BCE. Shi Hui was warning his belligerent companions that an attack on so virtuous and well-organized an opponent as Chu would be sure to fail:

> I have heard that, in using military force, one must examine the pretext before moving. A [state] that unceasingly practices virtue in its punishments, its government, its business affairs, its laws *(dian),* and its rituals is not to be attacked. . . . Last year Chu invaded Chen, and this year Zheng, but its people are not weary, and there is no resentment or criticism of the ruler: its government is so well ordered. When Chu attacked Chen, the affairs of its merchants, farmers, craftsmen and traders were not harmed. . . .
>
> When Wei Ao became Chief Minister, he selected the best *dian* of the state of Chu. . . . [T]he hundred officers move according to signals, and the army is ready for anything. [This shows] his ability to implement the ordinances *(dian).* In the ruler's appointments, appointees of his own surname *(neixing)* are chosen from among his relatives, while appointees of other surnames *(waixing)* are chosen from among his old companions. His choices do not ignore virtue, hard work does not go unrewarded, and kindness is shown to the aged.
>
> Travelers are treated with hospitality and exempted from service obligations.

High and low *(junzi xiaoren)* are distinguished by dress, the noble adhere to a constant standard of honor, while the mean follow graded rules of deportment, so that propriety is not violated.

Virtue established, punishments implemented, government perfected, state action timely, laws obeyed, rites followed: how can we make this state our enemy?[7]

This portrait has an air of impossible perfection: Shi Hui seems to be using an imaginary Chu to criticize current affairs in Jin. However, the speech neatly raises worthwhile questions about the Chu state: questions about social stratification; systems of social control for elites and commoners; the kinship and appointment systems; the treatment of traders, craftsmen, and travelers; the use of sumptuary laws; and the meaning of *dian*. These are all questions that we would like to have answered, not only for 597 BCE, but also for the last two decades of the fourth century BCE, the era of the texts from Tomb 2 at Baoshan.

The term *dian*, used in the above speech, appears frequently in passages related to law in early Chinese transmitted documents.[8] Creel explains the origin of this graph as a pictograph of "a book standing on a table . . . a book treated with special regard," and suggests that it can mean canon, statute, or archives.[9] One tale in the *Zanguoce* refers to a high Chu officer called *dianling*.[10]

Another tells the story of an early Chu hero who rescued the *ji ci zhi dian,* or "Chicken Order *dian*," from Wu's sack of the city of Ying in 505 BCE:

After the battles at Lake Ju when Wu had entered our capital, our ruler fled, the ministers followed, and our people were scattered everywhere. Menggu . . . left the fight to hurry to Ying.

"If the heir lives," said he, "the altars of Chu may yet survive."

He entered the great palace, bore off the *ji ci zhi dian*, and made his way by river to escape in the fens of Yunmeng. When King Chao reentered Ying, his five officials had lost the *fa* and the populace was in confusion. Menggu presented the *dian* and the officials regained their *fa;* the populace was thereby restored to order.[11]

While the story tells us nothing in detail about the contents of the precious text saved by Menggu, it implies that this *dian*, stored in the palace in the capital city where Shao Tuo served as minister of justice, held the key to effective government in Chu. Indeed, the story hints that *dian* were in some way prior to the *fa,* that other vital but ambiguous Eastern Zhou term from the discourse of law and social control.[12]

Famous *fa* (often translated as "laws" or "statutes") mentioned in pre-Qin books in connection with Chu include the *pu qu zhi fa,* or "Law on Hiding Fugitives," and the *mao men zhi fa,* or "Law of the Reed Gate."[13]

The *pu qu zhi fa* appears in a *Zuozhuan* story about a Chu official's success in forcing one of Chu's rulers to conform to ritual and legal rules, first as heir and chief minister and later as king. When the heir to the throne dared to use a "king-size" banner while hunting, his officer Wu Yu cut it down to the ritually correct size, saying, "Two lords in one state: who could stand it?"[14] Later, after succeding to the throne, the ruler built the Zhang Hua Palace and invited fugitives to fill it.[15] When a *hunren,* or gatekeeper (mutilated criminals often served in these positions[16]) belonging to Wu Yu fled into the Zhang Hua Palace, Wu Yu followed to get him back. However, a palace official refused to hand the fugitive over, saying, "The criminal liability of one who seizes a man in the king's palace is heavy indeed!" He then had Wu Yu himself arrested and brought before the king.

Wu Yu took this opportunity to give the king a lecture on the importance of preserving the social hierarchy, stretching from the king and feudal lords, at the top of the social ladder, to the servants and menials at the bottom. He cited a law of King Wu ordering a great rounding-up of fugitives at the beginning of the Zhou dynasty and noted that Chu's own King Wen had enacted the *pu qu zhi fa.*[17] Wu Yu explicitly argued that coercion was necessary to keep the lowliest subjects in their places: "If these flee, and [people are allowed to] shield them, there will be no one to fill the menial's place." In the end, the king grudgingly ordered Wu Yu: "Take your servant and go.[18]

The *mao men zhi fa* is mentioned in both the *Shuo Yuan* and the *Han Feizi* as a Chu ritual rule that is enforced even against the ruler's heir. The *Han Feizi* is most specific, using the anecdote of the *mao men zhi fa* to illustrate the following canon:

> Now, the lords of men may be anxious to know how to rule over the state, but unable to make rules beforehand in the way the teachers of singing have melodies composed beforehand. . . . Thus, who can cut open the boils of the people must be able to endure the same pain himself.[19]

The text drives this canon home with the story of King Zhuang of Chu rewarding a palace guard who had attacked the crown prince's chariot for entering an area forbidden under the Law of the Reed Gate. When the prince asked to have the guard punished, the king said:

> The law is that whereby the ancestral temple is revered and the altar of the grain and soil honored. Therefore, one who can establish the law, follow orders, and respect the altars is a [loyal] servant of the altars. How could he be punished?[20]

A final anecdote of Chu concerning written law occurs in the *Shiji* account of the life of the enigmatic figure Qu Yuan. That story begins with Qu Yuan at the court of King Huai of Chu, the very king whom Shao Tuo, the master of Tomb 2 at Baoshan, served as *zuoyin.* Qu Yuan himself is described as the king's *zuotu,* explained in the commentary as a personal assistant and translated by Watson as "aide."[21] The *Shiji* goes on to say that Qu Yuan was good at formulating edicts[22] and was (possibly for this reason) assigned to draft *xianling,*[23] or written laws, for Chu. Unfortunately, this assignment aroused the jealousy of his rivals at court, who seized the chance to criticize him:

Whenever he produces a law *(ling)*, Ping [Qu Yuan] puffs up his accomplishment, saying, "None but I could have done this!"

Believing this slander, and feeling perhaps that as king, he, rather than Qu Yuan, should get the credit for law-making, King Huai turned against Qu Yuan and ultimately removed him from his post at court.

The interplay between law and religion is a particularly tantalizing part of the Qu Yuan story. The above passage from the *Shiji* paints a picture of Qu Yuan's early career as an apparently quite secular legal aide to the king. However, the oeuvre for which Qu Yuan has been famous since Han times, the *Chuci*, is cast in the languages of religion: myth, sacred journeys, the fate of the soul, mystical questions, and what has been said by many scholars to be Chu's trademark, shamanism. Whether or not shamanism was peculiarly characteristic of Chu, its importance, for political and legal purposes, is the possibility of direct access for individuals to the forces and powers of the spirit world. It is conceivable that for someone merely to believe in the possibility of direct access to the spirits for anyone other than the ruler and his diviners could imply a vital challenge to the balance of power between ruler and subject.

While there is no guarantee that these textual fragments are more historical than legendary, they give us a hint of what some northerners, at least, thought about Chu law. On one hand, Chu was said to have been a complex, stratified society that valued its *dian,* legal documents that supported social hierarchy and order; on the other hand, Chu was said to have been willing to enforce its *fa,* its ritual rules and vagrancy laws, even against the king and his family. In addition, two hundred years after the fact, Sima Qian described the very ruler whom Shao Tuo served as having a jealous interest in the project of legislation. This chapter will glance at Shao Tuo's own documents to see whether Chu did indeed "make rules beforehand in the way the teachers of singing have melodies composed beforehand," whether its judges and officials actually followed the score in playing the instruments of state. Finally, in defining Chu through the examination of the grave documents of Shao Tuo, the chapter will focus on how underlying religious beliefs, whether or not shamanistic, might have affected Chu legal culture.

Tomb 2 at Baoshan

THE burial pit of Tomb 2 is almost square—34.4 by 31.9 meters in size—and was constructed with fourteen step-ledges down all four sloping sides. Robbers had dug a tunnel into the pit from the north side, but luckily got no farther than the first *guo,* or outer coffin, before giving up. The authors of Beijing 1991b speculate that methane gas produced by the decomposition of the contents of the *guo* may have driven the robbers off, leaving the tomb otherwise untouched for modern archaeologists.[24]

The wooden structure of the first *guo* was built resting on the bottom of the tomb over a small "waist pit," in which was buried a goat, together with wool and silk textiles. Like a wooden house,[25] the first *guo* contained not only a central chamber, in which reposed the

Figure 6.1 Tomb 2, Baoshan [after Beijing 1991b, vol. 2, pl. 3.1]

grave master's body within an inner *guo* and three nested *guan* coffins, but also four surrounding chambers. The rich furnishings of these chambers hint at Shao Tuo's privileged life
aboveground and reveal the hope that he might continue to enjoy a comfortable existence
underground after death. Ritual and eating vessels were found in the east chamber, at the
corpse's head; weapons and horse and chariot gear in the south, along his left side; an intricately built folding bed, bamboo containers and other items needed for life on the road, as
well as a bundle of blank bamboo strips, in the west chamber, at his feet; and pillows, bamboo
mats, boxes, and other comforts of daily life, together with two groups of inscribed bamboo
strips, a scraping knife for erasing scribal mistakes, and a hair writing brush, in the north
chamber, at the corpse's right hand.[26]

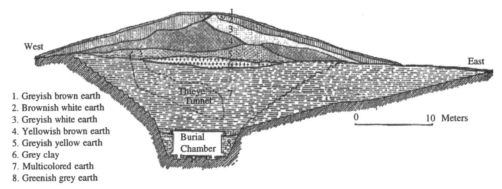

1. Greyish brown earth
2. Brownish white earth
3. Greyish white earth
4. Yellowish brown earth
5. Greyish yellow earth
6. Grey clay
7. Multicolored earth
8. Greenish grey earth

Figure 6.2 Drawing of Tomb 2, Baoshan [by Patrick Sheridan after Beijing 1991b, vol. 1, fig. 29]

Susan Weld

Archaeologists found the well-preserved skeleton of the tomb master inside the brilliantly decorated inner *guan*.[27] It was arranged on its back, legs extended, face turned to the right—turned, perhaps it would not be fanciful to say, toward the precious bundles of legal documents and divination texts in the north burial chamber.

Analysis of the skeleton led scholars Han Kangxin and Li Tianyuan to conclude not only that the tomb master was a thirty-five to forty-year-old male, but also that his skull and body type were closer to northern than southern regional physiognomy.[28] Whether this conclusion is valid, or would also be found to be valid for other high-ranking members of the Chu elite, as the authors seem to suggest, is a question that must await further study of a wider variety of Chu skeletal remains. However, scientific testing of Han and Li's hypothesis about the racial and ethnic composition and origin of the Chu elite may eventually shed light on any physiological "Chu difference."[29]

The Date of Tomb 2

MANY of the bamboo strips from Baoshan include dates in the form: year, month, day. As in the case of the contemporary quasi-legal document, the "E Jun tallies,"[30] each year was identified by important events that occurred in the previous year. One of the years so named in the strips is "The year following that in which the Grand Marshal Zhaoyang defeated the Jin army at Xiangling."[31] As the authors of Beijing 1991b point out, this battle can probably be identified with one reported in the *Shiji* for the sixth year of the reign of King Huai of Chu, or 323 BCE. If this identification is accurate, the Chu year-name corresponds to the next year, or 322 BCE.[32] Altogether seven years appear in the strips from Tomb 2, and the authors of Beijing 1991b have assigned Western-style dates to each of them as follows:

> "The year following that in which the Grand Marshal Zhaoyang defeated the Jin army at Xiangling": 322 BCE.
>
> "The year following that in which Chen Yu, the ambassador from Qi, offered ritual congratulations to the King": 321 BCE.
>
> "The year following that in which [the Chu noble] Luyang Gong[33] repaired the wall of the capital of Zheng, after the Chu army's [attack]": 320 BCE.
>
> "The year following that in which Jian Hu, ambassador of x, paid an incidental visit to Chu"[34]: 319 BCE.
>
> "The year following that in which Sheng Gong Bian, ambassador of Song, paid a formal visit to Chu": 318 BCE.
>
> "The year following that in which Xu Ying, ambassador of Eastern Zhou, presented ceremonial meats[35] at [the Chu capital of] Zai Ying"[36]: 317 BCE.
>
> "The year following that in which the Grand Marshal Zhuo Hua[37] came to the rescue of Fu": 316 BCE.

This last year appears on strip 267, which goes on to say: "In the sixth month, on the day *ding-hai,* the *zuoyin* was buried."[38] From this record we know that Shao Tuo's increasingly anxious divination inquiries about his worsening health were cut short by his death in the first half of 316 BCE.

The year names in the above list smack of Chu's efforts to establish itself as the ritual head of the contemporary world order: military victories, submissive gestures by other states, and Chu's lordly acts of generosity toward them. As Peters observes, tensions at this time were hottest between Chu and the state of Qin, to the northwest. This conflict would come to a head with the Qin sack of the Chu capital of Ying in 278 BCE, leading to Chu's retreat to the east, only thirty-eight years after Shao Tuo's death.[39]

The Documents from Baoshan

THE bamboo strips found in Tomb 2 fall into three main categories: grave inventory lists, found in the east, south and west burial chambers; divination strips, found in one pile of 57 in the north burial chamber; and legal or administrative documents, found in a separate heap of 231 strips beside the divination texts. While the placement of the divination and legal texts in two separate piles suggests a mental distinction between them, both groups were found in the same tomb chamber at the tomb master's right hand, and both must have loomed large in his personal and professional life. This chapter focuses on the legal documents, but it will conclude by briefly considering Chu law in light of what the divination texts tell us about the grave master's overarching ideas of religion and causation.

The cords that originally bound the strips in compact bundles had rotted by the time of excavation, and the strips, which probably floated for a time after the grave chamber had filled with water, had eventually become waterlogged and fallen to the bottom.[40] The water that filled the chamber (perhaps running in through the robbers' unfinished tunnel?) had the happy consequence of miraculously preserving the ink-inscribed documents: the ink of the inscriptions still stands out as legibly against the yellow background of the bamboo as if they had passed though Shao Tuo's hands yesterday.

Although the flooding of the chamber floated the strips somewhat out of their original order, the scholars who worked on them were able to arrange and number them, relying not only on their contents, but also on the shallow notches cut into them to hold the silk cords that bound the thin strips into orderly rolls.[41] Some of the strips had a slanting line drawn or scratched across their backs, perhaps to help illiterate workers bind them in the proper order; these lines also helped the modern workers in reconstructing that order. However, because of the difficulties of the script, arranging the strips is a task filled with difficulties and uncertainties, and scholars have pointed to a few instances where the ordering of the strips reflected in Beijing 1991b can be improved.[42]

As one can see by comparing the style, packing, variants, and stroke width of the graphs on the legal documents (strips 27–37, for example), it is very likely that several different scribes produced the documents. This would make sense in light of their contents, which include reports sent up to the central government by different local administrators and legal officials. On occasion the scribes also used punctuation marks: dots to separate the names in a series (strips 179–180), horizontal lines to set off the beginning of paragraphs or sentences (strips 171–178), and double horizontal strokes to indicate repetition or doubling of a graph or phrase (strip 7).[43] These features reveal the existence of a flourishing profession of legal scribes and copyists who supplied the record-keeping wants of the extensive Chu system of civil and judicial administration.

Contents of the Baoshan Legal Documents

THE 231 legal documents fall roughly into two groups: those supplied with section titles, written in larger graphs on the front of the first strip in the bundle (see strip 14) or on the back of one of the strips in the middle of the bundle (see the reverse of strips 33, 84), and those with no such titles. The four named groups consist of 1, the *jizhu,* or "Collected Register [Investigations]" (strips 1–13); 2, the *jizhuyan,* or "Collected Cases Arising from Register Investigations" (strips 14–18); 3, the *shouqi,* or "[Records of] Dates Assigned [for Disposition of Legal Matters]" (strips 19–79); and 4, the *shuyu,* or "Summaries of Legal Proceedings" (strips 80–102). The authors of Beijing 1991b group the remaining legal documents into three additional categories according to content: 5, records of the Chu central government's orders to local officials to lend money for purchase of seed grain, and efforts to secure repayment of those loans (strips 103–119); 6, relatively detailed records of particular investigations and hearings (strips 120–161); and 7, file notations of cases delegated to five named officials for disposition in the year 317 BCE (strips 162–196).[44]

Groups 1 and 2: Register Investigations and Cases

The first two groups of documents reflect the state's interest in making the *zhu,* or population registers—probably used to calculate the citizens' taxes and corvee liabilities—as accurate as possible.[45] This preoccupation fits well with Shi Wei's portrait of perfect social control over the Chu social hierarchy. Strips 1–2 and 7–9, for example, record the following events (to simplify the presentation of the texts used here, personal and place names will be replaced by Arabic letters where convenient):

> In 320 BCE,[46] the first month, the prefect A of W received a mandate from Wang Taizi (the royal heir), and under it verified the [registrations of the] people of W. Certain of their youths were found to be unregistered.[47] The *dian* registers in the archives in W should include two youths of *junzi* rank, B and C, who reside in X district in Y town; let them be registered. In 320 BCE, the second month, day *dingsi,* D, prefect of Z, believing that the prefect A of W was planning to verify the population of W, destroyed the *dian* registers. [Four named individuals fled]. Let them be arrested.

This case reveals both the state's determination to maintain correct registers and some local administrators' desire to escape state scrutiny.

In 321 BCE, the eighth month, on day *yiyou,* the king held court in the traveling palace in Lan Ying.[48] The prefect of X, the *damoao* A, sent out the order for all *bangren* [probably a city-dwelling low-level elite group] to submit their incorrect registers, husband the king's ink, and use it (?) to [rectify and] submit the incorrect registers of their underlings.[49] B's son C, one man, [was found to] live in Ying ward,[50] where Marshal Tu registered him;[51] C's son D, one man, and D's son E, one man, had not been registered on the *dian.*[52]

As a result of the investigations recorded in this group of strips, two youths of *junzi,* or noble, rank, and three generations of one *bangren*[53] family were added to the registers. The offenses of "keeping incorrect registers" and "failing to register youths" were paralleled in Qin law by *nihu,* "hiding households," and *aotong fufu,* "failing to add youths to the registers."[54] For such offenses, village elders could be sentenced to "redeemable shaving of the beard" under Qin law.[55] The Baoshan documents do not mention a particular penalty, but order that a prefect guilty of the offense be "immediately seized."[56]

Elsewhere in the Baoshan strips, the population registers are called *deng* as well as *zhu.* In one case the *zuoyin* ordered a local lord to check on the registration of the "builder" *(zaoshi)* A; after five witnesses inspected the documents, the local lord found A's registration correct and sent in the lineage register, *shideng,* (perhaps as proof).[57] In another case a ward chief was ordered to make sure to submit the names and residences of those who died in his ward;[58] the state had an interest in keeping the registers right up to date.

The use of the word *dian* in these cases makes one wonder whether the precious *ji ci zhi dian* restored to Ying by Menggu were no more than detailed population registers, reflecting rank, residence, and tax obligations—a practical method of social control still used in modern China. Peng Hao observes that the Baoshan strips imply all subjects of the state had to be registered from childhood, including those of *junzi* rank as well as *bangren,* or city-dwellers, and the apparently servile category of *guanren.*[59] While the terms do not precisely match, these groups probably reflect a society as complex, stratified, and, in theory at least, carefully controlled as that described by Shi Hui above. The system of total registration also fits well with the concern for recapture of fugitives expressed in Wu Yu's criticism of the Zhang Hua Palace.

In group 2 we find another registration case, in which the *dian* seems to have functioned as legal evidence of the ownership or affiliation of certain laborers:

> I, Ruo, the legal officer *(sibai)*[60] [in charge of] the charioteers of the Five Armies, dare to report to the "shining sun" [probably an honorary term for the Chu king himself[61]]: "The lord of Shaoxing, Pan Ke Jin, today seized my subordinates Deng A, Deng B, Deng C, and Deng D, with no just cause *(er wu gu*[62]*).* I reported this to the lord king; the lord king referred it to the noble *zuoyin;* the noble *zuoyin* referred it to Dan, the newly appointed director of inquisitions.[63] [He] ordered me to submit them [as evidence], but when both parties [were to] bring forward their *dian,* I had them while Shaoxing did not.[64] [Now] the direc-

Susan Weld

tor of inquisitions has not ruled in my favor, and the summer [field] work[65] of my laborers will soon be irreparably lost. I cannot present [my case] to the director, and do not dare not to report this to the king.[66]

The matter continues on the backs of strips 15, 16, and 17:

> The legal officer in charge of the charioteers of the Five Armies reports, saying: Jin, the lord of Shaoxing, seized his subordinates; the director of inquisitions did not decide in his favor; he is displeased. In the tenth month, on day *jiashen,* the king delegated [the matter] to the *zuoyin.*

This case shows a nice progression of the complaint up and down judicial channels, as well as a sketch of a hearing process, in which both sides were ordered to produce their *dian* as evidence of their right to the labor of certain workers. The procedure recalls that specified in the *Zhouli:* "By [requiring] the presence [of the two parties], [the minister of justice] deters accusations among the people; with the two [versions of] written evidence, he deters suits among the people."[67] One suspects that the complainant, the legal officer Ruo, was a person of some status in Chu who could afford to persist in taking his case repeatedly "all the way to the top."

An interesting feature of this case is the fact that the seized laborers all have the same family name of Deng.[68] On one hand, this circumstance might suggest that the status of *guanren* was hereditary in Chu. On the other hand, many of the cases reported in these strips concern similar groups of complainants or defendants with the same family names.[69] Future research may suggest a social explanation for this pattern, which resembles group robbery cases in the law clerk's manual from Shuihudi that involve several members of one family.[70] While the Shuihudi texts date to the Qin period, one must not lose sight of the fact that they were found only a few hundred miles east of Baoshan and belonged to a local official charged with governing Nanjun, the Qin prefecture carved out of the former Chu heartland.

Group 3: The Shouqi Strips: Assigning Dates for Legal Action

Most of the group of strips labeled "Shou Qi" follow the same highly abbreviated formula:

> Date 1 (year, month, day name)
> Name (geographical location, position, personal name) *shouqi*
> Date 2 (month, day name, as few as two or as many as forty or more days after
>   the first date)
> Statement of an official action framed in the negative
> Formula of harm suffered
> Name of the reporting officer (usually a *zheng,* or county magistrate) *shizhi*

The meaning of this formula has been much debated. Peng Hao believes that these strips record the initial stages of the handling of accusations in Chu.[71] In his view the structure tells us that routine handling of accusations was a two-step process: first, having filed his case on date 1, the complainant was assigned date 2 for a hearing to determine whether he had indeed sustained harm and whether his complaint could go to trial. Only if these two issues were resolved in the plaintiff's favor would the case go on to a trial.[72] Again, this procedure recalls the *Zhouli,* at least as interpreted by Maspero. While a tradition stretching back to the Han commentator Zheng Xuan read *minsong* and *minyu* as two different kinds of cases, namely, property disputes and criminal accusations, Maspero argues:

> [I]l en ressort clairement que les deux phrases du *Zhouli* sur "l'empechement," *jin,* des accusations, *song,* et "l'empechement" des proces, *yu,* que doit tenter le juge, en depit de leur symetrie qui a induit en erreur les commentateurs anciens, ne se rapportent pas a deux especes de proces differents, les proces civils et les proces criminals, mais bien a deux phases successives d'un meme proces (civil ou criminel suivant les cas), se deroulant depuis l'accusation jusqu'a la sentence.[73]

Whether or not Maspero's theory is correct for the royal Zhou, Peng Hao's interpretation of the Baoshan documents posits a two-step hearing procedure, as well as no obvious differentiation between the handling of property disputes and crimes.

Strip 29 is an example of a case that, under Peng Hao's interpretation, did not go to trial:

> Eighth month, day *jiaxu,* is the date on which Zhou Ren, a retainer of the *moao* of Liao, received an assigned date. On day *guiwei* [twenty days afterward], no trial. Investigation and interrogation [show that] harm was sustained. Prefect A recorded this case.[74]

Peng Hao's analysis of the meaning of the *shouqi* strips has been challenged by several Chinese scholars. The most persuasive alternative interpretation has come from Chen Wei, who understands the formula to be a demand sent down on date A from Shao Tuo's office in the central government to local officials to take specific judicial action before date B, or suffer the consequences. If we accept Chen Wei's reading, strip 29 would read:

> Eighth month, day *jiaxu,* Zhou Ren, a retainer of the *moao* of Liao, received the assignment. If he does not go to court on the day *guiwei* [twenty days after being assigned this date], harm will be suffered [or, there will be liability].[75]

The effect of Chen Wei's interpretation is to transform this group of strips from records of the *zuoyin's* dealings with the parties in various cases into internal bureaucratic communication and control, in which the plaintiffs have little part.

As Peng Hao points out, the sixty-one strips labeled *shouqi* include several instances where the same case is presented a second, or even a third or fourth, time.[76] Peng Hao suggests that a matter could be presented again after being rejected for trial, but no more than three times.[77] The phrase *san shou bu yi chu* does appear in strip 58, possibly meaning the offense of presenting the same accusation again after having been rejected three times. However, the inclusion of one case four times in this group (strips 46, 55, and 64), with no indication that the last instance was disapproved of, suggests that the rule cannot have been so simple. If we try to understand the repeated cases under Chen Wei's hypothesis, we end with an impression of an engaged but rather impotent Chu central government that had sometimes to order local officials up to four times to achieve compliance.

To give a sense of the time periods involved, this case was presented and heard (under Peng Hao's view) or ordered to be heard (under Chen Wei's view) on the following dates in 317 BCE:

strip 46: date received: ninth month, day *jiachen,*		0
[to be] heard: ninth month, day *wushen,*		+4
strip 52: date received: ninth month, day *jiyou,*		+5
[to be] heard: ninth month, day *guichou,*		+9
strip 55: date received: ninth month, day *guichou,*		+9
[to be] heard: ninth month, day *guihai,*		+19
strip 64: date received: tenth month, day *yihai,*		+31
[to be] heard: tenth month, day *wuyin,*		+34

Regardless of which interpretation is correct, this chart demonstrates the intense focus on time and time periods in the Chu judicial process.

Peng Hao comes close to Chen Wei's interpretation when he suggests that the emphasis on dates in the *shouqi* strips implies that contemporary legal procedure required officials to dispose of cases within a fixed time period.[78] He refers to a *Zhouli* passage that governs adjudication by magistrates at several levels:

> In general, adjudications by magistrates have fixed time periods. For [adjudications] in the capital, ten days; in the suburban areas, twenty days; in the [agricultural] hinterlands, thirty days; in the vassal's chief towns, three months; and in the allied states, one year. Within these periods, [the dispute] will be heard; outside of these periods, it will not be heard.[79]

The Han commentator Zheng Sinong compares these rules to those governing appeal in his day, in which a defendant could seek another investigation within three months of final adjudication.[80] The Qin documents from Shuihudi refer to a similar appeal procedure but hold that a *qiju* request could be entered only after final judgment.[81] Peng Hao cites Sun Yirang, however, for the proposition that the above passage regulates the officials, not the plaintiffs: "When the people come forward with matters for accusation, the magistrate must adjudicate them within a fixed time period."[82] While such a rule would make sense, there is quite a disparity among the periods between dates A and B in the *shouqi* texts: from just two days to as many as forty-four. However, others of the Baoshan documents show great dissatisfaction with the speed of adjudication. In strip 135, verso, Shao Tuo himself sends a complex case back down to the local official with the remark: "The case has gone on for a long time without any judgment. [Now] the king has ordered us to bring it to judgment."

A sampling of the official actions referred to in the last half of the *shouqi* formula reveals the breadth of duties required of persons named in the strips relating to legal matters:

> Interrogation of a defendant's wife and children; strip 20
>
> Filing an accusation *(gao)* in response to an assault incident; strip 22
>
> Reporting the names and residences of those who die in his district;
> strips 21, 32
>
> Paying gold plaque currency to a named group according to a mandate from
> the Chu capital; strips 43, 44

Strip 20 hints at what we see in the *shuyu* strips below: Chu legal authorities used some system of collective, kin-based responsibility to tighten their control over society.

Regardless of how one interprets these samples, this list shows the state's interest in having such duties performed predictably, on a predetermined schedule.

A parallel interest in time, and ways of bringing it within human control, appears in divination texts from Shao Tuo's tomb and elsewhere in Chu, which carefully limit their prayers and questions to fixed time periods, from a month to one or more years, beginning on a specified date.[83] After a series of prayers and sacrifices designed to appease spirits thought by the diviners to be causing trouble, the divination texts may note: "The [named spirits] are now all pacified. Within the stated period, there will be happiness."[84]

Group 4: The Shuyu Strips: Case Summaries

The *shuyu* strips contain more comprehensive records of the content of *song,* or accusations, than do the *shouqi* strips. The formula used in this group is somewhat different:

> Date [of accusation]
>
> Name [of plaintiff] *song*
>
> Name [of defendant] *wei yi,* or *yiqi* action complained of
>
> Date [of hearing]
>
> Name [of official] *shizhi*
>
> Name [of official] *weili* (?)[85]

Unlike the *shouqi* strips, this formula tells us something substantial about the nature of the crimes of which these defendants were being accused. A list of some of the actions complained of follows:

> Strip 80: metalworker A accuses metalworker B of injuring his younger
> brother C [all three share the same family name]
>
> Strip 81: A accuses B, the official in charge of weapons (?), of [illegally]
> taxing[86] his fields

Susan Weld

Strip 82: A accuses B, C, D, F, and G [all sharing one family name] of failing to divide [their] lands *(yi bu fen tian zhi gu)*[87]

Strip 84: A accuses B and C [who share the same family name], men of Sheng Furen,[88] of killing his older brother and servant

Strip 85: A accuses twenty-four named individuals [including two Song, four Huang, and six Deng] of receiving *(shou)* A's man [or men] and [enabling him or them to] escape[89]

The back of this strip has the following note: "As soon as the document is issued, bring them to court." The number of people mentioned in this summary indicates that public security may have required rapid action.

Strip 86: A accuses B of killing his younger brother

Strip 87: A accuses B, C, D, E, and F of receiving A's *qian?guan* G [who shares a family name with C and D] and [enabling him to] escape

Strip 88: A, the *sibai* [of a town in Chu], accuses B and C [who share the same family name and come from the same town] of *fanqiguan* (resisting or usurping office[90])

Strip 89: A accuses B of marrying/seizing his female servant/concubine *(qie)*

Strip 90: A accuses B and C [who share the same family name and reside in Fan Qiu's south *li*] of killing his brother. The strip continues with a report from a legal officer in Fan Qiu that there had been someone of the name C living in Fan Qiu's south *li,* but he had moved; there was no record of B

Strip 91: A accuses B and C [all three share the same family name, and B and C appear in the *shouqi* strips 34 and 39] of [illicit] burials on his land

Strip 92: A accuses B of snatching his son Dan and [asserts that] he found him in B's house *(er de zhi yu B zhi shi)*

Strip 93: A accuses B [who shares the same name] of seizing his heir[91]

Strip 94: A accuses the *dafu* of the royal graves of usurping land

Strip 95: A accuses B and C, saying that C (?) [unknown graph] his younger brother D and B killed him

Strip 96: A accuses B and C of killing his older brother

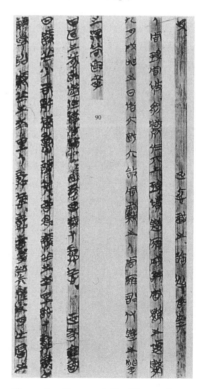

Figure 6.3 Representative *Shuyu* strips [after Beijing 1991b, vol. 2, pl. 130]

Chu Law in Action

Strip 97: A accuses B of seizing his wife

Strip 98: A accuses B of debt *(zhai)*[92]

Strip 99: A accuses his *guanren* (subordinates[93]) B, C, and D [who all share the
    same family name] of resisting or usurping official authority *(fanguan)* and
    fighting among themselves at Xindajiu [or the "New Grand Stable," a
    place we see the king establishing in strips 153 and 154]

Strip 101: A accuses B of squaring *(ju,* some kind of illegal survey?[94]) fields

Strip 102: A accuses Grand Intendant *(dazai)* B, Right Minister of Justice
    (yousikou[95]) C, D, and Prefect *(zheng)* E of judging illegally *(bufa)* in his
    older brother F's case

Strip 102 is the only place among these strips where we see the term *fa* used to mean something close to "law." While skimpy evidence, however, this case summary does seem to concern an individual's accusation against government authorities for failing to follow unspecified models or rules in making legal judgments: possibly an example of Chu officials failing to follow the "score," in Han Feizi's words.

From this list of the contents of several complaints, we can see that they included both property disputes and debt actions (which Anglo-American law would generally class as civil); murder, kidnapping, and rape (all criminal offenses); and malfeasance in office, illegal adjudication, and unauthorized taxation (administrative law matters). Most use the term *song* in the reporting formula, so it is clear that *song* was not limited to property crimes in the state of Chu.

Groups 5 and 6: Matters Relating to Government Loans and Other Investigations

The longer and more complex cases included in sections 5 and 6 reveal valuable clues not only about law, but also about the financial and social structure in Chu. Strips 103–119 relate to the king's edict in the sixth month of 322 BCE requiring three officials to lend gold to a (famine-stricken?) town for the purchase of seed grain. The edict stipulates that "[w]hen the term is up in the second month, the gold shall be fully repaid."[96] However, the edict is followed by a series of nine strips in which officials of various places list the amounts of the loans they made and state that "[t]hough the term is now past, the loan has not been repaid." Perhaps this series of strips records a Chu famine relief effort orchestrated by the king, the burden of providing money for seed grain to the stricken area being divided among a group of seven vassals or territorial administrators.

One of the cases in this group discusses the right to transfer land granted to an ancestor as a salary fief:

> The *zuozhi* [perhaps the assistant in charge of horses] Fan A had a salary fief in
> X place. When A died, his son Fan B succeeded him; when B died he had no
> son, so his younger brother Fan C succeeded him; when C died, he again had no
> son, so the *zuoyin* Shi(?) ordered that his paternal cousin Fan D be his successor.

While in D's hands, the salary fief became encumbered with debt, and Gu got hold of it.[97]

Gu apparently planned to divide the land thus acquired but was challenged by a successor in interest to the king, who asserted that Fan A did not have a (legal) successor to the fief. An official designated to settle the dispute ultimately declared that Fan A did indeed have a proper successor. In these two strips we may see a nascent development of the right to own and transfer real property. As in Europe, these kinds of rights were ultimately demanded by those with money to lend and a thirst for roots in the land. The concept of *hou*, or an heir who could ensure succession to real property, remained important in Chu, as we can see by the inclusion of the "heirless" *(ji wuhou)* in the group of unlucky spirits whose inauspicious influence was to be deflected in Shao Tuo's last divination texts.

Charge and Counter-Charge in a Murder Case

Strips 131–139 concern a complex case apparently originating with the plaintiff Shu Qing's accusation to the king that two residents of Yin, A and B, jointly murdered the plaintiff's older brother Ren on day *guisi* in the fourth month of 318 BCE.[98] When the plaintiff reported the matter to the official Zi Wei Gong, the latter commanded the right marshal of Wei to make up a written authorization for the plaintiff *(wei pu quan deng)* ordering that the two defendants be captured for him. As a result, A was captured and B committed suicide.

At this point, Zi Wei Gong referred the case to a Yin retainer with a request to reach a "thoughtful judgment" in the matter. However, the case then took a sudden turn, because we next read that the retainer not only failed to rule in the plaintiff's favor, but leaned in the other direction by arresting the father and another brother of the plaintiff, because of B's suicide. In response to this new counter-accusation, Shu Qing lists the names of six residents of Yin (five of whom share the family name Chen) and declares that "A and B together killed my brother Ren; all these know they killed him. I do not dare to fail to report this to Your Majesty."

Presumably in response to this report, the *zuoyin* forwarded the following order from the king to the Duke of Tang, apparently the overlord of Yin: "Shu Qing has accused A and B of killing his brother Ren, Yin retainers have captured A, but B committed suicide; the Yin retainers have seized [Shu Qing's] brother Cheng, and the case has long gone without judgment. The king orders that all be brought to judgment."

In the sixth month of 317 BCE a functionary was dispatched to Yin with the records in the case. By the seventh month the *sibai* of Yin announced that the official in charge of the case had sent the suit back to the prefect of Yin for resolution.

The parties then stated their opposing positions: the original plaintiff's brothers came forward to reiterate that the defendants had conspired to kill his brother and that he and his family had had no part in B's suicide. The other side countered by asserting that the brothers had slain B, and, what was more suspicious, the original plaintiff, Shu Qing, had fled town.

Given these directly contradictory statements, in the fifth month the official in charge of the case had both sides take an oath, 211 affiants in all. When the defendants' side took the oath, they all stated: "We testify of what we each have seen and heard: the plaintiff Qing murdered B, and Qing and his brothers all know that the defendants did not kill their brother." At this, Shu Qing's brother Cheng was arrested, but in only a few days he managed to tunnel out and escape.

According to royal order, the case was resubmitted to the *zuoyin*. Jun, the Duke of Tang, announced: "The king has ordered that this suit be delegated to me and that judgment be reached. When the prefect of Yin administered the oath, Qing fled and his brother Cheng tunneled to freedom; the rest of the parties are in custody and I will shortly try them. The king has ordered an official in charge to convey my orders, to bring justice to this long-delayed case. The Yin resident Cheng is ordered to give testimony." Four people of Yin, all sharing the family name Chen, and six retainers of Yin being present, the *zuoyin* reported the king's order to Zi Wei Gong, that Shu Cheng of Yin be put to the oath, as written in a document for proof. The case report continues: "When the witnesses on Cheng's side came forward, some were found to be unable to give testimony on his behalf: those belonging to the same *she* (shrine association?), ward, or office, and those more closely related than first cousins on the paternal side *(congfu xiongdi)*." Here the report unfortunately is cut short.

While the ultimate outcome of this case is unclear, these reports reveal that the official in charge of a hearing routinely made the witnesses swear an oath. The formula used in the report, "In X month, on Y day, the official in charge put them to the oath *(wei zhi meng),*" closely follows the language of the *Zhouli:*

> In the case of criminal accusations, [the Supervisor of Covenants, *simeng*] administers the oath to [the parties]. In general, when oaths are administered, each party furnishes a victim according to the size of his landed holdings and presents himself [at the covenant location]. When the oath has been executed, the *simeng* offers wine and the flesh of the victims [to the *mingshen,* or Supervising Spirits.][99]

The procedure for the *meng* oath is carefully described in several of the ritual classics, as well as in many stories in the *Zuozhuan.* In most descriptions, *meng* required oath takers to sacrifice an animal victim and smear its blood on their lips before announcing the oath to the *mingshen,* the "far-seeing" spirits called on to enforce the truth and sincerity of the words spoken.[100]

It is, of course, hard to say how much of the ceremony described in the *Zhouli* and other classical texts was included in the oaths administered in the Chu judicial process. However, this group of strips reveals the effort to use the threat of spiritual sanction to make oral testimony as reliable as possible. In addition, the case of the plaintiff Shu Qing suggests that in Chu, at least, each side could mobilize its own witnesses, rather than rely largely on the judge to find the witnesses, as was the case in later imperial practice. Indeed, the large number of witnesses described in this case makes one suspect that political, as well as judicial, factors may have been at play in the confrontation.[101] Perhaps the corollary to allowing the parties to present their own witnesses can be found in the rules we see in the same case strictly limiting the people who could testify to those who did not have a close, preexisting relationship and could therefore perhaps be presumed to be neutral.

Conclusion

THESE documents offer a very useful "inside perspective" on the Chu legal institutions that we glimpsed above in transmitted historical works.

First, they prove that Chu was indeed a complex society: the many official and unofficial titles and status groups mentioned in the texts promise years of fruitful research on the nature of Chu social stratification and the degree of government participation in it. One poignant case about those who occupied the lowest rungs of Chu society contains the following report by a local official:

> On day *jiachen,* a prison worker in the silk warehouse of the king's consort escaped. . . . I [came upon him] and was about to seize him, when he stabbed himself. I was able to prevent him [from doing much harm]; so reported.[102]

The prison worker's own testimony explains that he had taken a knife from the warehouse to try to cut off his leg irons and had managed to escape (into the street?) before being detected. It is these glimpses of the realities of life in the layered societies of early China that make the new documents especially valuable: through them, we can hear voices not felt to be worth preserving in the historical documents. This prison worker's story offers an ugly echo to Wu Yu's argument to the king that fugitives must be granted no mercy: "If these flee, and people are allowed to shield them, there will be no one to fill the menial's place."

Coercive methods of social control are very apparent in these documents. As Chen Wei has pointed out, the Chu authorities used a variety of methods of arrest, seizure, and detention to prevent defendants from absconding before trial. In the case of Shu Qing's accusation, one detainee committed suicide after arrest while another managed to escape from jail—an indication of the harsh conditions one could expect to find there. In addition, collective responsibility, at least of a defendant's wife and children, seems to have been the rule in Chu as elsewhere in the Zhou period.[103]

As to the Chu kings' practice of appointments, Shao Tuo himself is an example of a high appointee whose lineage originally split off from the royal house, taking Shao, the name of its royal ancestor, for a lineage name.[104] Shao Tuo's divination texts prove that he did not lose sight of this important connection with royalty. Again and again he has his diviners perform the *sidao* sacrifice to his lineal ancestors, beginning with King Shao—his direct link to the most powerful house of local ancestors.[105] The persistence of strong lineages so close to the royal house may have tended to dilute the Chu kings' authority. Indeed, the case summaries from Baoshan suggest that the Chu king's power was less than absolute, because we see him repeatedly sending down orders in specific cases without striking impact on the course of the adjudication.

An interesting angle to the question of Chu social structure will be the role of population and worker registers in both public and private social control. The emphasis on preserving the integrity of the registers looms large also in cases from the early Han period, showing how high was the degree of continuity between late Warring States Chu and early Han practices. In addition, despite the Han bias toward blaming all coercive legal techniques on Qin, the strips show that registration and collective responsibility in this region predated the Qin conquest.

The state's deep interest in the registers must have had an impact on naming practices in Chu. It is very likely that research on the Chu naming system will help to clarify the Chu social and political structure; perhaps such research will offer a way to understand the profusion of single surname groups, or *zu,* in the legal documents. Study of the cases on land inheritance and household division may ultimately shed light on the organization of the Chu elites. In this connection, it will be important to try to distinguish how far the cases found at Baoshan reflect elite, rather than popular, legal culture and affairs.

The cases on land tenure and grain loans offer insights into the economic basis of the Chu state, while analysis of the many place-names is already helping historical geographers in understanding the effective political and cultural reach of Chu power at the turn of the fourth century BCE. The tomb's evidence that the post of *zuoyin* required a considerable amount of travel, and the mention of "traveling" or "temporary" capitals of the state, suggest some of the methods Chu rulers used to try to maintain control over a state that had grown so rapidly in the preceding centuries.

However, many of these legal characteristics seem, from other sources, to have been true also in other Eastern Zhou states. A possibly distinctive aspect of Chu justice may be related to the region's reputation for religious excess and eccentricity. While the legal documents now available from both Qin and early Han emphasize the use of careful interrogation—backed by torture if necessary—as the way to secure truth in judicial proceedings, torture is not apparent in Shao Tuo's documents. Instead, judges and officials seem to have resorted to the judicial oath, relying, perhaps, on their subjects' deep belief in the existence of, and the court's access to, a complex pantheon of ancestors, ghosts, and spirits. Shu Qing's case shows how close such practice could come to being a mobilization of political support rather than an adjudication of facts at issue: his opponents were able to summon more than two hundred allies to join them in the oath. The fate of a judicial witness who gave false testimony under oath is suggested by the inclusion of the *mengzu,* the spirit of a person under a curse, among the spirits of unlucky humans—the *bugu* ghost of a stillborn child, the soldier fallen in war, the sailor drowned at sea, and the man dead without an heir—whom Shao Tuo's diviners exorcize in their struggle to cure his fatal illness.[106]

The ultimate abandonment of the judicial oath in China may have accompanied a paradigm shift in beliefs about causation in the period from the late Warring States to early Han. It seems to have been during this period that Chinese medicine shifted its emphasis from incantation and exorcism—an elite form of which is evident in Shao Tuo's deathbed divinations, prayers, and sacrifices—to recipes for rectifying the balance between yin and yang influences.

Susan Weld

· 96 ·

In the *Laws,* Plato explains why the judicial oath was no longer appropriate for the Greeks:

> [Rhadamanthus] appears to have thought that he ought to commit judgment to no man, but to the Gods only, and in this way suits were simply and speedily decided by him. For he made the two parties take an oath respecting the points in dispute, and so got rid of the matter speedily and safely. But now that a certain portion of mankind do not believe at all in the existence of the Gods, . . . the way of Rhadamanthus is no longer suited to the needs of justice; for as the opinions of men about the Gods are changed, the laws should also be changed. . . . [He] who obtains leave to bring an action should write down the charges, but not add an oath; and the defendant in like manner should give his denial to the magistrates in writing, and not swear.

Like Greece in the fifth century BCE, China was turning away from a world vision based on belief in the gods and confidence in direct access to their help; Chu may simply have been the last to make the change.

7

Towns and Trade

Cultural Diversity and Chu Daily Life

Heather A. Peters

The life of a Chu peasant most likely did not differ significantly from that of his Neolithic ancestor. Farmers have lived in villages and cultivated wet rice south of the Yellow River since the sixth millennium BCE.

The original territory of the state of Chu was located in the Dan River valley and in the upper reaches of the Han River valley—in other words, near the western end of the east-west line denoted by the Han and Huai Rivers that is conventionally taken as the dividing line between North China and South China. As Chu grew and spread eastward and southward, its territory always lay primarily south of this Han-Huai line. Chu therefore was a "southern" state not only in the eyes of its Central Plains neighbors to the north, but in fact geographically, topographically, climatologically, gastronomically, and (for these and other reasons) culturally. Chu agriculture was based on paddy rice and on a wide array of vegetable crops; its domestic animals included dogs, pigs, chickens, perhaps ducks, and water buffalo (in place of the oxen of the Central Plains states); and it was richly supplied with varieties of bamboo and undoubtedly used that plant to make a wide range of useful articles, including tools, weapons, baskets, mats, and small household goods. Chu also, as we shall see, had access through trade to a range of subtropical and tropical products, both for its own use and to trade northward. In all of these respects, Chu was the heir to cultural patterns of long standing in the regions south of the Han and Huai.

The earliest carbonized remains of paddy rice recently have been excavated at Pengtou-shan in northern Hunan Province.[1] The remains date to 6200 to 5800 BCE and are associated with crude, round-bottomed, unevenly fired undecorated pots. Archaeologists broadly divide the ensuing millennia into three major cultural traditions: the Daxi (3800–2800 BCE), the Chujialing (ca. 3200–2200 BCE), and the Qinglongchuan Phase III, now more frequently called Shijiahe (roughly 2200–2000 BCE).[2] The lives of these farmers, especially those from the Daxi and Chujialing cultures, were simple and unsophisticated. As far as we can tell from the archaeological record, their sites are devoid of monumental religious centers, major art traditions, or any indication that social change was in the making. From the archaeological data on the ceramic material associated with these cultures, we can outline an increasingly advanced ceramic and stone tool technology. The Chujialing pottery is the most distinctive. Some of it is eggshell thin and fashioned into tall, ring-footed cups created by using the wheel.

These Neolithic farmers lived in either square or round houses constructed of a combination of wood, bamboo, thatch, and some kind of mud or clay plaster.[3] A few houses associated with the Shijiahe culture were semisubterranean. Although Chinese archaeologists have not excavated entire villages in the Hubei-Hunan region, we can speculate that villages there were similar in size to excavated villages from the Yellow River region, such as Banpo and Jiangzhai,[4] which averaged between fifty to one hundred households.

The Chujialing farmers buried their dead in single pits in prone, extended positions.[5] Children in the Chujialing culture were usually buried in urns, indicating that they were ritually differentiated from adults, but other class distinctions are not yet evident. In a cemetery belonging to the later Shijiahe culture, bodies were found in supine flexed positions.

Recent data from the Shijiahe sites, however, imply that certain changes were occurring in this region. The discovery of elaborately detailed carved jade figurines,[6] for example, indicates a high level of technical expertise, which in turn strongly hints of developments that may prove significant in understanding the emergence of a civilization that contributed to what later came to be "Chu."

The transition from the second to the first millennium BCE saw a number of important innovations in the culture and society of archaic China. The emergence of early states during the Shang and Western Zhou periods, with their increasing social stratification, occurred around the same time as the introduction and use of bronze technology, which was used mainly to make ritual vessels and weapons. The peasants were no doubt affected by these social changes and during the Zhou period were incorporated into the state structure as slaves, forced labor, and military conscripts.[7] Although there is evidence for the beginning of the use of bronze and even iron for agricultural tools such as sickles and hoes during the sixth century BCE,[8] most farmers probably still grew their crops using tools made from stone, bone, shell, and wood.

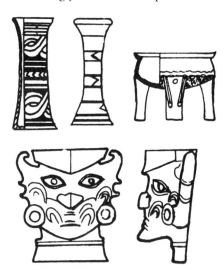

Figure 7.1 *(Top, left)* Daxi pottery cups. [after Zhang Zhiheng, 1982, fig.1]
(Top, right) Shijiahe thin-legged pottery *ding* from Qinlongquan, Hubei. [after Hubei kaogu xuehui, 1987, 39, fig. 1.5]
(Bottom) Shijiahe jade carving from Xiaojiawuji site, Hubei. [after Zhang Xuqiu 1992, fig. 2.3]

While peasant life may have remained more or less unchanged, or changed only very slowly, urban life in the walled towns and capitals of the Eastern Zhou period was clearly evolving. The towns and cities were centers of political and commercial activity.

Life in Chu Towns: Physical Layout of the Towns

THE settlement pattern of the Chu state did not differ markedly from the overall pattern outlined for the Eastern Zhou period in general. The largest and most important unit was the *guo,* translated as state or principality. Textual evidence suggests that *guo* sometimes consisted of only one walled settlement, a kind of city-state, but far more common were states that linked several settlements in a hierarchical network to a capital city where the king and his ministers and officials resided. The capital was called the *du* and its surrounding settlements were termed *yi*.[9]

By the middle of the Warring States period the network of hierarchically nested settlements was dominated by just seven major states, one of which was Chu.[10] There are currently fifty surveyed or excavated settlements associated with the Chu state that provide information about the physical layout of Chu urban centers (see the list of important archaeological sites in chapter 2). We can broadly classify Chu settlements into four types: 1, primary centers, such as capitals (*du cheng*); 2, secondary centers (*bie du*); 3, tertiary centers (*xian* and *yi*), most of which were originally small feudal city-states taken over by the Chu state; and 4, very small fortress-like settlements, found primarily on Chu's frontiers, which served military purposes.[11] From excavation reports on these settlements, we can get some sense of urban life.

An urban resident of Chu would have lived in a roughly rectangular-shaped settlement surrounded by a stamped-earth (*hangtu; pisé*) wall. The shape sometimes varied because of the settlement's placement within the natural landscape. Some, especially those with a military or defensive function, were backed by hills or bordered by rivers. Remains of moats encircling the city wall were found at many of the sites.[12] Whereas northern cities sometimes included burial grounds within the city walls, this was rarely the case in Chu cities.[13] Chu cemeteries were scattered in the countryside around the city.[14]

The interior space of excavated walled cities was broken up by stamped-earth mounds and platforms that served as the foundations for the temples, palaces, and residences of the elites. These buildings were constructed from wood, bamboo, and other perishable materials, but post holes and thousands of fired, unglazed roof tiles remain to give archaeologists some sense of their structure. While smaller settlements may have focused on a single activity, such as trade, larger urban centers clearly encompassed a gamut of activities—administrative, ritual, military, and commercial.

Jinancheng, a large walled city that has been well excavated, is eighteen kilometers north of Jiangling. It functioned as a primary urban center for Chu during the Warring States period.[15] This site, roughly rectangular in shape, covered an area of more than sixteen square kilometers and was surrounded by a moat. Unlike most Eastern Zhou settlements elsewhere, it had been built on top of a mound, not on a flat plain. The stamped-earth outer wall had been constructed in three parts: first, a foundation ten to fourteen meters wide was made by digging a trench and filling it with layers of stamped earth; this formed the core. Next, the core was covered with a thick layer of sloping, pounded earth measuring about ten to fifteen meters thick. Finally, an additional four-meter layer of "slope protection" was applied. This outer layer provided support for the wall and also helped to carry off heavy rainfall. The walls at Jinancheng were from thirty to forty meters thick at the base and narrowed to ten to twenty meters at the top.

The outer wall at Jinancheng was interrupted by twenty-eight breaks. Eight of these mark entryways into the city, and two of the eight were water gates. Two small rivers flowed though the settlement providing city residents with a water supply and drainage as well as an alternative form of transportation. The other six gates opened onto roads leading into the city. Wood from the remains of one of the gates over the waterways yielded a C-14 date of 480 ±47 BCE.

The interior space at Jinancheng, as expected, was broken up by a series of stamped-earth platforms on top of which had been built the palaces and temples. Large quantities of unglazed tiles were found on top of these platforms, suggesting that they supported different kinds of buildings. Based upon post holes found in platform 30, archaeologists suggest that a palatial-sized two-room building, measuring sixty-three meters east to west by fourteen meters north to south, sat on top of this foundation. Stamped-earth platforms were concentrated in the northeastern section of the city, suggesting to some[16] that this served as the residential area for the elites. Quantities of carbonized rice confirm a rice diet.

Certain areas within the walled enclosure were specialized craft areas. For example, pottery kilns were found in the southwestern section of the site. They were also concentrated along the banks of the two small rivers. Five of the kilns have already been excavated and were found to have produced roof tiles and daily wares. Traces of a bronze foundry were also located in the southwestern section of the site. Some scholars suggest that those industries located near the palace area were controlled by the Chu court.[17]

The Jinancheng site is distinctive for the large quantity of wells found within the city walls. Archaeologists reported finding more than four hundred constructed of various materials: entirely of earth, with ceramic collars (the majority), with wooden collars, and with bamboo collars. The bottoms of some of the wells were covered with a layer of tiles. Foot notches found in the walls of the wells very likely served the workman who dug the wells or cleaned and repaired them. The wells were also filled with shards from different kinds of jars —jars that may have been used to draw water from the well or to store water. Chinese archaeologists have suggested that wells served as sources of water as well as cool storage areas for food products during the long, hot summers.[18]

Another large and well-excavated Chu city is Shouchun in Shouxian, Anhui. Shouchun covered a huge area of 26.35 square kilometers, illustrating the trend of major political centers to increase in size during the Eastern Zhou period.[19]

Forts were generally very small settlements; most were about 0.1 kilometers square, and, because of their military and protective function, they were usually bordered by natural defenses in the landscape and were consequently less regular in shape. Two examples of forts are Caodian Fangcheng[20] in the Xiaogan region of eastern Hubei and Caowang Zuicheng in southeastern Hubei.[21] Caodian Fangcheng, which measures 0.11 square kilometers, is walled with battlements on three sides and a moat on the outside. Caowang Zuicheng is only .055 square kilometers in size. It is surrounded by well-preserved walls and is located near Tonglushan, an ancient copper mine active during the Eastern Zhou period, suggesting it might have been associated with protecting Chu control of bronze resources. Traces of metal casting were uncovered inside the walls.

From archaeological data we know that the urban elite lived in large buildings and were supported by a staff of artisans; textual descriptions provide more details of their lifestyles. For example, the *Zhanguoce* describes the northeastern metropolis of Linzi, the capital of the Qi state (whose archaeological remains cover an area of thirty square kilometers[22] and were contemporary to the Chu site of Jinancheng). Supporting a population of around seventy thousand households, its streets were so busy that the carriages rubbed rims and people rubbed shoulders. Its people were wealthy; they played musical instruments, gambled, raced hounds, and played ball.[23]

Although the bustle of Chu cities may have been similar, we do get some hints from the texts that Chu cities were architecturally distinctive and recognizably different from their northern counterparts. Chu palaces and towers were a source of admiration and imitation. In one tale, King Ling of Chu (r. 540–528 BCE) finished building a tower and invited other lords and princes to see it.[24] Duke Xiang of the northeastern state of Lu (home of Confucius), upon his return from a visit, insisted upon constructing at great expense a "Chu palace."[25] King Ping of Chu (r. 528–516 BCE) was criticized for his building excesses, which placed a financial burden on the people.[26] Given the pride and expense afforded buildings, we can conjecture that Chu capitals were architectural splendors.

The growth of urbanization and the splendor of the urban lifestyle in Chu was linked to Chu's control of foreign trade. While the archaeological record includes little material evidence of the commercial activity that changed the face of Chinese ancient cities during the Eastern Zhou period, textual descriptions can once again provide some hints. The *Zhanguoce* alludes to speciality markets, such as the sandalwood market,[27] and other texts of the period, for example the *Spring and Autumn Annals,*[28] hint at the activities of a lively and entrepreneurial merchant class.

Life in the City

WARRING States period poetry provides a glimpse of the elegance and sumptuousness of Chu life in the princely palaces. In the song "Summoning the Soul" from the famous collection of Chu (or "Chu-style") poetry, the *Chuci,* the poet writes:

> O Soul, come back! Return to your old abode . . .
> The chambers of polished stone, with kingfisher curtains hanging from
>   jasper hooks;
> bedspreads of kingfisher seeded with pearls, dazzling in brightness,
> arras of fine silk covers the walls;

damask canopies stretch overhead . . .

all kinds of good food are ready . . .

bitter, salt, sour, hot, and sweet . . .

ribs of the fatted ox, tender and succulent;

stewed turtle and roast kid, geese, braised chicken,

fried honeycakes of rice flour . . .

jade-like wine . . .

the lovely girls are drunk with wine. . . .[29]

In contrast to this vision of urban splendor, we see that the majority of everyday ceramic ware, found in both burial and settlement sites, is very plain and ordinary. In the Spring and Autumn period potters favored wares made with either a fine brownish paste or a sand-tempered gray paste. Both kinds were relatively high fired.[30] The ceramics found at the Hubei settlement sites of Jijiahu (Dangyang), Jinancheng, and Yicheng consist of a variety of gray, brownish-gray, black, and reddish pastes.[31] The Jijiahu site included some black-slipped wares.[32]

Most of the pottery was crudely made, either by hand or by slow wheel. The surfaces of the wares were either plain or decorated with cord marks, bowstrings, or simple geometric patterns such as hatching or crisscross marks. The types included cooking vessels such as steamers (types *li* and *zeng*) and pots called *fu;* an assortment of serving vessels such as various kinds of bowls, tall-stemmed cups, and the more elegant long-necked vases called *hu;* and different kinds of storage containers such as large urns called *weng* and smaller fat-bellied jars called *guan*. The wide distribution of these very similar wares throughout the core region of the Chu state implies that the wares were made for mass consumption, and most likely households purchased them at one of the local markets. We can imagine that these kinds of un-glazed ceramics were used on a daily basis in the households of all urban dwellers since they were the only kind of wares found at settlement sites.

The aristocratic Chu town resident, however, also used expensive bronze ritual vessels and refined lacquer cups and bowls, and dressed in exquisite embroidered silks and gauzes. There are many hundreds of examples of bronze ritual vessels from Chu tombs. In the tombs, the distinctive long-legged bronze *ding* tripods (fig. 3.1) were usually accompanied by an assort-ment of wine vessels (types *zun* and *hu*) and serving vessels (types *fu* and *dou*). Lacquerware eventually exceeded bronze in value.[33] According to the *Yantielun* (Discourses on salt and iron), a first-century BCE text, one lacquer cup was worth ten bronze cups. The text further points out that producing lacquer was very labor intensive, a trait that undoubtedly enhanced its value.[34]

It is the lacquerware, however, that helps to reinforce our impression of the elegance and sophistication of Chu elite life. The large quantities of lacquer objects retrieved from Chu burials in southern Henan, Hubei, and Hunan argue convincingly that although lacquerware is not unique to Chu, it occupied a position of unusual importance in Chu material culture. For example, more than 900 items (approximately two-fifths of the burial objects) excavated from the Yutaishan cemetery in Hubei were lacquerware,[35] and 110 of the 2,500 grave goods unearthed from Tianxingguan 1, a large-scale Chu tomb in Hubei, were lacquerware.[36]

Heather A. Peters

Lacquerware came in all shapes and sizes, from functional vessels such as elegant eared wine cups (fig. 3.10) to imitations of ritual vessels like *ding* and *dou* (pl. 4), to items unique to lacquer, such as grotesque guardian figurines (fig. 3.15), reclining deer, and drumstands crafted in the shape of birds (figs. 3.8, 3.9). Lacquerware was even fashioned into handles for weapons. The exquisite geometric designs on these objects illustrate the perfection of the lacquer tradition in Chu.

The songs of the *Chuci* also praised the rich bedspreads and curtains found in the royal bedchambers. Because of surprisingly good preservation in some of the Chu tombs in Hubei and Hunan, archaeologists have been able to retrieve and reconstruct some of the fabrics used by Chu aristocrats. These sumptuous silk textiles heavily embroidered with elaborate and intricate designs and the delicate fine-meshed gauzes completely accord with our mind's image of Chu luxury (fig. 3.2).[37]

Fortunately there are also well-preserved examples of Chu clothing.[38] Not only do we have examples of robes and garments from Chu tombs, but several Chu tomb figurines dressed in cloth clothes and adorned with hair have survived (pl. 6). From these we can see that during the Warring States period the dress and hairstyle of people living in Chu were very similar to those of persons living in the Central Plains region. The assertion of elites in the northern states that their clothing styles were uniquely civilized and that all others were barbaric seems, at first glance, to have provoked no dissent in Chu. Both men and women wore a wide-sleeved robe secured at the waist with a sash. Men wore their long hair bound up with a hairpin. They also wore a variety of hats.

Yet within this overall similarity between northern and Chu styles there were small differences, and those must be regarded as significant. Clothing is frequently a marker of ethnicity;[39] any ethnographer working in southwest China today can immediately identify a specific ethnic group based upon the type, color, decor, and weave of their head dresses and clothing.[40] Chu styles would have been readily identifiable as such in their own time.

There are also hints of more radical differences in dress revealed in Chu pictorial art. For example, some of the more fantastic and whimsical figures illustrated on the lacquerware have tent-like dresses or tunics with ragged hemlines, apparently worn over trousers. There is also some question as to whether or not Chu men tattooed their faces, a custom prevalent among the Wu and the Yue groups.[41] Some of the painted wooden burial figurines excavated from Changsha tombs have dots on their faces (fig. 4.1), which some scholars suggest represent tattoos.[42] However, other pictorial art representing Chu men does not depict tattoos, although many of the men depicted do have mustaches. It is possible that the figurines with the facial "tattoo" marks represent Wu-Yue people living within Chu society.

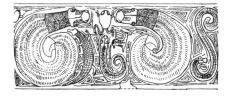

Figure 7.2 Decor featuring a tattooed man and animals on Spring and Autumn bronze *you* from Gangkou, Hunan [after Hunansheng bowuguan 1991, 148, fig. 6.1-2]

By the Warring States period the Chu aristocrat was living a life not dissimilar to that of his fellow aristocrats to the north, but certain aspects of his culture, both in content and in style, serve to remind us that the Chu noble was not exactly the same as his northern counterpart.

During the Eastern Zhou period the people living within Chu cities formed a complex social fabric. At the top were the titled aristocracy, most of whom were linked by kinship ties. In the middle sat a growing middle class of merchants and lower-ranked government officials, and at the bottom, as always, were the lower classes, whose lives may have been culturally distinct yet were intertwined with the Chu elites. In themselves these divisions are not remarkable; they are social distinctions found throughout the China of the time, which was a complex state society with a class structure. But the numerous excavated burials provide us with a means for sorting out broader cultural distinctions within Chu society.

It has long been understood that differences found among the dead reflect differences found among the living.[43] Of the more than three thousand burials located in the twenty-five locations surrounding Jiangling, Hubei, about eight hundred have mounds. Forty of the eight hundred have mounds taller than six meters with diameters of at least forty meters. The rest of the mounds are lower and smaller.[44] Thus it seems clear that the presence or absence of mounds, together with the size of those burials with mounds, is an important correlate of social distinction among Chu burials, just as it is for contemporary tombs in the north. We cannot forget that the labor required to construct these large-scale tombs and their mounds also serves as a marker of the authority and status the individual had in life.

If we follow the classification of Chu tombs by archaeologist Guo Dewei, the stratification of Chu society becomes evident. He divides Chu tombs into five feudal categories: the royal family, upper-ranking officials (landowners or enfeoffed lords), lower-ranking officials, the *shi* (a class derived from the landless sons of the aristocracy), and commoners.[45] Descriptions of examples of these tombs and their contents is a further reflection of urban life.

No Chu royal burials have yet been scientifically excavated, but we can assume they will be the largest and most grand. Based upon the remains of the destroyed and looted burials belonging to the late Chu kings in the Shouxian, Anhui, region and from the burials belonging to high-ranking elite, the royal burials will not only be lavish in scale, structure, and burial goods, but will also be accompanied by human sacrifice and sacrificial horse and chariot pits.

The burials of high-ranking ministers and enfeoffed lords were mounded and had tomb paths. Their outer coffins generally measured from seven to ten square meters and were divided into five or seven side and head compartments. Bronze ritual vessels were the most important category of burial good, although ceramic vessels imitating bronze vessels have also been unearthed. In addition, there were bronze bells and chimes, weapons, and horse and chariot trappings. Lacquer and jade objects also figured prominently. There may have been human sacrifice. Examples of these burials include Xiasi 1,[46] Tianxingguan 1,[47] Changtaiguan 1,[48] and Baoshan 2.[49]

Tianxingguan 1, for example, just outside Jiangling, is a large tomb with a mound. The mound is 7.1 meters high and covers a tomb pit measuring 43 by 37 meters at ground level. The walls of the tomb pit are graded in a series of fifteen step-ledges, and the tomb path leading down into the tomb is nineteen meters long. The surface of the outer coffin chamber is

61.5 square meters; it is divided into seven smaller compartments. The coffin chamber contained a set of three coffins. The tomb had already been pillaged before archaeologists excavated it, yet 2,440 burial items still remained. Among them were bamboo strips giving an inventory of the goods as well as the name and title of the tomb occupant, Lord Fancheng of Dishang (Dishang Jun Fancheng), who had been enfeoffed by a Chu king during the middle Warring States period.[50]

Another example is Baoshan Tomb 2, the source of the inscribed bamboo strips (see Weld, chapter 6) that have so greatly enriched our understanding of the Chu legal system. The remaining mound of the tomb is 5.8 meters high and has a diameter of 54 meters. The mound covers a pit measuring 34.4 by 31.9 meters at the top and 7.8 by 6.85 meters at the bottom. It has a 19.8 meter long tomb path; the tomb walls descend in a series of fourteen step-ledges. The grave goods included a lavish quantity of bronze ritual vessels, many of which were inlaid with gold and silver, along with weapons, pottery, lacquerware, and textiles, as well as 445 bamboo strips.[51] Inscriptions found on objects in the tomb identify the occupant as Shao Tuo, a senior official *(zuoyin)* of the Chu state. The tomb can be precisely dated to 316 BCE.

Tombs of lower-ranking officials included both ones with and without mounds. Most have a tomb path. The outer coffin chambers measure four to six meters in length and are divided into three to five compartments. Mortuary goods include both bronze ritual vessels and ceramic wares made to imitate bronze vessels. Most burials contained drums and lutes, but no bells or chimes. Chariot axles and horses' bits probably symbolized horse and chariot sacrifices. There were lacquerware and bronze weapons in all burials. Examples of burials of this rank include Wangshan 1,[52] Tengdian 1,[53] Niuxingshan 1 and 2,[54] Liuchengqiao 1,[55] Baizifan 5,[56] and Baishizi 1.[57] Most of the burials contained wooden figurines; a few of them had human sacrifice—for example, Baizifan 5, Liuchengqiao 1, and Baishizi 1. The scale of these burials pales in comparison to Lord Fancheng's burial. One of them, Wangshan 1, had a mound measuring only 2.8 meters tall with a diameter of 18 meters. The mouth of the pit was 16.1 by 13.6 meters; the walls were notched into five steps, and the tomb path extended 15.87 meters in length. There were only 400 burial goods, of which 160 were bronze. Recently analyzed and published inscribed bamboo strips unearthed from the tomb now reveal the occupant to have been Zhao Gu, a *daifu* (senior official) of the first rank.[58]

The majority of the over five thousand burials excavated in Henan, Hubei, and Hunan belong to the *shi* (petty aristocracy) and commoners. Burials belonging to the *shi* usually do not have mounds, although some have tomb paths. They usually have one outer coffin chamber and one inner coffin. Their outer coffin chambers measure 2.5 to 3.5 meters in length and are divided into only one or two compartments. The most important category of burial good is imitation bronze vessels made from pottery. A few burials contain musical instruments such as drums and zithers, and more than half have bronze weapons and lacquer objects. The simplest burials belong to commoners. Many are single-coffin tombs; some do not have a coffin. Initially, burial goods were simply utilitarian ceramics, but after the middle Warring States period, ceramics imitating bronze ritual vessels also appeared. Most graves contained a small amount of lacquerware and bronze weapons.

Diversity within Chu Culture and Society

CHU culture, as defined in the archaeological record, is a complex mix of diverse cultures. The current trend is to view Chu culture as a melting pot of diverse elements, melding its own indigenous traits with those from the Central Plains culture from the north, Ba and Shu from the west, the so-called "100 Yue" from the south, and Wu-Yue from the east.[59] Chu society, however, was not simply a mix of these elements, but was also a plural society in which a variety of ethnic groups each maintained its own distinctiveness while living side by side in the same area.[60]

Chu as a state did not consist of a single cultural unit. As in many states, Chu society was formed of hierarchical relationships between different groups that bonded them into patron-client relationships. The Chu state not only assimilated many of the differing elements within its initial boundaries, but as it expanded, pushing east, west, and south, it came into contact with still other groups, which it proceeded to absorb or accommodate.

Archaeological evidence for this melange of ethnic groups can be seen among the burial remains. Graves that are clearly non-Chu appear together with classic Chu tombs. In order to distinguish what is not Chu among these burials, it is essential to have a definition of a "Chu" type burial. Although some regional variation is present, the overwhelming similarity of the structure and mortuary goods of the thousands of burials surrounding former Chu settlements in Henan, Hubei, and Hunan serves as a diagnostic criterion to identify Chu culture (see Xu, chapter 2).[61]

Ethnic Plurality in Chu Society

THE most frequently encountered "other" elements come from the Yue and Ba cultures. Yue culture is traditionally associated with a vast cultural complex covering most of southern China, including Zhejiang, Fujian, Jiangxi, Hunan, Guangdong, Guangxi, and Yunnan. Yue culture is subdivided into regional groups ranging from the Yue state located in today's Zhejiang Province to the politically less complex Yue known as the "100 Yue" living in Hunan, Guangxi, and Guangdong. Although the "100 Yue" may not, in fact, constitute a single ethnic group as we would recognize it today, they are lumped together because of similarities in their material culture found in the archaeological record. They are associated with a hard textured proto-porcelaneous pottery, sometimes glazed, covered with stamped geometric designs; distinctive boot-shaped bronze axes; shouldered axes; and bronze vessels decorated with herringbone stripes, concentric circles, double "f" patterns and anthropomorphic motifs. Like the people in the Central Plains, they used *ding* tripods for cooking, but their *ding* were basin-shaped with spindly legs and sometimes had flared rims. These kinds of *ding* are known as Yue-style *ding*. The graves of people belonging to the Yue culture are longer and narrower than those belonging to Chu people, and they sometimes had a "waist pit" dug into the floor of the grave pit into which was placed a ceramic jar. In addition to the characteristic axes, Yue-style spears and swords are also distinctive.[62]

The presence of Yue in Chu society is archaeologically evident not only along the borders and frontiers of the Chu state, but also in its centers.[63] For instance, the Yutaishan cemetery near Jiangling is a classic example of a Chu burial ground. However, particular artifacts among the burial goods suggest contact with other cultures. For example, certain stylistic traits reflect northern Central Plains influence, such as the long-legged *li* and *ding* and long-necked *hu,* which are similar to ones found at Zhongzhoulu in Henan. Other artifacts, however, reflect the presence (not simply the influence) of outside cultural elements—for example, the six Yue-style *ding* found in the Chu burials at the Yutaishan cemetery. From burial 1 at Macheng in eastern Hubei, a porcelaneous jar covered with stamped geometric designs was excavated along with *ding, dui,* and *hu* vases of typical Chu style.[64] From burial 1 at Tianxingguan, Jiangling, a Yue-style spearhead was unearthed from what is a classic elite Chu burial. The inclusion of these non-Chu artifacts in Chu burials provides only ambiguous evidence about cultural plurality, but it clearly points to Chu contact with other cultural groups.

Archaeological sites in Hunan, however, are much more explicit in indicating that mixed populations of Yue and Chu people lived at the sites. At these sites, graves that are clearly non-Chu coexist in the same burial grounds with classic Chu burials.[65] Many of these sites, including Changsha,[66] also contain burials with contents that include both Chu and Yue artifacts—suggesting, not unreasonably, that the people who lived in these frontier regions were not bound by rigid ethnic or cultural boundaries in terms of the items they used.

Traveling west from Jiangling along the Yangtze around three hundred to four hundred kilometers into modern-day Sichuan, we find an area long associated by Chinese historians and archaeologists with the Ba culture. Traditionally, Chinese historians and archaeologists have associated nearly the entire eastern portion of Sichuan, extending into western Hubei along the Yangtze River, with the Ba people. Archaeological data confirm a cultural distinction between the remains of these people and those of the Chu; data also suggest that the two groups were in contact and maintained some kind of exchange relationship.[67] While textual evidence is sparse, references to Ba in the *Zuozhuan* suggest military and diplomatic contact between the Ba and the Chu, as well as alliances forged through marriage.[68]

Archaeological evidence of Ba-Chu intermingling consists mostly of weapons located in the Chu-dominated region of western Hubei along the Yangtze River.[69] For example, there is a particular bronze axe-like weapon called *ge* by some[70] and *qi* by others.[71] This weapon was excavated from a pit grave in Jingmen, Hubei, together with a Ba-style flat-hilted sword. The burial was grouped with four other burials containing typical Chu burial objects.[72] Willow-leaf, flat-hilted swords have also been retrieved from other sites in western Hubei, from the region extending from Ziguixian to Yichang and Shijiangxian. A so-called Ba burial was also reported unearthed from the Dangyang region in Hubei.[73] Characteristic Ba-type objects, such as a waisted ax (type *yue*) embossed with a tiger design and flat-hilted swords incised with tiger designs, have also been found in Chu burials in Changde and Yiyang in Hunan.[74] The juxtaposition of Ba-style burials alongside Chu-style burials suggests that while many of the weapons could be products of gift exchange, barter, or war booty, people from the two cultural groups did coexist.

Trade during the Eastern Zhou Period

TRADE was a primary force behind Chu expansion, especially into the southern tropics. The Chu state, located both north and south of the Yangtze River, sat on an interface between the south and the Central Plains. Given the fact that they played an integral part in the interaction spheres of the north, it is perhaps natural that entrepreneurs from Chu served as intermediaries in facilitating the movement of desired exotic products from western and southern frontier regions to the north.

Trade, or, more broadly, exchange, has always been a driving force of societies, whether complex or simple. Markets, in particular, are a focal point of human interaction. In China, ancient trade networks connected vast expanses of land, stretching across Central Asia and reaching down into modern Southeast Asia, crossing lands that only later became part of the Chinese empire.

Trade existed on different levels. First, there was local trade, the very old tradition of central market towns that link rural villages into economic networks providing the villagers and urban dwellers with the products they

Figure 7.3 Bronze cowry-shaped "ant-nose" coins [after Liu Zhiyi 1992: 80]

lack. These towns also served as important social centers. Markets of this sort were often held on fixed days of the week or month. A glimpse of the role markets may have played in an ancient local market economy can be found in ethnographic material drawn from the modern Xishuangbanna Autonomous Region in Yunnan Province.[75] There are small daily markets in nearly every town supplying basic foodstuffs and supplies. Certain roles seem to be associated with specific ethnic groups; for example, the Dai bring in vegetable produce from their gardens, while the Han Chinese tend to be the butchers. However, the weekly Sunday or Monday markets are special. Dai women who do not regularly bring products to the market will find something to bring on Sunday. For example, they will make special sticky-rice sweets, bring in some cloth, or sell eggs or vegetables. The markets are more festive on these days, and the social nature of the event is very noticeable.

In ancient China during the Eastern Zhou period local markets that may have been similar in nature to those of present-day Xishuangbanna undoubtedly played an important role in the lives of the people. Chinese texts describe the lively nature of market centers during the Eastern Zhou period.[76] We can imagine the farmers coming into town on market days to exchange their goods and to enjoy the sights of the town. The marketplaces brought together people of different social levels as well as of different cultural groups, including farmers, town dwellers, and wandering itinerant traders who brought goods from distant lands.

Long-distance trade may have functioned on at least two different levels. The first is the individual, who may have operated on a very local level, simply moving goods from one part of the country to the other, although in doing so he may have traveled great distances. This lifestyle persisted into modern times among the Haw, Chinese muleteer traders who transported goods from Yunnan down into Southeast Asia and back again until 1949. Some long-distance traders may also have had more prestige and operated on much higher state levels as agents for official commerce. Second, there was the state tribute system, in which the state itself required groups within its territory to bring in specific products on a regular basis. The state, in exchange, distributed "gifts" to the people bringing tribute.[77] Paleographical evidence from the Warring States period suggests an elaborate system of government-regulated trade.[78]

In looking at historical sources, it is apparent that although private merchants and traders existed, some merchants sustained a closer relationship with the rulers and the state than others. For example, during the eighth century BCE the Zheng ruler made an agreement with the merchants of Zheng. The merchants had helped the ruler to establish new territory, and under the agreement promised not to rebel. In exchange, the ruler of Zheng promised not to meddle in the affairs of the merchants.[79]

The "Biographies of the Money-Makers" (Huozhi) chapter of the *Shiji* lists the various economic resources of the different regions and how these resources were used and distributed (as of the Western Han period, when the *Shiji* was written). The chapter essentially describes the tribute system; it also abounds with stories of how specific individuals made their fortunes, and how they sometimes used their wealth to help their rulers. The chapter attempts to explain the principles of Eastern Zhou period economics, emphasizing the motive of profit *(li)*. It also describes the major economic centers, the people who lived in those centers, and their most important economic products; and it goes on to outline trade networks and the major communication routes such as roads, rivers, and canals. (In dealing with Chu, for example, it describes the region's main products and its extensive trade with adjacent areas.) Its focus on the persuasive theme that trade is a legitimate path to success and power suggests a tension between the rising merchant class and a government used to greater control over the economy.

The Chu Trader

THERE is Warring States period archaeological evidence for activities of Chu trade and exchange over a wide territory extending from the Henan and Hubei in the north, to Jiangsu in the east, to Sichuan in the west and down into Hunan, Guangxi, and Guangdong in the south. For example, in 1957 archaeologists unearthed a pair of bronze bamboo-shaped containers from the site of Qiujia Huayuan, Anhui, near Shounan.[80] Archaeologists believe that the two objects, called the "E Jun tallies," functioned as a kind of permit issued to a specific individual authorizing him to trade in a designated area. E Jun, or Prince E, the name of the individual mentioned in these inscriptions, is thought to have been a son or brother of King Huai of Chu (r. 328–298 BCE).

According to the inscription, Prince E had been given special trading privileges by the king. The "tallies" permitted him to buy goods cheaply and to sell them dearly. They exempted him from paying taxes while en route and entitled him to food and lodging while traveling. He also had to operate within some restrictions; for example, his traveling time was limited to one year, and the routes, which included both land and water, were carefully prescribed. The amount of goods he transported was also limited, both in quantity and type: he was permitted to transport only the amount of goods that could be carried by 150 boats, 50 carts, 500 horses, and 1,000 men. Further, he and his retainers were prohibited from carrying weapons. There was no indication, either on the tallies or from the texts, whether or not Prince E was trading on behalf of the king. It is certain, however, that he traded under royal protection, because he was carrying valuable goods without the benefit of his own armed men to guard him. We can only assume that Chu routes were protected from banditry by the ruler himself.

Two routes are outlined, one by land and the other by water. The water route travels from Echeng along the Yangtze, passes through Lake Dongting down along the Xiang River, and returns to Ying (which at the time the tallies were issued was probably located in Shouxian, Anhui). The land route also starts out from Echeng and terminates at Ying.

The inscriptions on these tallies also confirm other economic information found in contemporary historical sources, for example concerning taxes. There were possibly three categories of taxes: (1) the *li* tax levied on lodgings; (2) the *bu* business tax; and (3) the border tax paid when crossing outposts and stations.[81] The collection of taxes by the local elite certainly contributed to the growth of rich citizens beyond the direct control of the Chu court.

Chu Trade Relations

TEXTUAL and archaeological data on exchange with the central states is limited to political engagements, such as military or diplomatic treaties and the marriage arrangements that sometimes accompanied them. It is with the archaeological data retrieved from the south, a region neglected in the textual sources, that we discover some evidence regarding economic exchange and trade routes.

Chu rulers and traders, involved though they were with the contentious Central Plains states, found trade with resource-rich lands lying to their south and west most profitable. Chu merchants concentrated their interests on three regions: the Southwest, the Jiangnan, and the Lingnan regions. The Southwest includes the modern provinces of Sichuan, Yunnan, Guizhou, and western Guangxi. It is hilly and dominated by the Yunnan-Guizhou plateau sweeping down from Tibet. The relationship and contact between Chu and Ba—the principal ethnic group/state of the Southwest—outlined above was undoubtedly primarily motivated by economics. According to the *Huayang Guozhi*, Ba was a source for silk, hemp, fish, salt, copper, iron, cinnabar, lacquer, tea, and honey.[82] Archaeological data from the Ba region attest to frequent contacts and an exchange relationship between their peoples.

The Jiangnan region, which literally means "south of the Chang Jiang" (Long River, or the Yangtze River), includes the modern provinces of Hunan, Jiangxi, Zhejiang, and Fujian. Although hilly as well, this region is endowed with fertile river valleys, such as the Xiang River valley, which runs from south to north through Hunan Province. Both temperate and subtropical, this region served as a transition zone for Chinese expansion on its way to the truly tropical Lingnan region.[83] Lingnan, which means "south of the Ling mountain range," encompasses the modern provinces of Guangdong and eastern Guangxi and continues into northern Vietnam. The region was famous for its exotic products, such as kingfisher feathers, pearls, tortoises, aromatic and medicinal plants, and fragrant barks and resins.

Chu's Quest for Gold

IN the minds of many contemporaries, the Chu state was linked with gold. According to the *Zhanguoce*, "Gold, pearls, gems, rhinoceros horn, and ivory all come from Chu."[84] Although Chu ritual vessels were generally not made of gold, many Chu bronze vessels were inlaid with complex designs made from gold and silver or covered with gold leaf;[85] its currency, called *ying-yuan*, was minted from gold.[86] More spectacular, however, are the vessels made of gold (pl. 7) recently excavated from the burial of Zeng Hou Yi (see So, chapter 3, and Cook, chapter 5).[87] The quest for gold sources to maintain a steady supply both for use and trade was doubtless one reason for Chu expansion into lands to their south and southwest.

A passage in the *Han Feizi* states that "raw gold was found in the lands south of Jing (Chu)."[88] Some scholars link the "lands south of Jing" with the Mei Shui (Mei River) region (mentioned in the Tang period's *Man Shu*). The Mei Shui is associated with today's Jinsha Jiang (Golden Sands River), the name for the western section of the Yangtze that forms the southern border of Sichuan with Yunnan. In short, these authors locate the source of Chu's gold supply along the Yunnan-Sichuan border.[89]

The authors further suggest that Chu kings may have stationed an official representative in northern Yunnan as early as 500 BCE to oversee and control the exploitation of the gold and its shipment back to Ying, the Chu capital. One scholar[90] tried to link this hypothetical post with two burial sites, one near Chuxiong, Wanjiabei, in Yunnan,[91] and the other in the Ying-jiang region, about 160 to 179 kilometers southwest of Chengdu.[92] However, in both instances the connections prove very flimsy. The artifacts retrieved from these two cemeteries do not support the argument for Chu presence at either site—they reflect the local cultures.

There may have been sources of gold closer to Chu metropolitan centers. In the *Guanzi* it says, "The gold of the Ru and Han Rivers belongs to Chu."[93] The Ru and Han Rivers are found today in southern Henan. Other sources may have been in the south. The "lands south of Jing" may not have referred to the Sichuan-Yunnan region at all, but in fact to Hunan. We see in the "Biographies of the Money-Makers" chapter of the *Shiji* that in the Jiangnan region gold came from Yuzhang and bamboo from Changsha.[94] Panned gold could also be obtained in the Pingjiang region near the Hubei/Hunan border, around Changde and Taoyuan (near Lake Dongting).[95] A modern text on mining resources cites gold deposits in seventy-five prefectures in Hunan Province located to the east and west of the Xiang River.[96]

Archaeologically, there is clear evidence of a Chu presence in these regions—there is a definite spread of Chu burials and settlements south along the Xiang River, as well as additional sites found along the tributaries of the Xiang, both to the east and west. Several ancient mines in the western region of Hunan yielded copper and tin, which may have been important sources for the production of bronze ritual vessels.[97] The Mayang mine, for example, was an important source of natural copper.[98] Closer sources for copper were also available to the

Chu—for example, Tonglushan in southeastern Hubei,[99] and farther east, Ruichang in northwestern Jiangxi.[100]

Ivory, Pearls, and Incense

THROUGHOUT the ages, the lush tropical south, filled with exotic luxury goods, has lured the northern Chinese entrepreneur with its promise of great wealth. Adventurous Chinese businessmen have been willing to risk their lives transporting goods to and from these southern latitudes, by land or by sea, for at least a thousand years.[101] In the process of moving goods, they also moved themselves, and the large populations of overseas Chinese living in Southeast Asia today remind us of the continuing tradition of trade with regions far to the south.

During the Han period, Panyu, located near today's Guangzhou, was already an established trading center distributing tropical products. The *Shiji* states that "Panyu is the most important city in the area, being a center for pearls, rhinoceros horn, tortoise shell, fruit, and cloth."[102] Qin Shihuangdi, shortly after unifying his empire in 221 BCE, dispatched five armies for campaigns against the Yue because of "the expected gains from the lands of the Yue with their rhinoceros horns, elephant tusks, kingfisher feathers, and pearls."[103] Trade between the north and Panyu, so well established by the Han period, must have begun even earlier. Events from Qin Shihuangdi's quick decision to send armies into the region, to the posting of Han military garrisons south of the kingdom of Changsha[104] suggest a continued military presence by early rulers to control the flow of trade.

Chu was not only geographically closer to the Lingnan region than its northern neighbors, it was also closely identified with many products from the south, such as ivory, pearls, rhinoceros horn, kingfisher feathers, resins, and incense. For example, the exiled prince of Jin found it difficult to find a suitably luxurious present to thank the Chu king for his hospitality, because not only did the Chu king have beautiful women, jade, and silks, but also exotic products such as feathers, furs, ivory, and hides.[105] Kingfisher curtains and bedspreads seeded with pearls, mentioned in the *Chuci* songs, may have adorned the Chu royal palaces. Fragrant perfumes and incense may also have been used in shamanistic rituals.[106]

Ivory and rhinoceros products may have come from sources within the Chu state territory or from regions farther south. Both the *Shiji* and the *Han Shu* confirm that ivory, rhinoceros horn, and pearls were being transported up from south China at least as early as the Qin-Han period. Tang-period tribute lists record rhinoceros horn as tribute requested from southern Hubei, southeastern Sichuan, northeast Guangxi, and Hunan, as well as Annam (northern Vietnam).[107] Elephant tusks came mainly from Annam, although wild elephants were apparently still roaming the Yangtze River valley in 200 CE and in southern Fujian until 1050.[108] Chu royalty were known to have hunted rhinoceros in the marshy Yunmeng region east of Ying City.[109]

Other products, however, could only have come from the tropical south. The "Treatise on Geography" *(Dilizhi)* of the *Han Shu* mentions the Hepu district, located on the coast of Guangxi Province, which abounded with riches such as rhinoceros, elephants, tortoise shell, pearls, silver, copper, and fruit. Hainan Island, known then as Zhuhai (Shore of Pearls), was visited and even colonized by the Han period in order to secure access to its medicinal products, pearls, tortoise shell, ivory, and colorful or scented woods.[110] Chu pearls were unquestionably from tropical waters; the Hepu district in coastal Guangxi Province and Hainan Island were the most likely sources. Kingfisher feathers, likewise, were tropical products. According to the *Han Shu,* the tribute demanded from Chao Tuo, king of the Southern Yue, included one thousand kingfisher feathers, ten rhinoceros horns, five hundred purple cowries, forty pairs of live kingfishers, and two pairs of peacocks.[111]

Archaeologically, there is unfortunately little material evidence for these products, either in Chu sites or in sites in Guangdong or Guangxi. Kingfisher feathers are highly perishable, leaving little expectation that they would be preserved in the archaeological record. The complete absence of traces of rhinoceros horn is somewhat mysterious, although it is much more perishable than bone. One must also consider the possibility that it was already being ground up for medicinal purposes at this early date. In a non-Chu burial excavated near Luoyang in Henan, a sword was unearthed that is classified as coming from Chu because of its inscription, which reads: *fanyang zhi jin,* "metal of Fanyang." Fanyang, which belonged to Chu, was located in Xincai, Henan. The sword was sheathed in an ivory scabbard inlaid with pearls.[112]

The Southern Routes of the Chu Trader

By tracing the advance of Chu-type burials into Hunan along the Xiang River and its tributaries, pushing down toward the Lingnan region, we are, in effect, following the routes of Chu southern expansion during the Eastern Zhou. Both eastern and western Hunan are hilly and mountainous. The most obvious route of access from Hubei into Hunan is along the river systems. Starting in the metropolitan center in Jiangling, the trader would probably have traveled east by boat along the Yangtze River, then headed south through Lake Dongting and continued down the Xiang River. In southern Hunan, he would have run into the rugged Nanling mountain chain, which rises in northern Yunnan and sweeps east in an arc down through southern China.

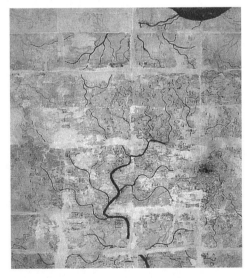

Figure 7.4 Map of Xiang River valley from Mawangdui, Tomb 3 [after Fu Juyou and Chen Songchang 1992, 151]

There are five possible passes in this mountain range that would have permitted access from Hunan and Jiangxi into the Guangxi-Guangdong region.[113] Pass 1 linked Jiangxi with Guangdong. Pass 2, located in southern Hunan near Yichang, allowed the traveler to cross the mountains from a tributary of the Xiang River and continue south to Panyu using the Wu

Jiang, a small river that linked up with the Bei Jiang. Pass 3 was near Pass 2. The difference between them was that the terrain on the Hunan side of the pass was rugged and less easily traveled. Pass 4 connected Hunan with Guangxi via a land route. Pass 5 seems potentially the most likely candidate for this early travel. Located just north of Xing'an in eastern Guangxi, it connects the Xiang River with the Gui River, which in turn flows into the Xi Jiang (West River), which leads to Panyu. The short stretch of land between the Xiang and Gui Rivers was eliminated by Qin Shihuangdi in 219 BCE, when he built the Xing'an canal immediately after becoming emperor in 221.[114] The speed at which Qin Shihuangdi built this canal suggests that this particular route was already well known.

Archaeological Evidence for Routes to the South

ARCHAEOLOGICAL evidence strongly suggests that the Chu state moved southward along the Xiang River and to the southwest along the western tributaries of the Xiang, possibly representing the Chu state's quest for metal sources. Classic Chu-type burials are found as far south as Zixing, the southernmost portion of Hunan, interspersed with non-Chu indigenous burials, evidence that further confirms Chu's multiethnic population.

The distribution of burials southward along the Xiang and thence eastward to Zixing seems to suggest that Chu traders might have been using Pass 2, which crossed over the Nanling Mountains from Hunan into Guangdong. However, at the moment the Guangdong side of the pass lacks archaeological data that would confirm this route. On the other hand, archaeological finds in the vicinity of Pass 5 do support the use of this pass for early trade.[115] The majority of burial goods found were local products, such as basin-mouthed *ding* tripods, boot-shaped axes, and double-shouldered axes. However, there are certain nonlocal artifacts (in a Gongcheng burial), such as the *ding* tripod with the hoof-shaped legs, the classic *zun*-type wine vessel, and bells, which indicate probable contact with Chu.

Thirty-six Warring States period burials belonging to members of the local elite in Guangdong are clustered along the Xi and Sui Rivers, in western Guangdong near the border with Guangxi.[116] The Xi connects with the Gui River in Guangxi and leads directly to Panyu. As with the Guangxi burials, the burial goods from these tombs reflect a mixture of cultural influences. Not only did the graves contain pottery and bronze—objects characteristic of the "100 Yue" culture—but many of them also yielded bronze ritual vessels that probably derived from Chu: for example, the inlaid bronze *ding* tripod and the *qiaohe*-type tripod vessels from the Luoding, Beifushan, site.[117] Another *qiaohe* tripod bronze vessel, this one excavated from the Sihui Niaodanshan burial,[118] was covered with surface decorations in the so-called Huai style, characteristic of Chu vessels. Chinese archaeologist Xu Huanbin strongly believes that many of these vessels came directly from Chu and that others reflect locally produced imitations of Chu vessels.[119] They suggest a market or exchange system using Chu ritual vessels to bargain with the local elites.

In sum, archaeological evidence points to a trade route that connected Ying with Panyu by first traveling south via the Xiang River into Hunan, then veering west across Pass 5 into eastern Guangxi Province, where the route continued along the Gui River. From the Gui, river traders proceeded along the Xi River into Guangdong Province and southward down to Panyu. The proliferation of Warring States period burials containing high-status bronze goods along all four of the rivers running south to Panyu in Guangdong suggests that the entire region benefited from this trade.

Conclusion

BY the Spring and Autumn and Warring States periods the region controlled by Chu had long adopted and assimilated many of the cultural traits of the Central Plains. While traces of indigenous culture are found within the archaeological record of the territory of Chu in its early historical phases, they are not in themselves sufficiently significant to mark Chu as having a distinct cultural tradition. Yet aspects of Chu civilization did clearly reflect meaningful cultural differences.

Chu's distinctiveness lies in the interstatial ecological niche it filled. Geographically, the Chu state lay on an interface between north and south China. It was centered, as outlined above, in the Jiangnan, a region that connected the temperate Central Plains to the north with the tropical Lingnan valleys and hills to its south. Chu straddled the Yangtze River, which serves as another marker separating the north from the south.

But this niche is more than one of simply linking two geographical regions; it is also economic and political. Based upon the current data, it seems extremely likely that Chu controlled access to certain easily transportable, high-value goods such as feathers, pearls, ivory, resins, and gold, but more important, Chu served as the mechanism for moving these goods from one place to another. In doing so, the Chu state provided much-needed services to the other states. It also must have managed to make a profit out of these activities; otherwise, there would have been little incentive to undertake what were clearly dangerous and risky ventures.

During this period none of the other states had the political and economic sophistication, combined with the geographical location, to carry out this role. The role gave the Chu state a stature and significance that allowed it to assimilate the culture of the Central Plains while maintaining a certain degree of independence manifested in the details of its culture. For example, the settlement pattern of Chu towns and cities did not differ significantly from those in the Central Plains, but the design of its buildings and palaces did. The Chu elite used ritual bronze vessels like their counterparts in the north, but they indulged themselves with the luxuries of the goods produced in or transported through Chu. In sum, the unique economic role played by Chu helped to produce and reinforce its individuality.

PART III

*The Spirit
of Chu*

8

Characteristics of
Late Chu Religion

John S. Major

Nᴏᴛ very much is known about Chu religion during most of the Zhou period. As Cook has shown in chapter 5, during the first centuries of the existence of the Chu state the rulers of Chu were ultraorthodox in their performance of Zhou-style ancestral rites. Later, as the center of power in Chu moved eastward and authority fell increasingly into the hands of locally based aristocratic "advisors" to the throne, such rites were coopted by members of that aristocratic class for their own ends. Nevertheless, the ancestral rites practiced in Chu were clearly related to beliefs, liturgies, and ritual norms common to the Central Plains states.

Because the population of Chu, throughout the state's long duration, was ethnically and linguistically heterogeneous,[1] it is reasonable to assume that there existed a range of local religious beliefs and practices at least among the common people, and probably extending into the ranks of local notables as well. Hardly any evidence of such beliefs and practices exists before the Warring States period, however, and it remains sparse until the very end of the Warring States and into the Han period.

The Question of Regionalism

Wʜɪʟᴇ it is possible and legitimate to talk about regional traditions in early China and to assert that such regional traditions did in fact exist, it is difficult to define them satisfactorily, or to meet the objections that are certain to be raised against them (however they are defined). With regard to intellectual and religious traditions, for example, it is often problematic to say that a particular cluster of thoughts and beliefs represents a regional tradition in early China because a case can be made that the same thoughts and beliefs were found in other areas beyond the supposed region in question. The same will be true for material culture, tomb architecture, and most other fields; some Chinese scholars have recently pointed out, for example, that some supposedly distinctive late Chu tombs share many elements of Qin tomb architecture.[2] On the other hand, early China was a very diverse place with strong and distinctive regional differences; this is manifestly true on the basis of a wide range of evidence.

The point requires further sharpening. The regional diversity of ancient China seems obvious, just as does the regional diversity of China today. Yet in Zhou dynasty China, as today, a "national" culture tended to mask regional differences at the elite level. Diplomats, philosophers, and free-lance political advisors (all likely to be members of at least the petty aristocracy) traveled widely in ancient China and generally seem to have felt reasonably at home culturally at whatever court they happened to be visiting. This notional uniformity of elite culture, in contrast to apparent cultural differences between regions of China, is fraught with opportunities for misunderstanding—and again this is as true for modern China as it is for the ancient period.

Von Falkenhausen has stated that "the distinctiveness of Chu music remains elusive, if not illusory."[3] He makes it clear that in his view the illusory nature of Chu music extends to Chu culture in general. This is a highly conservative position, based on the factual observation that most literary and archaeological remains for early and mid-Zhou Chu relate to the Chu cultural elite—which had much in common with Zhou elites everywhere. This conservative position is also, in my view, highly misleading, for several reasons: first, the cosmopolitan Chu elite ruled local populations whose cultures undoubtedly were marked by strongly distinctive regional characteristics. Second, in the later stages of Chu's political existence, the Chu elite itself became increasingly assimilated to the local populations of Chu's recently acquired eastern and southern lands. Third, therefore, it is reasonable to make careful inferences from late Chu evidence about the cultural characteristics of subelite Chu populations in earlier periods.

This chapter will examine a number of features of late Chu religion that can be described and analyzed with some degree of confidence. It will then go on to suggest ways in which Chu religious beliefs contributed important elements to the changing religious world of Han China broadly conceived. In the course of this investigation we shall also explore some links between the Chu religious world and other parts of East Asia extending beyond the Chinese cultural sphere.

Before inquiring further into the specific nature of Chu religion, however, it will be useful to take stock of what we know and how we know it. The most fundamental question to be raised in this regard is the extent to which we can isolate something called "Chu religion" at all. In order to define the part it is useful to begin by defining the whole. I take the minimum essential features of early Chinese religion—shared throughout the Zhou cultural sphere of influence—to include the following:

- Worship of a ruler's ancestors as necessary to the continued existence of a state
- Ascription of divine ancestors to the ruling house
- Worship of an aristocrat's ancestors as necessary to the continued existence of an aristocratic family

John S. Major

- For persons in every station in life, a sense of religious obligation to worship and honor ancestors, and to provide a male heir for the continuation of the family line
- A religious obligation to provide a proper funeral for one's parents, including grave goods and other ritual elements appropriate to their hierarchical status in society, with as much lavish pomp as was financially possible and ritually permissible
- Belief that each person has a complex soul—with both corporeal and ethereal components—often but not necessarily thought of as distinct *po* and *hun* souls
- State-sponsored rites of sacrifice and propitiation to high divinities, such as gods of the four directions or the four (or eight) winds, and the god of the soil
- Popular belief in, and rites directed toward, deities of local mountains, rivers, old trees, and the like, whether or not such rites were sanctioned by the state
- A requirement that religious buildings (including tombs) and the rites conducted in or about them be properly oriented in space in order to be efficaciously used

Religious beliefs and practices in Chu apparently encompassed all of these "Chinese" elements, but added special emphases to some and incorporated additional elements not known from elsewhere.

Huainan, Changsha, and Chu

As noted earlier, even in the Warring States period evidence for a distinctive Chu religion remains fragmentary and confusing. In neither the early nor the later phases of the Warring States period do the ritual inscriptions found on bronze vessels tell us anything about the religious life of ordinary people, nor much about the broader religious beliefs of members of the elite.

As this book has repeatedly emphasized, "Chu" by the end of the Warring States period referred primarily to eastern and southern regions that were incorporated into the state of Chu only very late in its historical existence, and that were probably always more Man and Yi or Wu and Yue than Chinese (as conventionally understood) in culture. By Han times, "Chu" meant, quintessentially, the culture of the lower Yangtze/lower Huai regions. As Sukhu shows in chapter 9, the kingdom of Changsha in Hunan became, in the imagination of the Han court, inseparable from the Qu Yuan myth, and likewise a symbol of exotic "Chu" culture.

Moreover, at least some aspects of Chu religion—those that belong in the realms of philosophy and religious cosmology—were part of an intellectual tradition that had some of its most important roots in the northeastern state of Qi. (It is worth noting that in the Han period the Warring States boundaries of Qi and Chu were redrawn so that the two states shared a common border along what is now the southern boundary of Shandong Province.) Other aspects of Chu religion apparently had links, or at least close analogies, with religious cultures in far-flung locations elsewhere in East Asia. The question of defining "Chu religion" thus becomes very complex.[4] To complicate matters still further, there are occasional tantalizing hints that Chu religious practices preserved some elements of Shang dynasty practices that had been eclipsed in the Central States by the Zhou ascendency.

Yet despite whatever difficulties one might have in giving "Chu religion" a precise definition, by the late Warring States period it becomes clear from both the textual and the archaeological record that the religious life of Chu was extraordinary indeed. A plethora of monster-masked gods, snake-wielding shamans, brawling cosmic deities, whistling tiger-fanged goddesses, and other remarkable beings give evidence of the diversity and special qualities of the Chu pantheon—a pantheon confirmed in the liturgical and celebratory poems of the *Chuci* and in the iconography of Chu ritual and funerary art. Specific evidence for late Chu beliefs and ideas is found in a number of texts—including the early strata of *Shanhaijing, Chuci,* parts of the Mawangdui corpus, and of the *Huainanzi*—that can be correlated with iconographic evidence from well-attested archaeological sites.

Is this, then, "Chu religion"? Yes—but the affirmative needs to be modified immediately by a reminder that the evidence here is strongest for the late, eastern-and-southern phase of Chu. The degree to which the features of Chu religion described below can be projected back in time and westward in space depends in part on one's taste for inference and, perhaps, for speculation. I would propose that Chu religion is characterized by at least the following special features that define its regional distinctiveness as compared with the mainstream religious tradition(s) of the Central Plains states:

- A special emphasis on spatial orientation and directionality in the definition of a religious cosmology; this feature is shared with "mainstream" ancient Chinese religion but accorded unusual importance in Chu
- Belief in, and rites directed at, gods of directions and months depicted as being masked, monstrous, or otherwise extraordinary in appearance
- An emphasis in religious iconography on a small and consistent set of animal images, most importantly snakes, dragons, predatory birds, and tigers (in part a legacy evolved from Shang dynasty motifs)
- Religious use of iconic and probably apotropaic figures depicted as having protruding tongues, bulging eyes, and (usually) antlers
- An unusual emphasis on hunting as an aspect of ritual behavior, and on hunting scenes as part of the decor of ritual bronze vessels
- Shamanism, mediumism, and other manifestations of spirit possession in a state of trance, together with
- A belief in the capacity of the temporarily disembodied human soul to undertake spirit journeys through time and space

Spatial Orientation and Religious Cosmography

A concern with spatial orientation is characteristic of ancient Chinese society in general and has exceedingly deep roots. Among the earliest manifestations of this cultural trait is the

Neolithic invention of animal emblems for the directions (of which the [Bluegreen] Dragon of the East and the [White] Tiger of the West appear to be the earliest). The extraordinarily early origin of these spatial emblems is confirmed by a burial at Puyang, northern Henan,[5] dating to ca. 4000 BCE; in addition to a dragon and tiger made of a shell mosaic flanking the east and west sides, respectively, of the interred corpse, there is at the corpse's feet a tree made of bones and shells, the most plausible interpretation of which is as an axial image representing cosmic centrality (perhaps the north pole). Also of great antiquity is the system of lunar lodges *(xiu),* which the Chinese devised in order to specify the location of various bodies in the heavens; it dates to no later than the late third millennium BCE.[6] A third instance of this early concern with directionality is a Neolithic bone plaque inscribed with an eight-pointed figure that apparently indicates the eight points of the compass.[7]

These examples are not specific to Chu, but there is ample evidence from later times for spatial orientation as a key element in Chu religion. There is, from the Shang period (excavated at Ningxiang near Changsha, Hunan), a magnificent square *ding* with a strikingly human-like *taotie* image on each of its four sides (fig. 8.1). This *ding* recalls a tradition in which Confucius was asked if it were true that the Yellow Emperor had four faces.[8] Whether or not one chooses to associate the Changsha *fangding* with the Yellow Emperor, its imagery of orientation to the four quarters is unmistakable. Another example is the lacquer coffer of Zeng Hou Yi decorated with images of the Northern Dipper, the Bluegreen Dragon, the White Tiger, and the twenty-eight lunar lodges, all demonstrating remarkable continuity of cosmological imagery over a period of many centuries (fig. 3.12).[9]

The Chu Silk Manuscript, translated by Li Ling in the appendix, provides still more evidence for the importance of spatial orientation in Chu religion. Both the layout and the content of the document make plain that its overriding religious concern is with the interplay of space and time. The Chu Silk Manuscript anticipates later ritual and astrological calendars, such as the "Yueling" of the *Lüshi chunqiu,* in emphasizing the importance of performing certain actions and refraining from others in each month of the year in order to ensure safety and good fortune for the community as a whole. Further literary evidence for this cosmolog-

Figure 8.1 Shang bronze *fangding* with four faces, Changsha, Hunan [courtesy of Avery Press]

ical consciousness is found in the "Summons of the Soul" and "Great Summons" poems of the *Chuci,* in which the shaman-interlocutor warns the soul against traveling in any of the cardinal directions. Still other literary evidence of Chu cultural origin, although of Han date, is found in the cosmological chapters of the *Huainanzi*[10] and in the almost mandala-like arrangement of the chapters of the *Shanhaijing.*[11]

Also important in emphasizing the spatial orientation of Chu religion is the famous funerary banner from Mawangdui Tomb 1, the tomb of the Lady of Dai (fig. 8.2). In this case the symbolism refers not so much to the four directions (although directional references are present in the banner's iconography) as to axial centrality. The banner reads from bottom to top as a cosmography, from the watery subterranean world of giant fish, a great serpent, and a squat-bodied giant (possibly a personification of Huntun: primordial undifferentiation or chaos), through the earthbound realm of the tomb and the palaces of the living, to the Changhe Gate of Heaven (guarded by birdbodied immortal officials) giving entry to the celestial world. Most scholars accept the suggestion, first made by Hulsewé, that many pictorial and literary documents found in tombs were intended to act as a sort of cosmic "road map" for the soul of the deceased.[12] That, I agree, is true of the Mawangdui banner, but I would interpret it also

Figure 8.2 Drawing of the Mawangdui silk funerary banner, Tomb 1. Note the depiction of the subcelestial world in the shape of a *hu* vessel, and the apotheosis of Lady Dai at the top center. [Drawing by Sandra Smith-Garcès; see Major 1993, 50]

John S. Major

Plate 1   Shaman holding spear with large leaf-shaped blade confronting a dragon, lacquer painting on a Xinyang zither [after Beijing, 1986 pl. 17.3]

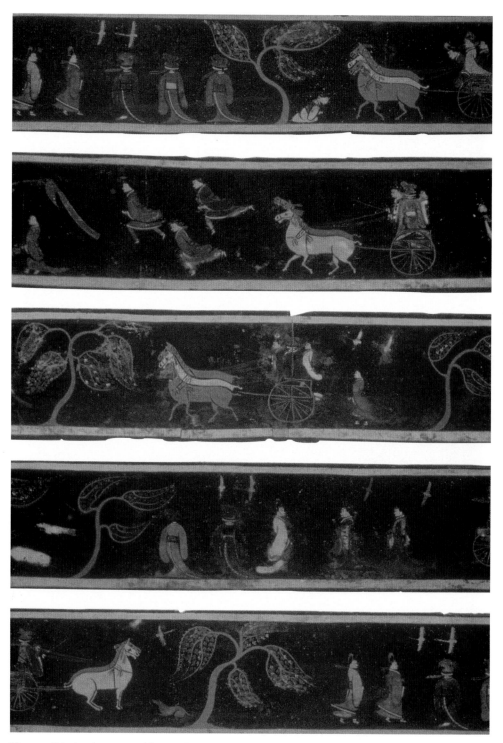

Plate 2 Painting from a round lacquer food container, Baoshan [after Beijing 1991b, vol. 2, pl. 8]

Plate 3 Lacquer screen, Wangshan [courtesy of Avery Press]

Plate 4 Lacquer *dou* from Zeng Hou Yi tomb, Suixian [courtesy of Avery Press]

Plate 5 Double
lacquer drinking
cup from Baoshan,
Tomb 2 [courtesy
of Susan Weld]

Plate 6 Wooden figurine from Mashan, Jiangling, Hubei [after Beijing 1985, pl. 31]

Plate 7 Cast gold vessel from
Zeng Hou Yi tomb [after postcard
from Hubeisheng bowuguan]

Plate 8   Funerary banner from Mawangdui Tomb 3 [after Fu Juyou and Chen Songchang 1992, 23]

Plate 9 The *liubo* set from
Mawangdui Tomb 3 [courtesy of
Avery Press]

Plate 10 Painted bronze mirrors
from Xinyang [after Beijing 1986,
pl. 13.3–13.4]

as a device for ensuring the proper cosmological orientation of the tomb (and
ary rites associated with it) for the benefit of the deceased.

Finally, as will be emphasized again below, various cosmologically charged obj
late Warring States and Han periods are strongly associated with Chu: bronze 1
cosmographical patterns, *liubo* game boards, and the astronomical/astrological
known as the *shi,* or cosmograph. Not only the famous mid-Han mirrors with
decor, but also designs antecedent to them—"mountain" mirrors, eight-tree mir
on—were apparently highly prized in Chu and elsewhere in southern China,
remains unclear if Chu was also a center for the manufacture of such mirrors. T
liubo, however it was played, had strong associations with both spatial orientation ar
cult of immortals; surviving evidence, including a magnificent *liubo* set from N
Tomb 3 (pl. 9), seems to indicate that the game occupied a particularly prominent
south. And while the *shi* cosmograph cannot be described as exclusively a Chu c
majority of cosmographs currently known were found in Chu tombs.[13] Moreover,
nomical chapter of the *Huainanzi*[14] is to a large extent concerned with principl
operation of the cosmograph, providing a further link between that instrument and
ary heritage of Chu.

This striking Chu emphasis on the religious importance of spatial orientation c
relates to other features of Chu religion, including both the pantheon and the belie
flight" spirit journeys undertaken by religious adepts. It also relates to the treatment of
endar and the calendrical gods, that is, time oriented in space.

Monsters and Gods

THE human realm of late Chu was seen as part of a wider cosmos of sacred mountair
associated divinities and astral projections, and a pantheon that ranged from local ;
deities to powerful high gods. The Chu predilection for positional astrology (using tł
mograph) and for such devices as TLV mirrors reflected a perceived need to mold l
actions to the demands of a larger numinous world. There is a striking tendency in C
to depict god figures as bizarre and often ferocious-looking monsters. It is also strikin
among the godlike figures depicted in Chu sources, divine personifications of the t
months occupy a particularly prominent place. The most famous example of the gods c
twelve months are the peripheral figures on the Chu Silk Manuscript, which have al
been described by So in chapter 3; see also Li Ling's translation of the Chu Silk Manus
in the appendix.[15] Less well known, but of considerable potential interest, are twelve s
masks from Matianping, Hunan (fig. 8.3).[16] It is unclear from early reports whether t
masks in fact form a single set; if they do, it would be plausible to regard them as possible
resentations of the twelve monthly/directional gods (The Matianping masks, however,
quite different in aspect from the peripheral figures of the Chu Silk Manuscript. The la
are drawn as full figures and are rather diverse in appearance; the masks are all variants on
basic *taotie* mask motif, depicting figures that are bug-eyed, fanged, and lacking lower jav
The months are of course named on the Chu Silk Manuscript; a different set of very u

Chinese sounding names for the months (*Shetige*, etc.) was in widespread use during the Han period.[17]

Clearly, the months were personified or deified in Chu religion. That the months were represented on the Chu Silk Manuscript by monsters with heads that resemble masks also raises the question of whether the months were portrayed by actors in masked rituals. The stone masks from the Matianping burial site were made for display, not for wearing; yet they may have had wearable counterparts. Childs-Johnson has studied masked rituals in the Shang;[18] it is interesting to speculate whether such rituals also were enacted in Chu in much later times.

Figure 8.3 Four of twelve stone masks from a W. Han tomb at Matianping, Hunan, perhaps depicting the gods of the twelve months [after Hunansheng bowuguan 1984, fig. 29]

One thing that is very interesting about all of these figures is that although some of them seem quite frightening looking, none appear to be malevolent; like the ferocious gods of Tibetan Buddhism, these deities might be dangerous, but their powers can be enlisted, under the right circumstances, to protect believers from truly malevolent forces in the cosmos. That there were also truly demonic and harmful figures is known, for example, from the text titled *Jie*, excavated at Shuihudi, which refers to many such, including a baleful whirlwind demon.[19]

In Chu religion as we now know it, the gods are not made in the image of man. Chu iconography includes a diversity of figures that can be interpreted as spirits or deities, from the hieratic figures on the coffin of Zeng Hou Yi to the dragon-imps on the coffin of the Lady of Dai, from the multiheaded, multilimbed peripheral figures of the Chu Silk Manuscript to the human-animal composites of the Mawangdui Silk Banner; what one does not find are deities that resemble ordinary, or even idealized, human beings.

A number of recent studies have advanced the identification of the gods of the Chu pantheon, working well back into the Warring States period. Such deities as Yan Di, Zhu Rong, Gou Mang, and Ru Shou, known from the "Heaven Questions" (Tianwen) of the *Chuci*, the Mawangdui text *Wuxingzhan*, and the *Huainanzi*, have strong ties to Chu religion and roots that go considerably deeper in time than the Han. Zhu Rong and Yan Di, among others, were regarded as founding ancestors of the Chu royal clan.[20] Yan Di, Zhu Rong, Gong Gong, and other gods (including some whose names are partly indecipherable) are mentioned in the "inner short text" section of the Chu Silk Manuscript. A continuing flow of new archaeological evidence on Chu religion continues to open new avenues of future research in sorting out the Chu pantheon; in particular, new evidence always opens new possibilities of correlating textual (especially ancient manuscript) and iconographic evidence. We already know many names of gods and goddesses, but it is not always clear how they relate to each other and to what extent they are the same as, or correspond to, deities in the north China tradition. There is a strong likelihood that deities from various ethnic groups (including the Central States Chinese) were adopted into the evolving religious culture of Chu and that in

turn the "barbarian" deities of Chu were assimilated to the traditional Chinese deities of the Central States. Such a process is well known, for example, in the assimilation of Babylonian and, especially, Egyptian deities into Roman religion.

A further important point about the Chu pantheon emerges from the text of the Chu Silk Manuscript. Modern scholars, relying on late Warring States and Han texts, have reached a consensus that Chinese cosmogony is unique in having an inception rather than a creation. Late cosmogonic texts, such as the famous opening passage of the astronomical chapter of the *Huainanzi,* do indeed depict a self-organized and self-evolving universe that becomes thus-of-itself *(ziran)* through the operations of the Dao, expressed physically through the permutations of *qi* manifested in yin, yang, and the five phases. But the widely held image of the Chinese universe as "uncreated" is in need of revision; the gods in the Chu Silk Manuscript are depicted unambiguously as cosmic creator-ancestors. Thus Han Huang-Lao cosmogony has its roots in Chu creation mythology dating to at least the fourth century BCE, but along the way a religious conception of cosmogony was altered to become a more philosophical and self-contained conception, probably by Zou Yan and his associates in the state of Qi during the third century BCE.

Snakes and Other Animal Motifs

ONE of the most striking impressions one gets from studying Chu religious iconography and from reading Chu religious texts is of how pervasive snakes, dragons, and serpent-bodied composite figures are in the remains of Chu culture. This is one of the most obvious ways in which Chu religious iconography, to a much greater extent than that of other areas of Zhou China, seems to preserve iconographic motifs from the Shang.[21] We have seen that the dragon-tiger pair as symbols of east and west dates back to Neolithic times; the bird (particularly a bird of prey) as a symbol of the south is also of great antiquity, attested through archaeoastronomical evidence to the pre-Shang period.[22] There is no direct evidence of similar antiquity for the snake as a symbol of the north (the Dark Warrior symbol of the north, a paired snake and turtle, is of late Warring States or Han date[23]), but there is ample evidence from at least the Shang period for the snake as an emblem of celestial divinity and centrality —that is, for a cosmological role symbolic of the north celestial pole and the axis of heaven. Moreover, the iconographic pairing of the bird of prey and the snake as symbolic opposites is of both very widespread distribution and great antiquity in the classical cultures of Eurasia and is likely of Neolithic origin. In China, as elsewhere, this symbolic pair took on the connotations of high-low, fiery-watery, celestial-earthly, and south-north; with the elaboration of five-phase *(wuxing)* theory in the Warring States and Han periods, the bird-snake pair took on the full range of yang-yin and fire-water correlative attributes.[24] The bird-snake motif shows up conspicuously on those familiar icons of late Chu religion, the funerary banners from Mawangdui Tombs 1 and 3. The banners depict the subcelestial world in the shape of a *hu* vessel defined on the top and bottom by an owl (bird of prey) and a snake, representing heaven and earth, and on the two sides by two intertwined dragons (pl. 8; fig. 8.2). The two dragons, substantially identical except for color, are perhaps to be understood as a dragon-tiger

Figure 8.4 Drawing of dragon-headed *shen* spirits handling and preparing to devour snakes from lacquered outer coffin, Mawangdui Tomb 1 [after Hunansheng bowuguan 1981, 377]

pair, in the familiar symbolism of east and west. In Han art, often very little visual distinction was made between the tiger *as a mythical/directional beast* and the dragon[25]—in other words, cosmologically the tiger is in effect a species of dragon. Certainly many dragons, pre-Han through Tang, are shown with elongated feline bodies, striding on long legs, while tigers of the same dates are conspicuously draconic.

Thus for the study of late Chu religion, we are able to interpret animal iconography on a number of levels. The correlative symbolism of five-phase theory gives us, in the first place, the dragon-tiger and bird-snake pairs: the dragon as birth/regeneration/wood/springtime, the tiger as death/destructiveness/metal/autumn; the bird of prey as south/potency/fire/heat/active, the snake as north/passivity/water/cold/hibernation. Beyond that, we read the bird as heaven and snake as earth or as the subterranean underworld. Further still, the bird is a symbol of ripeness, the snake a symbol of hibernal quiescence but also of regeneration and rebirth. One of the most conspicuous attributes of real-life snakes is that they shed their skins, undergoing, in effect, an auto-rebirth.

Although, as we have just seen, the iconographic meaning of the snake in Chu (and other Chinese) religious cosmology is by no means entirely negative, it is clear that in China, as elsewhere, snakes were also regarded as demonic, dangerous, and poisonous. (There is mounting evidence from studies of evolutionary psychology that an aversion to snakes is a hardwired, instinctual attribute of the human brain.) Thus an ability to control or manipulate snakes (or other serpentine creatures, such as dragons) was indicative of special, divinely bestowed powers. The issue of shamanism in Chu religion will be explored further below; here it is germane to note that *snake handling* was a common if not universal feature of north Asian shamanism: the shaman is invulnerable to the danger of snakes while possessed by his or her tutelary deity.[26] As we will remark upon again below, in works of Chu origin and of late Warring States/early Han date, such as the *Shanhaijing* and the *Huainanzi,* shamans are described as handling serpents.[27]

Many of the figures of Warring States and Han Chinese myth (known primarily from Chu or Chu-influenced sources) are "monstrous" in appearance, often serpent-bodied or otherwise reptilian. Gong Gong, Zhuan Xu, Gun, and Yü all have serpentine and/or arthropod characteristics. It is especially true that cosmic gods were depicted as demi-serpents: famous examples include Fuxi and Nügua, the Torch Dragon, the dragons of Thunder Marsh, and the denizens of the Yellow Emperor's realm at Chariot Pole Hill.[28] At the top center of the funerary banner from Mawangdui Tomb 1 is a being with a human torso and head and a serpent tail; the banner from Mawangdui Tomb 3 is different in details from the Tomb 1 banner, but it does show a male figure in the same position (accompanied by what seems to be a groom or bodyguard), equipped with a long serpentine tail, ascending to heaven on scaly fish-bodied steeds. Although various interpretations of these figures have been offered, it seems to me that the obvious reading is also the best one: these figures are the apotheoses of the occupants of the tombs, and their serpentine tails are indicative of their transformation into godlike (or divine ancestor) figures in the celestial realm (pl. 8; fig. 8.2).

It is obviously not the case that all Chinese, or all Chu, gods are depicted as being serpent-tailed; it is, however, true that all beings depicted as having a human head, or human head and torso, and a snake's tail are gods. The convention of depicting gods as serpent-tailed goes back at least to the Shang, and this is one of the many ways in which Chu religion seems to occupy a special position as the heir of Shang beliefs and practices. The Freer Gallery in Washington, D.C., has a famous *he* bronze vessel with a lid sculpted as a realistic human face topped with bottle-shaped horns; the lid sits atop the vessel so as to link with a serpentine tail that winds around the body of the vessel itself. Each leg of a *guang* vessel, also in the Freer collection, takes the form of a human head (with arms and upper torso) ending in a coiled serpentine tail.[29] I do not suggest that these Shang-era figures should be understood to be the same as Fuxi, Nügua, or any of the other gods whose names we know from the late Zhou period and beyond; rather, I point out that the Chu religious iconographers who depicted their celestial gods as serpent-bodied drew on a tradition already invested with the prestige of many centuries of ancient dynastic practice.

Finally, it is worth noting that while bird, snake, dragon, and tiger images appear on a variety of objects associated with ritual practices, they seem especially prominent in association with music—for example, on drum and bell stands (figs. 2.3, 8.5; pl. 1). This in turn leads to further lines of inquiry, too complex to pursue here but too important not to take note of, into the links in religious cosmology between music, the calendar, and directionality. We observe also that the large birds incorporated into the decor of drumstands sometimes are crowned with antlers; this leads us to yet another class of Chu iconographic materials.

Figure 8.5
Lacquer painting on a wooden zither of shaman holding two dragon-like snakes, Hubei, Xinyang, Tomb 1 [after Beijing 1986 pl. 2.3]

Characteristics of Late Chu Religion

The Antler-and-Tongue Motif

IN chapter 3 So has described the unique tomb guardian figures of Chu as works of religious art; here we shall try to understand their place in Chu religious belief and practice. The figures, known still from only a relatively small number of examples, are by no means identical, but they share some common features: most are vaguely reptilian in aspect and have prominent insect-like eyes; often but not always they are adorned with antlers. Almost invariably they exhibit a long, pendulous tongue. It is generally agreed that such figures were included in tombs to function as guardians, to repel evil or demonic forces from invading the tomb and disturbing its occupant. It is therefore not surprising that the figures should be ferocious of mien, but their special features still invite explanation. These apotropaic antler-and-tongue figures in their concrete manifestations are specific to Chu culture and thus fit into the Han view of Chu as "barbarian" and "other." At the same time, they fit into a system of symbolism that is deeply rooted in the human subconscious and that has analogues in other Asian cultures distributed over a wide area.[30]

One of the most striking characteristics of the antler-and-tongue motif is its obvious phallicism. But it is important to note in this regard the distinction between a penis and a phallus. The two words are often treated as synonyms, but they are not. The penis is a simple feature of male anatomy; the phallus is a symbolic device, eternally powerful and potent. The phallus can be a naturalistic depiction of an erect penis, or its symbolism can be displaced onto other features, such as a protruding tongue, horns, or antlers. Phallic figures themselves can be depicted as anatomically male, but also as female or androgynous. Symbolically, the point is not gender but power. In the case of the Chu antler-and-tongue figures, we seem to be dealing with the empowerment of the demonic—but the figures themselves are not baleful, but rather apotropaic. They are, in short, demons, or gods, harnessed (coerced?) to provide protection for the master of the tomb.

Examples of such coopted demons are known from other Asian cultures; one thinks, for example, of the Balinese Rangda (a baby-eating witch whose physical attributes include fangs, large, bulging eyes, a long, pendulous tongue, and wild hair) who nevertheless, suitably placated and honored in the Temple of the Dead (and kept under control by the protective, dragon-like Barong) protects the community from other witches, sorcerers, and the like. Similar also to the Chu antler-and-tongue figures are the fierce-aspect divinities of Tibetan Buddhism (and their antecedents in the Bon religion).

Phallic figures also commonly symbolize the idea of potency in connection with fertility. It is quite conceivable that these figures might have had, in addition to their apotropaic role, a function in promoting the generative processes of the yang (spring and summer, and phallic) on behalf of the tomb master.

These figures also obviously to some extent represent three-dimensional treatments of the *taotie* figure of bronze decor: large, vacuous eyes, horns or antlers, tiny, grasping arms, fiercely fanged upper jaws. The difference is that they are treated in the round and provided with lower jaws and lower bodies. But they clearly derive from the same symbolic representational

John S. Major

· 132 ·

system; thus we would expect their symbolism to include motifs of axiality and watchfulness against danger.[31]

Note that the Xinyang antler-and-tongue tomb guardian figures are depicted as grasping and gnawing on snakes. The pervasive snake imagery of Chu religious iconography has been discussed above; here it is enough to note that the gnawing of serpents by the antler-and-tongue guardian figures is no doubt a symbol of the conquest of death/danger/earthliness and possibly, by extension, also of the conquest of the ravages of time.

The huge eyes of these figures are possibly intended to represent cicada eyes—the resemblance anyway is very striking. The cicada was in China, from very ancient times, a symbol of rebirth, because of its emergence from the earth and its shedding of the husk-skin of its pupal stage; this no doubt accounts for the widespread practice in early China of placing a jade cicada in the mouth of an entombed corpse.[32] (Skin shedding and earthliness are thus iconographic features that the cicada shares with the snake). But the huge eyes of the figures also may appropriately be seen as indicating the vigilance of these figures in guarding their tombs, rather like the much later Buddhist "all-seeing heavenly king" temple guardian figures.

Finally, the antler motif has obvious links to shamanic practices. In the classic shamanism of northern Eurasia, the shaman, in preparation for being possessed by his familiar deity, dresses in an animal skin and an animal mask, often one topped by antlers (even if the skin and mask are not otherwise cervine).[33] This, too, has phallic connotations of the potency of the shaman in his state of possession; it also directly symbolizes the shaman's state of spiritual transformation by linking it with an "animal power."

Hunting Motifs

HUNTING scenes are prominent as part of the decor of Warring States bronze vessels and other figurative art from Chu—so much so that late Zhou bronzes decorated with hunting scenes have come to be known as "Huai style" bronzes. Hunting played a large role in royal and aristocratic life throughout China in the Shang and Zhou periods, but it seems to have taken on especially deep religious meanings in Chu culture.

Shang oracle bones record numerous instances of royal hunts; Childs-Johnson has proposed that *taotie* motifs on Shang bronzes represent (severally) the four large hunted beasts that were the special quarry of the Shang kings and whose flesh was offered ritually to the Shang ancestors and high gods—the buffalo, deer, wild sheep, and tiger.[34] Lewis, in turn, has pointed out that royal and aristocratic hunts continued in the Zhou period, serving as rallying events for the Zhou royal house (or the ruling houses of the several states), as occasions for the display of aristocratic virtues and etiquette, and as substitutes for warfare in carrying out military training and maintaining military preparedness.[35] The animals killed or captured in the hunt were also sometimes used as offerings in the royal or aristocratic ancestral temples.

The prominence of hunting scenes in Chu art leaves no doubt of its importance in Chu culture. It also is safe to assume that hunting in Chu culture represented a continuation, perhaps with different emphases, of Shang and Zhou practices. The significance of hunting was

Figure 8.6 Hunting scene of an immortal pursuing game (note feathered costume) etched onto a lacquer box from Mawangdui Tomb 3 [after Fu Juyou and Chen Songchang 1992, 62]

certainly also manifold, embracing meanings ranging from transformation magic to aristocratic leisure. We also see differences that may reflect the actual environmental circumstances of Chu; for example, while Chu hunting scenes often show large mammalian quarry, they are especially replete with depictions of the shooting of waterfowl.

K. C. Chang has proposed that changes in animal decor on bronzes from the Shang *taotie* to the Huai-style hunting scenes represents a change in attitudes in ancient China toward the natural world in general—a change, in Chang's view, from an awestruck reverence for the natural world and the animals that symbolized its spiritual dimension in the Shang to, by the Warring States period, a secular spirit symbolized by human power over the animal world—in particular, by human ability to slaughter large numbers of animals in the hunt.[36] This theory does not seem entirely satisfactory, however, both because large-scale royal hunting was as characteristic of Shang as of Zhou times, and because even the largest and bloodiest hunts of late Zhou times were more than merely occasions for the slaughter of beasts.

First, it is important to emphasize that large-scale hunting was an aristocratic privilege. We have seen (Cook, chapter 5) how the royal family of Chu and their aristocratic supporters were scrupulously orthodox in their performance of temple rites. It seems not unlikely that a fondness in Chu for ritual bronzes decorated with hunting scenes might betray a slightly defensive assertion of aristocratic status and mores on the part of the upper classes of that powerful but peripheral state. Cartmill has shown[37] that in medieval Europe, just at a time when the military prowess of the aristocracy was being challenged by new infantry tactics and weapons, hunting became the aristocratic activity par excellence; there grew up under those circumstances an elaborate etiquette of the hunt, a precise and abstruse language of venery, and an ascription of high prestige to stags, boars, and other objects of the chase.

Hunting as an element in aristocratic self-definition almost certainly was characteristic of Chu culture, as it was of early Chinese civilization in general. At least, the prestige of hunting in ancient China is not at issue; bronze vessels themselves were high-prestige goods, and if they were decorated with hunting scenes, the hunt must have shared in that atmosphere of prestige. More precisely, there is evidence that in Chu the deities of the suprahuman world, and perhaps also the souls of deceased ancestors, were believed to enjoy hunting. This is again

John S. Major

implicit in the decor of ritual bronzes; the liturgical and sacrificial aspects of rituals employing bronzes were addressed to gods and ancestors, but so, too, was the very decor of the bronzes themselves. Even more to the point, the dragon *shen* figures on the black lacquer coffin from Mawangdui Tomb 1 are portrayed as being engaged in hunting amid cloud-foliage decor that seems to suggest the celestial realm. The clear implication is that the occupant of the coffin is herself to be thought of as having departed to an otherworldly realm of aristocratic ease and privilege.

Hunting was not merely an occasion for pleasurable, strenuous exercise or participation in a controlled simulacrum of warfare; it was also an occasion for killing or capturing animals under circumstances that carried sacrificial connotations. We have seen that in the Shang, the use of animal masks and *taotie* designs on bronzes implies that animals (or at least some animals) were embodiments of divine spirits; this point has been explored in depth by Childs-Johnson. The same inference may be made on the basis of the metamorphic and composite imagery associated with the gods of Chu. As Campbell has pointed out, if animals are regarded as the embodiment of deities, one way of worshiping those deities is to sacrifice the animals and ritually offer their flesh to the gods.[38] Evidence from the Spring and Autumn period suggests that the link between hunting and sacrifice was a solemn obligation. As a remonstrating nobleman said to the Duke of Lu, "The lord does not shoot any bird or beast whose flesh is not offered in the sacrificial pots or whose hide, teeth, bones, horns, fur, or feathers are not used on the sacrificial vessels."[39]

In Warring States China, again emphatically in Chu, humans were deeply involved in the world of animals through rituals of exorcism and sacrifice. One important source of evidence for this is the "Monthly Ordinances" (Yueling) section of the *Lüshi chunqiu,* a text that is northern in origin but later became particularly associated with the Huang-Lao school (which in the Han was centered in Qi and Chu). In that text it is specified that game captured by the ruler in a ritualized hunt was a required part of the sacrificial offerings made at the suburban temples (the ancestral altars outside the cardinal direction gates of the capital) at each turn of the season throughout the year. In particular there appeared to be, in this religious cosmology, a royal obligation to procure mammalian game as summer turned into autumn, and fish as autumn turned into winter, to "lead in the *qi* of the season."[40] The widespread use of hunting motifs on Chu ritual bronzes may therefore also refer to the ruler's role as a "cosmic assistant," or facilitator, in bringing about the smooth and orderly succession of seasons in the annual cosmic round. And this of course returns to the point made earlier in this chapter about the importance of seasonal and directional orientation in Chu religious consciousness.

Shamanism and Spirit Possession

MANY aspects of Chu culture, and especially of Chu (and other early Chinese) religion, have been subjects of hotly contested scholarly debates; few such debates have been as vigorous as that about the existence and status of shamanism in ancient China. On one side are scholars who argue that shamanism, properly understood, is exclusively associated with Siberian and other northern Eurasian cultures, and therefore that it merely confuses the issue to use the word in connection with China at all. On the other extreme are scholars who see all ancient Chinese religion as essentially shamanistic. In a recent volume surveying the culture of ancient China,[41] K. C. Chang, for example, identifies the Neolithic grave at Xishuipo, mentioned above, flanked by a shell-mosaic dragon and tiger, as the "tomb of a shaman"; other contributors to the volume similarly use the term "shamanism" broadly in describing ancient Chinese religion.[42] While not subscribing to this broad view of ancient Chinese religion as shamanistic, I would argue that shamanism was a key part of early Chinese religion and especially of the religious culture of Chu.

In taking up the issue of shamanism, it is necessary in the first place to be clear what one is talking about. Hultkrantz has offered a definition that will form the basis for further discussion of shamanism in this chapter: a shaman is "a social functionary who, with the help of guardian spirits, attains ecstasy to create a rapport with the supernatural world on behalf of his group members."[43] This definition, without being overly restrictive, imposes two very important requirements: that the shaman personally have familiar guardian spirits, and that he (or she) must contact the spirit world in a state of ecstatic transport. In view of these requirements, I am not sure that the evidence currently available permits us to regard most ancient Chinese royal and aristocratic sacrificial rituals as shamanistic.[44]

On the other hand, the evidence for a shamanistic component of Chu religion is strong and diverse enough to be quite persuasive. The "Li sao," the "Nine Songs," and similar poems of the *Chuci* have long been seen by scholars as literary treatments of genuine experiences of shamanistic spirit possession, and arguments against that view have not been convincing.[45] These poems follow a fairly stereotypical pattern: a shaman, often employing erotic imagery, invites a god or goddess to take possession of her or his body; the ecstatic union, if successful, nevertheless comes to an end, leaving the shaman sad and bereft. These poems meet our test of shamanism proper: the deity invoked is specifically named, and the sexual imagery gives evidence of ecstatic union.

It might also be possible to argue that if the *Chuci* poems give evidence of shamanism, it is not necessarily the case that such shamanism was particularly a Chu phenomenon. But one making that argument would then have to explain how and why the *Chuci* poems were seen as such powerful items of Chu exotica in the Han period. And one might ask, too, why similar evidence for shamanistic practices is so lacking from the Central States.

The literary evidence for Chu shamanism is bolstered by other evidence that, although somewhat fragmentary and impressionistic, cumulatively is sufficient to carry some weight. One must consider, for example, the prevalence in Chu iconography of such images as snakes and human-animal composite figures, all of which have known shamanistic connotations in the religious cultures of Siberia and Northeast Asia. Closely related to this is the phenomenon of snake handling; in a typical passage, one of the most famous shamans of ancient China, the probably mythical Shaman Xian *(Wu Xian),* is described in *Shanhaijing* 7:

> Shaman Xian is north of Woman Chou Mountain. In his right hand he grasps
> a bluegreen snake, in his left hand he grasps a vermilion snake. He dwells on
> Dengbao Mountain, where the assembled shamans ascend and descend.

John S. Major

Another passage, from *Shanhaijing* 16, combines the motifs of snake regalia, shamanistic ascent to heaven, and ritual music:

> Beyond the Southwestern Sea, south of the Vermilion River and west of the Flowing Sands, there is a person who wears bluegreen snakes as ear ornaments and rides two dragons. His name is Hou Kai of Xia. He presented three slave women to Heaven, after which he received the nine *bian* songs and the nine *ge* songs and descended again.

An elaborately robed figure depicted on the remains of a lacquer *se* stringed musical instrument from Xinyang, shown holding a spear with a leaf-shaped blade and confronting a dragon, has been interpreted as a shaman; he could, in corroboration of this, be described as a reptile subduer (pl. 1). The shamanistic connotations of antlered figures have already been mentioned above; one might note also the specific use of antlered birds on Chu drumstands, in light of the well-known association between shamanism and drumming (not all drumming is shamanistic, but virtually all shamans employ drumming in their rituals).

One point that is still largely speculative is whether Chu shamans employed incense, psychoactive plant substances, alcohol, or other inhaled or ingested materials to aid in attaining a state of spirit possession. Comparative studies of shamanism would tend to suggest the use of such techniques, but specific evidence for their use in Chu is ambiguous or lacking (but see the incense burners described by So in chapter 3).[46]

Overall it seems quite clear that shamanism was an important component of Chu religion; it is still not clear how this shamanism fit into the total picture of Chu religion and whether, for example, shamanism played a part in the royal state ancestral cult. It could well be, however, that the "Invoker" of Chu rituals of sacrifice and feasting, whose role was described by Cook in chapter 5, played a role that was shamanistic according to Hultkrantz' definition cited above.

It may also be the case, as K. C. Chang argues, that shamanism has roots extending deep into the Neolithic period in several parts of China—this would not be the only instance in which Chu culture apparently inherited and preserved elements of very ancient (pre-Shang or Shang) practices.[47] Chu shamanism also might very well have links to the classic shamanism of Northeast Asia and Siberia; Chu most certainly had cultural links with the north via the Shandong and Liaodong peninsulas (i.e., the states of Qi and Yan).[48] There is ample evidence for later Chu links with Liaodong through the lacquer trade; there is evidence also for the travel of Chu goods, probably via the Amur valley, to the Lake Baikal region. For example, the Hermitage Museum in St. Petersburg has in its collection silk textiles from Noin Ula, Mongolia, that are virtually identical to those from Mawangdui Tomb 1. A piece of embroidered silk virtually identical to the one excavated at Mashan was found in a fourth-century BCE burial from a horse-riding nomadic culture at Pazyryk in southern Siberia. On one of the end panels of the black lacquer coffin from Mawangdui Tomb 1 (the one with hunting motifs, mentioned above) a horse is represented with twisted hindquarters, a classic nomadic way of depicting a fallen horse.[49] In an earlier article on Chu religion I suggested that Chu might have had links with the South Siberian corridor to West Asia and Europe, via, for example, the Indo-European Tocharian culture of ancient Xinjiang, and the Andronovo culture further to the north.[50] These links, which seemed rather speculative at the time, are now being substantiated at least in part through the work of Mair and his colleagues.[51]

The subject of ecstatic experience in Chu religious culture leads to still another area of inquiry. Shamanism as such was at least to some extent (in ways that are not yet fully understood) a formal and recognized part of Chu religion. But as Paper has pointed out in his rich and provocative new comparative study of Chinese religions, in Chu culture, along with shamanism there very likely existed religious practices—perhaps outside the structure of officially sanctioned rites—characterized by a more promiscuous spirit possession.[52] This was what Paper terms mediumism, in which participants in religious rituals go into trances and are possessed by spirits, speak in tongues, prophesy on behalf of the community, dance with wild, unbound hair, and otherwise engage in "lewd" conduct. (A crucial difference between this type of spirit possession and shamanism is that a medium—who might be any participant in an ecstatic ritual—does not necessarily have any formal training or lineage sanction to act as a conduit for the divine, and his or her possession is not by a particular, familiar, known, and named tutelary spirit.) Mediumism has been a part of Chinese folk religion for centuries (and remains so today), despite the frequent disapproval of formal religious authorities and overt hostility on the part of government. It is likely that what struck social authorities as the out-of-control excesses of mediumism were involved in the "lewd rites" *(yinsi)* of Chu so disapproved of by Chinese commentators to the north.[53]

If shamanism proper suggests ancient links between Chu and the north, mediumism betokens cultural attributes in common with the south, including the peninsular and island worlds of Southeast Asia. Mediumism is pervasive in the Malay world, for example. Thus it is significant that linguistic evidence suggests that the now very widespread and diverse Malayo-Austronesian peoples may have originated in the coastal regions of south China around present-day Fujian[54]—or, in other words, in ancient Yue, hard by the southern frontier of Chu. Ritual and iconographic links between ancient south China and the Malay lands of the South Seas have been explored by a number of scholars.[55] Reinforcing these similarities is concrete evidence of long-distance trade between Chu and places to the south, including a trade in sacred objects. Chu had known trade links with the Red River valley of Vietnam (see Peters, chapter 7), which in turn was in trade contact with the East Indies. Many temples throughout the Lesser Sunda Islands preserve Warring States or Han-era Dongson-type bronze drums; the "Moon of Pejeng" in a temple in central Bali is only the most famous of many such sacred objects.

We have already noted above, in connection with antler-and-tongue fierce protective deities, the additional possibility of ritual and iconographic ties between Chu religion and proto-Tibetan religions via the Shu and Ba cultures of Sichuan.

Both more evidence and additional research are still needed to sort out the complexities of Chu religion. But for the present it seems fair to reiterate that, as I proposed some years ago, Chu religion is of particular interest because Chu itself was ethnically diverse and because its culture was enriched by contacts and commonalities with other, sometimes far-flung, cultures of East Asia. Chu occupied a very special position as a crossroads of cultures in ancient East Asia.

Farflight: Cosmology and Spirit Journeys

As a direct consequence of the prevalence of shamanism (and mediumism) in Chu, the theme of the spirit journey played a significant role in Chu religion, as both literary and artistic evidence makes clear. "Farflight"[56] is the term I use to denote a specific kind of spiritual ascent characteristic of Chu. This quest for ecstatic union with a divinity whose realm is located on the very edge of the cosmos itself is the dominant theme of the "Li sao" and several other poems of the *Chuci* collection and is represented exquisitely in a painting on silk of a gentleman (or, presumably, his disembodied soul or astral projection) depicted as riding on a dragon. Soaring effortlessly through the sky, traversing thousands of *li* in a single day in a carriage drawn by dragon-like steeds, the spirit meets the goddess (or god) for a brief taste of divine immortality; as in the shamanistic hymns of the "Nine Songs," the journey ends on a note of virtually postcoital tristesse as the quester must return to the human world once again.

The spirit journey seems to have had multiple roots in Chu religious belief. As we have seen, the basic premise of shamanism—that the body of a medium can be inhabited for a time, under the proper ritual circumstances, by a god or by the departed soul of a dead person—would imply its obverse, that is, that the soul of a living person could depart temporarily to visit with the gods themselves. Second, the idea of the separability of the *po* and *hun* souls at death engendered the idea that the *hun* ethereal soul could, under some circumstances, achieve an apotheosis that would lead to immortality in a divine realm. This must have led naturally to the idea that the *hun* soul could be liberated from the body under circumstances short of death. Third, the idea (prominent in the *Zhuangzi*) of nurturing the vital essence *(yangqi)* as a means of prolonging life or even averting death similarly implied that life resided in a spirit or soul separable from the body itself. Xiwangmu, the Queen Mother of the West, became in later Sao-style poetry the quintessential object of the farflight quest journey, in part because in her mountain fastness of Kunlun she kept, in a jade vase, the elixir of immortality itself. Fracasso interprets Xiwangmu as, among other things, both a goddess of pestilence and a protectress against epidemics;[57] in the latter guise her elixir could be seen as, in effect, a medical cure for death itself.

In a number of respects, then, the farflight motif of Chu religion was a precursor of and contributor to the cult of immortality that was to play so dominant a role in Han religious life.[58] The liberation from the physical body that enabled the spirit to soar effortlessly from Penglai to Kunlun and beyond came to be seen as both a symbol and a consequence of *wusi*, "deathlessness." In the Han period, indefinitely extended longevity, achieved by means of yogic breath control, elixir alchemy, or other means of self-cultivation and attunement to the Dao, became and remained thereafter a key goal of the religious adept in China.

Huang-lao Daoism and Chu Influence on Han Culture

BY the end of the second century BCE there existed a definite and growing fad for Chu culture in fashionable Han social and intellectual circles. Of course, Liu Bang, the founder of the Han dynasty, himself was a "man of Chu." A southern flavor was evident at the Han court from the very beginning, in everything from clothing styles and lacquerware to poetry, not excluding an influx of would-be courtiers and advisors from the south. The trend accelerated during the time of Emperor Wu. (For an elaboration of these points see Sukhu, chapter 9.)

Under Emperor Wu, enthusiasm in Chang'an for things southern included an interest in the late Chu regional intellectual tradition. That tradition contributed importantly to the ideas of the current of thought (whether a closely organized "school" of thought or a looser intellectual trend is a matter of debate) called Huang-Lao, which in turn was closely linked to self-cultivation and the origins of early Daoism.[59] Textual and iconographic evidence supports the idea that Huang-Lao was strongly linked to a regional—southeastern (i.e., "Chu")—intellectual tradition, a tradition that also had roots in the third-century BCE Jixia Academy of the state of Qi (a close neighbor to the northeast of Chu's easternmost territories).

What do I mean by Huang-Lao? I have described elsewhere what I take to be the essential philosophical stance of Huang-Lao.[60] Here I would emphasize that Huang-Lao thought takes Dao as the highest expression of universal order and considers the natural order to have normative priority over the human order. The ruler thus must make his actions conform to the natural order, both by means of inner self-cultivation and outer acquisition of knowledge about the phenomenal world. The king must not act "contrary to nature"; rather, the proper stance of the king is *wuwei,* "non-striving" or "taking no action contrary to nature." It is worth emphasizing, too, that the Huang-Lao ruler was no passive slave of natural forces, but rather was so empowered by them as to be virtually invulnerable on his throne.

Huang-Lao thought underwent vigorous development at the court of Huainan during the reign of Liu An (r. 164–122 BCE); this in turn suggests a specific mechanism for the rapid proliferation of Huang-Lao ideas at the Han imperial court in the late second century BCE and into the following century.

There was first of all, of course, a natural spread of ideas through intellectual contacts, the wanderings of scholars, and the exchange of written materials. (As Sukhu points out in chapter 9, Liu An himself wrote a commentary on the "Li sao.") The capacity for the dissemination of materials is conspicuous in the similarities between the Mawangdui corpus, from the kingdom of Changsha, and the *Huainanzi,* from the kingdom of Huainan. The Huang-Lao movement, if on can call it that, was vigorous and intellectually powerful; its ideas would have spread comparatively rapidly. But a single event may also have had considerable impact: the confiscation of the library of Liu An in 122 BCE, after he committed suicide rather than face trial and execution for alleged crimes against the imperial throne.

We have a good standard of comparison, in the funerary goods from Mawangdui, to give us a hint of what Liu An's palace and academy buildings might have contained. The Mawangdui funerary library surely represented only a portion, and probably a minor portion, of the royal library at Changsha; the library at Huainan, a famous center of learning, must have been even larger and included versions of most if not all of the same texts. Imagine, then, the bundles of slips and rolls of silk that passed into the imperial collection. We can readily imagine, also, that the haul included *liubo* sets, bronze mirrors decorated with the "four mountains" pattern and other cosmographical symbols, *shi* cosmographs, *xingpan* lunar lodge dials, gnomons and shadow scales, and other scientific instruments (pl. 9). The arrival of all of this material in Chang'an (probably with at least some academicians, astrologers, and technicians in tow) must surely have had a dramatic impact. These materials from Huainan must have sharply advanced Huang-Lao theories at the Han imperial court at a time when

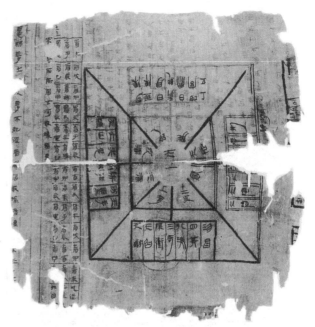

Figure 8.7 Chart showing the nine palaces of heaven and the twenty-eight lunar lodges, from a silk text called the "Yin-yang wuxing," Mawangdui Tomb 3 [after Fu Juyou and Chen Songchang 1992, 145]

those theories were not yet completely understood nor decisively influential in northern China. They certainly provided additional materials for Dong Zhongshu as he worked on his great philosophical synthesis during the decades immediately following Liu An's death (and note, in that synthesis, the blending of Yijing materials into Huang-Lao cosmology).

Chu Influence on the Han: Cosmographs, Calendars, Mirrors, and the Mother Goddess

I would like to suggest four specific cases of Chu cultural influence on the national intellectual and religious life of the Han.

The first is the *shi* cosmograph. This instrument consisted of a square "earth plate" on top of which was mounted a round and rotatable "heaven plate."[61] The cosmograph was used as an astronomical/astrological instrument; an image of the Dipper on the heaven plate was used as a pointer to indicate positional markings on the earth plate. This allowed the user to keep track of the movements of the sun and stars, and especially of the planet Jupiter, for the purpose of making astrological calculations. In the cosmological chapters of the *Huainanzi,* chapter 3, the "Treatise on the Patterns of Heaven," gives instructions for the use of the cosmograph.[62] This suggests that the cosmograph was highly valued by Liu An's scholars, and also that they expected readers of their treatise on astronomy to be fully familiar with it. The astrological meanings embedded in the cosmograph flow naturally from the positional, schematic cosmography that was a central tenet of Huang-Lao theory and reveal an ideological connection between the *Huainanzi* chapter and the rhymed "Heaven Questions" in the *Chuci*.[63]

Use of the cosmograph represented a new cosmological metaphor, one that replaced the old *gaitian* theory of cosmology. The original *gaitian* metaphor for the cosmos held that round heaven covered the square earth as a round chariot canopy covered the square passenger compartment.[64] But with the cosmograph, in order for the device to work at all the round heaven had to be smaller than the square earth. The absurdities that followed from making a physical model of the *gaitian* universe in this form—there would be no place to put the eight pillars that separated heaven and earth, and, as Wang Chong would later complain, the corners did not fit—hastened its abandonment in favor of the *huntian* theory.[65]

Figure 8.8 Antler-and-tongue figure of a shaman [courtesy of the British Museum]

A second specific influence of the Chu legacy, as exemplified by cosmological works such as the *Huainanzi* "Treatise on the Patterns of Heaven," is, I would suggest, the "Grand Inception" calendar reform of 104 BCE.[66] This event has been studied at length by a number of scholars, who have pointed out among other things the political benefits for the Han of abandoning the Qin calendar and promulgating their own. I would point out, in addition, that all of the astrological literature associated with the cosmograph was keyed, in the Chu tradition, to the so-called Xia calendar, in which the first civil month began in *yin,* the second month after the winter solstice.[67] The widespread use of the cosmograph, and credence in the astrology associated with it, would have been a powerful incentive to the calendar reform that was in fact carried out only fifteen years after Liu An's death.

A third specific piece of the Chu legacy, I believe, is the TLV mirror. The (disputed) earliest specimens of these mirrors do not predate 100 BCE; their main vogue as a cult item came late in the first century BCE and extended through the time of Wang Mang and into the Eastern Han.[68] Physically, the TLV pattern descends from the *liubo* game board, the earth plate of the cosmograph, and from certain precursor cosmological mirror patterns, such as the "four mountains" design. Conceptually, the TLV mirror is Chu and Huang-Lao in every respect and has its intellectual roots in the second century BCE. The Huang-Lao obsession with cosmic order is made manifest in these mirrors, magical objects that enabled their possessors to orient themselves in terms of the axis mundi, the eight mountains that formed the pillars of the universe, the multiple ninefold continents and provinces of the square earth, and the deities of the four directions. That this kind of schematic cosmography had achieved national significance can be seen in the institution of national sacrifices to the gods of the center and the four directions during the first century BCE.

Finally, I would suggest that the cult of Xiwangmu, Queen Mother of the West, which reached near-hysterical proportions at the end of the first century BCE and then settled down into religious respectability during the Eastern Han, is a clear example of Chu influence on China as a whole.[69] The earliest literary references to Xiwangmu occur in texts that may be identified as southern and Huang-Lao. Her manifestation as it is described in these texts may represent a long evolution from diverse sources, reflecting the ethnic diversity of Chu itself. The fierce-but-protective mien of Chu deity images in general may point to a common origin in early proto-Tibetan religious culture; Fracasso sees Tibetan influence on the early, ferocious image of Xiwangmu in particular.[70] In other respects Xiwangmu and her eastern counterpart, Dongwanggong, may descend from deities that, by the Warring States period at least, were accepted by the Chu royal house as representing the founding deities of their state.[71] Xiwangmu was often depicted in bronze on TLV mirrors; in the Eastern Han she became a favorite motif for tomb relief sculptures from Sichuan to Shandong. By post-Han times the tiger-fanged, whistling, terrifying goddess of the West had metamorphosed almost entirely into a beautiful, benevolent, wise, and immortal Daoist goddess, the mythical paramour of Emperor Wu of the Han.[72]

That elements of Chu religion and intellectual culture contributed so greatly to the larger culture of Han China is hardly surprising, given, as Sukhu shows in the following chapter, the hold that Chu achieved on the Han imagination.

9

Monkeys, Shamans, Emperors, and Poets

The Chuci *and Images of Chu during the Han Dynasty*

Gopal Sukhu

ACCORDING to tradition, Chinese poetry flows from two sources. The first is the *Shijing* (Book of Odes), the simple, moderate voice of the northern heartland. The second source is the *Chuci* (Chu Texts), the complex, lachrymose voice of the "barbarian" south. Although tradition canonized the first anthology, it is the second that had the greater influence during the formative period of the literature of the imperial age. Hawkes writes, "[W]hether traditional shaman songs or imitations of shaman songs or examples of the new secular poetry which developed out of them, they [the *Chu Texts*] all in one way or another, have their origins in Chu shamanism."[1] This contradicts the two-thousand-year-old tradition of *Chuci* exegesis, based on the earliest extant commentary, that of the second century CE imperial librarian, Wang Yi (d. 158 CE).[2] For Wang Yi the unifying factor

Figure 9.1 Drawing of Changsha silk painting of shamanka with phoenix and dragon [by C. Cook, after *Zhongguo gudai fushi yanjiu*, 18, fig. 2, and the cover of *Hunan kaogu jikan* 1]

in the anthology is an exemplary personality—that of its supposed main author, Qu Yuan, a fourth- to third-century BCE official in the royal court of Chu. According to Wang Yi the core of the *Chuci* is the work of Qu Yuan or work about him or in imitation of his literary style. Moreover, Wang Yi read the most shamanistic of the poems, the "Nine Songs" (Jiu ge) and the long, dolorous "Encountering Sorrow" (Li sao), as though they were allegories whose referent is the life of Qu Yuan. That life, according to the only biography—in the *Shiji* (Historical Records) of Sima Qian—is the classic story of the loyal minister rejected, banished, and driven to suicide by a benighted sovereign in the thrall of corrupt, sycophantic courtiers. Many centuries passed before scholars began to notice that Wang Yi's allegoresis made little sense of the poems.

By the end of the imperial age the subcommentaries to Wang Yi's annotations pullulated with the Chinese words for "strained," "arbitrary," and "mistaken," leaving later readers with the impression that Wang Yi was simply a defective commentator, although, for the more obscure passages, a necessary one. As Hawkes put it, "[T]he Later Han was an age of great scholars and exegetes, but Wang Yi was emphatically not of their number."[3] But Wang Yi did not invent the Qu Yuan myth, nor was his mode of exegesis extraordinary for his time. And while I would not contradict Hawkes about Wang Yi, I do not believe that it was primarily intellectual deficiency that misguided the writing brush of the imperial librarian. It was, rather, the hermeneutic culture the politics of the time engendered—specifically the politics of creating the images that would determine how the ancient state of Chu would be remembered.

Early Han Images of Chu: Chu Remembers Chu

WITH its defeat by the state of Qin in 223 BCE, the state of Chu lived on in the hearts of its remnant aristocracy as a desire for revenge. One of the Chu seers articulated this desire in a prophesy: "Even if only three families remain in Chu, the downfall of Qin will be in Chu."[4] The prophesy is famous because it was fulfilled. The overthrow of Qin was indeed effected mainly by two rebels from Chu, one an aristocrat, the other a commoner—Xiang Yu and Liu Bang, respectively. They in turn fought one another.

The aristocrat lost gloriously—falling only after cutting his own throat—and became a heroic legend. The commoner went on to become the somewhat embarrassing founder of the Han dynasty, which lasted four hundred years. He was a rough man with a drinking problem, as well as a womanizer—the image of the Chu provincial.

With his triumph the man of Chu had to leave Chu, while bringing its culture, in fragmentary form, to the political center of China, Chang'an. The sense of leaving home for good must have overcome Liu Bang as he passed through Pei, which was close to his birthplace:

> Kao-tzu [Gaozu, or Liu Bang] . . . started back to the capital, passing through his
> old home of P'ei [Pei] on his way. Here he stopped and held a feast at the Palace
> of P'ei, summoning all his old friends and the elders and young men to drink to
> their hearts' content. He gathered together a group of some hundred and twenty
> children of P'ei and taught them to sing and, when the feast was at its height,
> Kao-tzu struck the lute and sang a song which he had composed: "A great wind
> came forth; / The clouds rose on high. / Now that my might rules all within the
> seas, / I have returned to my old village. / Where shall I find brave men / To guard
> the four corners of the world?" He made the children join in and repeat the
> song, while he rose and danced. Deeply moved with grief and nostalgia, and

with tears streaming down his face, he said to the elders of P'ei, "The traveler sighs for his old home."[5]

Liu Bang's song is in one of the Chu modes. Pei was where he had been a village head under Qin rule. Liu Bang had been born and raised a commoner. Chu had not been his domain but his home. It was a Chu aristocrat, Xiang Yu, his eventual enemy, who had given him the title of prince of Han. He had to defeat this symbol of noble Chu to become emperor of the Han dynasty. In the passage we see Chu becoming for Liu Bang a state of nostalgia—a nostalgia that would overcome him and other members of the Han imperial household at various times throughout the first century or so of Han rule.

There was the time, for instance, when Liu Bang the emperor decided that he would replace the heir apparent, the son of Empress Lu, with the son of Lady Qi, one of his favorite concubines. The empress, upon learning this, sought the aid of the most perspicacious man at court, who advised her to attempt to win the support of four wise old men whom the emperor admired, but who refused to enter imperial service because they detested his boorishness. The empress followed the advice and brought the old men to court, where, at a palace banquet, they made clear their intention of lending their stature to the cause of the heir apparent. The emperor, swayed by this, abandoned his plan, whereupon

> The four men wished the emperor long life, and when they had finished that, they hastened to retire. The emperor watched them as they left. He summoned Lady Qi to come near and pointed the four men out to her, saying, "I want to replace the heir apparent, but with those four men upholding him, his wings are now full-grown and we would be hard put to hinder his rise. Empress Lu is now your true master." Lady Qi wept. The emperor said, "Dance a Chu dance for me, and I will sing a Chu song for you." And he sang, "The great swan flies high/and once he rises he goes a thousand miles/His pinions set/he crosses beyond the four seas/Even if I had an arrow for shooting high/where could I aim it?" He sang this several times as Lady Qi choked on sobs. The emperor rose to leave. The banquet was over.[6]

In this moment of crisis, it is the memory of a real Chu, brought back in song and dance, that consoles. Before he became emperor of all China, the ways of Chu were the only ones Liu Bang cared to know. An incident from that time illustrates this point and foreshadows cultural and political conflicts that would later develop at the Han court:

> Shusun Tong wore Confucian robes. The prince of Han [Liu Bang] detested them, so Tong changed them and wore the short tunic, in the style of Chu. The prince of Han was pleased.[7]

Shusun Tong was a Confucian from Qin who became one of Liu Bang's most trusted advisors. How much of a concession his change of clothes was may be surmised from another story from the *Shiji* where Xiang Yu, having sacked the Qin capital of Xianyang in the north, is advised to establish his capital there. But Xiang Yu thought it a better idea to return to Chu and establish his capital there. "To become rich and famous and then not go back to your old home is like putting on an embroidered coat and going out walking in the night. Who is to know about it?"[8] The man who attempted to convince Xiang Yu to stay in the north later remarked to someone else, "People say that the men of Chu are nothing but monkeys with hats on, and now I know what they mean!" To reject the civilized north for the barbaric south seemed unthinkable, and only a barely human southerner would consider it. So when Shusun Tong changed from the scholarly robes of the north to the short tunic of the south, he was making a concession to barbarism, but a barbarism that was on the rise, that he thought he could curb and eventually refine to his own benefit once it reached the north. So his concession was strategic and temporary.

The barbarism was not merely that of Chu. An aristocrat would surely have tolerated the Confucian robes. Rather, the barbarism was that of the lower-class men of Chu and various other states that had joined Liu Bang's army, hardly more than a rabble. Once they were in the capital, and Liu Bang was declared emperor,

> the emperor did away with the excessive protocol and laws of the Qin, selecting from them and simplifying them. His crowd of vassals, meanwhile, drank liquor and fought over who merited what. When they got drunk they shouted wildly, drew their swords, and struck the wooden pillars of the palace. The sovereign found this distressing. Shusun Tong, knowing that the emperor was growing increasingly disgusted at this, said to him, "Now a Confucian is not good at helping one in aggression and conquest, but can help with maintenance and development. I would like to call various scholars from the state of Lu to court and they, together with my disciples, will set up court protocol."[9]

When audience with the emperor was performed according to the Confucian protocol of Shusun Tong and his cohorts for the first time, the emperor declared, "Today, finally, I know the nobility of being an emperor."[10]

Court ritual was now Confucianized, but the imperial family was not. What Shusun Tong had effected was an aristocratic veneer for the upstart emperor. The northern Confucians saw through it all too easily. Of the Confucian scholars who were invited to court from the state of Lu (Confucius' state) to partake in the formulation of Han court ritual, two declined, protesting that "a reason for setting up ritual and music occurs only after an aristocratic family has had a hundred years' accumulation of moral power; then and only then can ritual and music be established for it."[11] The "accumulation of moral power" would eventually be produced artificially by historians who spuriously traced the emperor's family to the legendary Emperor Yao.[12] Such a pedigree made the Liu family both aristocratic and originally northern.

Had Liu Bang been an aristocrat, he could simply have continued the court protocol of Chu—that is, continued what he was used to. Liu Bang was distant enough from the aristocracy to find the ritual that prevailed among them baffling, and when Shusun Tong suggested fashioning a peculiarly Han court ritual, Liu Bang's first request was, "Can you manage to make it not difficult?"[13] Shusun Tong managed just that, but it was still necessary for all of the courtiers to practice it in preparation for the ritual audience with the emperor in the tenth month, to mark the seventh year from the founding of the dynasty. The question in court matters, then, was not whether or not to adopt Chu court protocol. (Even if Chu court protocol had been adopted, that protocol itself had been derived from northern models, since the ritual experts who were most in demand in all of the states were Confucian, i.e., heirs to the only models of court ritual, the Zhou forms of the north [see Cook, chapter 5].) The question was how to teach ritual to uncultivated commoners.

There were, however, rituals a Chu commoner would well have been familiar with: religious, especially shamanistic, rituals. This would have been true for most commoners in the Central States at the time. Chu, being on the periphery, preserved older (and indigenous) customs, and the difference between it and the other states was probably only one of degree. By the late Warring States period, however, Chu was one of the states singled out as a place where belief in shamans and ghosts was common. A text compiled under the kingdom of Qin (ca. 245 BCE) titled *Lüshi chunqiu* (The Springs and Autumns of Mr Lü), for instance, states, "The people of Jing (Chu) fear ghosts but the people of Yue seek blessings from them."[14] By the Han period the Chu preoccupation with shamans and spirits became a stereotype, as in this famous and unflattering picture of the Chu people from the *Han Shu* (History of the Former Han Dynasty):

> Watered by the Yangtze and the Han, Chu is a land of lakes and rivers, of well-forested mountains and of the wide lowlands of Jiangnan, where burning and flooding make the labors of ploughing and hoeing superfluous. The people live on fish and rice. Hunting, fishing and wood-gathering are their principal activities. Because there is always enough to eat, they are a lazy and improvident folk, laying up no stores for the future, so confident are they that the supply of food and drink will always be replenished. They have no fear of cold and hunger; on the other hand, there are no rich households among them. They believe in the power of shamans and spirits and are much addicted to lewd religious rites.[15]

The stereotype of the Chu people as shaman-thralled does not occur in any text earlier than *Lüshi chunqiu,* as far as I know. This makes sense since shamanism and various other forms of occultism were rife, and therefore nothing special, throughout the Central States, as was the case in most places in the world at the time. The characterization of Chu as barbaric or semi-barbaric, however, does occur earlier, and seen from the northern heartland, late-developing Chu appeared uncivilized. In general, Confucians and those under their influence were of course against shamanism. Mr Lü, or whoever wrote the *Lüshi chunqiu,* may well have been under the influence of the Confucians. It is odd that a criticism of occult practices should occur in his book since it was compiled under the rule of the first Qin emperor, who was notorious for his interest in the occult. For a Confucian living under Qin rule, the nearest target would have been the cruel emperor. Perhaps the writer was practicing the very Confucian art of hitting the nearest target by aiming at the one farthest away. Barbarous Chu no doubt served this purpose well. Chu also was put to this and other purposes during the Han.

According to the *Shiji,* the religious orientation of the Han imperial court was little different from that of the Qin. It was the wish of the Han founder, Liu Bang, that it should be this way. This commoner, who simplified the court ritual of Qin for use in the Han, was instinctively drawn to the elaborate religious ritual of Qin, which he largely preserved. In an unambiguous edict he said, "We consider sacrifice important and we honor worship. Under our rule the worship of the Lord on High and the sacrifices to the divinities of mountains and rivers that should receive sacrifice will be performed each according to its proper season as before."[16]

But what were the worship and sacrifices of Qin? The *Shiji* tells us, "When the Qin unified the world, [the emperor] ordered that the spirits of heaven and earth, of the famous mountains, and of the great rivers that had been customarily worshipped by the officials in charge of sacrifice be put in order, where possible." This "putting in order" of the spirits was of course the regularization of the sacrifices, according to time and liturgical mode. The officials in charge of sacrifice were not only the officials of the preunification State of Qin, they were the officials of all states now under Qin sway. The *Shiji* catalog of Qin dynasty sacrifices mentions deities of mountains, rivers, and other sites from every quarter of the empire. In addition, various heavenly bodies, the lords of heaven, obscure spirits such as the Chenbao (who were shaped like pheasants and emitted an intense light), and famous personages such as the Zhou kings and certain valorous generals were worshiped. Only a few of the sacrifices were of contemporary origin. The sacred legacy that Qin yielded to Han comprised many of China's most archaic religious practices.[17]

Liu Bang continued most of these practices and added to them, and he did not disappoint those who believed the stereotypes about the Chu predilection for shamanism. By his order the capital at Chang'an became a nexus of shamanic cults from all over China:

> In Chang'an he installed officers to carry out sacrifices and invocations. He also introduced female shamans. The shamans from Liang sacrificed to such forces as Heaven, Earth, the Sky Altar, the Celestial Waters, the Bedroom, and the Upper Hall. The shamans from Jin sacrificed to such forces as the Five Lords, the Sovereign of the East, the Lord Amidst Clouds, the Controller of Life, the Shaman Altar, the Shaman Temple, the Members of the Clan, and the First Cook. The shamans of Qin sacrificed to the Master of Altars, the Shaman Guards, and the two gods Zu and Lei. The shamans of Jing [Chu] sacrificed to such powers as the Lower Hall, the Shaman Ancestors, the Controller of Lives, and the Shimi Gruel God. The Nine Skies shamans sacrificed to the Nine Skies. All of the above sacrificed in the imperial palace at certain regular times. The Yellow River shamans sacrificed to the Yellow River at Linjin; the Southern Mountain shamans sacrificed to the Southern Mountain and to the Middle One of Qin. The Middle One of Qin is the second emperor of Qin.[18]

The Lord Amidst Clouds, the Controller of Lives, and the Yellow River are divinities also worshiped in the famous "Nine Songs" from the *Chuci*. It seems very likely that these *Chuci* songs, if they were known at the time, would have been used as hymns. The hymns recorded in the *Shiji* and the *Han Shu* as Han hymns are very similar to the Chu songs. (I have used the terms "song" and "hymn" here out of Sinological habit, but in fact they both translate the same Chinese word, *ge*.) The hymn to the Bedroom Divinity, known later as the Bedroom Divinity Who Brings Security to the Generation(s) *(Anshi Fangzhong),* a hymn to be performed by women to the accompaniment of strings (rather than bells and chimestones), was composed in the Chu mode, also by order of Liu Bang (as Emperor Gaozu).

During the first half century or so of Han rule, Chu culture was still a distinct entity in the Han imagination. It had spread through conquest to the center of a China finally unified under tolerable rule and was regenerating itself through those who still had memory of Chu as a political entity. But the peculiarly Chu aristocratic identity had been swept from the primary seats of sovereignty, first by Qin and again by a Chu commoner. And while Liu Bang and his cohorts held to their version of a Chu identity, the only definition of aristocracy available to them now was a northern one.

Han Remembers Chu

FOR the next few generations of the Han imperial house, Chu lived on as a culture that had to be self-consciously maintained, the more so as the culture that was actually lived moved farther and farther away from it. Rich rewards were given to those who could sing the classical songs of Chu (known as the *Chuci,* but not necessarily all the same as the core of the anthology that comes down to us by that name). Zhu Maichen, for example, who had spent decades in impoverishment so deep that his wife abandoned him, won favor with Emperor Wu because he could sing and explicate the old Chu songs. Sima Qian observed that Zhu Maichen once harbored a murderous grudge against someone who slighted him, and this sensitivity he attributed to Zhu Maichen's being "a Chu gentleman." We should remember, however, that the man who slighted him was instrumental in the downfall and death of the prince of Huainan, a close relative of Emperor Wu and probably the greatest champion of Chu culture of the Han dynasty.

Zhu Maichen was eventually appointed governor of Kuaiji and, before he lost everything to intrigue, rose to become one of the nine highest ministers of the empire.[19] Such examples encouraged the ambitious to study and imitate Chu poetry and music. Thus the culture of Chu became a metropolitan fad sustained by imperial nostalgia and sporadic literary discoveries from the princely provinces set up by the Han in the former Chu domains. Its foremost trendsetters were Jia Yi, Sima Xiangru, Mai Cheng, and the young Yang Xiong, all writers of the new form inspired by the *Chuci,* the *fu.*

Some of the early *fu* were emotionally intense musings on mortality or political failure with Confucian and/or Daoist overtones. Later, the long rhapsodic form became an even longer and more rhapsodic medium for extolling the splendors of the imperial court, usually with a section containing a token Confucian homily for the edification of the sovereign tacked on at the end. Yang Xiong would eventually turn away from the form, repudiating it with a term that later would be used by Ban Gu and others to characterize religious rites in Chu: *yin,* or "excessive." The Chinese word *yin* may also be translated as "lewd" or "lascivious." The use of the term by Yang Xiong was a harbinger of the rejection of Chu as a major source of culture for the Han imperial court.

Chu as Effigy of the Han Imperial House

To understand that sector of Han court politics that specifically influenced the reading of the *Chuci,* we must pay particular attention to the reign of Emperor Wu (r. 140–87 BCE), whose name means "the martial."

Emperor Wu expanded the borders of China to an unprecedented extent, but he was not satisfied with mere geopolitical power. His nearly fatal preoccupation is announced in Sima Qian's *Shiji* with characteristic understatement: "The present Son of Heaven in the beginning of his reign was especially devoted to the worship of divinities." As his armies and diplomatic missions journeyed ever more distantly into Manchuria, Korea, Central Asia, and Vietnam, Emperor Wu was at the same time involved in extending his influence into another dimension—the world of the gods. To effect this numinous campaign he employed a vast corps of ritual experts, magicians, and shamans. And as caravans laden with tribute surged toward the imperial capital, he hoped that corresponding signs of his cosmic power would be forthcoming from the realm of the spirits.

According to the *Han Shu,* such a sign was given in 120 BCE in the form of a spirit horse that emerged from the Wo Wei River near Dunhuang. One later commentator informs us that the horse had in fact been found along the banks of the river and that the story of its emergence from the river had been concocted. The emperor, however, seems to have believed the story of the equine miracle[20] and, some claim, used the occasion to set up the famous Music Bureau.[21] Be that as it may, the Music Bureau was commissioned to perform, at religious ceremonies, a hymn celebrating the arrival of the river horse and the "blood-sweating" horses of Ferghana, tribute from the northwestern campaigns. The song, which begins "The Grand Unity *(Taiyi)* offers tribute, the Heavenly Horse descends,"[22] goes on to describe the extraordinary features of the horses—their red color, which seems the result of scarlet sweat, their ability to go a thousand *li* in a single step, and their resemblance to dragons. Dragons are, among other things, the draft animals of the gods. That connotation is invoked toward the end of the poem wherein there is the exhortation: "Open the Gates [of Heaven] and take me over the Kunlun Mountains." The Gates of Heaven are located over the Kunlun Mountains. The "me" refers to Emperor Wu.

The hymn drew criticism from what Loewe calls the Reformist camp in Han court politics.[23] The Reformists were the heirs of classical Confucian political ideals. Their primary object of worship was an impersonal but somehow sentient force that they sometimes called heaven and sometimes called heaven and earth. They were strongly antishamanistic. The Modernists were their political rivals; they based their statecraft on the model of the Legalist

Qin dynasty and their religion on the eclectic, and sometimes shamanistic, cults supported by that regime.

The Reformists objected to the hymn on the grounds that "it had been composed and it had been performed in a religious context with the intention of commemorating the spectacular achievement of a reigning emperor."[24] The criticism, by a superintendent of the capital named Ji Yan, is recorded in the Treatise of Music in the *Shiji*:

> The kings of old composed hymns for the purpose of transmitting the charisma
> of the ancestors and transforming through education the myriad subjects. In the
> present case, Your Majesty has obtained horses and has composed poetry to sing
> of them, and the song is incorporated into the rites in the ancestral temple. Is it
> possible that the departed kings or the people will appreciate this music?[25]

I suspect that what particularly irked Ji Yan was the statement in the hymn: "The Grand Unity offers tribute." The phrase implies Emperor Wu's sovereignty over the divinity, a species of hubris especially abhorrent to the Confucian Reformist heart, since it assumes a personal relationship with a patron divinity. The passage later in the hymn wherein Emperor Wu demands that the heavenly horses take him to the gates of heaven only twists the knife in the wound.

This critic was unusually direct—so direct that one of Emperor Wu's other officials recommended that he and his whole family be exterminated as punishment. To avoid such dangers most critics framed their objections in indirect ways. A good example of this is Sima Qian's response to Emperor Wu's decision to institute the *feng* and *shan* sacrifices, which, far from transmitting ancestral charisma or transforming the masses, were performed in the strictest secrecy as a means to reach all of the powers of the cosmos. Emperor Wu, seeking to know how such sacrifices were to be properly conducted, questioned the most learned personages of his court. Most of his advisors shrugged their shoulders. Others offered conflicting accounts.

Sima Qian, however, responded that indeed the *feng* and *shan* sacrifices had been carried out in ancient times, and their performance sends pure offerings to all the countless spirits. Only the most virtuous rulers, however, and particularly those who had personally witnessed signs of heaven's approval, had presumed to undertake such hallowed and powerful rites. And since the rites had not been performed for some time, their proper form was now beyond recovery.

Whether the emperor felt the jab or not is hard to tell. He did, however, eventually perform rites he had been given to believe were the *feng* and *shan* sacrifices. Such information as he was able to obtain about them seems not to have come from his erudite advisors at court, but from itinerant shaman/magicians such as one Li Shaojun.

Li Shaojun was a man of obscure origins who claimed advanced age but minimal aging and deep knowledge of the occult. According to him, the *feng* and *shan* sacrifices were an important step on the road to immortality. As he instructed Emperor Wu:

If one sacrifices to the stove, it will deliver a certain object. Once it delivers the object, cinnabar can be transformed into gold. Once the gold has formed, if one fashions eating utensils of it, their use will augment one's lifespan. Once one's lifespan is augmented, that [the method of the *feng shan*] of the immortal denizens of the mysterious island of Penglai can be seen. Having seen that, if one performs the *feng* and *shan* sacrifices in that way, then one will never die. This is what Huang Di [the Yellow Lord] did.

After hearing such things as this from the lips of Li Shaojun, Emperor Wu began sending expeditions out to sea in search of the island of Penglai. He also began attempting to convert cinnabar and other substances into gold.[26] In 110 BCE he reinstituted (or rather, reinvented) the *feng* and *shan* sacrifices.

Chu in State Liturgy

SETTING aside the question of whether Sima Qian's implied objections to Emperor Wu's cultic practices were informed by a kind of rationalism, we need only compare his explanation of the *feng* and *shan* sacrifices with that of Li Shaojun to sense that two very divergent views on the nature of sacred ritual are in conflict here. The theory of ritual that Sima Qian sets forth for praise elsewhere in the *Shiji* is almost entirely derived from Confucian sources. According to it, for example:

> Ritual arises from humankind. People have desires. If one desires but does not obtain what one desires, then one cannot but feel resentment. If one's feeling resentment is without measure then one wrangles. If there is wrangling then there is disorder. The former kings detested this disorder; therefore, they instituted ritual and appropriateness to cultivate human desire, to fulfill human demands; that desire not be exhausted by objects, and that objects not be made to submit to [every] desire. That the two grow in mutual adaptation, that is why ritual arose. Therefore, what is known as ritual is nourishing/cultivating. It is with the grains and the five tastes that one cultivates the mouth. It is with pepper, thoroughwort, and perfumed roots that one cultivates the nose. It is with bells, drums, pipes, and strings that one cultivates the ear. It is with carving, openwork, and designs that one cultivates the eye, . . . Therefore, ritual is a cultivating.[27]

The word that I translate as "cultivate" also means to nourish or to feed. In this sense a more restricted and primitive notion of ritual resides, that is, blood sacrifice. This understanding of ritual was widespread even in Sima Qian's time. No one had thoroughly repudiated it, not even Confucius, as the following anecdote shows: Zigong wished to do away with the sacrificial sheep of the announcement rite of the new moon. The master (Confucius) said, "Si, you cherish the sheep, I cherish the rite."[28] According to one traditional commentary, the ritual of the announcement of the full moon, which was being carried on in the state of Lu, had already been abolished by the Duke of Wen, but the ritualists continued to sacrifice a sheep on the occasion of the new moon. Zigong, thinking this wasteful, suggested doing away with the sheep sacrifice as well. Confucius, unconcerned with the sheep, lamented the neglect of yet another of the ancient rituals.

Here Confucius seems implicitly to condone the violence and waste of sacrifice (the victim's meat may well have been eaten by participants, but Confucius' opinion has nothing to do with such practical considerations), and this is perhaps surprising to those of us, millennia away, who tend to associate Confucius with our "humanism," wherein there is no harbor for animal sacrifice. What concerns Confucius is not the sheep as "fellow creature" or item of exchange, but its transformation in the ritual context into food for spirits. We of course know that Confucius did not talk about spirits. He spoke of making sacrifices to dead parents "as if" they were present, whereas he could easily have simply stated that when one sacrifices something one is feeding the spirits of one's parents. He also spoke of serving the spirits, but keeping distant from them. Late Warring States Confucianism (I use this term in preference to "ruism"—preferred by many scholars—because it is more generally familiar) as expounded by Xunzi repeated and clarified what Confucius' position implied for them:

> [T]he sacrificial rituals originate in the emotions of remembrance and longing, express the highest degree of loyalty, love, and reverence, and embody what is finest in ritual conduct and formal bearing. Only a sage can fully understand them. The sage understands them, the gentleman finds comfort in carrying them out, the officials are careful to maintain them, and the common people accept them as custom. To the gentleman they are part of the way of man; to the common people they are something pertaining to the spirits.[29]

Here the spirits populate only vulgar interpretation and not the gentle mind, which finds comfort in what the rituals, despite their violence, express: loyalty, love, and so on. Further exemplification of this internal orientation of Confucian ritual occurs in a number of places in the literature, especially in a passage from the *Liji* quoted by Sima Qian:

> In general ritual begins at crudity, is perfected in external refinements, and ends at joy. Therefore, the height of perfection is when the internal state and [external] refinement are coterminous. Next in line is the case where sometimes the internal state predominates and sometimes the external refinement predominates. And last comes returning to the internal state in order to revert to the Grand Unity. Heaven and earth are thereby matched to each other; the sun and moon thereby cast light; the four seasons are thereby ordered; the stars and degrees of time thereby move; the Yangtze and the Yellow Rivers thereby flow; the ten thousand things thereby prosper; likes and dislikes are thereby moderated; joy and anger are thereby made appropriate. If one by means of ritual acts as subordinate, then one is compliant; if one by means of ritual acts as sovereign, then one will cast light.[30]

The Grand Unity in this passage is an impersonal concept, like heaven and earth, beyond frivolous mortal appeal. For Emperor Wu's shamans, however, it was a personal divinity whose features could be depicted and worshiped. The cult of Grand Unity involved such extravagances as an octagonal purple altar, images of the eight directions of the universe ornamented in particolored filigree, and cloth embroidered in hatchet-shaped patterns and jade. The Han histories also mention subsidiary shrines surrounding the main shrine and a corps of female musicians. We know of the details mainly through a memorial by Kuang Heng requesting their elimination. Kuang Heng eventually succeeded in influencing the court to abolish many state cults that the Confucians deemed objectionable, including that of the Grand Unity. One of the practices that seems particularly to have alarmed Kuang Heng in the Grand Unity rites was the burial of a model of the imperial chariot. Burial of slaughtered victims or carved images was a common feature of Han ritual sacrifice and magic. Whatever its particular significance was in the Grand Unity rites, the chariot was one of the traditional symbols of the state, and a traditionalist scholar like Kuang Heng could not but have read it thus: the martial emperor is willing to sacrifice the whole state for the sake of his supramundane enterprise.

Figure 9.2 Drawing of Taiyi centered between the Rain Master and the Thunder Lord over green and yellow dragons [after Li Ling 1992b, 23]

So disturbed was Kuang Heng by the burial of the carved image of the imperial chariot that when he edited the Han dynastic hymns, he expunged the line "Simurgh chariot and dragon scales"—that is, the imperial chariot's verbal image—from the hymn to the Grand Unity.[31]

Emperor Wu's offending hymn was composed in the Chu mode. Use of the Chu mode in the composition of religious music of course did not begin with Emperor Wu. We have seen that his ancestor, Liu Bang (Emperor Gaozu), used a variety of ancient modes, but preferred the Chu mode over all others in his maintenance and elaboration of the many and eclectic religious rites of the hated First Emperor of Qin. The Chu mode thus came to be associated with liturgical settings having strong overtones of the regime that had raised the cruelest hand against the old Confucian literati—the group with which the Han Reformists most closely identified.

Historians of the Later Han considered shamanistic rites the salient barbarian character-istic of Chu. The term "yin" (excessive), which, as we have seen, was used for the Chu rites, was also applied to Emperor Wu's rites. In the case of rites involving a ritual love relationship between the shaman and the invoked spirit, the word "yin" also carried the meaning "lewd."[32] Although it is not clear that Emperor Wu's rites were actually lewd and not merely excessive, they certainly drew criticism from the Reformists for a kind of promiscuity that was not merely sexual. The goal of Emperor Wu's vast ceremonies was to extend his earthly power into the celestial realms. To the Confucian mind it was an attempt to achieve an illicit inti-macy with the cosmic powers—illicit because it was direct. To use a late Warring States meta-phor, it was like a marriage arranged without relying on the proper go-betweens—which the Reformists conceived themselves to be.[33]

A desire to be in direct contact with divinity entailed also a will to escape the restraining force of cyclical history—or the Confucian version of it. It was to conceive of the dynasty as the First Emperor had conceived of it: as a line extending eternally into ever-increasing splendor, rather than as a circle whereon any point of departure is also a point of return. This cyclical time is of course derived from the agricultural time of the peasants, with its seasonal patterns of sowing and reaping, rearing and slaughter, activity and rest. Emperor Wu, in attempting, like the cruel First Emperor, to maintain far-flung armies of conquest and occu-pation as well as a continuous supply of ritual offerings, was overextending and impoverish-ing his peasantry—that is, ignoring the constraints of their circular time, the true source of dynastic time.

Emperor Wu's hymns in the Chu mode were to the Reformist ear songs of hubris, astral promiscuity, and economic foolhardiness. And under Emperor Wu the Chu mode spread to secular poetry and became the rage. The bridge between the hymns and secular poetry was a poem that was probably introduced to Emperor Wu by his uncle, Liu An, the prince of Huainan. The poem, called "Li sao" in Chinese, is usually translated in English under the title "Encountering Sorrow."

Encountering Sorrow and Han Political Reform

It is not difficult to fathom why Emperor Wu was attracted to the "Li sao"; it is full of shamanic imagery. It tells of divinations and conversations with shamans. Part of it describes the journey of a man with a shamanic title to the realm of the spirits in a chariot drawn by dragons. The poem was admired by Emperor Wu's critics as well, because, despite its imagery, the poem is a call for political reform, although it is vague about the precise nature of that reform. Perhaps in the state of Chu a political critique articulated through a shamanic con-ceit was no source of literary dissonance, but in the ideologically overcharged atmosphere of the Han court the shaman was an unfortunate medium for such a message.

Contending parties made this hybrid poem their battleground, waging a sort of herme-neutic guerilla warfare around and between its lines. Those whose objective was to remove the shaman had to do so without altering the text, which as the progenitor of an expanding, complex literary corpus, was rapidly filling literate memory. Their first tactic was to overwhelm the text with the life of its supposed author, Qu Yuan.

The earliest trace of the biographical reading of the "Li sao" is to be found in a work not included in the *Chuci* anthology, the "Diao Qu Yuan" (Mourning Qu Yuan) by Jia Yi (200– 168 BCE).[34] This trace is a paraphrase (or different version) of the famous line from the *luan* (envoi) of the "Li sao": "It is all over; there are no men in the state, no one who knows me" *(yi yi zai, guo wu ren mo wo zhi xi)*. In Jia Yi's poem, the line becomes: "It is all over, there is no one in the state who knows me" *(yi yi, guo qi mo wo zhi)*. Another famous "Li sao" line, "Again what is there to cherish in the old city" *(you he huai hu gu du)?* becomes: "Why need one cherish this old city" *(he bi huai ci du ye)*. Preceding these lines in Jia Yi's poem is the line: "I have heard that Qu Yuan drowned himself in the Milo River."[35] This indicates that Jia Yi was familiar with at least one aspect of the traditional biography of Qu Yuan that forms the basis of the allegorical reading of the poem. That he understood at least some of the poem according to that reading is evident in the line "Go through the nine regions looking for one's lord" *(li zhou er xiang qi jun xi)*, which is a gloss on Ling Fen's advice to consider the greatness of the nine regions and go elsewhere to seek a woman. (In the Jia Yi poem, "lord" [*jun*] is substituted for "woman" [*nü*], which accords with the reading we find later in Wang Yi.)

There are various images of mythical beasts, such as phoenixes and dragons, in the "Diao Qu Yuan" as well, but they are used in so conventional a manner that they shed no light on how the same images were read in the "Li sao." There is also the possibility that Jia Yi read those images in the poem as conventionally as he used them himself.

Jia Yi wrote the "Diao Qu Yuan" because he felt that he himself was reliving events from the life of Qu Yuan. Like Qu Yuan, he was a highly regarded, and thus envied, court advisor. Those who envied him accused him of opportunism and influenced his sovereign, Emperor Wen (r. 179–157 BCE) to banish him to the same region where Qu Yuan was supposed to have been banished, the city of Changsha. Jia Yi's poem was written near, and thrown into, the Xiang River in a tributary of which (the Milo) Qu Yuan was said to have drowned himself. This, at least, is what we are told by the Sima Qian biography of Jia Yi, which, against proper chronology, is set side by side with that of Qu Yuan in the *Shiji* in what is called a *liezhuan* (combined biography). This official biography of Qu Yuan was written sometime after the death of Jia Yi. How Jia Yi became familiar with the details of Qu Yuan's life to such an extent that he could see events of his own life mirrored in them is unclear, but it is not impossible that Jia Yi was himself one of the primary sources of data on the life of Qu Yuan.

Jia Yi was also the first to express disapproval of Qu Yuan's suicide. To do so he used the image of the coiled dragon, which protects itself by hiding in the watery depths, to represent the proper course for the gentleman. This dragon-like self-protection, the poem makes clear, did not exclude seeking out another king to serve.

The earliest historical mention of a poem called "Li sao" is in the *Han Shu* biography of Liu An, prince of Huainan (d. 122 BCE). (Huainan means "south of the Huai River"—part of what was once the state of Chu.) Liu An was called upon by his nephew, Emperor Wu, to produce a commentary *(zhuan)* for the "Li sao," which he did within a day of receiving the assignment. What was understood by "commentary" is a matter of debate. Some commentators say that it was a set of glosses and explications, like the Mao commentary on the *Shijing*. Others say it was actually a quasi-poetic appreciation of the "Li sao."[36] The parts of the *zhuan* that praise Qu Yuan and the "Li sao" are quoted without attribution in the biography of Qu Yuan in the *Shiji*[37] and with attribution in the *Li sao xu* (Preface to the "Li Sao") of Ban Gu (32–92), author of the *Han Shu*.[38] Wang Yi refers to it as an "explication" *(zhangju)* and implies that his own explication was based on that of Liu An.[39] It seems likely then that Liu An's *zhuan* contained both glosses and an appreciation of the poem:

> "Li sao" is like *li you* [encountering a source of worry]. Now heaven is man's beginning, father and mother are his roots. If a man is in straits he returns to his roots. Therefore people always cry, "God!" when they are being worked to the bone, or cry "father" or "mother" when their hearts are aggrieved. Qu Yuan walked a straight line on the right road; with every ounce of loyalty and knowledge he had he served his lord, but slanderers came between them—a case indeed of being "in straits." If one is faithful yet held suspect, loyal yet vilified, can one go on without resentment? Qu Yuan's "Li sao" was born of such resentment. In the *Airs of the States* there is eros without obscenity. In the *Minor Elegances* there is indignation without disorder. The "Li sao" can be thought of as a combination of the two.
>
> From Di Ku [the legendary sage king] to Duke Huan of Qi [r. 685–643 BCE], with Tang [first Shang king] and Wu [first Zhou dynasty king] in between, all of his mentions of historical figures are for the purpose of criticizing his own times. It makes clear the grandeur of the power of the Way and the principles of order and disorder without leaving anything out. His text is tight, his wording subtle, his intention pure, his behavior ethical. Words [that on the surface seem] trivial point to what is most important. The analogues that he raises, though near at hand, have far-reaching significance. His intentions are pure, therefore his references are to the fragrant. His conduct was ethical, therefore unto death he was not accepted [by his king]. Setting himself apart, he cleansed himself amid the filthy. He shed corruption as a cicada sheds its shell to float beyond the dust. He would harbor none of the world's dirt. He gleamed untainted. It is no exaggeration to say that the light of his intention rivaled that of the sun and moon.[40]

The above passage presents the characteristic style and the basic point of contention of *Chuci* criticism. The reading of the work merges with the reading of the author's personality. Comments on the style and wording of the work are, as it were, spoken in the same breath with comments on the mind and actions of the author. There is a cause-and-effect relation, if not a continuum, between the author's pure intention and his references to fragrant things. This conception of unity of intention and expression was formulated very early in the history of Chinese letters. It is summed up in the sentence "Poetry verbalizes intention" from the "Yao dian" chapter of one of the ancient Chinese "Classic of Documents," the *Shujing*. It is a definition of poetry that "became a dominant principle of Chinese poetic criticism and literary theory."[41] There was disagreement, however, about whether the intention expressed in the "Li sao" was a worthy one.

Liu An's favorable comparison of the "Li sao" with the *Shijing,* a Confucian classic, became the focal point of controversy. The classics were read as scripture. Scripture is the source of norms. It is beyond criticism. It is, instead, a criticism of the reader, or rather provides the occasion for the reader's self-criticism—an exhortation to alter behavior, attitude, and at times ontology to conform to the norm embodied in scripture. It also invites an unfavorable comparison of the world envisioned in scripture with both the real and the scripturally represented world. The norm may not be apparent in scripture, however, especially when the text was not fashioned with the idea of broadcasting norms in mind. It is then necessary to introduce a middleman, the commentator or interpreter, to tease the norms out of the text. In the case of a scripture with a known author, the actions of the author as set forth in a biography become part of the commentary of the text and an embodiment of the norm. The text is then seen to grow organically from the normative life of the author so that the one affirms and comments on the other.

At some point between the time of Liu An and that of Wang Yi, the term *jing* (scripture, or classic) was applied to the "Li sao." Whoever called the "Li sao" a *jing* was attempting to activate this style of reading for the words of the poem and/or raise the poem to the status of classic. But the "Li sao" never became a Confucian (or a Daoist) *jing;* we may infer that no consensus ever developed that it should be made one.

According to the *Han Shu,* Liu An's *zhuan* was written around the time Sima Qian put together his *Shiji.* And it is Sima Qian who next mentioned the "Li sao," in his famous letter to Ren An.[42] There Sima Qian mentions the poem in the same breath with the *Chunqiu* (Spring and Autumn Annals)—which was supposed to have been edited by Confucius—the *Yijing* (Book of Changes), Sunzi's *Bingfa* (Art of War), and the *Guoyu* (Discourses of the States), all works produced under duress by authors whose legitimate ambitions had been frustrated. At the time, Sima Qian was himself producing his *Shiji* under duress. It is odd, however, that whereas Sima Qian quotes hundreds of lines from the better poetry of Sima Xiangru and Jia Yi in his biographies of them, he does not quote the "Li sao" in the biography of Qu Yuan, citing instead the mediocre and spurious "Huai sha." Could it be that Sima Qian leaned toward the strain of the *Chuci* tradition that sought to rationalize the religious imagery in the "Li sao," preferring instead the pedestrian reworking (and interpretation) of the "Li sao"—the "Ai ying" and the "Huai sha"—over the multivalent masterwork itself? Some such reason would seem to be required to account for the absence of this most shamanic of the Chu texts from the *Shiji.*

The literary exclusion of shamanism presaged the eventual political exclusion of shamanism from the Han court. The character of some of Emperor Wu's shamans made them easy targets; Luan Da is a famous example. Originally a slave, Luan Da conned the emperor with some of the oldest ploys in the occult book: he promised magical production of gold, contact with the spirits, and the path to immortality if only he could be granted high office—so that the empowering spirits would not despise him. The emperor, who was an easy mark, therefore ennobled him to a rank above ministers of state. The shaman of course could not make good on his promises and was executed in the end for deceiving the emperor.[43]

We should remember, when confronted by examples of imperial gullibility, that most people at this time, noble or common, believed in such thaumaturgic power as the shamans and magicians claimed to have. Toward the end of Emperor Wu's reign, a well-established and trusted official took advantage of this superstition to engineer a witchcraft scare in the capital. The precipitating incidents involved the use of evil spells, false accusations, and of course shamans. Before the episode of mass hysteria was over, tens of thousands had died by execution or suicide. The purpose of it all was to provide a cover for the official's attack on Empress Wei's family, whose ire he had earlier incurred and now sought to deflect. He was eventually exposed, and the emperor had him executed and his shaman cohorts burned alive.[44] Incidents such as these no doubt made the emperor realize and lament that a good shaman is hard to find. There is no evidence, however, that he was ever persuaded that one would be impossible to find, despite the fact that he finally favored the Reformists and established their Confucianism as state orthodoxy.

Reform of state rites was not effected during the emperor's lifetime; it was carried out slowly and with many reversals during the succeeding reigns. One by one the cults of divinities inherited from the Qin, such as the Lord of Fire and the White, Green, and Yellow Lords, were abolished, as were Emperor Wu's cults to such divinities as Grand Unity and the Earth Queen. Although the existence of the gods was not denied, they were subsumed under the impersonal forces of heaven and earth. The ancient Zhou pattern of worship was, in the Han Confucian vision, "reestablished."

This explains why, as mentioned earlier, some of Emperor Wu's hymns were edited to accord with Confucian principles. The line in the hymn to the Heavenly Horse that reads, in Sima Qian's *Shiji,* "Grand Unity offers tribute" was altered, in Ban Gu's *Han Shu,* to read, "Grand Unity bestows," thus demoting the earthly Emperor Wu to his proper position— below the celestial powers.[45] In the meantime, it is clear that shamans were at some point prohibited from holding office because in the *Hou Han Shou* (History of the Later Han Dynasty) a man cites the fact that he is from a shaman family as reason for his inappropriateness for serving at court.[46]

By the second century CE the great Han scholars and exegetes were undertaking a hermeneutic campaign against shamanism that was bolder than any before. The conspicuously shamanistic "Li sao" provided a sort of test case. The text, while beautiful, said embarrassingly shamanistic things, so it had to be "taught" to speak as a classical scholar would before it could be admitted to higher literary society. The first step in that direction was to make the biography of Qu Yuan, with whom many Confucians could identify, the exclusive key to reading the text.

There was a challenge from within the Confucian camp, however, to this movement to raise the "Li sao," via Qu Yuan's biography, to "classic" status. The challenge was articulated by Yang Xiong (53 BCE−18 CE) in his "Fan sao" (Contre Sao). He prefaces his poem by asking rhetorically why someone like Qu Yuan, whose writing never failed to provoke tears and surpassed that of the celebrated Han poet Sima Xiangru, should have been rejected by his king.

The poem goes on to criticize Qu Yuan for not emulating Confucius, who, rather than commit suicide, left his state of Lu when he found his talents unwelcome there. This is essentially an extension of the criticism that Jia Yi articulated—suicide was not the proper course for a gentleman.

Ban Gu, in his *Li sao xu,* quoting Liu An's comparison of the "Li sao" to the classics, declares, "This statement appears to go beyond the truth." Because, says Ban Gu, quoting the *Shijing,* the noble thing is "to protect one's person" and not "show off one's talents and raise oneself above others," and certainly not commit suicide as Qu Yuan did. By doing this, Qu Yuan "lowered himself to the status of madmen." By the last Ban Gu meant people whose devotion to the Way made them act impetuously. Impetuosity included his "expressing his resentment of King Huai,"[47] his "ridicule of Pepper and Lan[48] and his contending amid the petty men who were endangering the state."

It is through Ban Gu that we get a hitherto rare shift of attention away from Qu Yuan to his text. Ban Gu quotes another fragment of the Liu An commentary where a reference to the Wuzi (fifth son) in the "Li sao" is identified as Wu Zixu (d. 484 BCE), a Spring and Autumn period figure from the state of Chu famous for having exhumed the body of the king of Chu, whipping it in revenge for the king's murder of Wu's father and brother. Ban Gu rightly points out that this is a gross misidentification and goes on to say that in identifying historical figures like Archer Yi, Jiao, Shao Kang, and the two Yao sisters, commentators like Liu An "have something to add or subtract according to what they know, but they still don't get it right. Therefore they pick and choose from all over the classics and the commentaries and take [the results] as an explication."[49] He then goes on to call the "frequent reference to [such things as] the Kunlun Mountains and after-death nuptials with Fu Fei" as "empty talk" with no basis in the orthodox classics. What we have here, besides a reading of the quest for celestial brides in the poem, is clear evidence that many of the allusions in the "Li sao" were as difficult for early Han scholars as they were for later scholars, if not more so.

Ban Gu, of course, knew his history. But even his commentary was seen as inadequate by Wang Yi, who criticized all the previous commentators for misreading characters and "contorting the meaning of the text." Besides that, Wang Yi took Ban Gu to task for criticizing Qu Yuan, citing other impetuous types like Wu Zixu, Bi Gan, and so on, who were recorded and approved of in the Confucian histories.

Along with affiliating Qu Yuan with Confucian heroes, Wang Yi affiliates the "Li sao" with Confucian texts:

> The text of the "Li sao," taking as its basis the *Shi* [Book of Odes] makes use of the *xing* and adduces analogues as metaphors. Therefore, fine birds and fragrant plants are used to correspond to persons of loyalty and integrity. Evil birds and foul-smelling things are used as comparisons for slanderers and sycophants, Ling Xiu and the Beautiful Person are used as comparisons for the sovereign, and Fu Fei and the beautiful women are comparisons for worthy ministers. Dragons and phoenixes are used to convey the noble person and the whirlwinds and rainbows are taken as [images of] the petty men.[50]

The *xing,* or "stimulus," is the use of "natural images, repeated with variations to open or sub-divide each stanza; they are juxtaposed without comment to the human situation . . . around which the poem centers and seem, at first glance, unrelated to it." The *xing* was isolated by early commentators "as one of three rhetorical devices of the Book of Odes [the others being comparison *(bi)* and exposition *(fu)*]."[51] The *xing,* if it occurs at all in the "Li sao," is the least frequent of the *Shijing* rhetorical devices to be observed there. Wang Yi mentions it first but offers no examples of it, preferring to point out many instances of comparison. His is clearly a vain attempt to trace the ancestry of the "Li sao" back to the *Shijing* by simply declaring that it uses this peculiarly *Shijing* rhetorical device.

The intellectual integrity of Wang Yi's other attempts to prove the filiation of the "Li sao" with other classics can be surmised from a passage from his postface, where he juxtaposes "Li sao" sentences with sentences from various classics and forcibly reads them against each other:

> The text of the "Li sao" depends on the Five Classics to establish its meaning. "I am the descendant of Lord Gaoyang" is [*Shijing* 245] "The one who first bore our people was [Lady] Yuan of Jiang." "Twisted *qiulan* to make a belt ornament" is [*Shijing* 83] "We will roam, we will ramble; her girdle stones are *qiong* stones and *ju* stones." "In the evening I pick the evergreens on the islet" is [*Yijing*] "The submerged dragon one does not employ." "Yoke up four dragons and make a chariot of a phoenix," is [*Yijing*] "At the right time yoke up six dragons and ride through the sky."[52]

The spuriousness of this method is not difficult to detect. Indeed, Liu Xie (d. ca. 523), who epitomizes the inability of traditional *Chuci* scholarship either to live with or without Wang Yi's readings, declared Wang Yi's judgments "unfactual" and "unperceptive" (he said the same about Ban Gu's for different reasons). Nevertheless, the question for Liu Xie and many other traditional scholars was not *whether* or not the "Li sao" should be compared with the classics, but merely how.[53]

Wang Yi's line-by-line annotations, however, have proved far more deleterious. According to Wang Yi, as is reflected in the Hawkes translation below, the beginning of the poem reads:

> Scion of the high Lord Gao Yang,
> Bo Yong was my father's name.
> When She Ti pointed to the first month of the year,
> On the day *geng-yin* I passed from the womb.[54]

Hawkes, in translating *jiang* as "passed from the womb," has followed Wang Yi's gloss on the word. Examination of Warring States and early Han literature reveals not one instance of the word used to mean "to pass from the womb," "be born," and so on. The usual meaning of the word is "to descend," usually from the sky, as do blessings from heaven, rain, birds that die in flight, and divinities. The last line quoted above should read something like: "On the day *geng-yin,* I descended from the sky."

If Wang Yi had glossed the word in its proper sense while insisting that the poem is an allegorical biography of Qu Yuan, he would have had to explain how it was that a minister of Chu descended from the sky. Autobiographies, however, had best have a birth at the beginning. He could, nevertheless, have taken descending from the sky as representing a birth, but then he would have had to admit that the speaker of the poem is a shaman or spirit, or both. He would then have had to allow the distasteful possibility that Qu Yuan, in writing this poem, had assumed the persona of the shaman. That, of course, could not be allowed, since Qu Yuan, for the exegetes of the second century, was a kind of hermeneutical agent whose mission it was to stamp out or at least domesticate Chu shamanism.

When the persona tells us that he descends into the world on the date Zhu Rong (God of Fire), an ancestral divinity of Chu, was appointed,[55] Wang Yi claims that it is simply Qu Yuan noting his own birthday. A few lines later, when the persona of the poem gives his name as Ling Jun, which is a shamanic title and means "Numinously Balanced" (or "Numinous Potter's Wheel"), Wang Yi intervenes by saying that the name is in fact part of a complex code that, when read properly, renders the name Qu Yuan.[56] Later in the poem the spirit/shaman flies through the air in a phoenix chariot in search of the goddess Fu Fei, but Wang Yi, no longer able to misread the literal, insists that this merely *represents* Qu Yuan's search for a like-minded scholar-recluse.[57]

The shamanic "Nine Songs" were also forced into the ill-fitting clothes of the Qu Yuan biography. "Xiang Jun" is a shamanic love song to the presiding divinity of the Xiang River. As in most of the "Nine Songs," the shamanic courtship is not successful, and toward the end of the poem the speaker throws a sleeve (according to Wang Yi) into the water as a pledge of love. Wang Yi naturally sees this speaker as Qu Yuan, who, in his frustration at the king's refusal to recall him from banishment, is threatening to take off his clothes, go naked, and join the barbarian tribes. This what-you-see-is-not-what-you-get hermeneutics is characteristic of much of the *Chuci* commentarial tradition.

Conclusion

THE Qu Yuan myth represents the final stage in the domestication of Chu, a process that commenced at the beginning of the Han dynasty, when memories of the ancient state were still fresh and its customs were still alive among those Chu commoners who became the Han aristocracy. The Confucian intelligentsia, on whom the survival of the dynasty greatly depended, called Chu barbaric for its shamanism, although shamanism flourished below them among the masses and above them among the aristocrats. Confucians made shamanism an emblem of what was excessive in the policies of the Han imperial house and used it as a target that could be struck with impunity in literature, political rhetoric, and the construction of history. Confucianism officially triumphed over shamanism, but shamanism lived on in both the general imagination and in texts. When the Confucians were politically weak, they chose to fight this remnant shamanism primarily by attacking texts; when they were strong, they drove both its practices and its practitioners out of state ritual as well. The commentary of Wang Yi reflects the equivocal nature of the Confucian triumph, because shamanism never wholly disappeared, either in the provinces or in the palace. Its traditions were of a higher antiquity than those of Confucianism. Its traditions underlay the ancient ritual tradition the Confucians claimed to transmit. This was indirectly recognized by Xunzi and his followers. For them, the ritual sacrifice was amenable to different levels of reading corresponding to levels of understanding that varied according to one's place in the social hierarchy. In the same way that the subject is an instrument for the sovereign, the literal and lowest reading of the ritual is merely the vehicle for the higher tenor of aristocratic understanding. The two levels exist separately but not independently. But in the Han dynasty the Confucians encountered again the incongruity that forced Confucius into teaching in the first place: an inability of those in the highest seats of sovereignty to interpret ritual sacrifice other than on the lowest level. Their response to this situation is exemplified by their desperate *Chuci* hermeneutics: they deny the vehicle, sometimes replacing it with the tenor, sometimes not—that is, where an unacceptable metaphor occurs, they sabotage it. For Wang Yi and his exegetical posterity, "to descend from the sky" is neither literally that nor a metaphor for birth; instead, it is, literally, Qu Yuan's birth. A shaman throwing a sleeve into a river is neither that nor a metaphor for anything else; it is, literally, Qu Yuan threatening to undress and go native. Qu Yuan becomes a kind of exegetical colonizer representing the forces of "civilization" in the barbarian texts of Chu. His life becomes their new and unwelcome context. And when we read him thus into the "Nine Songs" and the "Li sao," we get a taste of what "civilization" meant to many on whom it was imposed: distortion.

Conclusion

JOHN S. MAJOR

IN the foregoing pages we have attempted to define Chu—to delineate, in other words, a picture of Chu history and culture that mirrors the long and complex history of the state of Chu itself. We hope that our efforts will aid in making accessible to contemporary understanding a sense of Chu as a distinct, and distinctive, political and cultural realm within the large and diverse polity of early China. As the subtitle of this book suggests, we have concerned ourselves here with questions of "image and reality." The contributors have, we think, demonstrated that so much is now known from archaeological and textual sources about the state of Chu that it is no longer reasonable (if it ever was) to think of Chu as a historical, cultural, or geographical monolith. It is clear, too, that the image of Chu that has dominated Chinese historical thinking since the Han, and modern scholarship as well, derives primarily from an image of the "southern, barbarian" Chu created and nurtured during the Han period, an image that obscured the historical reality of pre-Han Chu. If we have succeeded in showing how the image of Chu has, over a long period of time, spread a veil over the reality of Chu, then the

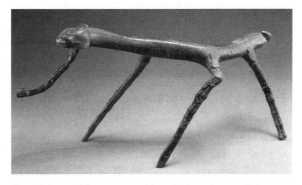

Carved dragon-like creature with a cicada at the top of the rear facing leg, a dragon biting a phoenix on the front facing leg, a long snake climbing up the withered front back leg, and a small snake biting a frog on the rear back leg, Mashan [courtesy of Xu Shaohua]

more complex and nuanced picture we paint here will, we hope, encourage people interested in ancient China to think beyond the level of an alluring but misleading stereotype of Chu culture.

We began with political history and historical geography, looking at Chu as one of many early states of the Zhou realm—a state ruled by an aristocracy of (at least nominal) northern lineage, but located in the middle reaches of the Han River valley, an area somewhat remote from the Central States. We saw how Chu gradually grew from being just one of many states to being one of the greatest kingdoms of pre-imperial China. In the process its center of gravity moved steadily east and south; at the same time its area increased, to encompass, at the height of Chu power, virtually the entire basin of the lower Yangtze River. In the course of this expansion Chu absorbed many states and peoples who were, in their own estimation and in the regard of the people of the Central States, "barbarians," or at the very least not wholly Chinese. (The question of who was Chinese, and by what criteria, was a contested issue at the time and remains a contested issue of historical interpretation; hence the quotation marks here around the word "barbarian.") These "barbarian" tendencies were encouraged by the far-flung networks of trade and cultural exchange that existed not only between Chu and the world of northern China, but with many non-Chinese regions as well, in the south, west, and north.

We saw, too, how the people of Chu evolved a distinctive style and decorative vocabulary in art, evolving new shapes and types of decor in bronze vessels and playing a leading role in the development of lacquerware and silk textiles. As Xu Shaohua suggests in his review of Chu archaeology, there is little evidence for a distinctive Chu culture during the Western Zhou period, when Chu was centered in the Han River valley. But there is little doubt that by the end of the Warring States period, and even more so in the early decades of the unified China of Qin and Han, Chu was culturally distinct from the states of the north—or at least both northerners and the people of Chu thought so. The phenomenon of Chu distinctiveness thus seems to have evolved over the course of time and as Chu became successively larger and more eastern and southern. The Chu rulers, conservative and even reactionary in their adherence to Zhou ritual norms for the early centuries of their reign, nevertheless gradually evolved new forms of ritual expression and new techniques of administrative control that reflected growing Chu cultural distinctiveness on the one hand, and the exigencies of socio-political circumstances on the other.

We saw, finally, how in the last century or so of the existence of the Chu state, and for some decades after its political (but not cultural) demise, Chu culture apparently was dominated by forms of religious and literary expression that were so striking as to impress themselves deeply in the consciousness of their neighbors to the north. In early Han China a set of cultural characteristics became widely identified as "Chu culture," and indeed these characteristics were seen as so exotically desirable that they became an important element in cultural fashion throughout China as a whole. They included the beautiful lacquerwares of Chu (analyzed by So in chapter 3), a shamanistic religious culture (Major, chapter 8), and the poetic forms of the *Chuci* anthology, reinvented as the Han rhymeprose rhapsody called the *fu* (Sukhu, chapter 9).

John S. Major

"Southern" culture—represented by distinctive bronze and lacquer vessels, superbly woven silk textiles, lacquer tableware, and other luxury goods; a sense of humid, semi-tropical ease and a wealthy, languid way of life; local styles of clothing and adornment; and most especially a literature of shamanic ecstasy and "farflight" spirit journeys—was, in the collective imagination of the Han capital and its political and literary elites, indelibly Chu. That Han perception has created problems ever since, because it was so strong, so vivid, and so pervasive in the available accounts of Chu (e.g., in the writings of Sima Qian) as nearly to preclude the possibility of thinking clearly about the centuries of Chu history that preceded the Han. For it is undeniably true that this stereotype of "Chu culture" is a product of the very last decades of the centuries-long existence of the Chu state, and of lands on the eastern and southern periphery of the enormous and diverse Chu territories. Having looked in detail at that history and at those territories, is it still permissible to acquiesce in the received wisdom and define Chu culture as the product of third- and second-century BCE Anhui and Hunan?

Our stance is not to reject the age-old conventional understanding of Chu culture, but to see it as one element in a larger set of historical and cultural realities that define Chu. In doing so, we are aware of the danger of appearing to accept the part as the whole, of allowing the stereotype to stand in for a more complex reality. It is all too easy, for example, to equate the Mawangdui tomb treasures with "Chu culture." But to imagine that the material culture, political and religious beliefs and rituals, and social and economic life of the Spring and Autumn period Chu rulers at Danyang or Ying were the same as those of the aristocrats entombed at Mawangdui would be, as this book has shown, to distort history beyond recognition.

At the same time, we think that the following two statements are true: that from the beginning Chu was culturally "special" because it represented an extension of Central States power into a peripheral region where indigenous peoples and their culture(s) were likely, over the long run, to modify significantly the Central States-style culture of the Chu ruling elite; and that the geographical, political, ethnic, and other forces that shaped the history of Chu led in the end to something that can be described meaningfully as "Chu culture." The Mawangdui finds might not typify the culture(s) of Chu for most of the historical existence of that state, but they do at least represent one particular epitome, in Hunan, of the Chu artistic and cultural tradition.

In other words, what we have tried to do here is not assert that the vivid image of "Chu culture" that people have had since the Han is wrong, nor suggest that that image needs to be discarded. Rather, we have tried to broaden our readers' understanding of Chu beyond that stereotypical image and to define Chu in terms of its long and complex history as an expanding state and an evolving culture. The phrase "Chu culture" perhaps will inevitably call to mind images of silk brocade and scarlet lacquer, shamanic rituals and poetic lamentations, and we have no quarrel with that; but we hope to have shown that "Chu culture," so conceived, has deep and complex roots that deserve attention in their own right.

Translation of
the Chu Silk Manuscript

LI LING AND

CONSTANCE A. COOK

Introduction

THE Chu Silk Manuscript is the only published and complete manuscript among several discovered in 1942 by tomb robbers in Zidanku, Changsha, Hunan. In 1946 the owner, Cai Jixiang, asked John H. Cox to carry these manuscripts to the United States, and they are now in the Arthur M. Sackler Gallery in Washington, D.C. The manuscript dates to about 300 BCE and was buried with a man approximately forty years old. The small size of the tomb and the apparent lack of bronze vessels in it suggest that the man was not an important official.

The Zidanku manuscripts can be compared to the Mawangdui Silk Manuscripts, dating to 168 BCE and also from Changsha. Both sets of manuscripts were found inside

Chu Silk Manuscript [courtesy of the Arthur M. Sackler Foundation, New York]

containers—the Zidanku manuscripts in a woven bamboo box and the Mawangdui manuscripts in a lacquer box. The latter also contained flutes, bamboo strips in rolls, oyster shells, and branches of plants. Some of the Mawangdui manuscripts were folded in a manner similar to the Chu Silk Manuscript. Other Mawangdui manuscripts were rolled around wooden tablets. The former were approximately the same size as the Chu Silk Manuscript, with a width of about forty-eight centimeters; the latter were much smaller, about twenty-four centimeters in width.

The Chu Silk Manuscript consists of both illustrations and texts; it is designed to resemble a divination board (*shi;* also sometimes called a diviner's board or cosmograph), which is itself a model of the cosmos.[1] This type of instrument, of which several have been found in Han tombs, consists of a round board symbolizing heaven that can rotate on a pivot on top of a square board representing the earth. There are essentially two types of divination board: one has a dial plate divided into the four directions, with eight degree markers, or points, indicated along with a central point called the Ninth Palace. In this palace and along the points are arranged the nine celestial gods. The second type of divination board has an additional set of twelve degree markers indicated to represent twelve divisions of time (such as hours or months) and the twelve matching gods. The central controlling god of the first type is Grand Unity *(Taiyi);* that of the second type is the Northern Dipper *(Beidou).*[2] In some examples, instead of degrees or points there are twelve blocks indicating the months, which are further marked into twelve smaller units.

The Chu Silk Manuscript is ringed by pictures of twelve gods representing the months. Each side represents a season, and each god is accompanied by a corresponding text of do's and don'ts for that month (much like the "Yueling" or "Monthly Rules" chapter of the *Liji*). In the four corners of the manuscript are pictures of trees, which represent the pillars holding up the heavens mentioned in Section B in the translation below. In the center of the manuscript, instead of Grand Unity or the Northern Dipper, is the main text. The main text is divided into two large sections, one twice as long as the other and each written upside-down relative to the other.

Each section of the text involves some aspect of the calendar. The Inner Long Text (positioned with winter on top, spring to the right, and summer below) concerns the year. The Inner Short Text (with summer on top, autumn to the right, and winter below) concerns the seasons. The brief texts around the rim, as indicated above, concern the months.

Generally, the writer of the manuscript was concerned that the calendar be used with proper respect and knowledge. Otherwise, the text threatens, cosmic collapse and evil catastrophic events would occur. The Inner Long Text consists of three tales or subsections: section A warns about unnatural events and demonic influences should the year be improperly calibrated or the calendar contravened (thus offending the [High] God). Section B shows the importance of a proper calendar in receiving a good and auspicious year from the gods. Section C warns that if the people are not respectful in their sacrifices to the God, they will run into trouble.

The Inner Short Text describes the divine creation of the calendar and how it brought order out of chaos. It also can be divided into three subsections: section A describes how the gods separated heaven and earth, regulated themselves according to hot and cold *qi* (i.e., yang and yin), and determined the four seasons by pacing out their boundaries. Section B describes how the gods supported the heavens with five pillars of different colors, and how the sun and moon emerged. Section C describes the division of time into days (and into groups of ten days) and of days into four time periods.

Translation

Chapter 1: Year (Inner Long Text)

Section A

If [. . . 3][3] and the length of the lunar months becomes too long or too short, then they will not fit the proper degree and spring, summer, autumn, and winter will [not] be [. . . 1] regular; the sun, moon, stars, and planets will erratically overstep their paths. When (the months) are too long, too short, contrary, or chaotic, (the growth of) the grasses and trees have no regularity. This is [called] *yao*, "demonic" (influences or omens). When heaven and earth create calamities, the Heaven's Cudgel *(Tianpou)* star creates (sweeping) destruction, sending (the destruction) down throughout all four regions (of the earth). Mountains collapse, springs gush forth geysers. This is called "contravention." If you contravene the years (and) the months, then upon entering the seventh or eighth day of the month there will be fog, frost, and clouds of dust, and you will not be able to function according (to heaven's plan). When heaven rains [. . . 3], it is a contrary month; keep still.[4] If it is the first, second, or third month, it is called *nizhongwang*, "death by a contrary end." [. . . 3] their country. If it is the fourth or fifth month, it is called *luanjiwang*, "death by a disordered cycle." [. . . 3]. In such a year, there will be trouble in the western territories, and if the sun and the moon get out of order, there will be halos surrounding (them) and trouble in the eastern territories. All under heaven will be at war and harm will come to the king.

Section B

Among the years, one is *deni*, "Favor and Affection," when if [. . . 6] the orbit of the five demonic (influences), then the grass, the trees, and the people will thereby [. . . 1 (achieve?)] regularity in the pace of the four [periods (of days, months, or years)]. When [. . . 2] demonic (influences) from above, the three seasons (spring, summer, and autumn) will thus proceed. In the year of Favor and Affection after three seasons have passed [. . . 1], [. . . 4] will fall. It is by numerical layout that the months are corrected to be only twelve [. . . 1]. If one disrupts a Favor and Affection (year), then there will emerge from the (underground) Yellow Pool [a . . . 4 (something evil)] which, moving in and out of [. . . 1 *tong* (some kind of channel)], will create misfortune for those below. When both the sun and the moon are in disorder, the stars and constellations will not shine. Once the sun and the moon have fallen into disorder, the division of the year will then [. . . 1], and the seasonal rains will come and go without regularity or constancy. One fears that the common people do not yet understand and take the (layout of) the calendar [. . . 1] (to be) invariable and unadaptable. The people consider [. . . 1] that the three constancies [the sun, the moon, and the stars?] will be destroyed, and the four risings [the four seasons?] will be ruined, thereby [. . . 1 (disrupting?)] the cosmic regularity. Only when the gods, the Five Governors [of the Five Phases], and the four risings are without problems and the reliable (calendrical) constancies guide the people will the Five Governors be illuminated and the Hundred Spirits be thus presented with sacrificial feasts. This is what is called *deni*, "Favor and Affection," when the many spirits are favorable. The God said: "Extend your respect to them! Never be disrespectful. When heaven creates good fortune, the spirits will then bring it to you. When heaven creates demonic (influences), the gods will (likewise) provide you with them. Be attentive and respectful in (your) preparations and the heavenly pattern will thus be the guiding standard. In the end, the heavenly [. . . 1 (pattern?)] will be the model for the people below. Respect it without fail!

Section C

If the people do not use [. . . 2] and travel along the mountains and rivers, streams and valleys without respect, then their sacrifices are not accepted and the God will bring them chaos. If the people can obtain enough provisions, they will not make trouble for each other. If they do not see [. . . 2], the halos will come. If the people do not understand the year, they will not offer sacrifices. If [. . . 1], it will be unfavorable for the people, there will be some [. . . 1 (trouble?)]. Affairs involving earth [such as plowing or building] will not be satisfactory; it will be inauspicious.

Chapter II: Seasons (Inner Short Text)

Section A

Long, long ago, Bao Xi of [. . . 2] came from [. . . 2] and lived in [. . . 2]. His [. . . 1] was [. . . 2] and [. . . 3] woman. It was confusing and dark, without [. . . 3], [. . . 2] water [. . . 1] wind and rain were thus obstructed. He then married Zuwei [. . . 1]'s granddaughter, named Nü Tian. She gave birth to four [. . . 1 (children)] who then helped put things in motion making the transformations arrive according (to Heaven's plan). Relinquishing (this) duty, they then rested and acted (in turn) controlling the sidewalls (of the calendrical plan); they helped calculate time by steps. They separated (heaven) above and (earth) below. Since the mountains were out of order, they then named the mountains, rivers, and four seas. They arranged (themselves) by [. . . 1] hot and cold *qi*.[5] In order to cross mountains, rivers, and streams (of various types) when there was as yet no sun or moon (for a guide), when the people traveled across mountains and rivers, the four gods stepped in succession to indicate the year; these are the four seasons.

Section B

The elder spirit is called Qing-[. . . 1]–gan (Green-?-Pillar), the second is Zhusidan (Red-Four-?), the third is Liuhuangnan (?-Yellow-?), and the fourth is [. . . 1]–mogan (?-Black-Pillar). After hundreds and thousands of years, the sun and the moon were finally born, (but) the Nine Continents were not level so the mountains [. . . 2 (collapsed?)]. Therefore the gods created [. . . 1] to cover (the Nine Continents). When the skydome shook, they used green, red, yellow, white, and black trees as supporting poles. Yan Di thereupon ordered Zhu Rong to make the four gods descend to set up the Three Heavens and with [. . . 2] distribute the four poles. He said: "If it is not a case of the Nine Heavens[6] crashing down, do not disturb(?) the heavenly powers." The God then finally made the movement of the sun and the moon.

Section C

Gong Gong calculated and set in motion the Ten Days [the Heavenly Stems] and the Four Times [periods, of a day, month, or year]. [. . . 4] spirits then stood still[7] making four [. . . 1] without resting. When the hundred spirits and the wind and rain became calendrically incorrect and disordered, he made the sun and the moon take turns working and resting. Thus we have the divisions of late night and morning, afternoon and evening.

Chapter III: Months (Surrounding Text)

Section A [First Month]

[The first month is called] Qu. (During this month) Yi will come. Do not [. . . 1] kill (living beings). *Renzi* and *bingzi* are inauspicious (days). If you make [. . . 1] and attack to the north, the general will come to evil, [. . . 5]. [The month's complete title is] Quyuxia, "Pick from Below."

Section B [Second Month]

[The second month is called] Ru. (During this month) you can send out an army and build a city, but you cannot marry off a daughter or take in slaves. Don't regret if you cannot accomplish both. [The month's complete title is] Ruciwu, "Such Is Military."

Section C [Third Month]

[The third month is called Bing.] (During this month) [. . . 5] marry, raise domestic animals, [. . . 3]. [The month's complete title is] Bingsichun, "Bing Controls Spring."

Section D [Fourth Month]

[The fourth month is called] Yü. (During this month) you cannot engage in any major affair. Shao Han [. . . 6]. If you take a wife, you will be the laughingstock of the country. [The month's complete title is] Yuqunü, "I Take a Wife."

Section E [Fifth Month]

[The fifth month is called] Gao. (During this month) the leader of the thieves will be [. . . 1 (un)]able to hide. If you do not see the moon at [. . . 2], you cannot offer sacrifices, for it is inauspicious. You can take [. . . 2] as slaves. [The month's complete title is] Gaochudu, "Gao Goes out and Is Visible."

Section F [Sixth Month]

[The sixth month is called] Qie. (During this month) you cannot send out the army. The navy will not [. . . 2]; it will be defeated and overturned. When you come to [. . . 3], you cannot offer sacrificial feasts. [The month's complete title is] Qiesixia, "Monkey[8] Controls Summer."

Section G [Seventh Month]

[The seventh month is called] Cang. (During this month) you cannot make an opening[9] [...
1]. It will be greatly unfavorable to the country. There will be a bird flying between the sky
and the land. [The month's complete title is] Cangmode, "Cang Is to Attain Nothing."

Section H [Eighth Month]

[The eighth month is called] Zang. (During this month) you cannot build a house or com-
mence (projects). Do not [... 1] or [... 1], for there will be great disorder in the country. To
take a woman (as a wife) is inauspicious. [The month's complete title is] Zangtu [... 1], "(?)."

Section I [Ninth Month]

[The ninth month is called] Xüan. (During this month) you can build a house, [... 3] moving, and then [... 4]. [The month's complete title is] Xüansiqiu, "Xüan Controls Autumn."

Section J [Tenth Month]

[The tenth month is called] Yang. (During this month) you (can)not engage in destructive
affairs, (but) you can [... 2] and rout evildoers in (all) four [directions]. [The month's complete
title is] Yang . . . yang, "(?)."

Section K [Eleventh Month]

[The eleventh month is called] Gu. (During this month) it is beneficial to invade and punish
other countries. You can attack cities, gather together people (to be soldiers), meet with lords
(of other countries), execute the chief criminals, and slaughter evildoers. [The month's complete title is] Gufenchang, "Gu Is Beneficial for Territorial Expansion."

Section L [Twelfth Month]

[The twelfth month is called] Tu. (During this month) you cannot attack cities, [... 8]. [The
month's complete title is] Tusidong, "Tu Controls Winter."

Notes

Note: Citations are by author, if known, and year of publication (an "author" is frequently a group or an institution). For anonymous journal articles, entries are listed by journal name and year of publication; anonymous books are listed by place and year of publication. The same conventions are followed in the bibliography.

Preface

1. We designate dates as Before Common Era (BCE) and Common Era (CE), corresponding to the familiar B.C. and A.D.; dates in this book should be assumed to be BCE unless otherwise noted.
2. For an examination of the pitfalls of relying completely on archaeological materials to define the cultural aspects of a people, see Renfrew 1987.
3. There are too many scholars of Chu to list individually. Wen Chongyi (1967) and Jao Tsung-yi (1985) were the first to attempt synthethic views of the Chu culture in light of archaeological material. The only book in a Western language on Chu culture is the recently published collection of papers from a Sackler Gallery symposium (Lawton 1991). In some ways, our book can be viewed as a sequel to the discourse on Chu presented in the Sackler volume. Li Xueqin, a scholar who has contributed extensively to our knowledge of Chu, presents a broad overview of the southern cultural region that has been traditionally associated with Chu (Lawton 1991, 1–22).
4. Barnard 1959.
5. K. C. Chang 1959.
6. Barnard 1974.
7. Barnard 1973.
8. K. C. Chang 1986, 422.

Introduction

1. The quote is attributed to Chen She. See *Shiji* 7, the biography of Xiang Yu; Burton Watson 1961, 68–104.
2. See Sima Qian's autobiography, *Shiji* 130. He was born north of the Wei River in Shaanxi and traveled extensively by river. Sima Qian identified Laozi, the putative author of the *Daodejing,* as a native of Chu serving the Chu court. See Loewe 1993, 270.

3. *Shiji* 129, "Huozhi," 26–28; cf. *Han Shu*, "Dilizhi" description.

4. *Shiji* 40.7.

5. *Guoyu*, SBBY ed., "Chuyu, xia," 18: 8b.

6. See Peters' exploration of Chu society, chapter 7; also where she discusses the question of a *man* ethnic group as well as the tales associated with early Chu kingship (1983, 35–42). See also Cook 1990, 4–8.

7. Cook 1990, 11–12; Shaughnessy 1991, 263–264; Rawson 1990, 146.

8. Shaughnessy 1991, 2–3; for his discussion of other Western Zhou bronzes mentioning attacks against Chu, see 204–208.

9. Li Xiandeng 1988. See also Peters 1983, 35–85; Cook 1990, 9–12 (for an examination of paleographical evidence).

10. See Cook 1994 for a discussion of the High Gods of Chu. Zhu Rong seems to be associated with stars as well as stoves. One wonders, too, if Danyang, "the Sunny side of Cinnabar [mountain or river]," the presumed site of the proto-Chu state, was not also a Han fiction.

11. *Han Shu*, "Dilizhi" no. 8 xia, *Han Shu buzhu* 28.65. For the Han definition of *yinsi*, see Stein 1979, 57. For a discussion of Chu rites, see Cook 1990, 269–281. The Han southerner Ying Shao never used the term *yinsi* to refer to Chu practices, but only to those of Kuaiji, the southeastern region in former Yue territory (*Fengsu tongyi tongjian* 9, 69).

12. See Sukhu, chapter 9.

13. *Shiji* 50.5. The capital was Pengcheng (modern Suzhou, Anhui), the site of popular Taoist and early Buddhist cult activities during the Later Han dynasty (Maspero 1981, 257). The Han vision of Chu is illustrated in the "Moneymakers" chapter of the *Shiji;* see Burton Watson 1961, 488–490. Sima Qian discussed the Han regions of Western Chu, Eastern Chu, and Southern Chu. He divided each into miniregions and related anecdotes regarding their individual cultural temperaments and natural resources. Pengcheng was the center between the Western and Eastern Chu regions. Southern Chu consisted essentially of all lands south of the ancient capital of Chu in Shouchun, Anhui, and all lands below the Yangtze, including Changsha. He claimed that Western and Southern Chu shared many similar customs. Southern Chu people, he claimed, were "fond of fancy phrases and clever at talking"; they were for the most part untrustworthy (Burton Watson 1961, 489). Eastern Chu, he noted, included the old city of Wu, a locus of many wandering scholars earlier, and a source of salt and metal (from nearby mountains). The city of Jiangling was in Western Chu and was known as a gateway to the Wu Mountain and the Ba region. It drew on the Yunmeng lakes for resources.

14. For the Huaiyi and Dongyi during the Western Zhou period, see Shaughnessy 1991, 176–181 passim.

15. Sima Qian noted that the Yue worshiped *gui* ("Huozhi," 40).

16. See Major and Sukhu, chapters 8 and 9, respectively. Perhaps it was during this time that the southerners became associated with snakes. See the definitions of the *man* and *min* as recorded by the 100 CE dictionary, the *Shuowen jiezi* (*Shuowen jiezi gulin zhengbu hebian* 10, 962–963). See the discussion of Chu's obsession with snakes in So and Major, chapters 3 and 8, respectively.

17. See Blakeley, chapter 4.

18. See Peters 1983 and chapter 7 of this book; Huang Gangzheng and Wu Mingsheng 1991.

19. This was the role of the occupant of Tomb 3 at Mawangdui. See studies by Gao Zhixi, Tan Qixiang, and Zhou Shirong on the military maps found in his tomb; Hunansheng bowuguan 1973, 305–337; Kaiya 1979.

20. Liu Shishan 1985.

21. See Sukhu, chapter 9.

22. *Shiji* 84: 23; Hawkes 1985, 53, pointed out that Qu Yuan was also a hero of Sima Qian.

23. Knechtges 1976, 17; Hawkes 1985, 18, 22, 35, 49–50.

1. The Geography of Chu

1. The most thorough compilation of conquered states made to date (He Hao 1989, 10–13) totals sixty-one. On tribal groups, see notes 58, 86, 87, and 89.

2. It is questionable whether Chu existed as a "state" (in either the ancient Chinese or modern anthropological

senses) in earlier times. There was an entity of some kind known as "Chu" in Shang times, but whether this was our Chu is a matter of considerable debate. Duan Yu (1982) follows the traditional view that it was. The epigraphic evidence, pro and con, has been debated between Wang Guanghao (1984 and 1985; 1988, 48–72) and Zhang Jun (1984b).

3. The dates for Western Zhou reigns herein generally follow Shaughnessy 1991, 241–287, slightly simplified. Some suspect that Chu assisted the Zhou in the conquest. The idea makes sense, but the evidence for it is not solid.

4. Western Zhou history and archaeology are treated in Hsu and Linduff 1989.

5. *Shiji* 40.5 (1932 ed.), 645; 1932 ed., 646. For discussions on Yu Xiong's specific role, see Shen Changyun 1983 and 1984; Li Jin 1989. General discussions of Chu relations with the Western Zhou may be found in Shu Zhimei and Wu Yongzhang 1980, Yang Kuan 1981b, Tang Jiahong 1985, and Duan Yu 1986.

6. This is the bone inscribed with "Chuzi lai gao," "the lord of Chu came to report"; see Gu Tiefu 1988, 26–31. There is some difference of opinion, however, as to whether this dates to before or after the conquest (material from Baoshan—see chapter 6—suggests the latter). It should be noted that several other "Chu" inscriptions in the same corpus (see Chen Quanfang 1988) do not necessarily relate to our Chu (see Wang Guanghao 1984).

7. *Shiji* 40.5–6 (645); *Zuozhuan*, Zhao 12/22.50. According to another tradition, enfeoffment had taken place earlier, under Yu Xiong's son or grandson (Xiong Li); see Blakeley 1988, 122. It has even been argued that the event had taken place under Yu Xiong (Sun Chong'en 1984, but see the response of Xu Jun 1982).

8. *Shiji* 33.12/553. Chen Changyuan (1985) argues that the Duke of Zhou's "flight" to Chu actually was an attack on Chu. (A *Guoyu* passage [14.7b] could be taken to contradict the impression given elsewhere that Zhou/Chu relations were on good footing during King Cheng's reign.)

9. Another factor may have been growing Chu independence while Zhou was preoccupied in other quarters.

10. The sources are not unanimous on the point. For discussions of the episode, see Wang Mingge 1988 and (more critically) Gong Weiying 1984.

11. This may have been prompted by the fact that circumstances at the Zhou court had become unstable. (It is sometimes held that Chu aided Zhou in a time of severe crisis under King Mu [r. 956–918], but there are good reasons to doubt this.) The Chu leader Xiong Qu reportedly adopted the royal title *(wang)* during the Zhou king Yi's time (865–858) and renounced it ("out of fear of Zhou") during the reign of the unsavory King Li (857–842); *Shiji* 40.6–40.7/631.

12. "Bamboo annals" (current version)—*Zhushu jinian*, xia 9a.

13. "Danyang" may have been the designation for an area, rather than the name of a settlement.

14. The designation of Ying as capital occurred either some time late in the reign of King Wu (740–690) or (as is usually assumed) at the outset of the reign of his successor, King Wen (689–675). However, it probably existed and was used as a base of operations earlier.

15. The Danyang phase might be termed "archaic." The outline of expansion given below suggests that the Ying phase should encompass two stages: one (formative?) in which Chu was active in a fairly narrow geographical range and another (florescence?) during which it interacted with other cultural groups far and wide.

16. Only the barest outlines on any of these fronts can be given here.

17. For details, see Blakeley 1988 and (to a lesser extent) Blakeley 1990.

18. Some scholars in this group posit a move from Zigui to Dangyang.

19. See Xu, chapter 2; So, chapter 3; Cook, chapter 5; and Peters, chapter 7.

20. For various reasons (including the location of Xiasi) a Chu location in the lower Dan valley position is usually posited. The close Chu/Zhou ties in the era surrounding the conquest, however, make it quite possible that Chu was at that time in the upper reaches of the Dan valley (in Shaanxi). The lower valley (in Henan), however, is still close enough to the Zhou center. (Some Southern School scholars have conceded that Chu was in the Dan valley in early Zhou times.)

21. See Shi Quan 1988 passim.

22. See Xu and Peters, chapters 2 and 7, respectively. It is worth noting, too, that extensive investigation has failed

to turn up any royal tombs in the vicinity. Jinancheng could have been a subsidiary capital in later times, or even a second "Ying" capital. (The Wu invasion of the Chu heartland in 506–505, discussed below, might have prompted a move southward from the more exposed Chu Huangcheng.) On the other hand, Jinancheng need not have been a capital city: the agricultural base of the area—not to mention its favorable position along trade routes—is sufficient to explain its considerable dimensions.

23. See Xu, chapter 2.

24. See Xu and Peters, chapters 2 and 7, respectively. Finding royal tombs will be as important a test for this proposal as for the southern ones—unless it turns out that kings were buried elsewhere (the Dan valley homeland?).

25. Some Southern School analysts have nominated Jijiahu (the first Ying to others in this camp, it will be recalled). It is highly improbable, however, that Western Zhou armies would have marched toward such a distant locale. Some within the Northern School have suggested one or another of the upland valleys west of Yicheng (in Nanzhang County or thereabouts), but there is no adequate evidence to that effect.

26. Significantly, this conclusion has been reached by both Northern and Southern School scholars (respectively, Shi Quan 1988, 349–353 and Taniguchi 1984, 12–13). The *identity* of the starting point (Ying or a secondary Danyang), however, remains open.

27. This was so for a campaign in 701 (Blakeley 1990). Shi Quan (1988, 181–185, 349–355) argues that the 703 campaign was launched from the Dan valley. He Hao (1989, 17–18) and others, however, take steps in the direction of deflating this idea, and there is more that can be said along this line. A march against Sui (in Handong, see below) in 706 must have originated in Hubei.

28. Traditional locations of placenames associated with Xiong Qu (see n. 11) would demand a Hubei locus for Chu at that time. There are more convincing locations, but these would still allow either a northern Hubei or southern Henan base of operations.

29. Neither the *Shiji* (4.42/68) nor the *Zuozhuan* (Xi 4, 5.15) mentions the Han River. Of the texts that do, the most reliable (and earliest) is the Old Text "Bamboo Annals," but its history is so fraught with problems that the reference to the Han it now contains could have been inserted long after the event.

30. On some of these, see Shaughnessy 1991, 3, 185, 204–208, 214. For discussions of the episode, see Wang Mingge 1988 and Gong Weiying 1983.

31. If Chu was situated north of the Han, there are at least two possibilities: (1) the Zhou force attacked Chu and then crossed the Han (with some further objective in mind); (2) Chu troops retreated to below the Han in the face of the Zhou assault.

32. A convenient summary of these struggles may be found in Maspero 1978, 169–221.

33. Zheng absorbed Xu's original locale (on which, see Li Xueqin 1985, 173–174) rather early on; Chu thereafter moved Xu to several other locations.

34. As we shall see below, Chu eventually absorbed both Cai and Chen and moved its capital to the latter in 278. On Cai and Chen materials, see Li Xueqin 1985, 184–185.

35. According to tradition, both Wu and Yue were centered below the Yangtze—Wu east of Lake Tai (southern Jiangsu) and Yue on Hangzhou Bay (Zhejiang); see Tan Qixiang 1982, 30. However, these may not have been their original locales, and there is no doubt that in Eastern Zhou times both expanded well north of the Yangtze (even beyond the Huai) and at times had their political centers there. On the archaeology of Wu and Yue and the problem of their locations, see Li Xueqin 1985, 195–198; Peters 1983, 226, 235–237, 238–242, 243, 246–247, 248–252, and 348; Xu, chapter 2; and Peters, chapter 7.

The locations of a good many states alluded to herein pose problems. I utilize the views I consider to be most reasonable and identify only some of the more controversial cases.

36. For four hundred years (with the exception of the Wu incursion of 506–505 discussed below) this functioned as an effective barrier to enemy penetration from the north into the Chu core region.

37. At the time, the term probably referred only to the area below the Ru River, but I use it *here* to include as far as the Ying.

38. About where the modern Wo River enters the Huai; see Tan Qixiang 1982, 29–30.

39. This story can be periodized in a number of ways. The scheme employed here takes into account the objectives of the present volume. Nor can the strategic considerations, intimately related to territorial expansion, be treated in depth here.

40. *Zuozhuan,* Huan 2/2.6, 19.

41. Chu may have attempted to extend its sway into Handong before this time. This would have affected Sui, which had kinship ties with Zheng and Cai. These, however, were very remote, and Handong was so distant from Zheng and Cai that strategic concerns are not a likely factor in their "fear of Chu." It is possible that Chu attacked Ruo (in the Dan valley) before 710, but Chu activity in the Dan valley, too, could hardly have been of immediate concern to Zheng and (even more so) Cai. Tang and Liao also may have been pressured by Chu before 710. (Liao was in the extreme southeast corner of the Nanyang Basin. Tradition assigns Tang to a nearby site [Li Xueqin 1985, 174; Tan Qixiang 1982, 29], but it was somewhat farther north; see Shi Quan 1988, 360–366.) He Hao (1989, 45–53) suggests that there were also moves against Shen and Lü (both near the center of the basin) by that time. The fact that the current Chu ruler (Wu) adopted the royal title *(wang)* may have been another factor, although exactly when this took place is not entirely clear and (according to one tradition) dated to slightly later. A recent discussion of the matter is by Shen Rusong (1990).

42. Sui is widely considered to be the Zeng of the Leigudun Tomb 1 (see Xu, chapter 2; So, chapter 3; and Cook, chapter 5), although not all are as yet convinced of this equation. Whether this Handong Zeng was in any way related to a Zeng in the Nanyang Basin is another unresolved issue. During the assault on Yun (701), Liao (see n. 41), Zhou (see n. 47), Er, and Zhen (see n. 49 and Blakeley 1990) were also involved.

43. Luo was situated in the Yicheng Plain (north of Chu Huangcheng); LuRong was on the edge of the Yicheng Plain, near Luo. Tradition assigns Jiao to a site near the Hubei/Shaanxi border, on the northern bank of the Han (see Tan Qixiang 1982, 29), but it was surely farther downstream and south of the river.

44. Deng was near the banks of the Han (just north of modern Xiangfan), not (as long assumed) farther north (in Dengzhou). See Shi Quan 1988, 105–126, and Li Xueqin 1985, 174.

45. It is this that lends considerable support to the Northern School view on the location of Chu at this time, because its proposals are far closer to the targets of these actions than the Southern School alternatives. Above all, it is highly improbable that attacks on Jiao (n. 43) and Ruo (n. 41) were launched from the banks of the Yangtze.

46. On Quan, see Shi Quan 1988, 354, n. 6; on Ran, see He Hao 1989, 36–44.

47. Zhou may have been here (see Shi Quan 1988, 182); it could hardly have been where tradition assigned it (on the Yangtze, east of Jiangling). In early times, there probably was a Yan state in the Yicheng plain, but by the time we read of it, its memory survived only in placenames. Kui (usually assigned to Zigui, along the Yangtze; Tan Qixiang 1982, 29) also may have been situated in this plain (see Shi Quan 1988, 180). (Eventually, Ruo was moved from the Dan valley to south of the Yicheng plain.)

48. Gu (just west of the Bend) and Jiao (see n. 43). Jun (farther upstream) and the upland groups retained their independence, although some "lands of the Pu" (perhaps in the foothills) were taken over by Chu in this time frame.

49. Logic would suggest that the western portions of Handong (Yun, Er, and Zhen) were incorporated at this time or not too long thereafter. In northern Handong, Sui remained at least nominally independent well into Warring States times. (The fate of Li or Lai, a small state northwest of Sui, is unknown). He Hao (1989, 219–221) argues that there was also a Huang state in Handong (different from a Huai valley state of the same name).

50. Situated there was a string of small polities: Bai, Fang, Dao, Dun, Xiang, Shenn, and Hu. In the western extreme of Fangcheng Wai was the territory of the state of Ying, but it is usually felt that it had been destroyed earlier by Zheng.

51. Xi was situated on the north bank of the Upper Huai; on the area, see Li Xueqin 1985, 158–160.

52. See Li Xueqin 1985, 171–173. Inscribed Lü bronzes (ibid., 173) are taken by some (see He Hao 1989, 234) as evidence that it survived for some time thereafter. However, even if correctly dated, the locale in which these were found raises the possibility that Lü remnants moved eastward to the Huai valley. (Toponyms in the

Upper Huai suggest a similar fate for the Shen elite.) The Nanyang Basin also may have been home to a Zeng state (see n. 42); but if so, it may have disappeared before Chu penetrated the basin.

53. On the locations of Tang and Liao, see n. 41.

54. The high points in this were the battles of Bi and Yanling and the 546 accomodation with Jin, mentioned below.

55. The fates of two other Upper Huai "Fan" states (one north of the river [see Xu Shaohua 1994, 131–136], the other ["Fann"] to the south) are unknown; the names of these states are known largely from inscribed bronzes. It is often held that several of the Fangcheng Wai states (Bai, Fang, Dao, and Hu) were incorporated during this phase, but there are strong hints that they survived into the 530s.

It was in this time frame also (ca. 611) that the Hanxi uplands and the more remote stretches of the Han were taken: the state of Yong (and probably Jun), several tribal groups (the QunMan, BaiPu, and some Rong), conceivably some Ba peoples, and the Hanzhong area (see n. 69). The history of Ba/Chu relations virtually requires that there were some Ba peoples along the Han in northwest Hubei. On the Ba and Chu interactions, see Peters, chapter 7, and Sage 1992, 47–60.

56. He Hao (1989, 11, 383) dates the fall of Jyang to the years 648–635, but this seems a bit early.

57. Shu, Shujiu, Shuliao, Shuyong, Zong, and Huan (the latter is alluded to only in rather late sources). Archaeological remains in this region are surveyed in Li Xueqin 1985, 194, and Peters 1983, 155.

58. Opinion has long held that Chao was considerably farther south (see Tan Qixiang 1982, 30). He Hao (1989, 193ff) makes a strong case, however, that it was northeast of Liu, thus not far below the Huai. He Hao (1989, 12, 384) dates the fall of Chao to 583–575, but when all things are considered, this is rather late.

59. The relevant site was Zhongli. There are problems with both proposals concerning its location: downstream from Zhoulai (Tan Qixiang 1982, 30) and upstream (Shi Quan 1988, 48).

60. The target is usually conceived of as the tradition-sanctioned Wu center south of the Yangtze (see n. 35), but this is highly improbable. One along the Lower Huai or in eastern Huainan (northern Jiangsu) makes more sense.

61. In Huaibei, Chu also took over the state of Yang sometime between 559 and 538 (He Hao 1989, 139–142).

62. At that time, presumably to forestall the need to deal with assaults on two fronts, Chu carried out a massive program of fortification and shifting around of the states in Fangcheng Wai and probably absorbed Bai, Dao, Fang, and Hu (see n. 50). In 529, Cai was moved southward (to XinCai), and Chu planted a client state in its homeland (see Xu Shaohua 1991).

63. Wu, however, managed two victories along the Huai in 504. This evidently raised Chu fears of another Wu thrust westward, because the Chu court once again abandoned Ying for safer quarters.

64. See n. 22.

65. Presumably in order to protect the western flanks of Fangcheng Wai, the semitribal Manshi (along the headwaters of the Ru River) was absorbed in 491.

66. The standard view is that this was the end of Chen, but He Hao (1989, 319–344) argues that both it and (later) Cai were shifted to Hubei and survived there (at least nominally) for some time thereafter.

67. On archaeological remains of Cai in Shouxian, see Xu, chapter 2, and So, chapter 3.

68. The allusion (*Shiji* 40.50/642) is to an attack by the state of Shu. However, because the geographical core of Shu was quite far to the west (in the Chengdu Plain) and because between it and Chu lay Ba peoples, it is probable that "Shu" is an error for "Ba." (It is relevant, also, that there had been two earlier Ba marches into Chu territory in Hubei.)

69. This ancient Hanzhong could hardly have been equivalent to the Hanzhong prefecture of imperial times, in the extreme upper portion of the valley. It was probably in the Hubei/Shaanxi border area. On Chu expansion into Sichuan and the cultural results, see Peters, chapter 7, and Sage 1992, 60–78.

70. Sage 1992, 107–112.

71. The only setback in the east came in 318, when Song appropriated some Chu lands in Huaibei.

72. Before this, Ba (in the face of Chu pressures from the east) had shifted westward to the Chongqing area (closer to Shu). On the Qin takeover and administration of Sichuan, see Sage 1992, 83–156, 199–201.

73. While the date of the destruction of Yue is debatable, Chu probably began to infiltrate the area after inflicting defeats on it in the late fourth century (333, 306), and historical sources allude to the creation of a "Jiangdong" commandary *(jun)* under King Huai (r. 328–299).

74. It is usually assumed that Qianzhong was south of the Yangtze, but this is debatable.

75. The traditional view is that this was accomplished by a two-pronged advance, down both the Han and Yangtze Rivers (see, for instance, Sage 1992, 145–146). That the Yangtze was involved, however, is uncertain from a number of angles (including, of course, the possibility that Ying was not on the banks of the Yangtze).

76. On Chu remains there, see Li Xueqin 1985, 184.

77. The dating of the destruction of Yue and the territorial implications are hotly debated questions.

78. Prior to this it had been moved within the Chu sphere and had been no more than a Chu client for some time.

79. Juyang was more centrally positioned in the Chu domains of the time.

80. On the remains there, see Xu, chapter 2, and So, chapter 3; Li Xueqin 1985, 163, 167.

81. Convenient summaries of this topic are those of He Hao (1989, 54–73) and Gu Tiefu (1988, 61–78).

82. Not considered here are three very complex questions: (1) a persistent tradition that a scion of Chu (Zhuang Qiao) established an outpost in Yunnan, which evolved into an independent state (see Peters, chapter 7; Peters 1983, 192, 215, 222, 341–343, 344–347; Li Xueqin 1985, 216–217; Sage 1992, 143–144); (2) the idea that there was a Chu presence of some sort in extreme western Sichuan, beyond Shu (see He Guangyue 1990, 18–19); and (3) that there was a Chu outpost in northwest Jiangxi.

83. King Cheng (r. 672–626) was supposedly commissioned by the Zhou king to put down a rebellion of the YiYue "of the South"; *Shiji* 40.13/633. See, however, Blakeley, chapter 4.

84. The *Shiji* (65.19/847) relates that the great Chu statesman of Warring States times, Wu Qi (ca. 381; see Blakeley, chapter 4), "pacified the BaiYue in the South." The *Zhanguoce* (Crump 1979, 230) alludes to Chu territory extending to Lake Dongting and Cangwu at this time.

85. See Blakeley, chapter 4.

86. The YiYue and BaiYue may well have been sub-Yangtze groups in Warring States times (although there was a "BaiYue" group north of the Yangtze in earlier times; see Shi Quan 1989). Locating them, however, is rendered difficult because they may have been widely distributed and because placing them must rely on very late sources (ibid., 338–339). "Dongting" is also mentioned. This unquestionably relates to the large lake in northern Hunan that still bears the name, and it is perfectly reasonable that this region (not far distant from the Chu remains of the Jiangling area) should have been within the Chu cultural (even political) sphere in Warring States times. Another placename, Cangwu, is taken to relate to an area in the deep south of Hunan, even extending into northern Guangdong.

87. The *Zuozhuan* (Xiang 13/15.39) has a Chu official stating that King Gong (r. 590–560) pacified the ManYi and launched a large-scale attack into Nanhai, thereby bringing these areas into the "Chinese" sphere of things. Even beyond the question of the historicity of this discourse, it may be noted that "ManYi" is a generic and geographically vague term; there were both Man and Yi north of the Yangtze, and the geographical significance of "Nanhai" is far from clear. (A parallel passage in the *Guoyu* [17.2b] mentions Nan-Hai, but not the ManYi.)

　　Finally, the *Zuozhuan* (523, Zhao 19/24.11) states that King Ping "attacked the Pu with a naval force." The use of naval forces against the Pu in 523 lends some credence to their being situated south of the Yangtze, but they need not have been very far below it, and some other river could have been involved. The latter possibility is reinforced by the fact that Chu had relations with a Pu group as early as Western Zhou times, and only a Southern School perspective on the location of Danyang would make it possible that these Pu were in Jiangnan. In fact, the idea that the Pu of 523 were in Jiangnan is based largely on events in 611 (in which the BaiPu figure). However, this involves the assumption that the Ying were at Jinancheng at the time; and a careful reading of the episode demonstrates clearly that the BaiPu of that time were situated in Hanxi, well north of the Yangtze. (It is possible, of course, that there were other Pu peoples in Jiangnan, or that the BaiPu moved there between 611 and 523.)

88. It is difficult, however, to say anything about the *nature* of the Chu presence. Something like frontier garrison posts would be the most logical supposition. (On Chu materials from Jiangnan, see Xu, chapter 2, and Peters, chapter 7.)

2. Chu Culture: An Archaeological Overview

1. Since the literature on Chu archaeology is massive, the citations in this chapter are for the most part limited to archaeological reports.

2. See discussion of the Chu Gong Ni *bo* and the Chu Gong Jia *zhong* in von Falkenhausen 1991, 53–54, and 97, n. 25; and Mackenzie 1991a, 109–110. For a discussion of Chu culture deriving from the north, see Luo Zhenyu 1983 (1.5.2–1.7.1); and Guo Moruo 1957 (*lu* 177, *kao* 164, *tu* 217–220). Mackenzie (1991a: 109–110) sees the *zhong* decor as typical of the north in the mid- to late Western Zhou (but follows Kane in seeing some differences in the calligraphy). Von Falkenhausen (1991, 53–54), who dates the *zhong* to the first half of the ninth century, suggests that it was made in a Zhou foundry. Complete sets of bells, and bells bearing inscriptions, are rarely found elsewhere. As von Falkenhausen (1991, 54–57) has suggested, the *zhong* (deriving from the *nao*) may have been an early southern innovation (taken up and revised in the north), but whether its origins had anything to do with Chu depends on Chu's location in Western Zhou times; see Cook 1993a. Early Spring and Autumn period bronzes, such as the Chu Ying *pan* and *yi,* were also in northern styles; see Rong Geng 1941, *tu* 856, *tuban* 842.

3. Hubeisheng Yichang diqu bowuguan 1992.

4. In some respects, such as ritual music (von Falkenhausen 1991, esp. 85–89, 94–95) and the formulae of bronze inscriptions (Cook 1990, passim), however, Chu usage continued to preserve northern traditions.

5. For instance, at Xiasi, Xichuan, and Henan (see Henansheng wenwu yanjiusuo 1991).

6. For example, at Zhaojiahu and at Yutaishan, Jiangling, Hubei (see Hubei Jingzhou diqu bowuguan 1982).

7. In the (late) middle Spring and Autumn period Xiasi Tomb 7 and Shanwan, Xiangyang, Tomb 6 (Hubeisheng bowuguan 1983b), we find mostly pairs (respectively, two each of *ding, fu,* and *yufou,* and one *zhan;* and two each of *ding, fu,* and *yufou*). The late Spring and Autumn Xiasi Tomb 10 had four *ding,* two each of *fu* and *yufou,* and one *dui;* and Shanwan Tomb 33 had two each of *ding* and *yufou* and one each of *fu* and *dui.*

8. The Wangsun Gao Spring and Autumn-era bell set from Xiasi (Xichuan) is the largest known to date; see von Falkenhausen 1991, 60–65.

9. Anhuisheng wenwu guanli weiyuanhui 1956; Hubeisheng bowuguan 1989.

10. The *ding/fu* set-form appears in Spring and Autumn tombs of northern states related to Zhou (such as Jin, Lu, and Zheng), but only as a variant practice.

11. See Mackenzie 1991a, 114.

12. Handong was occupied largely by Zhou-related states. See also the Chu *shengding* as exemplified by the middle Spring and Autumn period Kehuang *ding* recently discovered in a Chu tomb in Xichuan, Henan; Cao Guicen 1992b. Mackenzie (1991a, 120–122; see also 110–111) posits an eastern origin for certain of its features. Evidence for such an eastern origin derives from bronze inscriptions. For instance, there are ones of early Spring and Autumn date indicating relations with an unidentified Eastern Yi state (see Cook 1990, 327–328) and somewhat later ones showing intermarriage with the Upper Huai state of Jiang (see Cook 1990, 352–354).

13. For a discussion of eastern influence, see Rawson (1987) and Mackenzie (1991a, 114, 117–125 passim, 132). For examples of even-numbered sets, see the Yi-related tombs of Qufu (Shandong; Shandongsheng kaogu yanjiuso 1982) and the early Spring and Autumn period Upper Huai area tombs of Xinyang (state of Fan; Henansheng bowuguan 1981a) and Guangshan (state of Huang; Henansheng Xinyang diqu wenguanhui 1984).

14. Anhuisheng wenwu gongzuodui fanchengxian wenhua guan 1982b; Zhejiangsheng wenwu guanli weiyuanhui et al. 1984.

15. See Mackenzie 1991a, 109.

16. For example, in the following southern Hubei and Anhui tombs: that a low-ranking official (lower *dafu*),

Zhao Gu (Wangshan Tomb 1, Jiangling; Hubeisheng wenhuaju wenwu gongzuodui 1966), had five steps and the burial chamber was divided into three rooms; the tomb of a higher-ranking official (upper *dafu*), Zhao Tuo (Baoshan Tomb 2, Jingmen; Hubeisheng JingSha tielu kaogudui 1991), had fourteen steps and five rooms; the tomb of Pan Cheng (Tianxingguan Tomb 1, Jiangling; Hubeisheng Jingzhou diqu bowuguan 1982), a high official (upper *qing*), had fifteen steps and seven rooms; and, finally, the tomb of King You (Shouxian, Anhui) had nine rooms (the number of steps is unclear).

17. On the latter (and their influences on bronzes), see Mackenzie 1991a, 126–131. In the 558 tombs of the Yutaishan (Jiangling, Hubei) complex, 224 yielded various lacquer and wooden objects, in all about 1,000 pieces. Liuchengqiao Tomb 1 (Changsha, Hunan) held over 60 lacquer pieces. The Wangshan tombs (Jiangling, Hubei) contained over 200 lacquer pieces. In addition, Changtaiguan (Xinyang, Henan; Henansheng wenwu yanjiusuo 1983), Tianxingguan Tomb 1 (Jiangling, Hubei), and Baoshan Tomb 2 (Jingmen, Hubei) all contained a considerable number of lacquer and wooden ware. On the lacquered coffins from Leigudun Tomb 1 (state of Sui/Zeng, in Handong), see Thote 1991.

18. Hunansheng bowuguan 1972.

19. Hubeisheng bowuguan 1979; Anhuisheng wenwu gongzuodui fanchengxian wenhua guan 1979. On the Chu Wang Yinshen *zhan,* see Mackenzie 1991a, 136.

20. Finer examples have emerged from these Hubei tombs: Yutaishan Tomb 427 and Tomb 354 and Tianxingguan Tomb 1 (Jiangling); Baoshan Tomb 2 (Jingmen).

21. Xiong Chuanxin 1981.

22. In late Spring and Autumn to early Warring States Hunan tombs (Longdongpo, Changsha, and Deshan, Changde), we find iron scrapers and adzes. Yangjiashan Tomb 65 (Changsha) yielded a *ding* and an iron scraper, along with a steel sword. In Tomb 53 at Gangchang (Echeng, Hubei) was found a bronze *ding* with iron legs (Hubeisheng Echengxian bowuguan 1978); Huang Zhanyue 1976; Wagner 1988.

23. Hubeisheng bowuguan 1982b.

24. Yang Minghong 1986.

25. Chen Xianyi 1980b.

26. Hubeisheng Jingzhou diqu bowuguan 1989.

27. Hubeisheng bowuguan 1980c.

28. Yichang diqu bowuguan 1984.

29. Hubeisheng bowuguan 1983a.

30. Hubeisheng Jingzhou diqu bowuguan 1987.

31. Chu Huangcheng kaogu fajuedui 1980a.

32. *Zhongguo kaoguxue nianjian* 1991, 244.

33. Wang Shancai and Zhu Dejun 1980.

34. Jingmenshi bowuguan 1992.

35. Jingmenshi bowuguan 1998.

36. Beijing 1991b.

37. Hubei Jingzhou diqu bowuguan 1982.

38. Jianglingxian wenwu gongzuozu 1984.

39. Hubeisheng bowuguan 1973. The tombs in the Jiangling area are surveyed in Guo Dewei 1982.

40. Hubeisheng Jingzhou diqu bowuguan 1982.

41. Hubeisheng wenhuaju wenwu gongzuodui 1966.

42. Hubeisheng Jingzhou diqu bowuguan 1983; for Mashan, see Beijing 1985.

43. Hubeisheng Yichang diqu bowuguan 1992.

44. For a short notice on the discovery, see Zhang Yinwu and Li Fuxin 1983. Excavations (as yet unpublished) have been made by Wuhan University.

45. *Zhongguo kaoguxue nianjian,* 1990: 278. The chariot pit here is the largest and earliest so far found in Hubei. It suggests that there is an important elite tomb nearby, and its proximity to Chu Huangcheng lends some weight to the Northern hypothesis on the location of Ying.

46. Chu Huangcheng kaogu fajuedui 1980b. Further excavations made by Wuhan University have not yet been reported.

47. See Zhang Xixian 1983.

48. The Xixia and Nanyang sites are discussed in Han Weizhou 1956.

49. Hubeisheng bowuguan 1983b; Shi Quan 1988: 105–126.

50. Cao Guicen 1989; Henansheng wenwu yanjiusuo 1991: 332–344.

51. Nanyang diqu wenwudui 1982.

52. Cao Guicen 1992a.

53. Wang Rulin 1982.

54. Hubeisheng bowuguan 1983.

55. Wuhan daxue Jing-Chu shidi yanjiushi 1984.

56. Zhang Zedong 1983.

57. Hubeisheng bowuguan 1989 (on tomb 1); Hubeisheng bowuguan 1985; von Falkenhausen 1991: 70–75.

58. Dayexian bowuguan 1983.

59. Dayexian bowuguan 1984.

60. Echengxian bowuguan 1983.

61. Zhu Zhi 1958.

62. Cao Guicen 1981.

63. Shang Jingxi 1980.

64. Henansheng wenwu yanjiusuo 1988.

65. Henansheng wenwu yanjiusuo 1984.

66. Henansheng wenwu yanjiusuo 1986.

67. Ou Tansheng 1983.

68. Yang Lüxuan 1986.

69. Zan Hanqing 1983.

70. Li Shaozeng 1983.

71. Henansheng wenwu yanjiusuo 1983.

72. Henansheng Xinyang diqu wenguanhui 1986.

73. Zhumadian diqu wenhuaju 1988.

74. Henansheng Xinyang diqu wenguanhui 1981.

75. Anhuisheng wenhuaju wenwu gongzuodui 1964; Anhuisheng wenwu kaogu yanjiusuo 1987.

76. Anhuisheng Huailinxian wenguansuo 1983.

77. Anhuisheng wenwu gongzuodui 1982b.

78. Anhuisheng wenwu guanli weiyuanhui 1956.

79. Li Jingran 1936; Shouxian bowuguan 1986.

80. Jiangsusheng wenwu guanli weiyuanhui and Nanjing bowuguan 1965, 1974; Wu Shanqing 1977.

81. Anhuisheng wenhuaju wenwu gongzuodui 1963.

82. Anhuisheng wenwu gongzuodui 1982a; Yang Jiuxia 1988.

83. Qianshanxian wenwu guanlisuo 1986; Qianshanxian wenguansuo 1992.

84. Huaiyinshi bowuguan 1988.

85. Suzhou bowuguan kaoguzu 1981.

86. Li Ling and Liu Yu 1980.

87. Zhang Zhixin 1980.

88. Zhenjiangshi bowuguan 1984.

89. Shaoxing wenwu guanli weiyuanhui 1976.

90. Huang Xuanpei 1959.

91. Hunansheng bowuguan 1964.

92. Hunansheng wenguanhui 1958.

93. On the latter areas see Zhang Zhongyi and Peng Qingye 1984.

94. Hunansheng bowuguan 1963.

95. Chu wenhua yanjiuhui 1984: 73–74; *Zhongguo kaoguxue nianjian* 1986: 179.

96. Hunansheng bowuguan 1983.

97. Hunansheng bowuguan 1986b and 1985.

98. Hunansheng bowuguan 1986b.

99. Zhongguo kexueyuan kaogu yanjiusuo 1957; Hunansheng bowuguan 1959.

100. Hunansheng bowuguan 1972.

101. Hunansheng bowuguan 1980.

102. Peng Shifan 1980.

103. Cao Guicen 1989; Henansheng wenwu yanjiusuo 1991: 332–344.

104. Mackenzie (1991a: 141) notes that in Warring States times Chu cultural influence was greater on this region (that of Zeng/Sui) than on that of Cai (in the East). Von Falkenhausen (1991: 84–85) suggests that the mechanism for such influence (here and elsewhere) may have been through gifts of goods (such as bells) made in Chu workshops.

105. The close proximity of the Caowang Zuicheng settlement to the Daye mine suggests a close relationship between the two; on these, see Dayexian bowuguan 1984 and Xia Nai 1982.

106. Lutaishan (in Huangpi; Hubeisheng bowuguan 1982a), Guoerchong (in Huanggang; Huangzhou gumu fajuedui 1983), several in Echeng (Echengxian bowuguan 1983) and Daye (Xiong Yayun 1956; Chu wenhua yanjiuhui 1984: 27–28).

107. Cao Guicen 1989.

108. For a general discussion, see Wu Xinghan 1991.

109. Yin Difei and Luo Changming 1958.

110. Anhui Fuyang diqu zhanlanguan wenbozu 1987.

111. To which, it will be recalled from the previous chapter, Chu moved in 278.

112. Yang Zifan 1956; Liu Xinjian 1982.

113. Mackenzie (1991a: 139–140) seems to suggest (despite chronological difficulties on the basis of currently available materials) that there may have been Wu influences on Chu bronzes as early as mid-Spring and Autumn times.

114. For a survey of Chu cultural penetration into this area, see Liu Xin 1987.

115. Gu Tiefu 1982; Gao Zhixi 1980a and (for chronological revisions) 1987a.

116. Hunansheng bowuguan 1980; Hunansheng bowuguan 1986a.

117. Hunansheng bowuguan 1977.

118. Hunansheng bowuguan 1983.

119. Hunansheng bowuguan 1984.

120. Hunansheng bowuguan 1986.

121. He Jiejun 1991. It should be noted that Chu-style artifacts are also found in the South in areas beyond the geographical scope surveyed here (i.e., beyond the extent of the Chu political sphere); e.g., Sichuan (Sichuansheng bowuguan 1981), Guangdong (Guangdongsheng bowuguan 1973), and Guangxi (Guangxi Zhuangzu zizhiqu wenwu gongzuodui 1978). These materials may relate to Chu trade contacts and cultural exchange, on which see Peters, chapter 7 below.

3. Chu Art: Link between the Old and New

1. See Kuwayama 1983.

2. These finds were reported very briefly in an article in the August 30, 1992, issue, and in somewhat greater detail in the October 18, 1992, *Zhongguo wenwubao,* a newspaper published by the Beijing Cultural Relics Bureau, devoted to reports pertaining to cultural relics. The bronzes illustrated include a *ding,* inscribed and dated to the very end of the seventh century BCE, which shows the waisted profile, flat bottom, and outward flaring handles that were to become the hallmarks of the *shengding* closely identified with subsequent Chu burials (see also Mackenzie 1991a, 120–122).

3. A preliminary report was published in Wenwu 1980, 10: 13–20; this is superseded by a detailed monograph, Beijing 1991a.

4. See Beijing 1991a, 320–324 for a discussion of the date and occupants; a different interpretation is offered by Li Xueqin (1985, 157). The greater complexities of the problem are summarized in von Falkenhausen 1991, 58–61, esp. n. 52.

5. See Thorp 1988, 62, n. 9.

6. See So 1983 for an early discussion of the characteristics of Chu bronze art.

7. For example, the bronzes from the Marquis of Zeng's tomb in Suixian discussed below.

8. For a full report of the find, see Beijing 1989.

9. See designs on painted coffins of accompanying burials (Tokyo 1992, no. 87:1–2) and on lacquered wooden shields and leather armour plates (ibid., nos. 64:1–10, and 66).

10. The site was reported in *Jianghan kaogu* 1981, 1: 1–2; see Shu Zhimei 1984, n. 14–17, 66–67.

11. Beijing 1986.

12. Hubeisheng wenhuaju wenwu gongzuodui 1966, 33–56.

13. Beijing 1984.

14. Hubeisheng Jingzhou diqu bowuguan 1982, 71–116. Six of the seven tomb chambers at Tianxingguan have been plundered so that the published finds are only a small portion of what must have been an extensive original tomb inventory.

15. Beijing 1985. This tomb may date to as late as the early third century; see Xu, chapter 2.

16. Beijing 1991b.

17. Beijing 1986, colorplate 13:3–4, plates 37–47.

18. Some of the silks, lacquers, and bamboo are illustrated in Beijing 1985, colorplates 2–32; the bronzes are illustrated in plates 31–34.

19. See Beijing 1991b, plates 27–35; the most interesting examples are either inlaid, gilded, or representational in content (ibid., colorplate 11).

20. The more important bronzes from the find were exhibited in Beijing (see Beijing 1954); present locations for the inscribed vessels, many of which are scattered in various Chinese museums, are indicated in Ma Chengyuan et al. 1986–1990, 4: 660–679.

21. Beijing 1973, plate 178. See also Wang Zhongshu 1982, chap. 4, for a description of the status of the lacquer industry during Han times.

22. Mackenzie 1987; also Wang Congli 1987, 64–70.

23. See Thote 1991, 34–37; also in the same volume, 167.

24. Sixteen accompanying graves and a large horse-and-chariot pit with six chariots and nineteen horses were found at Xiasi, while Tomb 1 at Leigudun contained twenty-one sacrificial burials in separate chambers of the main tomb structure. Li Xueqin 1985, 158–161, discusses two other finds in Henan Province—Tomb 1 at Hougudui (reported in *Wenwu* 1981, 1: 1–8) and Tomb 1 at Baishizidi (reported in *Zhongyuan wenwu* 1981, 4: 21–28)—as well as Tomb 1 at Liuchengqiao in Changsha, Hunan Province (reported in *Kaogu xuebao* 1972, 1: 59–72), among his list of Chu burials and notes that they were also accompanied by human sacrifices.

25. The musical instruments found with the marquis in the east chamber include a small tambourine-like drum, a five-stringed *zhu* and a ten-stringed *qin* and five *se* (all plucked instruments), and two *sheng* mouth organs (Beijing 1989, 75–175; also von Falkenhausen 1991, 82–83, for a discussion of the significance of this phenomenon).

26. Beijing 1986, plate 44; Hubeisheng wenhuaju wenwu gongzuodui 1966, 37, fig. 9; Beijing 1984, plate 49; Beijing 1991b, plate 56:2–3.

27. See Rawson 1989.

28. Beijing 1991a, plates 73–76.

29. Beijing 1989, colorplates 17 and 18:1–3.

30. Beijing 1991a, colorplate 8 and plate 56.

31. Beijing 1989, colorplates 7–8, 11:1–3.

32. A virtually identical vessel has also been recovered from Tomb 1 at Wangshan (Beijing 1972b, n. 77). The Baoshan vessel contained remains of chicken bones. Lacquering on the inside of a bronze food vessel was clearly both decorative and functional, as the lacquer coating, like tin inside modern cooking and baking utensils, would have prevented contamination of the food.

33. See Beijing 1986, plates 64–65; Beijing 1991b, colorplate 11:1–2 and p. 239, fig. 158; Wen Fong 1980, n. 76; William Watson 1973, n. 125–127, etc.

34. Mackenzie has argued that both textile and carved wood designs have influenced bronze designs of the same period (see Mackenzie 1986, 1987, and 1991b).

35. Yang Xiaoneng n.d., plates 8–11.

36. See Bagley 1987, 34–35.

37. Evidence that the trend was kept alive during the Western Zhou is supplied by recent finds from Shaanxi (Beijing 1980, 2: 77) and Shanxi Provinces (Beijing 1990, n. 52).

38. Beijing 1989, plates 40 and 41:3, 51, 63; and 64:3–4.

39. The painting has often deteriorated to the extent that many such details are not immediately obvious, although close study and drawings have helped to recreate some of these figures for study (e.g., compare figures illustrated in Beijing 1986, colorplate 14 and plates 106–108, to drawings of them on p. 79).

40. See others from the same tomb in Beijing 1985, plates 40–42, and from Yutaishan (Beijing 1984, plate 71) and Baoshan 2 (Beijing 1991b, colorplate 14:1 and plate 84:1, 3). The Baoshan figures were also equipped with wooden swords (ibid., 254–257, figs. 168–170).

41. None of Gu's original works survived, of course, although what is believed to be close approximations of his works are in the collection of the British Museum and the Freer Gallery of Art (see Lawton 1973, 1–4, catalog 1).

42. See Sukhu, chapter 9; see also Hawkes 1985 and Mackenzie 1991a, 141–147.

43. See Major, chapter 8.

44. Beijing 1989, plates 121–124, or Tokyo 1992, n. 15–16. The Fuxi-Nügua element is discussed in detail by Guo Dewei (1981).

45. Beijing 1989, 355. For an account of the myth, see Bodde 1961, 394–395; see also Chantal Zheng 1992.

46. See Li Ling, appendix. Scholarship on this very important manuscript is exhaustive, with the major contributors including both Asian (Li Xueqin, Jao Tsung-i, Li Ling, Hayashi Minao) and Western scholars (Noel Barnard) alike (see Barnard and Fraser 1972). For a recent summary of the scholarship on the manuscript, see Lawton, 1991, 178–183; the bibliography lists the key publications on the subject by the scholars cited.

47. Suixian Leigudun yihao mu kaogu fajuedui 1979, 26, fig. 33; Li Ling in Lawton 1991, 181; and Li Ling 1991a.

48. The Xinzheng example is now in the National Historical Museum in Taibei. The Lijialou tomb was plundered when it was opened in 1923, and much of its contents are now dispersed. However, the majority of the bronzes recovered were published before they were dispersed (see Sun Haibo 1937).

49. A second wooden pedestal with inserted antlers was found in a separate chamber together with other objects of daily use. The relationship between the second object and the others in the same chamber is unclear.

50. The 156 Chu tombs at Yutaishan yielded 156 such figures in varying degrees of elaboration, one in each tomb (see Beijing 1984, 107–108, 110–111; plates 67 and 68:1–3). With the exception of one, all were placed in the head chamber of the grave. Interestingly, the large Tomb 2 at Baoshan is the only major Chu burial that did not have such a figure inside.

51. Beijing 1984, plate 66; Hubeisheng Jingzhou diqu bowuguan 1982, plate 23:6. Similar examples, with or without antlers and in various states of preservation, abound from Chu tombs (e.g., Beijing 1986, plate 90). Like the tomb figures, usually only one bird-tiger drumstand is found in a grave, and only the larger or richer graves of higher-ranking individuals would yield them.

52. Beijing 1986, colorplate 2:2–3; 3:1.

53. William Watson 1972, 70–72; Thote 1991, 38–39. Bird-snake combinations antedating much of the Chu representations discussed here have been found among artifacts recovered from sites in Shandong Province, suggesting that the origin of that combination may actually lie farther east (see Shandongsheng kaogu yanjiusuo

1982, plate 53:4; and Shandongsheng Jiningshi wenwu guanliju 1991, 469, fig. 13.1, plate 14:3; plate 15:6, and plate 16:1). Also, bronze vessels with bird-snake and shamanistic scenes have been recovered from sites in Henan, traditionally outside the realm of Chu control or influence (Weber 1968, figs. 42–45).

54. See Zhang Zhengming 1987, 264–265.

4. Chu Society and State: Image versus Reality

1. Much of this presumably had roots in an oral tradition.

2. This discussion sets aside problems with the idealized or "systematized" images found in texts such as the *Zhouli,* which are not directly relevant to the study of Chu.

3. A perusal of even a few entries in Loewe 1993 is sufficient to demonstrate this point.

4. Of course, to the extent that they relied on southern materials, not all of the blame lies with northerners. The images portrayed of Chu kings (discussed below), for instance, most probably derived from southern (oral?) sources.

5. Details and citations for much of what follows, especially as relates to the interplay between throne and lineages, may be found in Blakeley 1992b.

6. In Western Sinology, pre-Imperial China is conventionally characterized as "feudal." (The classic case for this was made by Granet 1952.) The idea, however, poses some significant conceptual problems (Blakeley 1976). Early on, I suggested the term "segmentary state" (ibid.), but I am now more inclined to favor "kinship state" (implicit in Blakeley 1992b and expanded on in Blakeley and Xu forthcoming). Military parameters of society and state are surveyed in Lewis 1990, 15–52.

7. These terms (and relevant ancient Chinese equivalents) are much debated by ethnographers (see, for instance, Kryukov 1966; Chun 1990). In the interests of simplicity, here "clan" simply refers to complex kinship units and "lineages" to their subunits. (See also n. 14.)

8. For an analysis of the role of ancestors and ancestral rites, see Savage 1985, 106–298, and Savage 1992. See also Cook, chapter 5, and Cook 1990, 1995, 1997.

9. See the introduction.

10. See Hsu and Linduff 1989, 147–185. For a critique of this traditional view, see Cook 1995.

11. In some territorial states, however, kinship units unrelated to that of the ruler did play significant roles; see n. 53.

12. The Zhou kings had an additional and unique religious role—responsibility for the cult of heaven, from which derived their license to rule (the Mandate of Heaven, *tianming*); see Eno 1990, 23–29, Hsu and Linduff 1989, 101–106; Savage 1992; Pankenier 1995.

13. This was an important factor in the decline of the authority of the Zhou kings over the territorial lords by the end of the first two centuries or so of the Zhou period.

14. *Xing* is usually translated (rather inappropriately, it can be argued) as "clan." It was, however, a far larger and less cohesive kinship structure than the *zong,* translated herein as "clan." (Little attention has been given to the extent to which the *xing* may have been based on fictive kinship ties and/or legendary connections.)

15. *Shiji* 40.6, 7/631, 632 (where Sima Qian demonstrates his ignorance of the ancient distinction between *xing* and *shi* by stating that the Zhou king "*xing*-ed [Chu as] Mi *shi*"). Allusions in bronze inscriptions to women of the Chu royal house include a graph taken by paleographers to be equivalent to *mi;* see Cook 1990, 336, 372.

16. Only in the case of (the presumably eponymous) Yu Xiong (on whom see Cook 1994, 4ff) did "Xiong" appear in the post-position (as personal name?). Zhu Junming (1987, 50–51) takes the relevant bronze-inscription graphs as equivalent to *yin* (drink), Zhang Zhengming and Zhang Shenlin (1983) as *shu* ("to strain" in wine production). Gong Weiying (1983, 79), on the other hand, reads *xiong* (of the texts) as a (mythical) three-legged turtle.

17. Zhang Zhengming and Zhang Shenglin 1983; Zhang Jun 1984a. Gong Weiying (1983) instead takes "Xiong" as a second *xing* of the Chu ruling house, but this defies the "societal logic" of ancient China (men were not referred to by their *xing* affiliation, and the evidence he offers of dual *xing* is spurious). In an entirely differ-

ent vein, Zhu Junming (1987) has argued that "Xiong" actually was not a native designation, but rather a pejorative one applied by Qin writers (in Warring States times). This would require that the *Shiji* Chu genealogy stemmed from a Qin source (a possibility, given the Burning of the Books in 213, under the Qin dynasty). However, it ignores that one Chu king has a "Xiong" designation in the *Zuozhuan* (Zhao 13/23.9; *Zuozhuan* references are to the 1983 edition) and, more tellingly, that there are several such allusions in bronze inscriptions (at least as currently understood; see Cook 1990, 482–489, 523–539).

18. Creel (1970, 334, n. 56) writes that "descendants in the direct line . . . from the founder of a *hsing* [*xing*] had no *shih* [*shi*] 'surname,' but only the *hsing.*" I would assiduously avoid the word "surname" for early China, but the point being made is valid: the main lineage of a territorial state (e.g., Chu) had no discrete designation (*shi;* i.e., lineage name). These were adopted only by collateral lineages (to distinguish them from the main line).

19. This would require linguistic practice at variance with the Central Plains (where the rulership title was in the post position). The connection with wine sacrifice derives from the graph readings cited in n. 16.

20. This is usually seen as a "usurpation" of a Zhou prerogative, but such a view is essentially an expression of the Northern Bias (or the "idealization" tendency of late Zhou times). In Western Zhou times the title was not unique to the Zhou, and other "peripheral" states (only marginally tied to the Zhou scheme of things), such as Wu and Yue, also employed it from early times (seemingly throughout their existence).

21. This function has been suggested, for instance, for the office of *Moao* (see below and n. 40, 72). *Ao* was probably equivalent to *yin.*

22. See, for instance, Liu Xinfang 1987, 75–76. Since graphs preceding "Ao" were in a number of cases demonstrably toponymns, it has been suggested that "X Ao" means "the Ao (-type leader) interred at X."

23. On the subject, see He Hao and Zhang Jun 1984, Liang Zhongshi 1988, and Tang Jiahong 1990.

24. *Zuozhuan,* Wen 1/8.7.

25. *Zuozhuan,* Zhao 13/23.13.

26. The latter follows hard on the heels of the account of King Gong's divination concerning an heir (discussed below). This reinforces the fact that it relates to unconventional successions.

27. Why this would be the case is not immediately apparent, but perhaps the idea was to insist that when all sons were candidates, the one who would be least likely to be involved in the struggle (i.e., the youngest) should succeed. A related factor may have been that succession by the youngest could still leave his elders as the true wielders of power.

28. *Zuozhuan,* Zhao 13/23.10–23.11. (All such passages herein are rather free paraphrases.)

29. I take this clause literally (and thereby presume the Ba woman below to have been a concubine). Commentators tend to take the phrases more figuratively, as alluding to the lack of a legitimate heir (see below), and then argue whether the Ba woman was consort or a concubine.

30. Gongzi Bi, who was on the throne for a few days in 529, during the rebellion against King Ling. King Ping maneuvered his death.

31. Gongzi Heigong, who was to be named prime minister in 529 (under the same conditions and with the same results as Gongzi Bi).

32. There is no indication of his position at court at this juncture. Perhaps he was a tutor.

33. He was later to oppose King Ling, aid King Ping in his rise to power, and serve as prime minister under the latter.

34. This foretells what was to happen after King Gong's death, when the youngest son (chosen by the spirits) was set aside (in favor of the eldest).

35. Or, to be more precise, what later commentators assumed to be the Zhou tradition. I am not aware, however, that it has been shown unequivocally that this included a strict rule of seniority.

36. This would make it possible for succession to go to a junior candidate and may be what prompted a (later or northern) misconception that sucession by the youngest was a common practice (or the set rule) in Chu.

37. The basic meaning of "X *shi*" was "lineage [called] X." Thus when applied to an individual (always a lineage head), it conflated him with the lineage in its entirety.

38. On these points, see Creel 1964, 179, n. 118; 180, n. 119.

39. Commentators have maintained that some of the Chu lineage names derived from those of their estates. The evidence, however, is not conclusive. In any case, there is no evidence that their lands were either extensive or administratively autonomous (see Blakeley and Xu forthcoming). (The absence of estates undoubtedly contributed to the relatively high level of centralization in Chu noted below).

40. If *"Moao"* was a state post (see below), it was the only major exception. (Some ritual roles may have been passed down hereditarily [see Zhang Jun 1984a, 98, n. 1], and there seems to have been a minor tendency toward hereditary tenure in local posts; see Blakeley and Xu forthcoming.)

41. Thatcher 1977–1978, 140–147.

42. The lack of estates in the countryside and the absence of hereditary office may have made Chu lineages somewhat more intensely concerned with obtaining and maintaining power and influence at court than their counterparts elsewhere.

43. See, for instance, the genealogical charts in Blakeley 1983. The point has been made by Zhang Jun (1984a, 96).

44. The lineage names of a number of individuals include "Xiong." Given its connection with kings (see above), it is quite probable that such lineages were segments of the royal clan. If so, the fact that such men are always found in low-level posts suggests that these lineages originated very early, although there is no way to say precisely when. (It could be, however, that these were lineages with roots in other Mi-*xing* states.)

45. There are problems, however, with this idea. Zhang Jun (1986) has attempted to sort them out but without definitive results.

46. It has long been assumed that the two graphs are interchangeable and that they thus referred to the same lineage. There is some reason to doubt this, but the arguments offered to date fail to solve some difficulties.

47. It was long held that the progenitor was a son of Wu. Zhang Jun's suggestion (1986, 183–185) that he was instead a brother of Wu has some merit.

48. *Mao* is probably a variant of *ao*, discussed above.

49. See Zhang Jun 1986, 180–182 and Li Ling 1991a.

50. This designation has occasioned much controversy (see Blakeley and Xu forthcoming), despite the fact that early commentators (e.g., Du Yu, *Zuozhuan*, Zhao 4/24.14) tied a Shenyin figure genealogically to King Zhuang.

51. See Wu Yufang 1992b. On a shadowy Jing collateral lineage, see below.

52. Blakeley 1979b, 89; Zhang Jun 1984a, 98–99.

53. See Blakeley 1977, 1979a, 1979b (p. 109 for a summary).

54. We encounter about a dozen lineages (represented by only one or two members) concerning which there is no hint of geographical origins.

55. For a survey of aliens in Chu in Spring and Autumn times, see Zhang Shenglin 1984.

56. Seven Qi princes: *Zuozhuan*, Xi 26/6.71; Guan Xiu: *Zuozhuan*, Ai 16/30.30.

57. Presuming that Song Mu was from the state of Song (*Zuozhuan*, Ding 5/27.46).

58. Bo Zhouli (*Zuozhuan*, Cheng 15/13.30, Xiang 26/18.9, Xiang 27/18.33) and perhaps Xi Wan (*Zuozhuan*, Zhao 27/26.3), on whom see below.

59. Guan Dingfu: *Zuozhuan*, under Ai 17/30.36, and presumably Guan Shefu (*Guoyu* 18.1a), on whom see Xiao Hanming 1986.

60. Members of Shen lineage (e.g., Shen Hai: *Zuozhuan*, Zhao 13/23.7) and the Peng lineage: e.g., Peng Zhongshuang: *Zuozhuan*, under Ai 17/30.36 (see n. 96); Peng Yu, known from a bronze inscription. See Blakeley and Xu forthcoming.

61. Xu Yan (*Zuozhuan*, Cheng 12/13.5) and, presumably, "Chu Xu Bo" (*Zuozhuan*, Xuan 12/11.14).

62. Zhen Yijiu (*Spring and Autumn* Xiang 24 [*Zuozhuan*, 17.20]; *Zuozhuan*, Zhao 4/21.16).

63. Zige (= Ran Dan): *Zuozhuan*, Xiang 19/16.31).

64. Deng Liao (*Zuozhuan*, Xiang 3/14.9).

65. Cai Wei (*Zuozhuan*, Zhao 13/23.3), Chao Wu (*Zuozhuan*, Zhao 13/23.4, etc.), and Fei Wuji (on whom see below).

66. Dao Shuo (*Zuozhuan*, Huan 9/2.57), presumably from the small state of that name (in central Henan.)

67. There were four figures bearing the lineage-name Pan (most notably Pan Chong, tutor to King Mu; e.g., *Zuozhuan*, Wen 1/8.7-8). If *pan* is a graphic variant of *fan*, the lineage probably originated in the state of Fan (located in Huaibei), and this would explain the presence of *shu* (uncle) in the designations of two Pan figures: Pan Wang (a.k.a. Shishu; *Zuozhuan*, Xuan 12/11.4,12) and Pan Dang (a.k.a. Shu Dang; *Zuozhuan*, Xuan 12/11.18).

68. Hubeisheng JingSha tielu kaogudui 1991, vol. 1—for Ruo: 353 (strip 70); Deng: 350 (strips 26, 27), 351 (strip 32), 358 (strip 129), 361 (strip 164), 362 (strip 172), 363 (strips 184, 189); Cai: 351 (strip 30), 358 (strip 130), 358–359 (strip 138), 361 (strip 167), 362 (strip 169), 364 (strip 193); Song: 350 (strip 18), 352 (strips 49, 51), 354 (strip 87), 361 (strip 164), 362 (strips 170, 175); Chen: 354 (strip 84), 358 (strip 138), 362 (strip 172), 362–363 (strip 181); Wu: 357 (strip 122); Zhou: 351 (strips 34, 39, 45), 352 (strip 60), 353 (strips 68, 74), 355 (strip 91), 359 (strip 141), 362 (strip 169), 363 (strips 183, 184, 190, 191); Huang: 353 (strip 71), 356 (strip 107), 358 (strip 138), 361 (strips 163, 164, 165), 362 (strips 170, 174, 180), 363 (strips 182, 184, 185, 187, 190). (One gets the feeling that these state names are functioning not as lineage names but as surnames in the sense that we understand the *"xing"* from Han times on.)

69. Also, two military captives (Guan Dingfu [n. 59] and Peng Zhongshuang [n. 60, 96]) of early Spring and Autumn times subsequently served Chu in important capacities.

70. On Chu central administration, see Liu Xianmei 1982; Xu Jun 1982; Zuo Yandong 1986; Thatcher 1977–1978 and 1985, 39–41; Li Jin 1989; and Liu Yutang 1990.

71. In modern times, Zhang Zhenze (1946) suggested that it had charge of the statutes.

72. Tang Jiahong (1988) and Cai Jingquan (1991) have suggested that it was so closely association with the Qu lineage that it, in effect, came to function as a designation for its lineage head. This, however, is unlikely, since in the Baoshan material we find *Moao* of other lineages in a number of local administrations (e.g., Hubeisheng JingSha tielu kaogudui 1991, vol. 1: 357, strip 121).

73. For example, the office of *lianyin* appears in texts (e.g., *Zuozhuan*, Xuan 12/11.22) and *aoyin* in the Baoshan materials (i.e., Hubeisheng JingSha tielu kaogudui 1991, vol. 1: 356, strip 110).

74. More than two dozen different "-*yin*" offices appear in the Baoshan materials, far more than are encountered in the sources for Spring and Autumn times. About one-fourth appear to be central posts, the rest, local.

75. For example, *Zuozhuan*, Xuan 11/10.50 and Cheng 16/13.35.

76. See *Zuozhuan*, Zhuang 4/3.8 and under Ai 17/30.36.

77. See Wen Chongyi 1976, 46–51; Shu Zhimei and Wu Yongzhang 1980; Tang Mingli 1991; and especially Song Gongwen 1988, 1–230.

78. This was the office of the occupant of Baoshan Tomb 2. See Weld, chapter 6.

79. Hubeisheng JingSha tielu kaogudui 1991, vol. 1: e.g., 359, strip 145.

80. Ibid., 355, strip 89.

81. For example, Ibid., 351, strip 38.

82. Ibid., 360, strip 155.

83. For example, Ibid., 351, strip 38.

84. Presumably the same as *Gongzheng*.

85. See Yang Fanzhong and Zhu Maxin 1981; Creel 1964, 172-174. The subject is thoroughly reviewed in Blakeley and Xu forthcoming.

86. A supposedly earlier (sixth-century) case is highly suspect; see Blakeley and Xu forthcoming. He Hao has been engaged in an extended analysis of the chronology and locations of Chu fiefs; see He Hao 1984, 1991; He Hao and Liu Binhui 1991.

87. He Hao presumes that the considerable number of *jun* means that power was quite decentralized. He may, however, be overly influenced by a passage in *Han Feizi* (SBBY ed., 4.10a) complaining of the excess of

fengjun in Chu, because this applies ony to the last (Eastern) phase of Chu history (the era of Huang Xie). Both He Hao and Chen Wei (1996, 101–107) presume that these *jun* were enfeoffed *(feng),* but the latter appropriately suggests that they were under significant central control, and therefore the possibility must be considered that the *jun* were heads of *jun* (commanderies or prefectures) rather than the holders of fiefs. (It may be significant, too, that much of the central government apparatus was mirrored in the structure of local government.) See also Weld, chapter 6; Peng Hao 1991; Luo Yunhuan 1991b; and Chen Wei 1995a, 1995b.

88. Given the inadequacies of the sources, little can be discerned about the kings of Warring States times. The only kings from that era on whom we have any meaningful information are those who reigned during the period covered in some detail by the only quasi-historical *Intrigues of the Warring States* (*Zhanguoce;* see Loewe 1993, 4). On that basis, King Huai (r. 329–299) and his son, King Qingxiang (r. 299–263), may have exercised some degree of authority (although the former died a captive in Qin).

89. For a statistical analysis of lineage participation in court affairs, see Blakeley 1979b.

90. This was Gongzi Yuan, who is discussed below.

91. Wang Yi, as quoted in *Shiji jijie* (*Shiji* 84.12/985). If the graph *yuan* is equivalent to *wei* (see above), the Wei lineage also appears in the Baoshan materials. Hubeisheng JingSha tielu kaogudui 1991, vol. 1: 350, strip 28; 352, strip 56; 355, strip 90.

92. Wu Yufang (1992a) has suggested that it was in fact the Xiang lineage (of the great anti-Qin rebel leader, Xiang Yu).

93. Wang Yi, as quoted in *Shiji jijie* (*Shiji* 84.12/985), defined it as being in charge of the three lineages mentioned above. If so, however, this would be a practice unique to Chu, there being no known corallary elsewhere of several lineages being grouped together in this way.

94. See Hubeisheng JingSha tielu kaogu dui 1991, vol. 1: 352–353, strip 62; 353, strip 67; 357, strip 121; 358, strip 130; 361, strip 157; 362, strip 176. This does not mean that there were no Qu figures at court, however, as the Baoshan materials are overwhelmingly concerned with local matters.

95. See He Hao 1992. The occupant of Wangshan Tomb 1, Jiangling, was also of the Zhao lineage.

96. Of the exceptions, one (Peng Zhongshuang, n. 60, 69) was rather early (early seventh century) and the other (Wu Qi, see below) rather late (in the early fourth century). I consider the evidence for two others proposed by Song Gongwen (1988, 39–40, 45–46) to be shaky at best.

97. Other than his rise, resignation, and the episode recounted below, the *Zuozhuan* alludes to him at only three points, all in a rather offhand manner. Elsewhere, he appears only in the *Lunyu* (n. 99) and in a unique (hence, suspect) episode in the *Shuoyuan,* and is mentioned in passing in the *Qianfulun.*

98. *Zuozhuan,* under Xuan 4/10.29.

99. *Lunyu,* 5.18.

100. See the genealogical chart in Blakeley 1992b, 38–39. (The complex nature of the Dou lineage represented there, however, reflects traditional understanding and may not be entirely accurate.)

101. Note that while Ziwen's mother (Bobi's wife) is the daughter of a lord, the same is not claimed of Ruo Ao's wife (the mother of the next ruler, Xiao Ao).

102. In this scenario, the fall of the Ruo Ao lineages in 605 (see above) could represent the main lineage (and its kings) emerging from under a genealogical cloud that had kept it at a disadvantage vis-à-vis the Dou lineage.

103. *Zuozhuan,* Xuan 12/11.5–11.7.

104. See Blakeley 1992b, 14–15.

105. *Shiji* 119.2–119.4/1246; translated in Nienhauser 1991, 218–222 passim.

106. Moreover, the trope of "thrice serving" is found in the *Lunyu* (5.18) instead in connection with Ziwen (for whom there is absolutely no independent evidence of such a career pattern).

107. On problems with the historicity of the Sunshu Ao stories, see Nienhauser 1991, 218–222, and Gu Tiefu 1988, 285–319.

108. Another source of confusion concerning the role of kings in Chu (in the recent literature) is the assumption that the relatively high degree of centralization there necessarily translated specifically into royal authority. This is a false assumption.

109. As will be seen below, however, Ping was evidently not the most forceful of personalities.

110. According to discourses recorded in both the *Zuozhuan* (Zhao 12/22.49–22.50) and the *Shiji* (40.26/636), Ling considered requesting a gift of tripods from the Zhou king. This is sometimes taken as an allusion to the "nine *ding*" that (at least in later imagination) served as the symbol of universal sovereignty (supposedly coveted also by King Zhuang; see below). Even if historically realiable (by no means a certainty), the context of the episode really suggests a less imposing expectation. Nevertheless, when the totality of Ling's actions and personality are taken into account, it would not be surprising if he hoped to supplant the Zhou kings.

111. *Shiji* 40.13/633. For uncritical treatments of King Cheng, see Peng Mingzhe 1986 and Wei Chang 1990.

112. If, however, the YiYue were located in Jiangnan, the absence of that segment of the episode from the *Zuozhuan* is not surprising, as it alludes very little to that region (see Blakeley, chapter 1).

113. For example, by Wei Chang (1988) and Zhao Hua (1987).

114. *Zuozhuan*, Xuan 4/10.28–10.29.

115. According to the *Shiji* variants (and other sources that treat the tripods).

116. *Zuozhuan*, Xuan 3/10.19–10.21. Variants appear in *Shiji* 4.74/76 and 40.19–40.20/634.

117. See Gu Tiefu 1988, 273–284. (For an uncritical treatment of the subject, see Zhao Zhongwen 1990.)

118. *Shiji* 40.17–17/634.

119. One of the few Chinese scholars to question the historicity of the episode (echoed in a number of other works) is Tan Qixun (1982).

120. He had played an ambiguous role in a military campaign in 611 (i.e., at the end of his first three years on the throne) and may have been involved behind the scenes in power struggles leading up to the 605 episode (see Blakeley 1992b, 12–13).

121. A fully legitimate Hegemon was recognized as such (at least as a formality) by the Zhou king, which was not the case with Zhuang of Chu. On the realities of the hegemonies, see Rosen 1978 and Liu Pujiang 1988.

122. An earlier (632) defeat by Jin and its allies at Chengpu did deflect Chu efforts at territorial acquisition away from the "core" states of the Yellow River. Nevertheless, thereafter (and throughout Zhuang's reign) Chu and Jin continued to struggle for the allegiance of the pettier states, and even a major Chu victory (at the Battle of Bi) 597 did not really change this.

123. The allusions to him, scattered in Warring States and Han texts, generally serve the ideological purposes of the authors/compilers. They are, however, rather consistent in their treatment of him. Studies of Wu Qi include Guo Moruo 1940, He Chongen 1985, Li Hengmei 1987, Okada 1981, Sun Kaitai 1985, and Wei Chang 1989. For a translation of the *Shiji* biography of him and a discussion of problems with it, see Goodrich 1981–1983.

124. A number of its members appear in the record, beginning with Wu She's grandfather, Can (e.g., *Zuozhuan*, Xuan 12/11.10).

125. *Zuozhuan*, Zhao 15/23.35, Zhao 19/24.11, Zhao 21/24.47, Zhao 24/25.16–7, Zhao 27/26.5–26.7, 9–10. The only study of the material is that of Matsumoto 1980.

126. See Blakeley 1992b, 27.

127. For a typically uncritical treatment of the material, see Wang Weiping 1986; for an excellent evaluation of it, see Johnson 1981.

128. The same theme lies at the core of the Qu Yuan saga; see Sukhu, chapter 9.

129. Other factors, of course, must have been at work. In terms of north-south competition, for instance, the wet-field agriculture of most of the Chu area (in contrast to the dry-field type of the Yellow River plain) surely was an important one. For a step in the direction to elucidating this important topic, see Pu Shipei 1989.

5. The Ideology of the Chu Ruling Class: Ritual Rhetoric and Bronze Inscriptions

1. This famous tale was first narrated in the *Zuozhuan*, Xuan 3 (606 BCE); a slightly abbreviated version appears in the *Shiji*, "Chu Shujia" 19; and a slightly variant version of the *Zuozhuan* narration is preserved in the *Chushi taowu* 14. See also Blakeley 1992b.

2. For the nine sacred caldrons see K. C. Chang 1983, 93–97. The Chu king Ling's rationale for expecting the Zhou to hand the nine sacred caldrons over to him was that his ancestors had been slighted in earlier Zhou gift-giving rituals. Now that Chu was more powerful, the Zhou should be willing to give the most treasured gift (*Zuozhuan, Zhao* 12).

3. Blakeley, chapter 4.

4. *Guoyu,* 1987 ed., "Chuyu, xia," 203–205.

5. Ibid.

6. Cook 1995. Guan Shefu noted that *wushi* were employed by a household for lineage mortuary feasts. *Guoyu,* 1987 ed., "Chuyu, Xia," 203–205.

7. Kane 1974–1975; Cook 1993b, 1997.

8. See Stanley Tambiah's discussion of how words, especially those summarizing myth, act through recitation to invoke spirits (Tambiah 1968, especially 175–185).

9. Savage 1992 interprets these same inscriptions in a Confucian light, insisting on the late reading of *de* as "virtue," although he is certainly correct in interpreting this virtue as associated with the "royal model emulation" of Kings Wen and Wu. For slightly different readings, see Cook 1990, 212–259; for their role in a potlatch feast, see Cook 1993b, 1997.

10. For the use of *ming* 'luminous' as a signifier of matters associated with the dead, see Maspero 1933. The Shang and early Zhou graph read later as *de* was initially a verb associated with "visiting" border peoples (Serruys 1980, 359). See Cook 1995; see also Du Naisong 1981 and Jao Tsung-yi, "Some Further Observations" (Barnard 1976, 152–154). "Visiting" border peoples was commonly combined with "punishing" (*fa* or *zheng*) them.

11. Cook 1997.

12. Archaeological evidence suggests that this practice may have been imported from the south in the middle of the Western Zhou period (von Falkenhausen 1991, 56–58).

13. Von Falkenhausen 1988, 676–684.

14. The feast is best described in the *Shijing* song, "Chuci" (Mao no. 209), translated by Waley (1953, 209–211) and discussed by von Falkenhausen (1988, 679–681). Many of the songs preserved in this collection describe the clan feast; see Waley's sections: "The Clan Feast," "Sacrifice," and "Music and Dancing." See also Childs-Johnson 1984, Cook 1993b, and Cook 1997. For a description of the foods, see K. C. Chang 1974b.

15. Xu Zhongshu 1936; Cook 1990, 162–211.

16. These date from the sixth to fifth centuries and belong to Jin in the northwest, Qi in the northeast, and Cai in the central southern region. The Son of Heaven *(tianzi)* by this time was reduced to a symbolic representative of the old order; as such, he may have been viewed as having religious or magical powers (see Ma Chengyuan et al. 1986–1990, inscription nos. 887, 850, 587–589).

17. Rubbings and a transcription are found in Henansheng Danjiangkuqu wenwu fajue dui 1980, 17, 27–30; Ma Chengyuan et al. 1986–1990, no. 644; von Falkenhausen 1988, 1076–1116; Mattos 1997; Cook 1990, 385–396, 406–408.

18. Li Xueqin 1985, 156–157. For discussions on the identity of the tomb occupant, see Li Ling 1981 and 1996; Wu Shiqian 1984; Henansheng Danjiangkuqu wenwu fajue dui 1980, 20; Chen Wei 1983, 32–38. Weizi Ping's kinship rank is incised on the bronze "Chu Shuzhisun," "Grandson (or descendant) of a younger male sibling of the royal Chu family." It is possible Ping and Wu were second cousins by the marriage of one of Wu's granduncles to a Wei lineage woman. His father was also a *lingyin,* Sunshu Ao (Song Gongwen 1988, 266; see n. 21 below). Chu elite often had bronzes of earlier date buried with them in their tombs. In the Heshangling section of the Xichuan burial ground, for example, six inscribed *shengding* belonging to Ke Huang (of the Dou lineage, one the the few survivors of the Ruo Ao massacre in 605; see Blakeley, chapter 4) were discovered in Tomb 1, dating to either 475 or 418 BCE (Qiu Shi 1992).

19. For details of Wu's career as *lingyin,* see Song Gongwen 1988: 225-230.

20. Cattle bone chips were found in the vessels. The vessel was referred to as *shangyi caiding;* both terms refer to a kind of meat sacrifice (Cook 1990, 104–105, 139–141, 149). For a discussion of which types of *ding* are used with which type and cut of sacrificial animal, see Li Ling 1996.

21. See the *Zuozhuan*, Xuan 12 (597 BCE), where Jin officers discuss the strength of Chu and the role of Wei Ao as the chief steward *(cai)* in selecting the "Statutes of Command" *(lingdian)* by which to order the army. Wei Ao, also known as Sunshu Ao and Wei Ailie, was also a *lingyin* (see Song Gongwen 1983, 70; 1988, 12).

22. *Shijing*, Mao 273, "Shi Wan," trans. by Waley 1953, nos. 221, 230.

23. *Zuozhuan*, Xuan 12.

24. *Zuozhuan*, Xiang 18.

25. Von Falkenhausen 1988, 1083 (based on earlier discussions of intertextuality by Sun Qikang 1983 and Liu Xiang 1983). The Wangsun Gao *zhong* was found in the same tomb as the Wangzi Wu *ding* (M2 at Xichuan, Henan). Von Falkenhausen 1988, 1079, notes that the rhetoric of this inscription reveals a "purposeful manipulation of current ritual language for ideological/ritual ends." The Wangsun Yizhe *zhong* was found in the hills outside of Yichang, Hubei, in 1884 and is dated to 551 BCE based on the identification of Yizhe as Zhuishui, the Lingyin Zinan. Zinan became *lingyin* after Zigeng because Weizi Ping apparently refused the offer (Li Xueqin 1980; Sun Qikang 1983; Liu Xiang 1983; Cook 1990, 411–419; Ma Chengyuan et al., 1986–1990, no. 650).

26. Cook 1990.

27. See the Qin Wu Gong bells, the Qin Gong *gui,* and the Jin Jiang *ding* (Ma Chengyuan et al. 1986–1990, nos. 917–920, 885).

28. Fanyang was probably the name of the southern bronze foundry, possibly located north of the Ru River in Henan (Li Xueqin 1985, 279; Luoyang bowuguan 1980, 492). The closest ancient mining sites discovered thus far are in southeastern Hubei (Li Xueqin 1985, 182–183). Another, in northwestern Jiangxi, was also most likely active at that time. A sword inscribed with the words "the bronze of Fanyang" was found in a Warring States tomb in Luoyang (Luoyang bowuguan 1980). It was found with a string of pearls and a lacquer sheath; see Peters, chapter 7.

29. See the Jin Gong *dian* (511–475 BCE), the Xu Wangzi Tong *zhong* (late Spring and Autumn), and the Cai Hou vessels (519–491 BCE). Curiously, the Yun'er *zhong*, a Xu bell inscription believed to be from the same scribal hand as the Wangzi Wu, Wangsun Gao, and Wangsun Yizhe bells, does not have *meng* for *ming*. The Cai inscriptions reflect fifth-century changes; they do not refer to *mengsi* but to a related rite, the *meng changdi* 'the luminous/covenant autumnal sacrificial rite.' The autumnal rite *(chang)* was also mentioned in late Warring States Chu inscriptions. In Western Zhou times, *chang* was a "tasting" ritual that took place in the king's private quarters. There is no evidence of it being originally associated with Autumn (Liu Yu 1989, 511'513). The term *di* can be traced back to Shang and early Western Zhou usage, when it referred to a one of several rites involving a commemorative feast to the High God in honor of the patrilinial ancestors (Shima 1979; Liu Yu 1989). The Shuyin *bo* inscription, Qi bell, dated to around 553–548 BCE, referred to the ritual as *mengxu*.

30. *Zuozhuan*, Cheng 12.

31. *Zuozhuan*, Cheng 13. The Song ruler acted as mediator. The actual text of the covenant was agreed upon outside the west gate of the Song capital. The feasting simply acted to seal the agreement in the presence of the ancestral spirits. For the proper etiquette of feasts, see Yang Kuan 1963.

32. *Zuozhuan*, Cheng 14.

33. *Zuozhuan*, Xi 22, 30; Cheng 14; Zhao 1. Most of the odes sung can be found in the *Shijing* collection.

34. *Zuozhuan*, Zhao 11.

35. *Zuozhuan*, Ai 15.

36. Li Xueqin 1985, 176–182.

37. For a detailed analysis of the Zeng Hou Yi bell inscriptions as they relate to early musical theory, see von Falkenhausen 1988, 746–841.

38. Hubeisheng bowuguan 1989.

39. Chang Yuzhi 1987; Cook 1990, 54–56, 62–66.

40. Ikeda 1981, 785–806.

41. Qing accounts of an ancient city of Xiyang locate it north of Suixian in southern Henan (see Cook 1990,

484–485), but it must have been closer to Anlu, the site outside of Suixian where the two bells were found during the Northern Song period.

42. Cook 1997. For traveling in the Shang, see Keightley 1983b, 552–554; for the movements of the king as a dating device, see Shaughnessy 1991, 76–81. For an example of a feast held outside a Zhou sacred center, see the Chang Xin *he* or the later E Hou Yufang *ding* (Ma Chengyuan et al. 1986–1990, nos. 13 and 26).

43. The inscription has left out the word for "to treasure" (*bao*, often replaced with the homophonous word *bao* 'preserve'), leaving the nonsensical: "may he eternally, it, use to present sacrificial offerings." If the inscription was read out loud, however, the homophones "eternal" (*yong*) and "use" (*yong*) could function as loans for each other, producing the phrase "may he use it and eternally present sacrifices." Both expressions "use it" (*yong zhi*) and "eternally present offerings [in the lineage mortuary feast]" (*yong xiang*) evolved out of Western Zhou usage and were in common use later. (There are many examples from the Upper Huai River region; see Ma Chengyuan et al. 1986–1990, nos. 598, 603, 608, 613, 614, 620). A Spring and Autumn period Zeng inscription considered to be from a different Zeng state in Shandong has *yong bao yong zhi xiang* (Ma Chengyuan et al 1986–1990, no. 691). The Cai vessels, dating to 518 BCE, found in Shouxian, Anhui, share the Zeng variant writing of *zuo* with the semantic "speech" element (Ma Chengyuan et al., 1986–1990, nos. 587–589).

The graph for "it" (*zhi*) appears with a number of different significs, such as the mouth or dagger. These are found in the sense of "it" in bronzes entombed with Zeng Hou Yi and on a Cai dagger-axe. When the graph should be read as *zhi* is obvious not only from the syntax of the phrase but from the formulaic nature of the phrase. The phrase has evolved from Western Zhou style blessings (Cook 1990, 162–207). The Cai Gongzi Jia *ge* has, in the same style of script as the Zeng bronzes, "[Made] for the use of Cai Gongzi" (Ma Chengyuan et al. 1986–1990, no. 601). Zeng bells also use the variant, but for another homophone (see Ma Chengyuan et al. 1986–1990, nos. 702ff). Luo Yunhuan (1988) notes that the epigraphical styles of the Chu Yin Zhang *zhong* and *bo* bells do not match. He suspects that the *bo* inscription was by a Chu scribe and the *zhong* inscription, like the Zeng Hou Yi inscriptions, was by a Zeng scribe (who perhaps copied from the Chu bell).

44. Both weapons are now in the Palace Museum of Beijing. For a photo of the sword, see Liu Jie 1934, 4. Rubbings are available in Ma Chengyuan et al. 1986–1990, nos. 656–657.

45. Yin was a royal Chu surname. It corresponded phonetically to the surname Xiong found in the received texts. (For a summary of past discussions, see Cook 1990, 526.)

46. Liu Binhui (1984, 348) dates the sword to the early years of King Hui's reign. A similar formula to "use it on travels; use it on military expeditions" was used on southeastern Spring and Autumn period ritual vessels from Chen and Xu. See Ma Chengyuan et al. 1986–1990, nos. 580, 567.

47. For other bird-script examples, see Rong Geng 1964, especially the inlaid dagger-axes discovered in Shouxian, Anhui (items 16 and 17). For a discussion of the Chu blade, see 287 (435 in reprint) and for the photo, see plate 1 (440 in reprint). Dong Zuobin (1953) claimed that bird script derived from the ornate Shang script found especially in clan signs. Ma Guoquan (1983) explained that bird script did not evolve directly from the Shang. It was popular in the southeastern inscriptions of the late Spring and Autumn period through the Warring States period. It was also popular during the first half of the Han period. Ma Guoquan speculated that the interest in "bird," "insect," and "fish" scripts prevalent in the south and southeastern states of Wu, Yue, Song, Cai, and Chu may have been related to religious beliefs that derived ultimately from the Shang. The Chu blade inscription, he claims, is composed of both bird and insect script (158).

48. Li Xueqin 1985, 163; Cook 1990, 523–525.

49. See Zhu Dexi 1954; Zhu Dexi and Qiu Xigui 1973; Hao Benxing 1983; He Linyi 1991; and Huang Xiquan 1991. These authors overlooked a food-service caldron made by a royal descendant of the Wu house in the Spring and Autumn period with terminology similar to the Chu Warring States inscriptions (see Ma Chengyuan et al. 1986–1990, no. 548). It seems that the early Wu scribes and these later scribes shared a common ritual tradition. For further discussion, see Cook 1995.

50. Li Xueqin 1985, 167.

51. There may have been others, but the excavation site has been destroyed. The vessels and some weapons, now

disintegrated, were found in a dike (Li Ling and Liu Yu 1980, 29–30). They were on display at the Jiangsusheng bowuguan in Nanjing in 1988. Only the *jian* and *dou* vessels are inscribed. The inscriptions are incised on preexisiting vessels, as was typical of the late Warring States period.

52. See Li Ling and Liu Yu 1980; He Linyi 1984; Liu Binhui 1984, 354; He Hao 1985; and Cook 1990, 205–207, 556–558.

53. Some of the rhetoric was preserved in a few short Warring States inscriptions from the state of Qi and on the lengthy late Warring States inscriptions of Zhongshan. The former retain bits of the sixth-century rhetoric and the latter were obviously influenced by contemporary philosophical and storytelling traditions. It is very likely that evidence from other states was destroyed during the Warring States period. It was common practice to cast vessels from the metals captured from one's enemies (e.g., see the late Warring States Chu inscription stating that fact, Ma Chengyuan et al. 1986–1990, no. 664).

54. Li Ling 1990.

6. Chu Law in Action: Legal Documents from Tomb 2 at Baoshan

1. The preliminary excavation report on this discovery was published in *Wenwu* in 1988. Hubei sheng JingSha tielu kaogudui Baoshan mudi zhengli xiaozu 1988, 1–14. The same issue of *Wenwu* also contains a number of special studies of the discoveries at Baoshan: Wu Shunqing, Xu Menglin, and Wang Hongxing 1988, 15–24; Baoshan mudi zhujian zhengli xiaozu 1988, 25–29; Hu Yali 1988, 30–31, 29; Wang Hongxing 1988, 32–34.

2. See, generally, Beijing 1991b, 1–5. The same press has also published a separate volume on the bamboo strips and plaque found in Tomb 2 at Baoshan (Beijing 1991c). This volume includes photographs of the strips, an annotated transcription, a description of their contents, a discussion of the script, and a preliminary findings list of the graphs used. Beijing 1991b adds to these an appendix by Peng Hao on what the strips reveal of the Chu legal system. A useful glossary of the graphs in the strips, together with a comparison of some with other epigraphical forms, and photographs of the strips with a transcription arranged alongside appears in Zhang Guangyu 1992.

3. In 1990, the Jingmen City Museum carried out a survey of the Chu cemeteries between Jingmen City on the northwest, the Han River on the east, and the old Chu capital of Ying on the southwest. Jingmenshi bowuguan 1992, 19–27. The museum archaeologists counted 22 cemeteries and 227 mounded elite graves, some arranged in regular rows on elevated, stepped terraces. This survey shows that Baoshan was included in Jinan's densely populated "funerary suburbs." See also Li Xueqin's review of the archaeological record in this area in 1985, 163–166. There is currently no consensus on the identification of a particular archaeological site as the earliest Chu capital of Ying, although Jinancheng, as well as Chu Huangcheng, in Yichengxian, and Jijiahu, in Dangyangxian, have all been raised as possibilities. See Blakeley 1985–1987 and 1990, and also Blakeley, chapter 1.

4. The title *zuoyin* appears in the *Zuozhuan* account of intrigue in the Chu court leading up to the extermination of the kindred and faction of Xi Yuan, *zuoyin* at the time of his death in 514 BCE. See *Zuozhuan*, Zhao 27: 906–910, ch. 52.14b–52.21b. Unfortunately, the story in Zhao 27 tells us little of the functions of the office, apart from the information that the *zuoyin* led a military force to cut off the invading Wu army. See Thatcher 1977–1978, 145–146, which translates *zuoyin* as "vice administrator on the left"; and Blakeley 1977, 208–243.

5. The *Zhouli*, a "systematizing" text thought to have been composed long after the end of the Western Zhou government that it purports to describe, puts an official called *da sikou* at the top of a well-articulated system of penal and civil administration. Use of English terms like "legal," "penal," and "judicial" in this context should not obscure the fact that the boundaries of the *da sikou*'s jurisdiction do not coincide seamlessly with these familiar Western categories. *Zhouli*, 516, ch. 34.13a, et seq. (Shisanjing zhushu ed.). See also Sven Broman's (1961) discussion of terms used for judicial officials in so-called "free" texts, thought by some scholars to present a more contemporary and authentic portrait of Zhou times. For the problematique of "systematizing" vs. "free" texts, see, e.g., Karlgren 1946.

6. Trans. Lau 1979, 126–127.

7. *Zuozhuan*, Xuan 12: 390–391, ch. 23.5b–23.6a.

8. For example, *dian* appears in the ode "Tang," in the *Shijing*, where King Wen of Zhou chastizes the latter-day Shang rulers for abandoning Shang's ancient virtue:

> Yin does not use the old (ways); but though there are no old and perfected men *(sui wu lao cheng ren)* there still are the statutes and the [penal] laws *(shang you dian xing);* you have not listened to them; the great appointment therefore is tumbling down.
> (Karlgren 1950a, 216)

Here the poet refers to written punishment texts, *dian xing,* as a source of authority that can be a substitute for authoritative humans.

9. Creel 1970, 124–125. See also Creel 1980, 29.

10. *Zhanguoce* 5.48a; Crump 1979, 277.

11. *Zhanguoce* 5.8b; translation modified from Crump 1979, 235. As elsewhere, the romanization has here been changed to pinyin. Peters makes note of this anecdote in her Ph.D. dissertation (Peters 1983, 44–45). In a recent commentary on the passage, apparently written before the publication of the Baoshan discoveries, Xu Jun reads the name of this legal text as *feng ci zhi dian,* or the "Phoenix Laws," and links it to an ancestral Chu belief in the phoenix as a protective spirit. Xu Jun 1986, 66–67. Crump solves the puzzle of the "Pecking Order Statutes" by elision, translating the phrase as simply "the books of law."

12. As we shall see below, the term *dian* does appear in the legal documents from Shao Tuo's grave, where it means population registers, lists of residents grouped by household *(shi)* and kept in local government archives *(yufu),* or lists of workers assigned to various officers.

13. These "laws" are cited in Peng Hao 1991, 548–554.

14. *Zuozhuan*, Zhao 7: 758–759, ch. 44.2b–44.3a.

15. The harboring of fugitives and criminals was a common element in Eastern Zhou formulaic depictions of evil rulers, as Wu Yu notes later in the same passage. Perhaps this focus can be traced to the enforcement problem faced by early states in a period when lawbreakers could get to the next jurisdiction in only a few hours.

16. For example, there is a group of Zhou architectural bronzes that include the figure of a one-legged door-keeper standing by a temple or palace gate. A recent find in Shanxi is a wheeled animal cart, like a zoo on wheels, complete with a door on hinges guarded by a one-legged keeper (see Rogers 1998, plate 42).

17. Kong Yingda, Tang author of the *shu* commentary on the *Zuozhuan,* says he does not know what the name of this law meant, but he cites Fu Qian, an earlier commentator quoted in a Han commentary, who said: "*Pu* means veiled; *qu* means hidden. This was a law about fugitives" (*Zuozhuan*, Zhao 759, ch.44.4a–44.4b). Kong Yingda does not make his discomfort with this explanation explicit, but it may stem from the discrepancy between the *Zuozhuan*'s quotation from the *pu qu zhi fa,* which concerns the concealing of stolen property ("He who conceals a robber's booty shall be held to the same liability as the robber"), and Fu Qian's explanation, which suits the situation in the Zhang Hua Palace much better. The legal device of making one individual liable for the penalty that is specified (by statute) for another is frequently used in the Qin legal documents found in 1975 at Shuihudi. The formula is usually [*yu X*] *tong zui* X, "liable to the same extent as X." See items D14, D15, D16, in Hulsewé 1985, 124–125; Shuihudi Qinmu zhujian zhengli xiaozu 1978, 157–158. This practice, which is limited in the Shuihudi documents to robbery (as in the *Zuozhuan* example), was different from co-adjudication, which specified that a criminal's household, village chief, and the members of his "group of five" would be liable to some degree for certain of his crimes. See D18 in Hulsewé 1985, 125–126; Shuihudi Qinmu zhujian zhengli xiaozu 1978, 159–160.

18. *Zuozhuan*, Zhao 7: 759–760, ch. 44.3a–44.5a.

19. *Han Feizi*, 1960 ed., ch. 13.1b, 9b–10a; Liao 1939, vol.2: 87–88.

20. *Han Feizi*, 1960 ed., ch. 13.9b; Liao 1939, vol.2: 108–110.

21. *Shiji* 1932 ed., 84.2, translated in Burton Watson 1961, vol. 1: 499–501. In the article cited above, Thatcher

seems to have suspected that Chu officials were functionally, or at least politically, divided into "right" and "left" moieties. If so, and if the *Shiji* account is to be trusted, Shao Tuo and Qu Yuan would have served the same king at the same time in the same left "moiety." Thatcher 1977–1978: 145–146.

22. "Skilled in the use of words" is Burton Watson's rendition of *xian yu ci ling* (Burton Watson 1961, 499).

23. *Xian* in the phrase *xianling* may mean to "promulgate" or "publicly display," as in the *Zhouli* reference to the "display" of minor punishments in the marketplace. *Zhouli*, "Diguan," "Sishi" (Market supervisor), 221, ch. 14.24 a–b (Shisanjing zhushu ed.).

24. Beijing 1991b, 45.

25. See the discussion of a possible Eastern Zhou transition in funerary symbolism from the tomb as temple or shrine to the tomb as a small world to be inhabited in the afterlife, in Lawton 1991, 167–174.

26. For a detailed account of the shape of the *guo* and *guan,* and the contents of the various chambers, see Beijing 1991b, 45–277.

27. The dragon and phoenix interlace on the inner *guan* seems to echo the patterns on the double coffin of Leigudun Tomb 1 studied by Thote (1991).

28. Beijing 1991b, 404–416.

29. See Major 1978, 228–230. In the future, human bone from the thousands of Chu graves dug since the 1950s will offer a valuable resource for defining Chu populations. Bone chemistry analysis can reveal differences between the diet, stature, and lifelong health of north and south, rich and poor, countryman and city dweller. It can help read, from the bones of the Chu peoples, the consequences of social stratification, as well as patterns of matri- and patrilocality and degrees of genetic differentiation that are now only speculative parts of the effort to define Chu.

30. This bamboo-shaped tally, made of bronze inlaid with gold, was discovered in Anhui at the site of Qiujia Park, east of the county seat of Shouxian. See Wenwu bianji weiyuanhui 1979b, 233–234. The tally reads, in part: "All those who send goods must use tallies and passports," and specifies the quantity limits and permissible traveling routes for its bearer. It reveals Chu's interest in controlling the flow of people and goods through the state. See Peters, chapter 7.

31. See strip 103.

32. See Beijing 1991b, 46; *Shiji,* "Chu shijia," ch. 40.

33. In these strips generally, an individual's feudal titles are indicated by the name of the fief, in this case Luyang, and rank, in this case *gong,* usually translated as "duke."

34. This translation follows the interpretation of Li Tianzhi, who prepared the transcription and annotations included in Beijing 1991b and 1991c. See Beijing 1991c, 47, n. 193.

35. As noted in Beijing 1991b, 41, this rite was properly performed by a subject to his lord. See *Zhouli*, "Tianguan," "Shanfu," 57–59: ch. 4.1a–6b. It must have been a proud day when the tattered remnant of the royal Zhou performed this ritual to Chu.

36. See Beijing 1991c, 41, and Beijing 1991b, 587.

37. Beijing 1991c, 57.

38. Beijing 1991b, 330; Beijing 1991c, 38.

39. Peters 1983, 270–295.

40. Beijing 1991b, 93.

41. Beijing 1991c, 4–9.

42. See, for example, Chen Wei 1994.

43. Beijing 1991c, 9.

44. Beijing 1991c, 10–11.

45. Accounts in the *Zuozhuan* refer to Chu efforts to survey lands and carry out a census of households. See Cheng 2: 429, ch. 25.22a *(nai da hu); Xiang 25: 623–624, ch. 36.14a–36.16b (shi pi fu, shu jia bing).*

46. Year names in passages noted herein will be translated into the Western form dates listed above.

47. Beijing 1991c, 17. My understanding of this strip and those discussed below relies heavily on the analysis furnished in Beijing 1991b, 265–277; the philological footnotes appended to the transcription of the strips

in Beijing 1991c, 16–67; the article on Chu law and legal administration by Peng Hao in Beijing 1991b, 548–554; and the article by Chen Wei on judicial administration, 1996b, 1–6.

48. As noted in Beijing 1991b, 373, n. 27, Lan Ying is one of the three previously unknown Ying cities mentioned in the strips. Liu Binhui and He Hao discuss the meaning of city names written in the form "X Ying" and propose possible geographical locations for all five Ying cities with this kind of name in appendix 24 of Beijing 1991b, 564–568. See also Blakeley, chapter 1.

49. Beijing 1991c, 17, 10.

50. Perhaps a ward of the capital at Ying?

51. This strip suggests that registration of city residents was in some cases (or for some purposes) the responsibility of an official called *sima tu,* or "Marshal of the Conscripts."

52. Beijing 1991c, 17.

53. The status of *bangren* in Chu may have been equivalent to that of *guoren,* a subgroup of the Eastern Zhou elite that lived in the cities and wielded a certain amount of political power. See Du Zhengsheng 1979, 21; and Lewis 1990, 53–96.

54. Hulsewé 1985, 177; Shuihudi Qinmu zhujian zhengli xiaozu 1978, 222.

55. Hulsewé 1985, 115; Shuihudi Qinmu zhujian zhengli xiaozu 1978, 143–144.

56. Strip 6.

57. Strips 12–13.

58. Strip 32.

59. Beijing 1991b, 548–549.

60. The *sibai,* or "supervisor of harms," seems to function in these strips as a specialist in matters of public security.

61. See the use of the same term, *xiangri,* in strips 131–139.

62. For the legal meaning of the term *wugu* in Han times, see Hulsewé 1955, 251. Here, as in Hulsewé's examples, it is tempting to see in *wugu* a vestigial theory of human liability that attached whenever one stepped outside of a specified, traditional, and positively defined path of proper behavior. Such a theory would offer a stark contrast to theories of liability underlying Western positive law. If correct, this interpretation would have the advantage of combining in the term *wugu* both "without just cause" and "without precedent."

63. *Xinzao* and *xinyin* seem to be official titles. Personal communication from Li Ling, May 1993. While their function is unclear, this case suggests that in Chu, at least, by this late period, it included some forms of adjudication or mediation. If we read *xin* as a variant of *xun* 'to question or interrogate,' the last half of the title might be translated as "Director of Investigations," which suits the context quite well.

64. The *Zuozhuan* records a dispute between two royal Zhou ministers in which representatives of the two parties were called to present their arguments before a mediator. The dispute was solved when one party was unable to present evidence for his side that would rebut the other side's evidence. Xiang 10: 542–543, ch. 31.12a–31.13b.

65. The notation on the back of strip 15 mentions a date in the tenth month, probably well into the busy harvest season.

66. Strips 14–17.

67. *Zhouli,* "Qiu guan: Da sikou," 517, ch. 34.15b; Biot 1851, 311. Scholars have puzzled over the meaning of *liang ji* in this passage. The Han commentator Zheng Xuan suggested that *ji* meant the same thing as Han *quan,* or contracts inscribed on wood that were divided in half, so that each party would have a version that could be verified by rejoining the halves. This explanation gains some support in the Baoshan strips because of their mention of a "three part sealed tally," referred to as evidence of a worker's registration. See strips 12–13. The Tang commentator Jia Gongyan observed that Zheng Xuan may have simply meant that *ji* were similar to contracts in being documents essential to the suit, as in the *Zuozhuan* case noted above. *Zhouli,* loc. cit.; *Zuozhuan,* Xiang 10: 542–543, ch. 31.12a–31.13b. Maspero was one of the first Western sholars to focus on the *Zhouli's* careful rules of judicial procedure; he interprets this phrase as follows: "il [the minister] demandait aux deux parties de lui presenter leurs titres justificatifs" (He [the minister] requires both parties to present

proof of their claims) (Maspero 1934–1935: 270). His outline of Zhou procedure included five stages: accusation *(song)*, hearing requiring the presence of both parties *(liang zao)*, pleadings *(ji, ci,* in this case *dian?)*, deposit of arrows or metal (perhaps as earnest money, to deter frivolous suits), and judgment. Ibid., 271.

68. It is possible that the word *xing* was not yet used in Chu to mean surname, as the order to register inhabitants' deaths includes only place of residence, first name *(ming)*, and kin group or "family name" *(zu)*. Strip 32.

69. See, for example, strips 80, 82, 85, 131–139.

70. Hulsewé 1985, 158; Shuihudi Qinmu zhujian zhengli xiaozu 1978, 209.

71. Beijing 1991b, 552–554.

72. Li Ling suggests that the reason many of the *shouqi* cases could not be tried and resolved was that the defendant could not be produced in court *(bujiang ti ying)*. Personal communication, June 12, 1993. See, for example, strips 19, 21, 25.

73. Maspero 1934–1935, 271–272.

74. Strip 29.

75. Chen Wei 1993, 74–79.

76. Beijing 1991b, 552. The matters repeated on more than one strip include those recorded on strips 46, 52, 55, and 64 (appears four times); 22, 24, and 30 (three times); 27 and 32, 31 and 50, 34 and 39, 41 and 48, 38 and 60, and 45 and 57 (two times each).

77. Beijing 1991b, 553.

78. Ibid., 552.

79. *Zhouli* 533, ch. 35.22a–35.22b.

80. Ibid. This is the interpretation followed by Biot in his translation (Biot 1851, 350): "il y a un certain nombre de jours fixe (pour l'appell)." Recently published transcribed texts from an early Han grave at Zhangjiashan, just west of the city of Ying, include an example of the successful assertion of a *qiju* appeal by a convict, apparently two months after judgment had been executed on him. Jiangling Zhangjiashan Hanjian zhengli xiaozu 1995, 31–32.

81. Shuihudi Qinmu zhujian zhengli xiaozu 1978, 200–201; Hulsewé 1985, 152–153.

82. Sun Yirang 1987, quoted in Peng Hao 1991.

83. Strips 197–249.

84. Strip 215.

85. Currently, scholars in China differ in their interpretations of this graph. He Linyi, for example, has concluded that it should be read as *li,* with the meaning of judge or hearing official. See *Shuowen,* 6A.3, "Anciently, *li* and *li* had the same pronunciation and were used interchangeably. Thus there was no distinction between *dali* and *dali* (high judge)." Chen Wei, however, believes that it means an assistant to the legal scribe whose name, as recorder, appears at the end of many of the strips (Chen Wei 1995c, 78).

86. This reading assumes that the authors are correct in reading *zheng* as a loanword for *zheng,* or tax, as used in the *Zhouli* passage exempting certain award fields from *guozheng,* or government tax. Beijing 1991b, 377, n. 130; *Zhouli,* 455, ch. 30.3b.

87. This looks very like the legal reflection of a modern *fenjia* dispute. See, e.g., Cohen 1970.

88. The authors of Beijing 1991c interpret this name as referring to a consort of King Sheng of Chu (45).

89. This offense is reminiscent of the *pu qu zhi fa,* and Wu Yu's criticism of the king's harboring fugitives in the Zhang Hua Palace, above, p. 104.

90. For this reading of *fanqiguan* I am indebted to Li Ling.

91. The word used here is *hou.* The annotators of the transcriptions in Beijing 1991b read *hou* as meaning descendants, whereas Peng Hao suggests that the word should be read as inheritance (Beijing 1991b, 378, n. 156, and 551). Since *hou* does appear in strips 151–152 from this grave, first as a verb meaning "to succeed to [property rights]" and then as a noun meaning "one who inherits, or succeeds to [property rights]," the former reading has a slight edge over the latter.

92. Reading as *ze* with the Beijing 1991c annotators, 46.

93. See above, p. 114–115.

94. Beijing 1991c, n. 165; 46. This reading is currently the subject of disagreement; Li Ling suggests that this graph should be read instead as *huo* (personal communication, June 12, 1993).

95. Here we see reference to the legal official, *sikou,* mentioned in the *Zhouli.* See above, p. 101, and n. 5. Li Tianzhi suggests that in this context the term might refer to the *sikou* listed in inscriptions on weapons from the state of Han—low-level officials in the government workshops. While this interpretation would fit well with the nature of *sikou* in the Shuihudi legal documents, this strip seems to refer to a judicial, decision-making role for the officials listed as defendants. See Beijing 1991c, 41, n. 46.

96. Beijing 1991c, 24.

97. Strips 151–152.

98. See the discussion of the case in Chen Wei 1994.

99. *Zhouli,* 541–542, ch. 36.6a–36.7a; Biot 1851, 359–361.

100. See Weld 1990, chap. 3.

101. See Gulliver 1979.

102. Strips 141–144.

103. Strips 122–123.

104. See Beijing 1991b, 385, n. 360; strip 200.

105. See, for example, strips 200, 203.

106. Strips 197–249.

7. Towns and Trade: Cultural Diversity and Chu Daily Life

1. Personal communication, 1991, Archaeology Department, Peking University; 1992, Archaeology Department, Peking University.

2. Zhongguo shehui kexueyuan kaogu yanjiuso 1984, 125–137. For the Shijiahe culture, see Shihe kaogudui 1990 and Zhang Xuqiu 1991.

3. K. C. Chang 1986, 215–217, 226; Zhongguo shehui kexue yuan kaogu yanjiusuo 1984, 134.

4. Xi'an Banpo bowuguan 1963; K. C. Chang 1986, 110, Xi'an Banpo bowuguan 1975, 280–284, 263.

5. Zhongguo shehui kexue yuan kaogu yanjiusuo 1984, 125–137.

6. Zhang Xuqiu 1992; Shihe kaogudui 1990.

7. K. C. Chang 1980, 194–195; 220–230.

8. Li Xueqin 1985, 285–287.

9. K. C. Chang 1976b, 62–64.

10. Gu Zuyu, 9–27.

11. Chen Zhenyu 1992, 65.

12. Chen Zhenyu 1992.

13. Chen Zhenyu 1993, 56.

14. The discovery of a large Eastern Zhou cemetery serves to mark the presence of an Eastern Zhou settlement even if traces of that settlement have not yet been found or excavated.

15. Chen Zuquan 1980a; Hubeisheng bowuguan 1980b, 1982b.

16. Chen Zhenyu 1992, 66.

17. Liu Binhui 1981a, 110.

18. Hubeisheng bowuguan 1982b, 2: 497.

19. Chen Zhenyu 1992, 63; Qu Yingjie 1992, 81–88.

20. Xiaogan diqu bowuguan 1990.

21. Dayexian bowuguan 1984.

22. Chen Zhenyu 1993, 52.

23. Crump 1970, 157–158; *Guoyu* 25.16.

24. *Zuozhuan,* Zhao 7: 612, 616.

25. *Zuozhuan,* Xiang 31: 559, 563.

26. *Zuozhuan,* Zhao 19: 674, 675.

27. Crump 1970, 203–204; *Guoyu* 30.1b; Yang Kuan 1981a, ch. 3.

28. See below, n. 79.

29. Hawkes 1985, 226–228.

30. Hubeisheng Jingzhou diqu bowuguan 1984, 54.

31. Chen Zuquan 1980a, 1980b; Hubeisheng bowuguan 1980b, Hubeisheng bowuguan 1982b, 1: 325–350, 2: 477–507; Hubeisheng wenwu guanli weiyuanhui 1965; Chu Huangcheng kaogu fajuedui 1980a, 1980b.

32. Yang Quanxi 1980b, 1980c.

33. See So, chapter 3.

34. Wang Zongshu 1982, 83.

35. Hubeisheng Jingzhou diqu bowuguan 1980, 39; Hubeisheng Jingzhou diqu bowuguan 1984, ch. 4, sec. 4.

36. Hubeisheng Jingzhou diqu bowuguan 1982, 91.

37. Beijing 1985.

38. Ibid.; Hunansheng bowuguan 1973.

39. Wobst 1977.

40. Observation based upon fieldwork conducted in the Xishuangbanna, Yunnan Province, from February 1988 to April 1989.

41. *Shiji* "Wutaibo Shijia," 1445.

42. K. C. Chang 1972, 31. These figures might also represent men of Wu or Yue cultural influence. This was the dominant cultural substratum in the Changsha area before a Chu military presence in the Warring States period.

43. Hertz 1907; Van Gennep 1908.

44. Jingmenshi bowuguan 1992; Tan Weisi 1980, 11.

45. Guo Dewei 1983.

46. Henansheng Danjiangkuqu wenwu fajue dui 1980; Beijing 1991a.

47. Hubeisheng Jingzhou diqu bowuguan 1982, 71–116.

48. Pei Mingxiang et al. 1957.

49. Hubeisheng JingSha tielu kaogudui Baoshan mudi zhengli xiaozu 1988, 1–14; Beijing 1991b.

50. Hubeisheng Jingzhou diqu bowuguan 1982, 111; Guo Dewei 1980, 78.

51. See Hubeisheng JingSha tielu kaogudui 1991.

52. Hubeisheng wenhuaju wenwu gongzuodui 1966.

53. Hubeisheng Jingzhou diqu bowuguan 1973.

54. Hunansheng bowuguan 1980.

55. Hunansheng bowuguan 1972.

56. Guo Dewei 1980.

57. Guo Dewei 1980, Hubeisheng Echengxian bowuguan 1983.

58. Chen Zhenyu 1979.

59. Guo Dewei 1988; Guo Shengbin 1991.

60. For a discussion of plural society, see Smith 1965.

61. Chen Yaojun 1980; Gao Zhixi 1980a; Guo Dewei 1988; Hubeisheng wenwu guanlichu 1959, 622; Li Shaolian 1983; Li Xueqin 1985; Pei Mingxiang et al. 1983; Peng Hao 1982; Wang Jin 1988.

62. Bai Yue minzu yanjiu weiyuanhui 1985; Feng Yuhui 1984; Fu Juyou 1982; Gao Zhixi 1980b; Gao Zhixi and Xiong Chuanxin 1980; Guangdongsheng wenwu guanli weiyuanhui et al. 1964b; Guangxi Zhuangzu zizhiqu wenwu gongzuodui 1984; He Jisheng and He Jiediao 1986; Jiang Yingliang 1980, 39–58; Jin Zegong 1984; Peng Hao 1984; Song Shuhua 1991, ch. 2; Tieshan zhongxue Zhenghexian wenwuguan 1979; Wu Mingsheng 1982, 1983; Yang Hao 1961; Yang Yaolin and Xu Huanbin 1985; Zhang Chao 1984; Zhejiangsheng wenwu guanli weiyuanhui et al. 1984.

63. The following provide overall summaries of Yue-Chu presence in the Hubei-Hunan region: Gao Zhixi 1987b; Guo Shengbin 1991; Liu Yutang 1987; Tong Enzheng 1986; Wu Yongzhang 1990.

64. See Guo Shengbin 1991, 65, 66.

65. For example, Yue burials are found in Hengshan (Tieshan zhongxue zhenghexian wenwuguan 1979), Dao-xian and Qiuyang (in the north) (Gao Zhixi 1980b), Yueyang, Zhuzhou, Shaoshan, Miluo, Xiangtan (Qiu Shihua and Cai Lianzhen 1978), Xiangxiang, Hengyang (Feng Yuhui 1984), Leiyang (Hunansheng bowuguan 1985b), and Zixing (Fu Juyou 1982; Wu Mingsheng 1982, 1983).

66. Jin Zegong 1984.

67. Peters 1983; Peters, chapter 6; Sage 1992, ch. 3.

68. *Zuozhuan,* Huan 9: 53; Zhuang 18: 97; Zhuang 19: 98; Wen 16: 274, 275; Ai 18: 851. See also Sage 1992, 60–66; Chen Wenxue 1991, 58.

69. Chen Wenxue 1991; Wang Jiade 1991.

70. Ma Chengyuan 1963, 1965; Wang Liutong 1963.

71. Yu Weichao 1963, 1964.

72. Wang Liutong 1963.

73. Yu Weichao 1980, 29.

74. Gao Zhixi and Xiong Chuanxin 1980, 58.

75. Observations based upon fieldwork conducted in Xishuangbanna, Yunnan Province, from February 1988 to April 1989.

76. *Shiji,* "Huozhiji."

77. Yu Ying-shih 1967.

78. For detailed information on the Baoshan bamboo strips and bronze tally, see Weld, chapter 6.

79. *Zuozhuan,* Zhao 16: 661, 664; Wang Yü–ch'üan 1951, 30.

80. Shu Zhimei and Wu Yongzhang 1980; Wenwu bianji weiyuanhui 1979, 234; Yin Difei and Luo Changming 1958.

81. Yang Kuan 1981a, 104.

82. Tong Enzheng 1979, 30.

83. Schafer 1967.

84. Crump 1970, 241; *Guoyu* 35.4.

85. Beijing 1991b.

86. There are four types of Warring States period Chu currency: (1) gold *yingyuan,* also called *yingcheng;* (2) gold discs called *bing;* (3) bronze cowries; and (4) silver shovel-shaped coins called *bu.* The gold *yingyuan* derives its name from the legend stamped on each of the sixteen to twenty small squares that comprise one plaque. *Ying* refers to Ying, the Chu capital, and *yuan* is believed to designate a specific weight (see Gao Zhixi 1972 and Li Jiahao 1973). Although *yingyuan* plaques were not consistent (weights range from 259 to 270 grams and gold content fluctuated between 91 and 98 percent), archaeologists assume that the central government controlled their production and distribution (see Zhang Pusheng 1959 and Hubeisheng Jingzhou diqu bowuguan 1972).

    The bronze cowries are the earliest as well as the most numerous currency. They are also called *yiqian* (ant-nosed money) or *guilian qian* (ghost-faced money) because of their peculiar legend giving them an ani-mate appearance (see Li Jiahao 1973, 192). They average 3.5 grams per coin.

    The silver spade-shaped coins have been found only at the settlement site near Guchengcun, Fugou, Henan (Henansheng bowuguan, Fugouxian wenhua guan 1980).

    Although there has been no proper research and analysis on how coins were used in the Warring States period economy, the distribution of these coins roughly coincides with the area Chu assimilated during the Eastern Zhou period.

87. Beijing 1989; Tokyo 1992.

88. *Han Feizi,* 1960 ed., 237.

89. Xu Zhongshu 1977; Xu Zhongshu and Tang Jiahong 1981.

90. Xu Zhongshu 1977.

91. Yunnansheng wenwu gonzuodui et al. 1978, 1983.

92. Sichuansheng wenguanhui, Ya'an diqu wenhuaguan, Yingjingxian wenhuaguan 1984; Sichuansheng wenwu guanli weiyuanhui 1988; Li Xiao'ou and Liu Jiming 1984.

93. *Guanzi*, "Jinghongjia" section cited in Hou Dejun 1985.

94. *Shiji*, "Huozhiji," 3268.

95. Gu Tiefu 1982, 82.

96. Zhu Xia 1953, 72.

97. Gao Zhixi and Xiong Chuanxin 1980, 51.

98. Hunansheng bowuguan 1985a.

99. Hunansheng bowuguan 1973, 251; Hubeisheng Tonglushan kaogu fajue dui 1975; Zhongguo shehui kexue yuan kaogu yanjiu suo tonglushan gongzuodui 1981.

100. Bagley 1993, 36.

101. Wang Gungwu 1958.

102. *Shiji*, "Huozhiji": 3268; translation from Burton Watson 1961, 346.

103. *Huainanzi* 18, also cited in Wang Gungwu 1958, 8, and Taylor 1983, 17–18.

104. The maps found in Mawangdui Tomb 3 also suggest the military importance of the Changsha region.

105. *Zuozhuan*, Xi 23: 185, 187.

106. Several poems in the *Chuci* mention perfumes and fragrances during the trancing ceremonies. For example, see Hawkes 1985, 102, 108.

107. *Xin Tang Shu*, "Dilizhi"; also cited in Schafer and Wallacker 1957–1958, 225.

108. Wiens 1954, 34.

109. *Chuci*, "Zhao Hun" verse 230, translated in Hawkes 1985.

110. Schafer 1952; 1969, 12.

111. *Han Shu*, ch. 95, 9b; Wang Gungwu 1958, 13.

112. Luoyang bowuguan 1980; see Cook, chapter 5.

113. Aurousseau 1923, 142.

114. *Huainanzi* 18, also cited in Taylor 1983, 17–18.

115. Burials excavated both at Yinshanling, Pingle (Guangxi Zhuangzu zizhiqu wenwu gongzuodui 1978), and Gongcheng (Guangxi Zhuangzu zizhiqu bowuguan 1973, 30–34, 41), in northeastern Guangxi Province, might very well indicate indigenous villages along the Chu trade route.

116. See He Jisheng 1985; He Jisheng and Yang Shaoxiang 1983; Guangdongsheng bowuguan 1975; Guangdong sheng wenwu guanli weiyuanhui et al. 1963a, 1964b; Guangdongsheng bowuguan et al. 1986; Guangdong sheng bowuguan, Zhaoqingshi wenhuaju fajue xiaozu 1974; Guangdong sheng bowuguan 1983.

117. Guangdongsheng bowuguan et al. 1986.

118. Guangdongsheng bowuguan 1975.

119. Xu Huanbin 1982.

8. Characteristics of Late Chu Religion

1. See Peters, chapter 7.

2. Li Ling (private communication); see also Lothar von Falkenhausen in the "Discussion" section of Lawton 1991, 174; also Xu, chapter 2.

3. Von Falkenhausen 1991, 95.

4. See Major 1978.

5. See Puyangshi wenwu guanli weiyuanhui et al., 1988, illustration on 4; also in K. C. Chang 1994, 64.

6. See Nivison 1984b.

7. Li Ling 1991b. For evidence of directionality in Shang religious cosmology, see Allan 1991.

8. For the Changsha square *ding,* see National Gallery of Art 1975, 52; Hayashi 1972, 168–169; and Munsterberg 1986, 208–210. The anecdote about Confucius is recounted in Bodde 1961 (reprinted in Bodde 1981, 45–84, on 50; the source is a lost passage from the *Shizi* (fourth century BCE), quoted in a later encyclopedia.

9. Some scholars argue that because Zeng was a state independent of Chu, the Zeng Hou Yi finds cannot be used to make arguments about Chu culture. As will already have become evident, the authors of this book regard Zeng as having been firmly within the cultural orbit of Chu.

10. Major 1984, 1993.

11. Fracasso 1983.

12. Hulsewé 1965.

13. On the cosmograph, see Loewe 1979; Li Ling 1991b; Field 1992 (and note that the translation "cosmograph" for shi is Field's); Major 1993; and Ecke 1994. With regard to mirrors, Jenny So has pointed out to me that "the few stone or clay casting molds with [the TLV] design have so far come primarily from the north." (Private communication; see also So and Bunker 1995, n. 69.) The question of the meaning of the TLV pattern itself may soon be solved, perhaps along with the significance of the game of *liubo;* a report in Zhongguo wenwu bao (Oct. 29, 1995: 1) contains a photograph of a silk text found in a Han tomb at Yiwan, Shandong, showing a TLV pattern (a *liubo* board?) with what appear to be explanatory captions. Frustratingly, the photograph is not clear enough to allow the characters on the silk text to be read, and the accompanying article provides no useful information; one looks forward eagerly to the publication of this material in detail. Meanwhile, see Rawson 1996, 159–161, for more on *liubo* boards.

14. Major 1993. The *Huainanzi* is of course of Han date (139 BCE), but the court of Huainan was in a part of Anhui that had long been under Chu control.

15. See also Hayashi 1972.

16. These remarkable *taotie*-like masks, excavated in Hunan, were reported in Hunansheng bowuguan and Huaihua diqu wenwu gongzuodui 1984; see the illustration on p. 57. It may be that the use of masks as funerary goods was more common in early China than has been generally realized. See, for example, a set of masks from Fangshan County, near Beijing (in what was then the state of Yan), dated to the early Western Zhou period; these and some other comparable masks are illustrated in Rawson 1996, 114–116. Masks from the (presumptively) Ba culture site at Sanxingdui are illustrated in the same volume, 67–69.

17. For a discussion of the names of these months, see Major 1993, 120–122.

18. Childs-Johnson 1995.

19. For *Jie* as a demonographic text, see Harper 1985. The whirlwind demons were discussed by Robert Chard in "The Spirit Whirlwind in Early China," a paper presented to the annual meeting of the Association for Asian Studies in Boston in March 1994.

20. See Cook 1994. Riegel (1989) identifies Gou Mang and Ru Shou as tutelary gods of the east and west, respectively, and considers them to be precursor deities to Dong Wang Gong and Xi Wang Mu. Allan (1979, 1991) has written about Shang roots of later Chinese divinities. For a modern overview of early Chinese mythology, see Birrell 1993. See also Sukhu, chapter 9, especially n. 55.

21. For a study of snake motifs in Shang art, see Munsterberg 1986.

22. Pankenier 1981–1982.

23. Major 1986.

24. Liu Dunyuan 1982.

25. For the dragon and tiger as paired icons, see, for example, Dièny 1987, 229.

26. Snake handling as a sign of divine protection is found in many societies; familiar modern examples include the Hopi and Zuni Pueblo cultures of the American southwest and certain Pentecostal Christian sects of the southern Appalachians.

27. Major 1993, 199.

28. For serpent-bodied deities in the *Huainanzi* and cognate texts, see Major 1993, e.g., 204–206.

29. Both vessels are illustrated in Munsterberg 1986, 202, 209, 175. See also Hentze 1953, fig. 3. Jenny So comments (private communication), "We have increasing evidence to support a southern provenance for [these] Freer bronzes . . . the *he* from Hunan or environs, the *guang* from southwest Shaanxi or environs." It is not immediately clear to me how this information should be evaluated, but it would seem to indicate both that an interest in serpentine motifs in cultures in the Yangtze Basin is very ancient, and that "southern" religious

ideas, including an interest in serpentine motifs, had some impact on Shang ritual practices and religious beliefs.

30. Salmony 1954.

31. Childs-Johnson 1994, 1995. It is not clear to what extent, if any, the Chu antler-and-tongue figures are related to the much earlier, presumptively Ba culture, figures from Sanxingdui, Sichuan (see Rawson 1996, 60–69); certain formal features, most especially an emphasis on large and sometimes protruding eyes, suggest that a research project into the possible relationship between the Sanxingdui and Chu figures might yield interesting results.

32. Hentze 1953; Li Ling 1992. This use of the cicada is found in Shang symbolism of transformation; see Childs-Johnson 1995.

33. This motif can be seen in an amazingly wide range of contexts, from the Paleolithic cave paintings of southern France to the Gundestrup Bowl (discovered in Denmark but probably of Thracian manufacture), to the Sythian burials at Pazyryk and Noin-Ula, to ethnographic materials on Siberian and Korean shamanism collected within the last century.

34. Childs-Johnson 1995.

35. Lewis 1990, 145–152.

36. K. C. Chang 1976a.

37. Cartmill 1993.

38. Childs-Johnson 1996; Campbell 1988, 147–179; see the photo in Campbell (151) of a Siberian bear cult, where the corpse of a sacrificed bear is being ritually offered some of its own flesh to eat. On the relationship between hunting and sacrifice, see also Burket 1983, e.g., 47: "For the ancient world, hunting, sacrifice, and warfare were symbolically interchangeable." See also Riegel 1982.

39. *Zuozhuan,* Duke Yin, year 5, quoted in Lewis 1990, 18. See also Childs-Johnson 1995.

40. Major 1993, 247, 256.

41. Murrowchick 1994; see especially K. C. Chang 1994 in that volume.

42. Among other issues, some scholars have debated whether the word *wu* can properly be translated as "shaman"; Mair 1990 traces the word to the Persian "magus." Other scholars argue for a gender component in shamanism, proposing, for example, that *wu* means "shamanka," while *ling* means "shaman." (On this view, the many *wu* whose names are recorded in Warring States and Han texts would of course have to be seen as female, which would entail some serious rethinking of early Chinese religion).

43. Hultkrantz 1973.

44. Childs-Johnson's persuasive arguments for at least some Shang rites as *masked* performances, however, force a reconsideration of the character of these sacrificial and divinatory rituals; see Childs-Johnson 1994, 1995.

45. Hawkes 1985; Waley 1955.

46. Fung 1994, 55. See also So's discussion of incense and censers in Chu culture in chapter 3; also Peters, chapter 7, note 106. The Chu fondness for incense may hint at a ritual use by shamans of psychoactive smoke on appropriate occasions.

47. K. C. Chang 1994.

48. See, for example, So 1995, Introduction, 20.

49. Lubo-Lesnichenko 1989. I am grateful to Jenny So (private communication) for some of this information. See So and Bunker 1995 for details on the items discussed in this paragraph; the same book (n. 70–71) discusses tuning keys for *qin* stringed instruments with northern and Achaemenid motifs.

50. Major 1978.

51. Victor Mair, private communication, and Mair 1993; Barber 1999.

52. Paper 1995.

53. The nature of these "lewd" rites has been an important focus of Cook's research; see, for example, Cook 1990, 272–274. See also Sukhu, chapter 9.

54. Cavalli-Svorza 1991.

55. Hentze 1953; several of the contributors to Barnard and Fraser 1972.

56. Schafer 1977 uses the term "farflight" to translate *zhaoyao*, a pair of stars at the end of the Northern Dipper that served as the dipper's pointer in its function as a celestial time dial; I adopt the same word here to refer to celestial spirit journeys.
57. Fracasso 1985; see also Major 1993, 201.
58. Yü Ying-shih 1965; Loewe 1979.
59. Roth 1991.
60. Major 1993, 8–14; see also Roth 1991 and Csikszentmihalyi 1994, 7–24 ff.
61. Li Ling 1991b; Field 1992.
62. See Major 1993, 92–94, 106–108, 118–120, etc.
63. Field 1992. I will explore these links further in my forthcoming book, *Essays on the Huainanzi*.
64. Major 1993, 35, and fig. 2.4.
65. I will explore these cosmographic issues further in essays on visualizing the round heaven and square earth and on the cosmic pillar in my forthcoming book, *Essays on the Huainanzi*.
66. Cullen 1993.
67. Pankenier 1992.
68. Ecke 1994.
69. See Cahill 1993; also n. 13 above.
70. Fracasso 1985.
71. Riegel 1989.
72. Cahill 1993.

9. Monkeys, Shamans, Emperors, and Poets: The *Chuci* and Images of Chu during the Han Dynasty

1. Hawkes 1985, 39.
2. See *Chuci Buzhu* 1983, 1.
3. Hawkes 1985, 28.
4. *Shiji*, 1985 ed., *Juan* 7: 300. See also Burton Watson 1961, 72.
5. Translation by Burton Watson 1961, 140.
6. *Shiji*, 1985 ed., 2047.
7. Ibid., 2721.
8. Burton Watson 1961, 86.
9. *Shiji*, 1985 ed., 2722.
10. Ibid., 2723.
11. Ibid., 2722.
12. *Han Shu*, 1983 ed., *Juan* 1B:215a: 59.
13. *Shiji*, 1985 ed., 2722.
14. *Lüshi chunqiu*, vol. 6, ch. 10 ("I bao"), 101.
15. Hawkes 1985, 18.
16. *Shiji*, 1985 ed., ch. 28, 1378.
17. Ibid., 1355, "Feng shan shu."
18. *Shiji*, 1985 ed., 1378.
19. Ibid., *Juan* 122: 3143. See also Burton Watson 1961, 315–316; and *Han Shu, Juan* 64.
20. According to *Han Shu* 6.19b: "In the New Territories of Nanyang there was a certain Bao Lizhang who ran afoul the law in the time of Emperor Wu and was sent to the garrison farms at Dunhuang. Several times along the banks of the Wo Wei River he saw wild horses, among whom there was a strange one, different from all the rest, drinking the waters of the river. Lizhang first made a man of clay, in the hand of which he put a bridle, along the banks of the river. Later the horse began playing around the figure and eventually became accustomed to it. After a long while Lizhang took the place of the clay man, took the horse, and offered it as tribute to the emperor. In order to make the horse seem supernatural he claimed that it had

emerged from the river." See also Loewe's discussion of the hymn to the "Heavenly Horses," etc., event in Loewe 1987, 196–199.

21. See Loewe 1987, 196, n. 11.

22. This first line I have translated from the text quoted in the *Yueshu* section of the *Shiji*, 1985 ed., 1178. The *Han Shu, Liyuezhi*, 22.26b has, instead of "the Grand Unity offers tribute" (*Taiyigong*), "the Grand Unity bestows" (*Taiyikuang*), a difference I will discuss later.

23. See Loewe 1987, preface.

24. Loewe 1987, 199.

25. *Shiji*, 1985 ed., 1178.

26. Ibid., 1385.

27. Ibid., *Juan* 23: 1157.

28. *Lunyu*, LYZY ed., *juan* 4: 59. See also Waley 1938, 98.

29. Xunzi, translation in Burton Watson 1963, 110.

30. *Shiji*, 1985 ed., 1170.

31. *Yuefu shiji*, 4.

32. See Cook, chapter 5; also Cook 1990, 271–275.

33. *Guanzi*, GZJZ ed., 6.

34. See translation in Knechtges 1968, 8–9.

35. *Wen Xuan*, zhuan 60, 1303.

36. See *Han Shu*, ch. 44, 1025, "Huainan Hengshan Jibei Wang zhuan."

37. It seems likely, as many scholars have suggested, that the quote from the *Li sao zhuan* was interpolated into the *Shiji* not by Sima Qian but by a later hand. The *Li sao zhuan*, according to the *Han Shu*, was being composed around the same time the *Shiji* was being written. It is therefore unlikely that Sima Qian had access to the *Li sao zhuan*. This would explain why it is mentioned in the *Han Shu* biography of the prince of Huainan and not the earlier *Shiji* version. See Tang Bingzheng 1985, 19; see also Hawkes 1985, 51–66.

38. Quoted in *Chuci buzhu*, 49.

39. Ibid., 48.

40. *Shiji*, 1985 ed., *Juan* 84: 2482; cf. Hawkes 1985, 55–56.

41. See Chow Tse-tsung 1968, 155.

42. See translation in Birch 1965, 95.

43. See *Han Shu* 18.10b and 25A.27a.

44. Loewe 1987, 37–90.

45. See *Han Shu* 22.26 and *Shiji* 24.7.

46. See Waley 1955, 12; and *Hou Han Shu* 83.15a.

47. This refers to King Huai of Chu, not the much later prince of Huainan, Liu An.

48. "*Lan*" is sometimes (mis)translated as "orchid"; "Pepper and Lan" here refers to loyal and upright officials, who on the complex imagery of the poem are given floral names.

49. *Chuci buzhu*, 49.

50. Ibid., 2–3.

51. Pauline Yu 1987: 47-48.

52. *Chuci buzhu*, 52.

53. Pauline Yu 1987, 108–111.

54. Hawkes 1985, 68.

55. Most specialists in the field agree that Zhu Rong was the ancestral spirit of the Chu royal house. In the *Shiji*, in the section on the Chu hereditary house, it says, "The ancestors of Chu originate from Zhuan Xu Gao Yang. Gao Yang was the grandson of Huang Di, and the son of Chang Yi. Gao Yang begat Cheng. Cheng begat Juan Zhang. Juan Zhang begat Chong Li. Chong Li occupied the office of Governor of Fire for Di Ku Gao Xin and had very great accomplishments. He was able to light and warm [*rong*] the world. Di Ku

named him Zhu Rong. When Gong Gong rebelled, Di Ku sent Chong Li to punish him but he [Chong Li] did not complete the mission. So Di Ku punished Chong Li on the *geng-yin* day, made his younger brother Wu Hui his descendant, and appointed him to the post of Governor of Fire, and he [Wu Hui] became Zhu Rong." From this passage we learn that Zhu Rong is a designation, like Gao Yang, that is not limited to one person. In a recently discovered Bao Shan bamboo manuscript, Zhu Rong figures as one of the distant ancestors of Chu called upon in divination. This would of course make him the distant ancestor of Qu Yuan, if there was a Qu Yuan. See Wang Guanghao 1988, 6–20.

56. *Chuci buzhu,* 4.

57. *Chuci buzhu,* 31.

Appendix: Translation of the Chu Silk Manuscript

This introduction has been abstracted by Cook from Li Ling, *Reconsidering the Chu Silk Manuscript,* draft ms., May 15, 1994. The English translation was initially revised by Michael Puett, then further revised by Constance Cook in consultation with John Major.

1. For more on the *shi,* see Major, chapter 8. See also Li Ling 1991b; Field 1992; and Major 1993, 39–43.

2. *Beidou* is the familiar Big Dipper constellation in Ursa Major. For the Dipper as the "hand" of a celestial "clock," see Major 1993, 88–94, 106–108.

3. Obliterated or untranslatable text is marked in the translation with ellipses. The numbers following the ellipses indicate the number of missing graphs. Words with unclear or debated meanings are marked with question marks. Words not in the Chinese text (missing but obvious from the context) are bracketed, as are words or phrases added in English to clarify the meaning of the Chinese text. Words or phrases added solely for the purpose of making the Chinese text read smoothly in English are placed in parentheses. For detailed annotations of the text, readers are referred to Li Ling 1985 and additional comments in a forthcoming article by Li Ling in *Guwenzi yanjiu.*

4. Li Ling follows Li Xueqin's understanding of the word *run,* used here as a verb (and therefore not in the sense of the adjective, which when modifying the word "month" refers to "an intercalary month" [i.e., an extra month in a leap year]); see Li Xueqin 1982 (eds.)

5. This is a reference to the sequential growth and waning of yin and yang.

6. The Nine Heavens, like the Nine Continents of Earth, were envisioned as being divided into nine equal regions, not as nine tiers (as commonly conceived). See *Huainanzi,* ch. 3, "The Treatise on the Patterns of Heaven"; and Major 1993, 69–71.

7. See n. 4 above for the translation of *run* as a verb meaning "to keep still"; that sense, however, does not necessarily seem appropriate here. This sentence is fragmentary and difficult to interpret. (eds.)

8. For the interpretation of *qie* as "monkey," see Cook 1994, 6.

9. An opening would include such activities as the digging of a well or the making of doors or windows.

Bibliography

Abbreviations

BEFEO	*Bulletin d'École Français d'Êxtreme-Orient*
BMFEA	*Bulletin of the Museum of Far Eastern Antiquities*
BSOAS	*Bulletin of the School of Oriental and African Studies*
EC	*Early China*
HKJ	*Hunan kaogu jikan* 湖南考古輯刊
HJAS	*Harvard Journal of Asiatic Studies*
HXKG	*Huaxia kaogu* 華夏考古
JAS	*Journal of Asian Studies*
JAOS	*Journal of the American Oriental Society*
JESHO	*Journal of the Economic and Social History of the Orient*
JHKG	*Jianghan kaogu* 江漢考古
JHLT	*Jianghan luntan* 江漢論壇
JZSZXB	*Jingzhou shizhuan xuebao* 荆州師專學報
KG	*Kaogu* 考古
KGTX	*Kaogu tongxun* 考古通訊
KGXB	*Kaogu xuebao* 考古學報
KGXJ	*Kaoguxue jikan* 考古學集刊
TP	*T'oung Pao* 通報
WW	*Wenwu* 文物
WWZLCK	*Wenwu ziliao congkan* 文物資料叢刊
WY	*Wenwu yanjiu* 文物研究
ZYWW	*Zhongyuan wenwu* 中原文物

Allan, Sarah. 1979. "Shang Foundations of Modern Chinese Folk Religions." In Sarah Allan and Alvin P. Cohen, eds., *Legend, Lore and Religion in China*. San Francisco: Chinese Materials Center.

———. 1981. *The Heir and the Sage: Dynastic Legend in Early China*. Taibei: Chinese Materials Center.

———. 1991. *The Shape of the Turtle: Myth, Art, and Cosmos in Early China*. Albany: State University of New York Press.

An Zhimin 安志敏. 1973. "Changsha xinfaxian di Xi Han bohua shitan" 長沙新發現的西漢帛畫試探. *KG* 1973.1: 43–53.

Anhui Fuyang diqu zhanlanguan wenbozu 安徽阜陽地區展覽館文博組. 1978. "Anhui Fengtai faxian Chuguo 'Ying dafu' tongliang" 安徽風台發現楚國'郢大腐'銅量. *WW* 1978.5: 96.

Anhuisheng Huaining xian wenguansuo 安徽省懷寧縣文管所. 1983. "Anhui Huaining chutu Chunqiu qingtongqi" 安徽懷寧出土春秋青銅器. *WW* 1983.11: 68–71.

Anhuisheng wenhuaju wenwu gongzuodui 安徽省文化局文物工作隊. 1963. "Anhui Huainanshi Caijiagang Zhaojia gudui Zhanguo mu" 安徽淮南市蔡家崗趙家孤堆戰國墓. *KG* 1963.4: 204–212.

———. 1964. "Anhui Shucheng chutu di tongqi" 安徽舒城出土的銅器. *KG* 1964.10: 498–503.

Anhuisheng wenwu gongzuodui fanchengxian wenhua guan 安徽省文物工作隊繁昌縣文化館. 1979. "Anhui wenwu kaogu gongzuo xin shouhuo" 安徽文物考古工作新收獲. In Wenwu bianji weiyuanhui 1979: 229–239.

———. 1982a. "Anhui Changfeng Yanggong fajue jiu zuo Zhanguo mu" 安徽長丰楊公發掘九座戰國墓. *KGXJ* 1982.2: 47–60.

———. 1982b. "Anhui Fanchang chutu yipi Chunqiu qingtonqi" 安徽繁昌出土一批春秋青銅器. *WW* 1982.12: 47–50.

Anhuisheng wenwu guanli weiyuanhui 安徽省文物管理委員會 and Anhuisheng bowuguan 安徽省博物館. 1956. *Shouxian Cai Hou mu chutu yiwu* 壽縣蔡侯墓出土遺物. Beijing: Science Press, 1956.

Anhuisheng wenwu kaogu yanjiusuo 安徽省文物考古研究所. 1987. "Shucheng Fenghuangzui faxian liang zuo Zhanguo XiHan mu" 舒城鳳凰嘴發現兩座戰國西漢墓. *KG* 1987.8: 723–727.

Archaeology Department, Peking University. 1992. *Treasures from a Swallow Garden*. Beijing: Wenwu Press.

Aurousseau, Leonard. 1923. "La Première conquête chinoise des pays annamite." *BEFEO* 23: 10–263.

Bagley, Robert W. 1987. *Shang Ritual Bronzes in the Arthur M. Sackler Collections*. Cambridge: Harvard University Press.

———. 1993. "An Early Bronze Age Tomb in Jiangxi Province." *Orientations*, 20–36.

Bai Guanxi 白冠西. 1957. "Yingyuan kaoshi" 郢爰考釋. *KGTX* 1957.1: 112–115.

Bai Yue minzu yanjiu weiyuanhui, 白越民族研究委員會 ed. 1985. *Bai Yue minzu shi luncong* 百越民族史論叢. Guangxi Renmin Press.

Bamboo annals. See *Zhushu jinian*.

Baoshan mudi zhujian zhengli xiaozu 包山墓地竹簡整理小組. 1988. "Baoshan erhao mu zhujian gaishu" 包山二號墓竹簡概述. *WW* 1988.5: 25–29.

Barber, Elizabeth Wayland. 1999. *The Mummies of Ürümchi*. New York: W. W. Norton.

Barnard, Noel. 1959. "New Approaches and Research Methods in Chin-Shi-Hsüeh." *Memoirs of the Institute for Oriental Culture* 19: 1–31.

———. 1972. "The Ch'u Silk Manuscript and Other Archaeological Documents of Ancient China." In Barnard and Fraser, 77–102.

———. 1974. *The Origin and Nature of the Art of Ancient Ch'u* (Studies on the Ch'u Silk Manuscript, 3). Canberra: Australian National University Monographs on Far Eastern History 6.

———. 1976. *Ancient Chinese Bronzes and Southeast Asian Metal and Other Archaeological Artifacts*. Melbourne: National Gallery of Victoria.

Barnard, Noel, and Donald Fraser, eds. 1972. *Early Chinese Art and Its Possible Influence in the Pacific Basin*. 3 vols. New York: Intercultural Arts Press.

Beijing. 1954. *Chu wenwu zhanlan tulu* 楚文物展覽圖錄. Beijing: Historical Museum.

———. 1962. *Archaeology of New China*. Wenwu Press.

———. 1972a. *Wenhua dageming qijian chutu wenwu* 文化大革命期間出土文物, ed. by the work team for the exhibition of excavated cultural relics. Vol. 1. Beijing: Wenwu Press.

———. 1972b. *Historical Relics Unearthed in New China*. Beijing: Wenwu Press.

———. 1973. *Changsha Mawangdui yihao Han mu* 長沙馬王堆一號漢墓. Beijing: Wenwu Press.

———. 1980. *Shaanxi chutu Shang Zhou qingtongqi* 陝西出土商周青銅器. Vol. 2. Beijing: Wenwu Press.

———. 1984. *Jiangling Yutaishan Chu mu* 江陵雨台山楚墓. Beijing: Wenwu Press.

———. 1985. *Jiangling Mashan yihao Chu mu* 江陵馬山一號楚墓. Beijing: Wenwu Press.

———. 1986. *Xinyang Chu mu* 信陽楚墓. Beijing: Wenwu Press.

———. 1989. *Zeng Hou Yi mu* 曾侯乙墓. 2 vols. Beijing: Wenwu Press.

———. 1990. *Wenwu jinghua* 文物精華. Beijing: Wenwu Press.

———. 1991a. *Xichuan Xiasi Chunqiu Chu mu* 淅川下寺春秋楚墓. Beijing: Wenwu Press.

———. 1991b. *Baoshan Chu mu* 包山楚墓. 2 vols. Beijing: Wenwu Press.

———. 1991c. *Baoshan Chujian* 包山楚簡. Beijing: Wenwu Press.

Bellingwood, Peter. 1991. "The Austronesian Dispersal and the Origin of Languages." *Scientific American*, July 1991, 88–93.

Biot, E., trans. 1851. *Le Tcheou-li*. 3 vols. Paris.

Birch, Cyril. 1965. *Anthology of Chinese Literature*. New York: Grove Press.

Birrell, Anne. 1993. *Chinese Mythology: An Introduction*. Baltimore and London: The Johns Hopkins University Press.

Blakeley, Barry. 1976. "Notes on the Feudal Interpretation of China." *EC* 2: 35–37.

———. 1977. "Functional Disparities in the Socio-Political Traditions of Spring and Autumn China. Part I: Lu and Ch'i." *JESHO* 20(2): 208–241.

———. 1979a. "Functional Disparities in the Socio-Political Traditions of Spring and Autumn China. Part II: Chou, Sung, Cheng." *JESHO* 20(3): 307–343.

———. 1979b. "Functional Disparities in the Socio-Political Traditions of Spring and Autumn China. Part III: Ch'u and Ch'in." *JESHO* 22(1): 82–118.

———. 1983. *Annotated Genealogies of Spring and Autumn Period*. Taibei: Chinese Materials Center.

———. 1985–1987. "Recent Developments in Chu Studies: A Bibliographic and Institutional Overview." *EC* 11–12: 371–387.

———. 1988. "In Search of Danyang." *EC* 13: 116–152.

———. 1990. "On the Location of the Chu Capital in Early Chunqiu Times in Light of the Handong Incident of 701 B.C." *EC* 15: 49–70.

———. 1992a. "A Chu Studies Update." *Early China News* 5: 1, 3–5.

———. 1992b. "King, Clan and Courtier in Ch'u Court Politics." *Asia Major* ser. III, 2: 1–39.

Blakeley, Barry, and Xu Shaohua. Forthcoming. "The Origins of the *Xian* Revisited: Local Government in Spring and Autumn Period Ch'u."

Bodde, Derk. 1961. "Myths of Ancient China." In Samuel Noah Kramer, ed., *Mythologies of the Ancient World*. New York: Doubleday and Co., Inc.

———. 1981. *Essays on Chinese Civilization*, ed. Charles Le Blanc and Dorothy Borei. Princeton: Princeton University Press.

———. 1991. *Chinese Thought, Society, and Science*. Honolulu: University of Hawai'i Press.

Broman, Sven. 1961. "Studies on the Chou-li." *BMFEA* 33: 1–89.

Brooks, E. Bruce, and A. Taeko Brooks. 1998. *The Original Analects: Sayings of Confucius and His Successors*. New York: Columbia University Press.

Bulling, Annaliese. 1960. *The Decoration of Mirrors of the Han Period*. Ascona, Switzerland: Artibus Asiae.

———. 1974. "The Guide of the Souls Picture in the Western Han Tomb in Ma-Wang-Tui near Ch'ang-sha." *Oriental Art* 20: 158–173.

Bunker, Emma C. 1993. "Gold in the Ancient Chinese World: A Cultural Puzzle." *Artibus Asiae* 53 (1, 2): 27–50.

Burket, Walter. 1983. *Homo Necans: The Anthropology of Ancient Greek Sacrificial Ritual and Myth*. Berkeley: University of California Press.

Cahill, Suzanne. 1993. *Transcendence and Divine Passion: The Queen Mother of the West in Medieval China*. Stanford: Stanford University Press.

Cai Jingquan 蔡靖泉. 1991. "Chuguo di Moao zhi guan yu Qushi zhi zu" 楚國的莫傲之官與屈氏之族. *JHLT* 1991.2: 70–74.

Cammann, Schuyler. 1948. "The 'TLV' Pattern on the Cosmic Mirrors of the Han Dynasty." *JAOS* 68: 159–167.

Campbell, Joseph. 1988. *Historical Atlas of World Mythology*. Vol. 1: *The Way of the Animal Powers*. Part 2: *Mythologies of the Great Hunt*. New York: Harper and Row.

Cao Guicen 曹桂岑. 1981. "Chudu Chencheng kao" 楚都陳城考. *ZYWW*. Special issue: 37–40.

———. 1983. "Shi tan Chuguo huobi" 試探楚國貨幣. In Henansheng kaoguxuehui 河南省考古學會編, eds., *Chu wenhua yanjiu lunwen ji* 楚文化研究論文集. Zhongzhou shuhua Press, 124–139.

———. 1989. "Henan Chu wenhua di faxian yu yanjiu" 河南楚文化的發現與研究. *HXKG* 1989.3: 63–67.

———. 1992a. "Henan Xichuan Heshangling Xujialing Chu mu fajueji" 河南淅川何尚嶺徐家嶺楚墓發掘記. *Wenwu tiandi* 文物天地 1992.6: 10–12.

———. 1992b. "Henan Xichuan Chunqiu Chumu jiankao" 河南淅川春秋楚墓簡考. *Zhongguo wenwu bao* 中國文物報, Sept. 18, 1992: 3.

Cartmill, Matt. 1993. *A View to a Death in the Morning: Hunting and Nature through History*. Cambridge: Harvard University Press.

Cavalli-Svorza, Luigi L. 1991. "Genes, Peoples, and Languages." *Scientific American,* November 1991: 104–110.

Chan, Ping-leung. 1962. "*Ch'u Tz'u* and Shamanism in Ancient China." Ph.D. dissertation, Ohio State University.

Chang, K. C. 1959. "A Working Hypothesis for the Early Cultural History of South China" (English summary). *Bulletin of the Institute of Ethnology, Academia Sinica* 7: 75–103.

———. 1972. "Major Aspects of Ch'u Archaeology." In Barnard and Fraser, vol. 1, 5–52.

———. 1974a. "Urbanism and the King in Ancient China." *World Archaeology* 6(1): 1–14.

———. 1974b. "Food and Food Vessels in Ancient China." *Transactions of the New York Academy of Sciences*. Second series, 35: 495–520.

———. 1976a. *Early Chinese Civilization: Anthropological Perspectives*. Cambridge: Harvard University Press.

———. 1976b. "Towns and Cities in Ancient China." In K. C. Chang 1976a, 61–71.

———. 1976c. "A Classification of Shang and Chou Myths." In K. C. Chang 1976a, 155–173.

———. 1977. *The Archaeology of Ancient China*. 3d ed. New Haven: Yale University Press.

———. 1980. *Shang Civilization*. New Haven: Yale University Press.

———. 1983. *Art, Myth, and Ritual: The Path to Political Authority in Ancient China*. Cambridge: Harvard University Press.

———. 1986. *The Archaeology of Ancient China*. 4th ed. New Haven: Yale University Press.

———. 1994. "Ritual and Power." In Murrowchick, 60–69.

Chang Yuzhi 常玉芝. 1987. *Shangdai zhouji zhidu* 商代周祭制度. Beijing: Zhongguo shehui kexue chubanshe.

Changsha tielu chezhan jianshe gongcheng zhihuibu wenwu fajuedui 長沙鐵路車站建設工程支會部文物發掘隊. 1978. "Changsha xin faxian Chunqiu wanqi di gang, jian he tie qi" 長沙新發現春秋晚期的鋼, 劍和鐵器. *WW* 1978.10: 44–48.

Chen Changyuan 陳昌遠. 1985. "'Zhou Gong ben Chu' kao" 周公奔楚考. *Shixue yuekan* 史學月刊 1985.5: 15–19.

Chen Hanping 陳漢平. 1986. *Xi-Zhou ceming zhidu yanjiu* 西周冊命制度研究. Shanghai: Xuelin.

Chen Quanfang 陳全方. 1988. *Zhouyuan yu Zhou wenhua* 周原與周文化. Shanghai: Shanghai Renmin chubanshe.

Chen Wei 陳偉. 1983. "Xichuan Xiasi erhao Chumu muzhu ji xiangguan wenti" 淅川下寺二號楚墓墓主及相關問題. *JHKG* 1983.1: 32–33, 38.

———. 1993. "Guanyu Baoshan 'Shouqi' jian di dujie" 關於包山 "受期" 簡的讀解. *JHKG* 1993.1: 74–79.

———. 1994. "Baoshan Chu sifajian 131–139 hao kaoxi" 包山楚司法簡 131–139 號考析. *JHKG* 1994.4: 67–71, 66.

———. 1995a. "Baoshan zhujian suojian Chuguo di xian jun yu fengyi" 包山竹簡所見楚國的縣郡與封邑. In *Changjiang wenhua lunji* 長江文化論集. Wuhan: Hubei jiaoyu chubanshe, 339–346.

———. 1995b. "Baoshan Chujian suojian yi li zhou di chubu yanjiu" 包山楚簡所見邑里州的初步研究. *Wuhan daxue xuebao* 武漢大學學報 1995.1: 90–98.

———. 1995c. "Guanyu Baoshan 'Shuyu' jian di jige wenti" 關於包山"疋獄"簡的幾個問題. *JHKG* 1995.3: 75–79.

———. 1996a. *Baoshan Chujian chutan* 包山楚簡初探. Wuhan: Wuhan University Press.

———. 1996b. "Guanyu Baoshan Chujian suojian di sifa zhidu" 關於包山楚簡所見的司法制度. Paper presented at the conference Dong Zuobin xiansheng bainian danchen jinian wenzixue guoji xueshu yanjiuhui.

Chen Wenxue 陳文學. 1991. "Chunqiu Zhanguo shiqi Chu Ba guanxi shitan" 春秋戰國時期楚霸關係試探. *JHKG* 1991.2: 57–60.

Chen Xianyi 陳賢一. 1980a. "Jinancheng Nanyuan Shuimen mugou jianzhu di fajue" 紀南城南垣水門木构建筑的發掘. In Hubeisheng bowuguan 1980b, 36–50.

———. 1980b. "Jiangling Zhangjiashan yizhi di shijue yu tansuo" 江陵張家山遺址的試掘與探索. *JHKG* 1980.2: 77–86.

Chen Yaojun 陳耀鈞. 1980. "Shilun Jiangling Chumu di tedian" 試論江陵楚墓的特點. *JHKG* 1980.2: 31–35.

Chen Zhenyu 陳振裕. 1979. "Wangshan yihao mu di niandai yu muzhu" 望山一號墓的年代與墓主. In Wenwu bianji weiyuan hui 1979, 229–236.

———. 1981. "Luelun jiuzuo Chu mu di niandai" 略論九座楚墓的年代. *KG* 1981.4: 319–331.

———. 1992. "Dong Zhou Chucheng di leixing chuxi" 東周楚城的類型初析. *JHKG* 1992.1: 61–70, 10.

———. 1993. "Dong Zhou Chucheng di bijiao yanjiu" 東周楚城的比較研究. *JHKG* 1993.1: 51–60.

Chen Zhongfu 陳忠富. 1980. "Yi Cheng 'Chu Huang Cheng' yizhi di jige wenti" 宜城"楚皇城"遺址的幾個問題. *JHLT* 1980.5: 85–86, 92.

Chen Zuquan 陳祖全. 1980a. "1979 nian Jinancheng gujing fajue jianbao" 一九七九年紀南城古井發掘簡報. *WW* 1980.10: 42–49.

———. 1980b. Jinancheng 1979 nian gujing di fajue 紀南城一九七九年古井的發掘. In Hubeisheng bowuguan 1980b, 88–94.

Cheng Xinren 程欣人. 1964. "Hubei Xiaogan Yezhu Hu Zhong faxian dapi Chuguo tongbei" 湖北孝感野豬湖中發現大批楚國銅貝. *KG* 1964.7: 369.

Childs-Johnson, Elizabeth. 1984. "Relationship between Symbolism and Function in Ritual Bronze Art of the Shang: New Archaeological and Bone Inscriptional Evidence." Ph.D. dissertation, New York University, Institute of Fine Arts, 1984.

———. 1988. "Dragons, Masks, Axes and Blades from Four Newly-documented Jade-producing Cultures of Ancient China." *Orientations,* April, 1988, 30–41.

———. 1994. "The Ghost Head Mask and Metamorphic Shang Imagery: A Prolegomenon to the Study of Oracle Bone Evidence for Exorcism, Spirit Invocation and Related Shamanic Practices." *EC* 20: 79–92.

———. 1995. "The Demon Who Devours but Cannot Swallow: Human to Animal Metamorphosis in Shang Ritual Bronze Imagery." In Beijing University Department of Archaeology, eds., *Chinese Archaeology Enters the Twenty-First Century Symposium Papers.* Beijing: Beijing University.

———. 1996. "Metamorphic Imagery in Early Chinese Art: *Long*-Dragons, *Feng*-Phoenixes, *Gui*-Spirit Masks and the Spirit Journey." *Kaikodo Journal,* February, 1998: 30–52.

Chow Tse-tsung. 1968. "The Early History of the Chinese Word *Shih* (Poetry)." In Chow Tse-tsung, ed., *Wen-lin: Studies in the Chinese Humanities.* Madison: University of Wisconsin Press.

Chu Huangcheng kaogu fajuedui 楚皇城考古發掘隊. 1980a. "Hubei Yicheng Chu Huangcheng kancha jianbao" 湖北宜城楚皇城勘查簡報. *KG* 1980.2: 108–113, 134.

———. 1980b. "Hubei Yicheng Chu Huangcheng Zhanguo Qin Han mu" 湖北宜城楚皇城戰國秦漢墓. *KG* 1980.2: 114–122.

Chu wenhua yanjiuhui 楚文化研究會. 1984. *Chu wenhua kaogu dashiji* 楚文化考古大事記. Beijing: Wenwu Press.

———. 1987. *Chu wenhua yanjiu lunji* 楚文化研究論集. Vol 1. Wuhan: Jing Chu shushe.

———. 1991. *Chu wenhua yanjiu lunji* 楚文化研究論集. Vol 2. Wuhan: Hubei Renmin chubanshe.

Chuci buzhu 楚辭補注. 1983. Hong Xingzu 洪興祖, ed. Commentary by Wang Yi, with subcommentary by Hong Xingzu. *Zhongguo gudian wenxue jiben congshe* 中國古典文學基本叢書 edition. Beijing: Zhonghua shuju.

Chun, Allen J. 1990. "Conceptions of Kinship and Kingship in Classical Chou China." *TP* 76: 16–48.

Chunqiu (Spring and Autumn annals). 1907. See *Zuozhuan* 1907 ed.; see also Legge.

Chushi taowu 楚史檮杌. n.d. Wu Yan 吾衍, ed. *Gujin yishi* 古今逸史. In Yan Yiping 嚴一萍, ed., *Baibu congshu jicheng* 9, 2. Taibei: Yiwen Press.

Cohen, Myron. 1970. "Developmental Process in the Chinese Domestic Group." In Maurice Freedman, ed., *Family and Kinship in Chinese Society*. Stanford: Stanford University Press.

Cook, Constance A. 1990. "Auspicious Metals and Southern Spirits: An Analysis of the Chu Bronze Inscriptions." Ph.D. dissertation, University of California, Berkeley.

——. 1993a. "Myth and Authenticity: Deciphering the Chu Gong Ni Bell Inscription." *JAOS* 113(4): 539–550.

——. 1993b. "Ritual Feasting in Ancient China: A Preliminary Study, I." *The Second International Conference Volume on Chinese Paleography*. Hong Kong: The Chinese University of Hong Kong Press, 469–487.

——. 1994. "Three High Gods of Chu." *Journal of Chinese Religions* 22: 1–22.

——. 1995. "Scribes, Cooks, and Artisans: Breaking Zhou Tradition." *EC* 20: 241–277.

——. 1997. "Wealth and the Western Zhou." *BSOAS* 60(2): 253–294.

Creel, Herrlee G. 1964. "The Beginnings of Bureaucracy in China: The Origin of the *Hsien*." *JAS* 23(2): 155–184.

——. 1970. *The Origins of Statecraft in China: The Western Chou Empire*. Chicago: University of Chicago Press.

——. 1980. "Legal Institutions and Procedures during the Chou Dynasty." In Jerome A. Cohen, Randle Edwards, and Fu-Mei Chang Chen, eds., *Essays on China's Legal Traditions*. Princeton: Princeton University Press: 26–55.

Crump, James I., trans. 1970. *Chan-kuo Ts'e*. Oxford: Clarendon Press.

——. 1979. *Chan-kuo Ts'e*. 2d ed., revised. San Francisco: Chinese Materials Center, Inc.

Csikszentmihalyi, Mark. 1994. "Emulating the Yellow Emperor: The Theory and Practice of HuangLao, 180–141 B.C.E." Ph.D. Dissertation, Stanford University.

Cullen, Christopher. 1980. "Some Further Points on the *Shih*." *EC* 6: 31–46.

——. 1981. "The Han Cosmic Model: A Rejoinder to Donald Harper." *EC* 7: 130–133.

——. 1993. "Motivations for Scientific Change in Ancient China: Emperor Wu and the Grand Inception Calendar Reforms of 104 B.C." *Journal of the History of Astronomy* 24: 185–203.

DeWoskin, Kenneth. 1983. *Doctors, Diviners, and Magicians of Ancient China: Biographies of Fang-shih*. New York: Columbia University Press.

Diény, Jean-Pierre. 1987. *Le Symbolisme du dragon dans la Chine antique*. Paris: Collège de France, Institut des Hautes Études Chinoises.

Dong Zuobin 董作賓. 1953. "Yindai di niaoshu" 殷代的鳥書. *Dalu zazhi* 6(11): 345–347.

Du Erwei 杜而未. 1966. *Fenglin guilong kaoshi* 鳳麟龜龍考釋. Taibei: Commercial Press.

Du Naisong 杜迺松. 1981. "Xi Zhou tongqi mingwen zhong di 'de' zi" 西周銅器銘文中的德字. *Gugong bowuyuan yuankan* 故宮博物院院刊. 1981.2: 86–109.

Du Zhengsheng (Tu Cheng-sheng) 杜正勝. 1979. *Zhoudai chengbang* 周代城邦. Taibei: Lianjing Press.

Duan Yu 段渝. 1982. "Chu wei Yin dai nan fu shuo" 楚為殷代南服説. *JHLT* 1982.9: 59–63.

——. 1986. "Lun Zhou Chu zaoqi di guanxi" 論周楚早期的關係. *Shehui kexue yanjiu* 社會科學研究 1986.5: 101–108.

Eberhard, Wolfram. 1968. *The Local Cultures of South and East China*. Leiden: E. J. Brill.

Ecke, Tseng Yuho. 1994. "Cosmic Mirrors." In Toru Nakano et al., *Bronze Mirrors from Ancient China: The Donald H. Graham, Jr. Collection*. Chicago: Paragon Book Gallery Ltd.

Eliade, Mircea. 1964. *Shamanism: Archaic Techniques of Ecstasy*. Trans. by Willard R. Trask. New York: The Bollingen Foundation.

Eno, Robert. 1990. *The Confucian Creation of Heaven*. Albany: State University of New York Press.

Feng Yongxuan 馮永軒. 1981. "Shuo Chu du" 説楚都. *JHKG* 1981.2: 13–21.

Feng Yuhui 馮玉輝. 1984. "Hengyangshi Miaopu, Wuma Guicao, Maoping gumu fajue jianbao" 衡陽市苗圃五馬歸槽茅坪古墓發掘簡報. *KG* 1984.10: 800–886.

Fengsu tongyi tongjian 風俗通義通檢. 1987. Centre franco-chinois d'études sinologiques No. 3. Reprint. Shanghai: Guji shudian.

Field, Stephen. 1992. "Cosmos, Cosmograph, and the Inquiring Poet: New Answers to the 'Heaven Questions.'" *EC* 17: 83–110.

Fong, Mary H. 1991. "Tomb Guardian Figurines: Their Evolution and Iconography." In George Kuwayama, ed., *Ancient Mortuary Traditions of China*. Los Angeles: Los Angeles County Museum of Art, 84–105.

Fong, Wen, ed. 1980. *The Great Bronze Age of China*. New York: Metropolitan Museum of Art.

Fracasso, Riccardo M. 1981. "Manifestazioni del simbolismo assiale nelle tradizioni cinese antiche." *Numen* 28(2): 194–215.

———. 1983. "Teratoscopy or Divination by Monsters: Being a Study on the *Wu-tsang Shan-ching*." *Hanxue yanjiu / Chinese Studies* (Taibei) 1.(2): 657–700.

———. 1985. "Holy Mothers of Ancient China: A New Approach to the Hsi-Wang-Mu Problem." Taibei: mimeograph.

Fu Juyou 傅舉有. 1982. "Zixing jiushi Chunqiu mu" 資興舊市春秋墓. *HKJ* 1982.1: 25–31.

Fu Juyou and Chen Songchang 陳松長. 1992. *Mawangdui Hanmu wenwu* 馬王堆漢墓文物 (added title in English: *The Cultural Relics Unearthed from the Han Tombs at Mawangdui*). Changsha: Hunan Publishing House.

Fung, Christopher. 1994. "The Beginnings of Settled Life." In Murrowchick, 50–59.

Fuyang diqu zhanlanguan 阜陽地區展覽館. 1973. "Anhui Fuyang diqu Chutu di Chuguo jin bi" 安徽阜陽地區出土的楚國金幣. *KG* 1973.3: 162–166, 170.

Gao Zhixi 高至喜. 1972. "Hunan Chumu zhong chutu di tianping yu fama" 湖南楚墓中出土的天平與法馬. *KG* 1972.4: 42–45.

———. 1980a. "Shilun Hunan Chumu di fenqi yu niandai" 試論湖南楚墓的分期與年代. In *Zhongguo kaogu xuehui* 1980, 237–248.

———. 1980b. "Hunan faxian di jijian Yuezu fengge di wenwu" 湖南發現的几件越族風格的文物. *WW* 1980.12: 48–51.

———. 1987a. "Zailun Hunan Chu mu di fenqi yu niandai" 再論湖南楚墓的分期與年代. In Chu wenhua yanjiuhui 1987, 24–34.

———. 1987b. "Churen ruxiang di niandai he Hunan Yue Chu muzang di fenbian" 楚人入湘的年代和湖南越楚墓葬的分辨. *JHKG* 1987.1: 57–63.

———. 1991. "Mawangdui Hanmu di Chu wenhua yinsu fenxi" 馬王堆漢墓的楚文化因素分析. *Hunan bowuguan wenji* 湖南博物館文集. Changsha, 76–81.

Gao Zhixi and Xiong Chuanxin 熊傳新. 1980. "Churen zai Hunan di huodong yiji gaishu" 楚人在湖南的活動遺跡概述. *WW* 1980.10: 50–60.

Girardot, N. J. 1983. *Myth and Meaning in Early Taoism*. Berkeley and Los Angeles: University of California Press.

———. 1976. "The Problem of Creation Mythology in the Study of Chinese Religions." *History of Religions* 15(4): 289–318.

Gong Weiying 龔維英. 1983. "Chu di zuxing you er shuo" 楚的族姓有二説. *JHLT* 1983.1: 78–79.

———. 1984. "Zhou Zhao Wang nan zheng shishi suoyin" 周昭王南征史實索隱. *Renwen zazhi* 人文雜志 1984.6: 81–83, 45.

Goodrich, Chauncey S. 1981–1983. "Ssu-ma Ch'ien's Biography of Wu Ch'i." *Monumenta Serica* 35: 197–233.

Graham, A. C. 1989. *Disputers of the Tao*. LaSalle, Ill.: Open Court Publishing Co.

Granet, Marcel. 1952. *La feodalité chinoise*. Oslo: A. Aschehoug.

Gu Tiefu 顧鐵符. 1954. "Changsha 52.826 hao mu zai kaoguxue shang zhu wenti" 長沙52-826號墓在考古學上諸問題. *WWZLCK* 1954.10: 68–70.

———. 1982. "Jiangnan dui Chuguo di gongxian yu Chuguo di kaifa Jiangnan" 江南對楚國的貢獻與楚國的開發江南. *HKJ* 1982.1: 82–86.

———. 1984. *Chuguo minzu shulue* 楚國民族述略. Hubei: Hubei renmin chubanshe.

———. 1988. *Xiyang chugao* 夕陽芻稿. Beijing: Zijincheng.

Gu Zuyu 雇祖禹. *Dushi fangyu jiyao* 讀史方輿紀要. Vol. I (17th century; various editions).

Guangdongsheng bowuguan 廣東省博物館. 1973. "Guangdong Deqing faxian Zhanguo mu" 廣東德慶發現
戰國墓. *WW* 1973.9: 18–22.

———. 1975. "Guangdong Sihui Niaodanshan Zhanguo mu" 廣東四會鳥旦山戰國墓. *KG* 1975.2: 102–108.

———. 1983. "Guangdong Luoding chutu yipi Zhanguo qingtong qi" 廣東羅定出土一批戰國青銅器. *KG*
1983.1: 43–48.

Guangdongsheng bowuguan et al. 1973. "Guangdong Deqing faxian Zhanguo mu" 廣東德慶發現戰國墓.
WW 1973.9: 18–22.

———. 1986. "Guangdong Luoding Beifushan Zhangguo mu" 廣東羅定背夫山戰國墓. *KG* 1986.3: 210–220.

Guangdongsheng bowuguan, Zhaoqingshi wenhuaju fajue xiaozu 肇慶市文化局發掘小組. 1974. "Guangdong
Zhaoqingshi Beiling Songshan gumu fajue jianbao" 廣東肇慶市北嶺松山古墓發掘簡報. *WW* 1974.11:
69–80.

Guangdongsheng wenwu guanli weiyuanhui et al. 廣東省文物管理委員會. 1963a. "Guangdong Qingyuan
faxian Zhoudai qingtong qi" 廣東清遠發現周代青銅器. *KG* 1963.2: 57–61.

———. 1963b. "Guangdong Shixing Baishiping Shan Zhanguo yizhi" 廣東始興白石坪山戰國遺址. *KG*
1963.4: 217–220.

———. 1964a. "Guangdong Zengcheng, Shixing di Zhanguo yizhi" 廣東增城, 始興的戰國遺址. *KG* 1964.3:
143–151, 160.

———. 1964b. "Guangdong Qingyuan di Dong Zhou muzang" 廣東清遠的東周墓葬. *KG* 1964.3: 138–142.

Guangxi Zhuangzu zizhiqu bowuguan 廣西壯族自治區博物館. 1973. "Guangxi Gongcheng xian chutu di
qingtong qi" 廣西恭城縣出土的青銅器. *KG* 1973.1: 30–34, 41.

———. 1984. "Jinnianlai Guangxi chutu di Xian Qin qingtong qi" 近年來廣西出土的先秦青銅器. *KG*
1984.9: 798–806.

Guangxi Zhuangzu zizhiqu wenwu gongzuodui 廣西壯族自治區文物工作隊. 1978. "Pingle Yinshanling
Zhanguo mu" 平樂銀山嶺戰國墓. *KGXB* 1978.2: 211–250.

———. 1984. "Guangxi Zhuangzu zizhiqu hexian chutu yipi Zhanguo tongqi" 廣西壯族自治區賀縣出土一
批戰國銅器. *KG* 1984.9: 853–854.

Guanzi. 1873 ed. *Guanzi jiaozheng* 管子校正 edition, commentary by Dai Wang 戴望, 1873. Various reprints.

Gulliver, Philip H. 1979. *Disputes and Negotiation: A Cross-Cultural Perspective.* New York: Academic Press.

Guo Dewei 郭德維. 1980. "Zeng Hou Yi mu bingfei Chumu" 曾侯乙墓并非楚墓. *JHLT* 1980.1: 76–79.

———. 1981. "Zeng Hou Yi mu zhong qikuangshang ri, yue he Fuxi, Nügua tuxiang shishi" 曾侯乙墓中漆筐
上日月和伏羲, 女媧圖象試釋. *JHKG* 1981.1: 56–60.

———. 1982. "Jiangling Chu mu zongshu" 江陵楚墓綜述. *KGXB* 1982.2: 155–182.

———. 1983. "Chumu fenlei wenti tantao" 楚墓分類問題探討. *KG* 1983.3: 249–259.

———. 1988. "Shilun Chumu di fenqu" 試論楚墓的分區. Paper presented at the International Scholarly
Conference on Chu History, Wuhan.

Guo Moruo 郭沫若 (alias Mo Shi 末碩). 1940. "Shu Wu Qi" 述吳起. *Dongfang zazhi* 東方雜志 44(1): 38–48.

———. 1957. *Liang Zhou jinwenci daxi tulu kaoshi* 兩周金文辭大系圖錄考釋. Beijing: Science Press.

Guo Shengbin 郭勝斌. 1991. "Lun kaoguxue Chu wenhua di wenhua goucheng" 論考古學楚的文化構成. In
Hunansheng bowuguan 1991, 64–71.

Guoyu 國語 (Discourses of the states). Traditionally said to be compiled by Zuo Qiuming during the Chunqiu
period. Probably anonymously compiled during the third and fourth centuries BCE.

———. SBBY ed. *Sibu beiyao* ed. Reprinted. Taibei: Zhonghua shuju, 1966.

———. 1987 ed. *Guoxue jiben* ed. Shanghai: Xinhua shuju.

Han Feizi 韓非子 (The book of Master Fei from the state of Han). Compiled by the followers of Han Feizi (d.
233 BCE) 1960 edition: *Han zi qianjie*, ed. Liang Qixiong. Zhonghua shuju. 2 Vols. Beijing: Xinhua shudian.

———. SBBY ed. *Sibu beiyao* ed. Reprinted. Taibei: Zhonghua shuju, 1966.

Han shu 漢書 (Book of Han; History of the former Han dynasty). Compiled by Ban Gu 班固 (ca. 82 CE).

———. 1975 ed. Zhonghua Shuju ed. 中華書局出版. Beijing: Xinhua Shudian.

———. 1983 ed. Zhonghua Shuju ed. 中華書局出版. Beijing: Xinhua Shudian.

Han Weizhou. 1956. "Henan Xixiaxian ji Nanyangshi liang gucheng diaocha ji." *KGTX* 1956.2: 46–50.

Hao Benxing 郝本性. 1983. "Shouxian Chuqi jidou zhuming kaoshi" 壽縣楚器集脰諸銘考釋. *Guwenzi yanjiu* 古文字研究 1983.10: 205–213.

Harper, Donald J. 1978. "The Han Cosmic Board (*Shih*)." *EC* 4: 1–10.

———. 1980. "The Han Cosmic Board: A Response to Christopher Cullen." *EC* 6: 47–56.

———. 1985. "A Chinese Demonography of the Third Century B.C." *HJAS* 45: 459–498.

Hawkes, David. 1985. *Ch'u Tz'u: The Songs of the South.* 2d ed. Harmondsworth, England: Penguin Books, 1985.

Hayashi, Minao 林巳奈夫. 1967. "Chugoku kodai no shinpu" 楚國古代の神巫. *Tōhō gakuhō* 東方學報 (Kyoto) 38: 199–224.

———. 1972. "The Twelve Gods of the Chan-kuo Period Silk Manuscript Excavated at Ch'ang-sha." In Barnard and Fraser, Vol. 1, 123–186.

———. 1973. "Kan kyo no zuhyo ni, san ni tsuite" 漢鏡の圖柄二三について. *Tōhō gakuhō* 東方學報 (Kyoto) 44: 1–65.

———. 1984. "Iwayuru 'taotie' mon wa nani o arawashita mono ka" 所謂饕餮文は何を表はしたぢのか? *Tōhō gakuhō* 東方學報 (Kyoto) 56: 1–97.

He Chongen 何崇恩. 1985. "Ping Wu Qi ji 'Wuzi'" 評吳起及 "吳子." *Xiangtan daxue xuebao* 湘潭大學學報 2: 101–106.

He Guangyue 何光岳. 1988. *Chu yuanliu shi* 楚源流史. Changsha: Hunan renmin chubanshe.

———. 1990. *Chu mieguo kao* 楚滅國考. Shanghai: Shanghai renmin chubanshe.

He Hao 何浩. 1984. "Zhanguo shiqi Chu fengjun chutan" 戰國時期楚封君初探. *Lishi yanjiu* 歷史研究 1984.5: 100–111.

———. 1985. "Eling Jun yu Chunshen Jun" 邸陵君與春申君. *JHKG* 1985.2: 75–78.

———. 1989. *Chu mieguo yanjiu* 楚滅國研究. Wuhan: Wuhan chubanshe.

———. 1991. "Lun Chuguo di fengjunzhi di fazhan yu yanbian" 論楚國的封郡制的發展與演變. *JHKG* 1991.5: 72–77.

———. 1992. "Wen Pingye jun di shenfen yu Zhaoshi di shixi" 文坪夜君的身分與昭氏的世系. *JHKG* 1992.3: 68–70, 78.

He Hao and Liu Binhui 劉彬徽. 1991. "Baoshan Chujian fengjun shidi" 包山楚簡封君釋地. In Hubeisheng JingSha tielu kaogudui 1991, 569–579.

He Hao and Zhang Jun 張君. 1984. "Shilun Chuguo di junwei jichengzhi" 試論楚國的君位繼承制 *Zhongguoshi yanjiu* 中國史研究 1984.4: 3–13.

He Jiejun 何介鈞. 1991. "Hunan wanqi Chu mu ji qi lishi beijing" 湖南晚期楚墓及其歷史背景. In Chu wenhua yanjiuhui 1991, 112–124.

He Jisheng 何紀生. 1985. "Guangdong faxian di ji zuo Dong Zhou muzang" 廣東發現的几座東周墓葬. *KG* 1985.4: 360–364, 348.

He Jisheng and He Jiediao 何介鈞. 1986. "Gudai Yuezu di qingtong wenhua" 古代越族的青銅文化. *HKJ* 1986.3: 215–239.

He Jisheng and Yang Shaoxiang. 1983. "Guangdong Guangningxian Tonggugang Zhanguo mu" 廣東廣寧縣銅鼓崗戰國墓. *KGXJ* 1983.1: 111–119.

He Linyi 何林儀. 1984. "Chu Eling Jun sanqi kaobian" 楚邸陵君三器考辨. *JHKG* 1984.1: 103–104.

———. 1991. "Chuguan sishi" 楚官肆師. *JHKG* 1991.1: 77–81.

Henansheng bowuguan 河南省博物館. 1981a. "Henan Xinyangshi Pingqiao Chunqiu mu fajue jianbao" 河南信陽市平橋春秋墓發掘簡報. *WW* 1981.1: 9–14.

———. 1981b. "Henan Xichuanxian Xiasi yihaomu fajue jianbao" 河南淅川縣下寺一號墓發掘簡報. *KG* 1981.2: 119–127.

Henansheng bowuguan, Fugouxian wenhua guan 扶溝縣文化館. 1980. "Henan Fugou Gu Chengcun chutu di Chu jin yinbi" 河南扶溝古城村出土的楚金銀幣. *WW* 1980.10: 61–66.

Henansheng Danjiangkuqu wenwu fajue dui 河南省丹江庫區文物發掘隊. 1980. "Henansheng Xichuanxian Xiasi Chunqiu Chumu" 河南省淅川縣下寺春秋楚墓. *WW* 1980.10: 13–20.

Henansheng kaogu xuehui 河南省考古學會. 1983. *Chu wenhua yanjiu lunwenji* 楚文化研究論文集. Vol. 1. Zhongzhou shuhua chubanshe.

———. *Chu wenhua mizong* 楚文化覓蹤. Zhengzhou: Zhongguo guji chubanshe.

Henansheng wenwu yanjiusuo 河南省文物研究所. 1983. *Xinyang Chu mu* 信陽楚墓. Beijing: Wenwu Press.

———. 1984. "Henan Huaiyang Ma'anzhong Chumu fajue jianbao" 河南淮陽馬鞍冢楚墓發掘簡報. *WW* 1984.10: 1–17.

———. 1986. "Shang Cai Zhuanwachang Zhanguo Chu mu qingli jianbao" 上蔡磚瓦廠戰國墓清理簡報. *ZYWW* 1986.1: 4–6.

———. 1988. "Henansheng Yexian jiuxian yihao mu di qingli" 河南省葉縣舊縣一號墓的清理. *HXKG* 1988.3: 1–18.

———. 1991. *Xichuan Xiasi Chunqiu Chu mu* 淅川下寺春秋楚墓. Beijing: Wenwu Press.

Henansheng Xichuanxian wenguanli 河南省淅川縣文管理, Nanyang diqu wenguanli 南陽地區文管理. 1981. "Henan Xichuan xian Xiasi yihao mu fajue jianbao" 河南淅川縣下寺一號墓發掘簡報. *KG* 1981.2: 119–127.

Henansheng Xinyang diqu wenguanhui 河南省信陽地區文管會. 1981. "Gushi Baishizi di yihao he erhao mu qingli jianbao" 固始白獅子第一號和第二號墓清理簡報. *ZYWW* 1981.4: 21–28.

———. 1984. "Chunqiu zaoqi Huangjun Meng fufu mu fajue baogao." 春秋早期黃君孟夫婦墓發掘報告. *KG* 1984.4: 302–337.

Henansheng Xinyang diqu wenguanhui 河南省信陽地區文管會. 1986. "Luoshan Tianhu Shang Zhou mudi" 羅山天湖商周墓地. *KGXB* 1986.2: 153–198.

Hentze, Carl. 1953. "Mythologische Bildsymbole im alten China." *Studium Generale* 6: 264–277.

Hertz, Robert. 1907. *Death and the Right Hand.* Trans. Rodney and Claudia Needham. Reprinted, Glencoe, Ill.: Free Press, 1960.

Hightower, James R. 1954. "Ch'ü Yüan Studies." In *The Silver Jubilee Volume of the Zimbun-Kagaku-Kenkyuso.* Vol. 1. Kyoto, 92–233.

Hou Dejun 後德俊. 1985. "Churen di cai jin fangfa" 楚人的采金方法. *JHLT* 1985.3: 72.

Hou Han shu (History of the Latter Han dynasty) 後漢書. Compiled by Fan Ye 范曄 (c. 440 CE). 1983 ed. Zhonghua Shuju edition 中華書局出版. Beijing: Xinhua Shudian.

Hsu Choyun and Katheryn M. Linduff. 1989. *Western Chou Civilization.* New Haven: Yale University Press.

Hu Guangwei. 1934a. "Shouchun xinchu Chu Wang ding kaoshi" 壽春新出楚王鼎考釋. *Guofeng, Juan* 4, no. 3: 1–4; no. 6: 1–4.

———. 1934b. "Anhuishengli tushuguan xinde Shouchun chutu chu Wang tuodingming shi" 安徽省立圖書館新得壽春出土楚王鉈鼎銘釋. *Guofeng, Juan* 5, no. 8/9: 1–2.

Hu Yali 胡雅麗. 1988. "Baoshan Erhao mu qihua kao" 包山二號墓漆畫考. *WW* 1988.5: 30–31, 29.

Huainanzi 淮南子 (compiled under the direction of Liu An, king of Huainan, 139 BCE). 1926. Edition of Liu Wendian 劉文典, *Huainan honglie jijie* 淮南鴻烈集解. Shanghai: Commercial Press. Reprinted, Taibei, 1969.

Huainingxian wenwuguanlisuo 懷寧縣文物管理所. 1983. "Anhui Huainingxian chutu Chunqiu qingtongqi" 安徽懷寧縣出土春秋青銅器. *WW* 1983.11: 68–71.

Huaiyinshi bowuguan 淮陰市博物館. 1988. "Huaiyin Gaozhuang Zhanguo mu" 淮陰高庄戰國墓. *KGXB* 1988.2: 189–232.

Huang Gangzheng 黃綱正 and Wu Mingsheng 吳銘生. 1991. "Zhangguo Changsha Chucheng chulun" 戰國長沙楚城初論. In Chu wenhua yanjiu hui 1991, 167–175.

Huang Xiquan 黃錫全. 1991. "𩰬𩰖 kaobian 考辨." *JHKG* 1991.1: 63–69, 72.

Huang Xuanpei 黃宣佩. 1959. "Shanghaishi Jiadingxian Waigang gu mu qingli" 上海市嘉定縣外岡古墓清理. *KG* 1959.12: 685–686.

Huang Zhanyue 黃展岳. 1976. "Guanyu Zhongguo kaishi yetie he shiyong tieqi di wenti" 關於中國開始冶鐵和使用鐵器的問題. *WW* 1976.8: 62–68.

Huangzhou gumu fajuedui 黃州古墓發掘隊. 1983. "Hubei Huangzhou Guoerchong Chumu fajue jianbao" 湖北黃州國儿沖楚墓發掘簡報. *JHKG* 1983.3: 13–22.

Bibliography

Hubei kaogu xuehui 湖北考古學會. 1987. *Hubeisheng kaogu xuehui lunwen xuanji* 湖北省考古學會論文選集. Wuhan.

Hubeisheng bowuguan 湖北省博物館. 1973. "Hubei Jiangling Taihuiguan Chu mu qingli jianbao" 湖北江陵太暉觀楚墓清理簡報. *KG* 1973.6: 337–344.

———. 1974. "Hubei gu Kuang zhi yizhi diaocha" 湖北古礦治遺址調查. *KG* 1974.4: 251–254.

———. 1979. "Hubeisheng wenwu kaogu gongzuo xin shouhuo" 湖北省文物考古工作新收穫. In Wenwu bianji weiyuanhui 1979, 295–309.

———. 1980a. *Suixian Zeng Hou Yi mu* 隋縣曾侯乙墓. Beijing: Wenwu Press.

———. 1980b. *Chudu Jinancheng* 楚都紀南城. Wuhan: Hubei Provincial Museum.

———. 1980c. "Dangyang Jijiahu Chucheng yizhi" 當陽季家湖楚城遺址. *WW* 1980.10: 31–41.

———. 1982a. "Hubei Huangpi Lutaishan liang Zhou yizhi yu muzang" 湖北黃陂魯台山兩周遺址與墓葬. *JHKG* 1982.2: 37–61

———. 1982b. "Chudu Jinancheng di kancha yu fajue" 楚都紀南城的勘查與發掘. *KGXB* 1982.3: 325–350; 4: 477–508.

———. 1983a. "Dangyang Fengshan, Yangmugang yizhi shijue jianbao" 當陽馮山, 楊木崗遺址試掘簡報. *JHKG* 1983.1: 43–50.

———. 1983b. "Xiangyang Shanwan DongZhou muzang fajue baogao" 襄陽山灣東周墓葬發掘報告. *JHKG* 1983.2: 1–35.

———. 1985. "Hubei Suizhou Leigudun erhao mu fajue jianbao" 湖北隨州擂鼓墩二號發掘簡報. *WW* 1985.1: 16–36.

———. 1989. *Zeng Hou Yi mu* 曾侯乙墓. Beijing: Wenwu Press.

———. 1991. *Zeng Hou Yi mu wenwu yishu* 曾侯乙墓文物藝術. Wuhan: Hubei meishu chubanshe.

Hubeisheng bowuguan 湖北省博物館, Beijing gongyi meishu yanjiusuo 北京工藝美術研究所 [1985]. *Hubei Zeng Hou Yi mu chutu wenwu tu'an xuan* 湖北曾侯乙墓出土文物圖案選 [n.p.]: Changjian wenyi chubanshe.

Hubeisheng bowuguan Jiangling gongzuo zhan 湖北省博物館江陵工作站. 1984. "Jiangling Xieshan Chu mu" 江陵溪山楚墓. *KG* 1984.6: 515–527.

Hubeisheng Chushi yanjiuhui 湖北省楚史研究會 et al. [1985]. *Chushi yanjiu zhuanji* 楚史研究專輯. Hubei: Wuhan shifan xueyuan.

Hubeisheng Dayexian bowuguan 湖北省大冶縣博物館. 1983. "E Wangcheng yizhi diaocha jianbao" 鄂王城遺址調查簡報. *JHKG* 1983.3: 23–28.

———. 1984. "Dayexian faxian Caowang zui gucheng yizhi" 大冶縣發現草王嘴古城遺址. *JHKG* 1984.4: 66.

Hubeisheng Echeng xian bowuguan 湖北省鄂城縣博物館, Egang jijian zhihui bu wenwu xiaozu 鄂鋼基建指揮部文物小組. 1978. "Hubei Echeng Egang 53 hao mu fajue jianbao" 湖北鄂城鄂鋼五十三號墓發掘簡報. *KG* 1978.4: 256–260.

———. 1983. "Echeng Chu mu" 鄂城楚墓. *KGXB* 1983.2: 223–254.

Hubeisheng JingSha tielu kaogudui 湖北省荆沙鐵路考古隊. 1991. *Baoshan Chumu* 包山楚墓. 2 vols. Beijing: Wenwu Press.

———. 1992. "Jingmen jian jiawan muzang he yao zhi fajue jianbao" 荆門簡家灣墓葬和窯址發掘簡報. *JHKG* 1992.1: 28–34.

Hubeisheng JingSha tielu kaogudui Baoshan mudi zhengli xiaozu 湖北省荆沙鐵路考古隊包山墓地整理小組. 1988. "Jingmenshi Baoshan Chumu fajue jianbao" 荆門市包山楚墓發掘簡報. *WW* 1988.5: 1–14.

Hubeisheng Jingzhou diqu bowuguan 湖北省荆州地區博物館. 1972. "Hubei Jiangling shouci faxian yingyuan" 湖北江陵首次發現郢爰. *KG* 1972.2: 67.

———. 1973. "Hubei Jiangling Tengdian yihao mu fajue jianbao" 湖北江陵藤店一號墓發掘簡報. *WW* 1973.9: 7–17.

———. 1980. "Jiangling Yutaishan Chumu fajue jianbao" 江陵雨台山楚墓發掘簡報. *KG* 1980.5: 391–402.

———. 1982. "Jiangling Tianxingguan yihao Chumu" 江陵天星觀一號楚墓. *KGXB* 1982.1: 71–115.

———. 1984. *Jiangling Yutaishan Chumu* 江陵雨台山楚墓. Beijing: Wenwu Press.

Bibliography

——. 1987. "Hubei Qianjiang Longwan faxian Chuguo daxing gongdian jizhi" 湖北潛江龍灣發現楚國大型宮殿基址. *JHKG* 1987.3: 19–21.

——. 1989. "Hubei Jiangling Jingnansi yizhi di yi, er ci fajue jianbao" 湖北江陵荊南寺遺址第一，二次發掘簡報. *KG* 1989.8: 679–692.

Hubeisheng shehui kexueyuan lishi yanjiusuo 湖北省社會科學院歷史研究所. n.d. *Chuguo biannian ziliao* 楚國編年資料. Wuhan: Hubeisheng shehui kexueyuan lishi yanjiusuo.

——. 1981. *Chu wenhua xintan* 楚文化新探. Hubei: Hubei renmin chubanshe.

Hubeisheng Tonglushan kaogu fajue dui 湖北省銅綠山考古發掘隊. 1975. "Hubei Tonglushan Chunqiu Zhanguo gu kuangjing yizhi fajue jianbao" 湖北銅綠山春秋戰國古礦井遺址發掘簡報. *WW* 1975.2: 1–12.

Hubeisheng wenhuaju wenwu gongzuodui 湖北省文化工作隊. 1966. "Hubei Jiangling sanzuo Chu mu chutu dapi zhongyao wenwu" 湖北江陵三座楚墓出土大批重要文物. *WW* 1966.5: 33–55.

Hubeisheng wenwu guanlichu 湖北省文物管理處. 1959. "Hubei diqu gu muzang di zhuyao tedian" 湖北地區古墓葬的主要特點. *KG* 1959.11: 622–624.

Hubeisheng wenwu guanli weiyuanhui 湖北省文物管理委員會. 1965. "Hubei Yicheng 'Chu Huang cheng' yizhi diaocha" 湖北宜城"楚皇城"遺址調查. *KG* 1965.8: 377–382.

Hubeisheng Yichang diqu bowuguan 湖北省宜昌地區博物館. 1992. *Dangyang Zhaojiahu Chumu* 當陽趙家湖楚墓. Beijing: Wenwu Press.

Hulsewé, A. F. P. 1955. *Remnants of Han Law*. Leiden: E. F. Brill.

——. 1965. "Texts in Tombs." *Asiatische Studien / Études Asiatiques* 18/19: 78–89.

——. 1985. *Remnants of Ch'in Law*. Leiden: E. F. Brill.

Hultkrantz, Åke. 1973. "A Definition of Shamanism." *Temenos* 9: 25–37.

Hunansheng bowuguan 湖南省博物館. 1959. "Changsha Chu mu" 長沙楚墓. *KGXB* 1959.1: 41–60.

——. 1963. "Hunan Changde Deshan Chu mu fajue baogao" 湖南常德德山楚墓發掘. *KG* 1963.9: 461–473, 477.

——. 1964. "Hunan Shimenxian gucheng ticheng yizhi shijue" 湖南石門縣古城堤城遺址試掘. *KG* 1964.2: 104–105.

——. 1972. "Changsha Liuchengqiao yihao mu" 長沙瀏城橋一號墓. *KGXB* 1972.1: 59–72.

——. 1973. *Changsha Mawangdui yihao Hanmu* 長沙馬王堆一號漢墓. 2 vols. Beijing: Wenwu Press.

——. 1977. "Hunan Shaoshanguan qu Xiangxiang DongZhou mu qingli jianbao" 湖南韶山灌區湘鄉東周墓清理簡報. *WW* 1977.3: 36–54.

——. 1980. "Hunan Xiangxiang Niuxingshan yi, erhao daxing Zhanguo muguo mu" 湖南湘鄉牛形山一，二號大型戰國木槨墓. *Wenwu ziliao congkan* 3: 98–112.

——. 1981. *Mawangdui Hanmu yanjiu* 馬王堆漢墓研究. Changsha: Hunan Provincial Museum.

——. 1983. "Hunan Zixing jiushi Zhanguo mu" 湖南資興舊市戰國墓. *KGXB* 1983.1: 93–121.

——. 1985a. "Hunan Mayang Zhanguo shiqi gu tongkuang qingli jianbao" 湖南麻陽戰國時期古銅礦清理簡報. *KG* 1985.2: 113–124.

——. 1985b. "Leiyang Chunqiu, Zhanguo mu" 耒陽春秋戰國墓. *WW* 1985.6: 1–15.

——. 1986. "Guzhang Baihewan Chu mu" 古丈白鶴灣楚墓. *KGXB* 1986.3: 339–360.

——. 1991. *Hunan bowuguan wenji* 湖南博物館文集. Changsha: Yuelu Press.

Hunansheng bowuguan, Changde diqu wenwu gongzuodui 常德地區文物工作隊. 1986a. "Linli Jiuli Chu mu fajue baogao" 臨澧九里楚墓發掘報告. *HKJ* 3: 87–111.

Hunansheng bowuguan, Huaihua diqu wenwu gongzuodui 懷化地區文物工作隊. 1984. "Hunan Xupu Matianping Zhanguo Xi Han mu fajue baogao" 湖南漵浦馬田坪戰國西漢墓發掘報告. *HKJ* 2: 38–69.

Hunansheng Chushi yanjiuhui 湖南省楚史研究會. 1987. *Chushi yu Chu wenhua yanjiu* 楚史與楚文化研究. Changsha: Qiusuo zazhi.

Hunansheng wenguanhui 湖南省文管會. 1958. "Hunan Xiangyin gu Luocheng di diaocha yu shijue" 湖南湘陰古羅城的調查與試掘. *KGTX* 1958.2: 10.

Ikeda Suetoshi 池田末利. 1981. *Chūgoku kodai shūkyō shi kenkyū (seido to shisō)* 中國古代宗教史研究 (制度と思想). Kyoto: Tokai daigaku shuppankai.

Jao Tsung-i 鏡宗頤. 1969. *Jing-Chu wenhua* 荊楚文化. Taipei: Institute of History and Philology, Academia Sinica.

———. 1972. "Some Aspects of the Calendar, Astrology, and Religious Concepts of the Ch'u People as Revealed in the Ch'u Silk Manuscript." In Barnard and Fraser 1972, 113–122.

———. 1976. "The Character *te* in the Bronze Inscriptions." In Barnard 1976, 145–154.

Jiang Tingyu 蔣廷瑜. 1980. "Cong Yinshanling Zhanguo mu kan Xi'ou" 從銀山嶺戰國墓看西甌. *KG* 1980.2: 170–178.

———. 1982. "Chuguo di nanjie he Chu wenhua dui Lingnan di yingxiang" 楚國的南界和楚文化對嶺南的影響. In *Zhongguo kaogu xuehui* 1982, 67–73.

Jiang Yingliang 江應樑. 1980. "Bai Yuezu shu yanjiu" 百越族屬研究. *Xinan minzu lishi yanjiu jikan* 西南民族歷史研究季刊, no. 1: 39–58.

———. 1983. *Daizu shi* 傣族史. Sichuan Minzu Press.

Jianghan kaogu 江漢考古. 1989. "Sannianlai di kaogu shouhuo" 三年來的考古收獲. *JHKG* 1989.2: 104–112.

Jianglingxian wenwu gongzuozu 江陵縣文物工作組. 1984. "Hubei Jiangling Chu zong diaocha" 湖北江陵楚宗調查. *KGXJ* 4: 196–207.

Jiangling Zhangjiashan Hanmu zhujian zhengli xiaozu 江陵張家山漢墓竹簡整理小組. 1985. "Jiangling Zhangjiashan Hanjian gaishu" 江陵張家山漢簡概述. *WW* 1985.1: 9–15.

Jiangsusheng wenwu guanli weiyuanhui 江蘇省文物管理委員會 and Nanjing bowuguan 南京博物館. 1965. "Jiangsu Liuhe Chengqiao Dong Zhou mu" 江蘇六合程橋東周墓. *KG* 1965.3: 105–115.

———. 1974. "Jiangsu Liuhe Chengqiao erhao Dong Zhou mu" 江蘇六合程橋二號東周墓. *KG* 1974.2: 116–122.

Jin Zegong 金則恭. 1984. "Changsha xian chutu chunqiu shiqi Yuezu qingtong qi" 長沙縣出土春秋時期越族青銅器. *HKJ* 1984.2: 35–37.

Jingmenshi bowuguan 荊門市博物館. 1992. "Jishan Chu zong diaocha" 紀山楚冢調查. *JHKG* 1992.1: 19–27.

———. 1998. *Guodian Chumu zhujian* 郭店楚墓竹簡. Beijing: Wenwu chubanshe.

Johnson, David. 1981. "Epic and History in Early China: The Matter of Wu Tzu-hsü." *JAS* 40(2): 255–271.

Kaiya Ichiryu 海野一隆. 1979. "Chizugaku teki michi yori suru Makimitai shutsudo chizu no kentō" 地圖學的見地よりする馬王堆出土地圖の檢討. *Tōhōgakuhō* 東方學報 51: 51–82.

Kane, Virginia. 1974–1975. "The Independent Bronze Industries in the South of China Contemporary with the Shang and Western Chou Dynasties." *Archives of Asian Art* 28: 77–107.

Karlgren, Bernhard. 1941. "Han and Huai." *BMFEA* 13: 1–125.

———. 1946. "Legends and Cults in Ancient China." *BMFEA* 18: 199–366.

———. 1950a. *The Book of Odes: Chinese Text, Transcription, and Translation.* Stockholm: Museum of Far Eastern Antiquities.

———. 1950b. "The Book of Documents." *BMFEA* 22: 1–81.

———. 1957. *Grammata Serica Recensa.* Stockholm: Museum of Far Eastern Antiquities (reprinted from *BMFEA* 29).

Keightley, David N. 1983a. "The Late Shang State: When, Where, and What?" in Keightley 1983b, 523–564.

———. ed. 1983b. *The Origins of Chinese Civilization.* Berkeley: University of California Press.

Keller, Andrea. 1992. "Nügua als Protagonistin im Schöpfungsgeschehen nach frühchinesischen Quellen." *Chinablätter* 19: 233–246.

Knechtges, David R. 1968. "Two Han Dynasty *Fu* on Ch'u Yuan: Chia I's *Tiao Ch'u Yuan* and Yang Hsiung's *Fan-sao.*" In David R. Knechtges, *Two Studies on the Han* Fu *(Parerga, 1).* Seattle: Far Eastern and Russian Institute, University of Washington.

———. 1976. *The Han Rhapsody: A Study of the Fu of Yang Hsiung (53 B.C.–A.D. 18).* Cambridge: Cambridge University Press.

Kryukov, M. V. 1966. "Hsing and Shih." *Archiv Orientalni* 34: 535–553.

Kuwayama, George. 1983. "The Cultural Renaissance of Late Chou." In George Kuwayama, ed., *The Great Bronze Age of China: A Symposium.* Los Angeles: Los Angeles County Museum of Art, 56–63.

Lau, D. C. 1979. *Confucius: The Analects.* Harmondsworth, England: Penguin Books.

Lawton, Thomas. 1973. *Chinese Figure Painting*. Washington, D.C.: Freer Gallery of Art.

———. 1982. *Chinese Art of the Warring States Period: Change and Continuity*. Washington, D.C.: Freer Gallery of Art.

———. 1991. *New Perspectives on Chu Culture during the Eastern Zhou Period*. Washington, D.C.: Arthur M. Sackler Gallery, Smithsonian Institution.

Legge, James, trans. 1872. *The Chinese Classics*. 5 vols. Vol. 5, parts 1 and 2: *The Ch'un Ts'ew, with the Tso Chuen*. Oxford: Oxford University Press, 2d ed. Reprinted, Taipei, 1972.

Leigudun erhao mu qingli fajuedui 擂鼓墩二號墓清理發掘隊. 1981. "Suizhoushi Leigudun erhao mu chutu yipi zhongyao wenwu" 隨州市擂鼓墩二號墓出土一批重要文物. *JHKG* 1981.1: 1–2.

Lewis, Mark Edward. 1990. *Sanctioned Violence in Early China*. Albany: State University of New York Press.

Li Binghai 李炳海. 1991. "'Chuci ~ Jiuge' di dongyi wenhua jiyin" 楚辭 ~ 九歌 的東夷文化基因. *Zhongguo shehui kexue* 中國社會科學 1991.4: 101–112.

Li Hengmei 李衡梅. 1987. "Zhongguo lishi shang yong buhui momie di renwu—Wu Qi" 中國歷史上永不會磨滅的人物———吳起. *Wenshi zhishi* 文史知識 1987.12: 63–68.

Li Jiahao 李家浩. 1973. "Shilun Zhanguo shiqi Chuguo di huobi" 試論戰國時期楚國的貨幣. *KG* 1973.3: 192–196.

Li Jin 李瑾. 1989. "Lun woguo gudai 'huozheng' zhiguan zhi laiyuan ji qi fazhan" 論我國古代火正職官之來源及其發展. *Shixue yuekan* 史學月刊 1989.1: 17–22.

Li Jingran 李井然. 1936. "Shouxian Chu mu diaocha baogao" 首先楚墓調查報告. *Tianye kaogu baogao* 田野考古報告 1: 213–279.

Li Ling 李零. 1981. "'Chu Shuzisun Peng' jiujing shi shei?" 楚叔之孫佣究竟是誰? *Zhongyuan wenwu* 1981.4: 36–37.

———. 1985. *Changsha Zidanku Zhan'guo Chu boshu yanjiu* 長沙子彈庫戰國楚帛書研究. Beijing: Zhonghua shuju.

———. 1986. "Chuguo tongqi mingwen biannian huishi" 楚國銅器銘文編年匯釋. *Guwenzi yanjiu* 古文字研究 13: 353–397.

———. 1990. "Formulaic Structure of Chu Divinatory Bamboo Slips." *Early China* 15: 71–86.

———. 1991a. "Chu gu zuyuan shixi di wenzixue zhengming" 楚古族源世系的文字學證明. *WW* 1991.2: 47–54, 90.

———. 1991b. "'Shi tu' yu Zhongguo gudai di yuzhou moshi" 式圖與中國古代的宇宙模式. part 1. *Jiuzhou xuekan* 九州學刊 1991.4: 5–52; part 2, 1991.7: 49–76.

———. 1991c. "On the Typology of Chu Bronzes." Trans. and ed. by Lothar von Falkenhausen. In *Beiträge zur allgemeinen und vergleichenden Archäolgie*, vol. 11. Mainz-am-Rhein: Philipp von Zabern Verlag.

———. 1991d. "Discussion." In Lawton 1991, 178–183.

———. 1992. "Huti fangfu, zhijin he liandan" 戶體防腐, 冶金和煉丹. *Wenwu tiandi* 文物天地 1992.4: 17–20.

———. 1992b. "Hubei Jingmen 'bing bi Taisui' ge" 湖北荊門「兵避太歲」戈. *Wenwu tiandi* 1992.3: 22–25.

———. 1993. "Baoshan Chu jian yanjiu (zhan bu lei)" 包山楚簡研究 (占卜類). In *Zhongguo dianji yu wenhua luncong* 中國典籍與文化論叢. Beijing: Zhonghua shuju, 425–448.

———. 1996. "Zailun xizhou Xiasi Chu mu—du *Xizhou Xiasi Chu mu*" 再論淅州下寺楚墓———讀『淅州下寺楚墓』. *WW* 1996.1: 47–60.

Li Ling and Liu Yu 劉雨. 1980. "Chu Elingjun sanqi" 楚鄂陵君三器. *Wenwu* 1980. 8: 29–34.

Li Shaolian 李紹連. 1983. "Chu wenhua qiyuan di jige wenti" 楚文化起源的幾個問題. In Henan Provincial Archaeological Committee, eds., *Chu wenhua yanjiu lunwen ji* 楚文化研究論文集. Vol. 1. Zhongzhou shuhua Press, 96–105.

Li Shaozeng 李紹曾. 1983. "Qisi gucheng zhi diaocha" 期思古城址調查. *ZYWW*. Special issue: 59–60.

Li Taohua 李兆華. 1990. "Jingmen shi Xiangling Gang, Dong Zhou yizhi yu mudi qian yi" 荊門市響嶺崗東周遺址與墓地淺議. *JHKG* 1990.4: 62–69, 95.

Li Xiandeng. 1988. "Shilun Chu wenhua de xingcheng ji tedian" 試論楚文化的形成幾特點. International Conference on Chu History and Culture, Wuhan, Hubei. Typescript.

Li Xiao'ou 李曉鷗 and Liu Jiming 劉繼銘. 1984. "Sichuan Yingjingxian lietai Zhanguo tukeng mu qingli jianbao" 四川榮經縣烈太戰國土坑墓清理簡報. *KG* 1984.7: 602–606.

Li Xueqin 李學勤. 1980a. "Lun Han-Huai jian di Chunqiu qingtong qi" 論漢淮間的春秋青銅器. *WW* 1980.1: 54–58.

———. 1980b. "Cong xinchu qingtongqi kan Changjiang xiayou wenhua de fazhan" 從新出青銅器看長江下游文化的發展. *WW* 1980.7: 67–38; 8: 35–40.

———. 1982. "Lun Chu boshu zhong di tianxiang" 論楚帛書中的天象. *HKJ* 1: 68–72.

———. 1984. *Dong Zhou yu Qindai wenming* 東周與秦代文明. Beijing: Wenwu Press.

———. 1985. *Eastern Zhou and Qin Civilizations.* Trans. K. C. Chang. New Haven: Yale University Press.

Li Yujie 李玉潔. 1988. *Chu shi gao* 楚史稿. Kaifeng: Henan daxue.

Liang Zhongshi 梁中實. 1988. "Chuguo zhi ju heng zai shaozhe" 楚國之舉恆在少者. *JHLT* 1988.3: 59.

Liao, Wen-kuei. 1939. *The Complete Works of Han Fei Tzu: A Classic of Chinese Legalism.* 2 vols. London: Probsthain.

Liu Binhui 劉彬徽. 1980. "Shilun Chu Danyang he Ying du di diwang yu niandai" 試論楚丹陽和郢都的地望與年代. *JHKG* 1980.1: 45–46.

———. 1981a. "Chu Ying du jianzhi kao" 楚郢都建制考. In Hubeisheng shehui kexueyuan lishi yanjiusuo, *Chu wenhua xintan*, 102–117.

———. 1981b. "Jinan Cheng kaogu fenqi chutan" 紀南城考古分期初探. *JHKG* 1981.2: 29–35.

———. 1984. "Chuguo youming tongqi biannian gaishu" 楚國有銘銅器編年概述. *Guwenzi yanjiu* 古文字研究 9: 331–372.

———. 1986. "Hubei chutu liang-Zhou jinwen guobie niandai kaoshu" 湖北出土兩周金文國別年代考述. *Guwenzi yanjiu* 13: 239–251.

———. 1995. *Chu xi qingtongqi yanjiu* 楚系青銅器研究. Hubei: Hubei Educational Press.

Liu Dunyuan 劉敦愿. 1982. "Shilun Zhanguo yishupin zhong di niao she xiangdou ticai" 試論戰國藝術品中的鳥蛇相鬥題材. *HKJ* 1: 73–81.

Liu Jie 劉節. 1934. *Chuqi tushi* 楚器圖釋. Beijing: Beijing Library.

Liu Pujiang 劉浦江. 1988. "Chunqiu wu Ba bian" 春秋五霸辯. *Qi Lu xuekan* 齊魯學刊 1988.5: 36–41, 11.

Liu Shishan 劉世善. 1985. "Changsha Wang Wu Rui ji qi muzang kao" 長沙王吳芮及其墓葬考. *Changsha shizhi tongxun* 長沙史志通訊 1985.1: 51.

Liu Xiang 劉翔. 1983. "Wangsun Yizhe zhong xinshi" 王孫遺者鐘新釋. *JHLT* 1983.8: 76–78.

Liu Xianmei 劉先枚. 1982. "Chu guan yuanliu kaosuo" 楚官源流考索. *JHLT* 1982.8: 57–61.

Liu Xinfang 劉信芳. 1987. "Chuguo zhu Ao soyi" 楚國諸傲瑣議. *JHLT* 1987.8: 75–79.

Liu Xing 劉興. 1987. "Cong Jiangsu Dong Zhou shiqi yicun kan Chu wenhua di dong jian" 從江蘇東周時期遺存看楚文化的東漸. In Chu wenhua yanjiuhui 楚文化研究會 1987, 281–292.

Liu Xinjian 劉心健 and Wang Yanchang 王言暢. 1982. "Shandong Feixian faxian Ying yuan" 山東費縣發現·郢爰·. *KG* 1982.3: 288.

Liu Yu 劉雨. 1989. "Xi Zhou jinwen zhong di jizuli" 西周金文中的祭祖禮. *KGXB* 1989.4: 495–522.

Liu Yutang 劉玉堂. 1987. "Lun Hubei jingnei gu Yuezu di ruogan wenti" 論湖北境內古越族的若干問題. *Minzu yanjiu* 民族研究 1987.2: 35–42.

———. 1990. "Chu guan bu kao" 楚官補考. *JZSZXB* 1990.3: 89–93.

Liu Zhiyi 劉志一. 1980. "X-zi xinkao" 咒字新考. *JHKG* 1992.3: 79–80.

Loewe, Michael. 1978. "Man and Beast: The Hybrid in Early Chinese Art and Literature." *Numen* 25(2): 97–117.

———. 1979. *Ways to Paradise: The Chinese Quest for Immortality.* London: George Allen and Unwin.

———. 1982. *Chinese Ideas of Life and Death: Faith, Myth and Reason in the Han Period (202 B.C.–A.D. 220).* London: George Allen and Unwin.

———. 1987. *Crisis and Conflict in Han China.* London: George Allen and Unwin.

———, ed. 1993. *Early Chinese Texts: A Bibliographical Guide.* Berkeley: Society for the Study of Early China.

Loveday, Helen. 1989. "A Study of the Regional Styles Present in the Material Culture of the State of Chu in the Warring States Period." Ph.D. dissertation, Wadham College, Oxford University.

Lubo-Lesnichenko, E. I. 1989. "'Uigur' and 'Kirghiz' Paths in Central Asia." *Works of the Hermitage Museum (Trudy gosudarstvennogo ordena Lenina Ermitazha)* 27: 4–9.

Lunyu 論語. ZZJC ed. The Analects, attributed to Confucius and his followers, c. 450–250 BCE. *Lunyu zhengyi* 論語正義, ed. Liu Baonan 劉寶南, 1866. *Zhuzi jicheng* 諸子集成 ed., Beijing: various reprints.

Luo Yunhuan 羅運環. 1988. "Lun 'Chu Wang Xiong Zhang zhong' xi Zeng ren fangzhi" 論『楚王熊章鐘』系曾人仿制. Typescript.

———. 1991a. "Guwenzi ciliao suojian Chuguo guanzhi yanjiu" 古文字資料所見楚國官制研究. In Chu wenhua yanjiu hui 1991: 270–289.

———. 1991b. "Lun Baoshan jian zhong di Chuguo zhouzhi" 論包山簡中的楚國州制. *JHKG* 1991.3: 75–78.

Luo Zhenyu 羅振玉. 1983. *Sandai jijin wencun* 三代吉金文存. Beijing: Zhonghua shuju.

Luoyang bowuguan 洛陽博物館. 1980. "Henan Luoyang chutu 'Fanyang zhi jin' jian" 河南洛陽出土 "繁陽之金" 劍. *KG* 1980.6: 488–492.

Lushi chunqiu 春秋. Attributed to Lu Buwei, ca. 245 BCE. *Zhuzi jicheng* ed. Shanghai: Shanghai shudian.

Ma Chengyuan 馬承源. 1963. "Guanyu 'Dawu wuqi' di mingwen ji tuxiang" 關於·大武舞戚·的銘文及圖像. *KG* 1963.10: 562–564.

———. 1965. "Zai lun 'Dawu wuqi' di tuxiang" 再論·大武舞戚·的圖象. *KG* 1965.8: 413–415.

Ma Chengyuan et al., eds. 1986–1990. *Shang-Zhou qingtongqi mingwenxuan* 商周青銅器銘文選. 4 vols. Beijing: Wenwu Press.

Ma Guoquan 馬國權. 1983. "Niaochongshu lun'gao" 鳥蟲書論稿. *Guwenzi yanjiu* 古文字研究 10: 139–176.

Ma Shizhi 馬世之. 1985. "Guanyu Chu zhi bie du" 關於楚之別都. *JHKG* 1985.2: 68–74.

Mackenzie, Colin. 1986. "The Evolution of Southern Bronze Styles in China during the Eastern Zhou Period." *Bulletin of the Oriental Ceramic Society of Hong Kong* 7: 31–48.

———. 1987. "The Chu Tradition of Wood Carving." *Colloquies on Art and Archaeology in Asia* 14: 82–102.

———. 1991a. "Chu Bronze Work: A Unilinear Tradition or a Synthesis of Diverse Sources?" In Lawton 1991, 107–158.

———. 1991b. "The Influence of Textile Designs on the Art of the Warring States Period." Paper delivered at the annual meeting of the College Art Association, Washington, D.C.

———. 1993. "Meaning and Style in the Art of Chu." In Whitfield, 119–149.

Mair, Victor H. 1990. "Old Sinitic *M'aq, Old Persian *Maguš*, and English Magician." *EC* 15: 27–48.

———. 1993. "Progress Report for a Project Entitled 'A Study of the Genetic Composition of Ancient Dessicated Corpses from Xinjiang (Sinkiang), China.'" *Early China News* 6: 1, 4–8.

Major, John S. 1978. "Research Priorities in the Study of Chu Religion." *History of Religions* 17(3/4): 226–243.

———. 1984. "The Five Phases, Magic Squares, and Schematic Cosmography." In Henry Rosemont, Jr., ed., *Explorations in Early Chinese Cosmology*. JAAR Thematic Studies 50/2. Chico, Calif.: Scholar's Press, 133–166.

———. 1986. "New Light on the Dark Warrior." In N. J. Girardot and John S. Major, eds., *Myth and Symbol in Chinese Tradition* (symposium issue, vols. 13 and 14 of *Journal of Chinese Religions*). Boulder, Colo.: Society for the Study of Chinese Religions, 65–86. Rev. version in Major forthcoming (a).

———. 1993. *Heaven and Earth in Early Han Thought: Chapters Three, Four and Five of the Huainanzi*. Albany: State University of New York Press.

———. Forthcoming (a). *Essays on the Huainanzi and Other Topics in Early Chinese Intellectual History*. Albany: State University of New York Press.

———. Forthcoming (b). "Some Questions Do Have Answers: 'Tianwen' and *Huainanzi*." In Major, forthcoming (a).

Maspero, Henri. 1933. "Le Mot *ming*." *Journal Asiatique* 22: 249–296.

———. 1934–1935. "Le serment dans la procedure judiciaire de la Chine antique." *Mélanges Chinois et Bouddhiques* 3: 270.

———. 1978. *China in Antiquity*. Trans. Frank A. Kierman, Jr. Amherst: University of Massachusetts Press.

———. 1981. *Taoism and Chinese Religion*. Trans. Frank A. Kierman, Jr. Amherst: University of Massachusetts Press.

Matsumoto Tamio 松本民雄. 1980. "Shunju Sokoku Hi Mugoku gaidan" 春秋楚國費無極外傳. *Bunka* 文化 43(3, 4): 22–76.

Mattos, Gilbert L. 1997. "Eastern Zhou Bronze Inscriptions." In Shaughnessy 1997, 85–123.

Munsterberg, Hugo. 1986. *Symbolism in Ancient Chinese Art*. New York: Hacker Art Books.

Murrowchick, Robert E., ed. 1994. *China: Ancient Culture, Modern Land*. Cradles of Civilization, II. Norman: University of Oklahoma Press.

Nanyang diqu wenwudui 南陽地區文物隊 et al. 1982. "Xichuanxian Maoping Chu mu fajue baogao" 淅川縣毛坪楚墓發掘報告. *ZYWW* 1982.1: 42–46.

National Gallery of Art. 1975. *The Exhibition of Archaeological Finds of the People's Republic of China*. Washington, D.C.: National Gallery of Art.

Nie Fei 聶菲. 1991. "Mawangdui Hanmu yishupin yu wu wenhua" 馬王堆漢墓藝術品與巫文化. In Hunansheng bowuguan.

Nienhauser, William H., Jr. 1991. "A Reexamination of 'The Biographies of Reasonable Officials' in the *Records of the Grand Historian*." *EC* 16: 209–233.

Nivison, David S. 1982–1983. "1040 as the Date of the Chou Conquest." *EC* 8: 76–78.

———. 1983. "The Dates of Western Chou." *HJAS* 43(2): 481–580.

———. 1984a. "Stems and Branches: Toward a Unified Theory of the Calendar." *duduan 02*. Stanford: Privately circulated.

———. 1984b. "Evolution of the Chinese Lunar *hsiu* System." *duduan 03*. Stanford: Privately circulated.

Nivison, David S., and Kevin D. Pang. 1990. "Astronomical Evidence for the *Bamboo Annals'* Chronicle of Early Xia." *EC* 15: 7–95.

Okada Takumi 岡田功. 1981. "Sokoku to Go ki hempo" 楚國と吳起變法. *Rekishigaku kenkyū* 歷史學研究 490: 15–30.

Ou Tansheng 歐潭生. 1983. "Xinyang Chu Wangcheng shi Chu Qingxiang Wang di linshi guodu" 信陽楚王城是楚頃襄王的臨時國都. *ZYWW*. Special issue: 52–54.

Pankenier, David W. 1981–1982. "Astronomical Dates in Shang and Western Zhou." *EC* 7: 2–37.

———. 1982. "Early Chinese Positional Astronomy: The *Guoyu* Astronomical Record." *Archaeoastronomy* 5: 10–20.

———. 1983–1985. "Mozi and the Dates of Xia, Shang, and Zhou." *EC* 9–10: 175–183.

———. 1992. "The *Bamboo Annals* Revisited, Part I: Problems of Method in Using the Chronicle as a Source for the Chronology of Early Zhou." *BSOAS* 55(2): 272–297; "Part 2: The Congruent Mandate Chronology in *Yi Zhou shu*." *BSOAS* 55(3): 498–510.

———. 1995. "The Cosmo-Political Background of Heaven's Mandate." *EC* 20: 121–176.

Paper, Jordan. 1995. *The Spirits Are Drunk: Comparative Approaches to Chinese Religion*. Albany: State University of New York Press.

Pei Mingxiang 裴明相 et al. 1957. "Woguo kaogu shishang di kongqian faxian—Xinyang Changtaiguan fajue yizuo Zhanguo da mu" 我國考古史上的空前發現——信陽長台關發掘一坐大墓. *WWZLCK* 9: 21–22.

———. 1983. "Chu wenhua zai Henan fazhan di licheng" 楚文化在河南發展的歷程. In Henansheng kaogu xuehui 1983, vol. 1., pp. 23–48.

Peng Hao 彭浩. 1982. "Chu muzang zhi chu lun" 楚墓葬制初論. In Zhongguo kaogu xuehui 1982, 33–40.

———. 1984. "Woguo liang Zhou shiqi di yueshiding" 我國兩周時期的越式鼎. *HKJ* 2: 136–141.

———. 1991. "Baoshan Chujian fanying di Chuguo falü yu sifa zhidu" 包山楚簡反映的楚國法律與司法制度. In Hubeisheng JingSha tielu kaogudui 1991, 548–554.

Peng Mingzhe 彭明哲. 1986. "Luelun Chu Cheng Wang cheng Ba" 略論楚成王稱霸. *Xiangtan daxue xuebao* 湘覃大學學報 1986.3: 76–81.

Peng Shifan 彭適凡. 1980. "Jiangxi diqu chutu Shang Zhou qingtongqi di fenxi yu fenqi" 江西地區出土商周青銅器的分析與分期. In Zhongguo kaogu xuehui 1980, 181–194.

Peters, Heather. 1983. "The Role of the State of Chu in Eastern Zhou Period China: A Study of Interaction and Exchange in the South." Ph.D. dissertation, Yale University.

Pi Daojian 皮道堅. 1995. *Chu yishu shi* 楚藝術史. Hubei: Hubei Educational Press.

Pirazzoli t'Serstevens, Michèle. 1982. *The Han Dynasty*. Trans. Janet Seligman. New York: Rizzoli International.

Porter, Deborah. 1993. "The Literary Function of K'un-lun Mountain in the *Mu T'ien-tzu chuan*." *EC* 18: 73–106.

———. 1996. *From Deluge to Discourse: Myth, History, and the Generation of Chinese Fiction*. Albany: State University of New York Press.

Pu Shipei 浦士培. 1989. "Chunqiu Zhanguo shiqi Jiangling diqu daozuo qiantan" 春秋戰國時期江陵地區稻作淺探. *JZSZXB* 1989.3: 89–92.

Pulleyblank, E. G. 1983. "The Chinese and Their Neighbors in Prehistoric and Early Historic Times." In Keightley 1983b, 411–466.

Puyangshi wenwu guanli weiyuanhui 濮陽市文物管理委員會 et al. 1988. "Henan Puyang Xishuipo yizhi fajue jianbao" 河南濮陽西水坡遺址發掘簡報. *WW* 1988.3: 1–6.

Qian Linshu 錢林書. 1981. "'Yan Ying' jie" 鄢郢解. *JHLT* 1981.1: 94–95.

Qianshanxian wenguansuo 潛山縣文管所. 1992. "Anhui Qianshan Zhangfashan jiuhao Zhanguo mu" 安徽潛山章法山九號戰國墓. *JHKG* 1992.4: 22–24.

Qianshanxian wenwu guanlisuo 潛山縣文物管理所. 1986. "Qianshanxian Zhangfashan qingli yi zuo Zhanguo mu" 潛山縣章法山清理一坐戰國墓. *WY* 1986.2: 14.

Qiu Shi 求實. 1992. "Henan Xizhou Heshangling Chu mu niandai chuyi" 河南淅州和尚嶺楚墓年代芻議. *Zhongguo wenwubao* 中國文物報 18: 3.

Qiu Shihua 仇士華 and Cai Lianzhen 蔡蓮珍. 1978. "Taoqi di reshiguang ciding niandai jieshao" 陶器的熱釋光測定年代介紹. *KG* 1978.5: 344–351.

Qu Yingjie 曲英杰. 1992. "Chudu Shouchun Yingcheng fuyuan yanjiu" 楚都壽春郢城復原研究. *JHKG* 1992.3: 81–88.

Rao Zongyi. See Jao Tsung-i.

Rawson, Jessica. 1987a. "Western Zhou Sources of Interlaced Motifs." In Rosemary Scott and Graham Hutt, eds., *Style in the East Asian Tradition*. Colloquies on Art and Archaeology in Asia, no. 14. London: Percival David Foundation of Chinese Art, 38–64.

———. 1987b. *Chinese Bronzes: Art and Ritual*. London: The British Museum.

———. 1989. "Chu Influences on the Development of Han Bronze Vessels." *Arts Asiatiques,* tome 44, 84–99.

———. 1990. *Western Zhou Ritual Bronzes from the Arthur M. Sackler Collections,* vols. 2a and b. Cambridge: Harvard University and the Sackler Museum.

———. 1996. *Mysteries of Ancient China: New Discoveries from the Early Dynasties*. London: British Museum Press; New York: George Braziller Inc.

Renfrew, Colin. 1973. *The Explanation of Culture Change: Models in Prehistory*. Pittsburgh: University of Pittsburgh Press.

———. 1990. *Archaeology and Language: The Puzzle of Indo-European Origins*. Cambridge: Cambridge University Press.

Rickett, W. Allyn. 1960. "An Early Chinese Calendar Chart." *TP* 48: 195–251.

———. 1985–1998. *Guanzi*. 2 vols. Princeton: Princeton University Press.

Riegel, Jeffrey K. 1982. "Early Chinese Target Magic." *Journal of Chinese Religions* 10: 1–18.

———. 1989. "Kou-mang and Ju-shou." *Cahiers d'Extrême-Asie* 5 (special issue on Taoist studies, II): 55–83.

Robinet, Isabelle. 1976. "Les Radonnées extatiques des taoïstes dans les astres." *Monumenta Serica* 32: 159–273.

Rogers, Howard, ed. 1998. *China 5000 Years: Innovation and Transformation in the Arts*. New York: The Guggenheim Museum.

Rong Geng 容庚. 1941. *Shang Zhou yiqi tongkao* 商周彝器通考. Beijing: Harvard-Yenching Institute.

———. 1964. "Niaoshu kao" 鳥書考. In Wang Mengdan 王夢旦, ed., *Jinwen lunwenxuan* 金文論文選. Hong Kong: Zhuda: 391–442.

Rosen, Sydney. 1978. "Changing Conceptions of the Hegemon in Pre-Ch'in China." In *Ancient China: Studies in Early Civilization*. Hong Kong: The Chinese University Press, 99–114.

Roth, Harold D. 1991. "What is Huang-Lao?" Paper presented at the Fiftieth Annual Meeting of the Association for Asian Studies, New Orleans.

Sage, Steven F. 1992. *Ancient Sichuan and the Unification of China*. Albany: State University of New York Press.

Salmony, Alfred. 1954. *Antler and Tongue: An Essay on Ancient Chinese Symbolism and Its Implications*. *Artibus Asiae*, supplementum 13. Ascona, Switzerland: Artibus Asiae Publishers.

Savage, William Elliot. 1985. *In the Tradition of Kings: The Gentleman in the Analects of Confucius*. Ph.D. dissertation, University of Michigan.

———. 1992. "Archetypes, Model Emulation, and the Confucian Gentleman," *EC* 17: 1–25.

Schafer, Edward H. 1952. "The Pearl Fisheries of Ho-P'u." *JAOS* 72: 155–168.

———. 1967. *The Vermillion Bird*. Berkeley: University of California Press.

———. 1969. *Shore of Pearls*. Berkeley: University of California Press.

———. 1977. *Pacing the Void: Tang Approaches to the Stars*. Berkeley: University of California Press.

Schafer, Edward H., and Benjamin Wallacker. 1957–1958. "Local Products of the T'ang Dynasty." *JAOS* 4: 213–248.

Schneider, Laurence. 1980. *The Madman of Ch'u: The Chinese Myth of Loyalty and Dissent*. Berkeley: University of California Press.

Serruys, Paul L-M. 1981. "Towards a Grammar of the Language of the Shang Bone Inscriptions." In *Zhongyang yanjiuyuan guoji hanxue huiyi lunwenji* 中央研究院國際漢學會議論文集 (Proceedings of the International Conference on Sinology: Section on Linguistics and Paleography; 7 vols.) 2. Taipei: Academic Sinica, 313–364.

Shandongsheng Jiningshi wenwu guanliju. 1991. "Xueguo gucheng kancha he muzang fajue baogao." *KGXB* 1991.4: 449–495.

Shandongsheng kaogu yanjiuso 山東省考古研究所. 1982. *Qufu Luguo gucheng* 曲阜魯國古城. Jinan: Qilu Publishing Co.

Shang Chengzuo 商承祚. 1957. *Shike zhuan wen bian* 石刻文編. 2 vols. *Kaoguxue zhuankan* 考古學專刊, no. 4. Beijing.

Shang Jingxi 尚景熙. 1980. "Caiguo gucheng diaocha ji" 蔡國古城調查記. *Henan wenbo tongxun* 河南文博通訊 1980.2: 30–32.

Shaoxingxian wenwu guanli weiyuanhui 紹興縣文物管理委員會. 1976. "Zhaoxing Fenghuang shan mu guo mu" 紹興鳳凰山木槨墓. *KG* 1976.6: 392–394.

Shaughnessy, Edward L. 1985–1987. "The 'Current' *Bamboo Annals* and the Date of the Zhou Conquest of Shang." *EC* 11–12: 33–60.

———. 1991. *Sources of Western Zhou History: Inscribed Bronze Vessels*. Berkeley: University of California Press.

———. 1997. *New Sources of Early Chinese History: A Guide to the Reading of Inscriptions and Manuscripts*. Berkeley: Society for the Study of Early China and the University of California, Institute of East Asian Studies.

Shen Changyun 沈長云. 1983. "'Yu Xiong wei Wen Wang zhi shih' jie" 鬻熊為文王之師解. *JHLT* 1983.6: 79.

———. 1984. "Ping Yu Xiong wei huoshi shuo" 評鬻熊為火師說. *JHLT* 1984.1: 80–81.

Shen Rusong 沈茹菘. 1990. "Chungqiu Huan Gong ernien 'Cai Hou Zheng Bo hui yu Deng' jie — jian shuo chunqiu chuqi zhongyuan xingshi" 春秋桓公二年蔡侯鄭伯會於鄧解──兼說春秋初期中原形勢. In Yin Da 尹達 et al., ed. *Jinian Gu Jiegang xueshu lunwenji* 紀念顧頡剛學術論文集, vol. 1. Chengdu: BaShu shushe, 343–357.

Shi Quan 石泉. 1988. *Gudai Jing-Chu dili xintan* 古代荊楚地理新探. Wuhan: Wuhan daxue.

———. 1989. "Chunqiu BaiPu diwang kaobian" 春秋百濮地望考辯. In Tang Jiahong 唐嘉弘, ed., *Xian Qinshi lunji* 先秦史論集. Zhengzhou: Zhongzhou guji, 337–349.

Shihe kaogu dui 石河考古隊. 1990. "Hubeisheng Shihe yizhi qun yijiu baqi nian fajue jianbao" 湖北省石河遺址群1987年發掘簡報. *WW* 1990.8: 1–16.

Shiji 史記 (Records of the historian). Compiled by Sima Qian (145–86? BCE).

———. 1932 ed. *Shiki kaichū kōshō* 史記會注考証, ed. Takikawa Kametarō 瀧川龜太郎. Tokyo. Reprinted, Taipei: Chung-hsin Publishing Co., 1977.

———. 1961. See Watson 1961.

———. 1972 ed. Beijing: Zhonghua Shuju ed.

———. 1985 ed. Beijing: Zhonghua Shuju ed.

Shima Kunio 島邦男. 1979. "Disi" 禘祀. *Guwenzi yanjiu* 古文字研究 1: 396–413.

Shouxian bowuguan 壽縣博物館. 1986. "Shouxian Shuangqiao Zhanguo mu diaocha" 壽縣雙橋戰國墓調查. *WY* 1986.2: 11–13.

Shu Zhimei 舒之梅, ed. 1984. *The Unearthed Cultural Relics from Leigudun, Suizhou, Hubei Province.* Hong Kong: The Museum of Chinese Historical Relics.

Shu Zhimei and Wu Yongzhang 吳永章. 1980. "Cong Chu di lishi fazhan kan Chu yu Zhongyuan diqu di guanxi" 從楚的歷史發展看楚與中原地區的關係. *JHLT* 1980.1: 65–70.

Shuihudi Qinmu zhujian zhengli xiaozu 睡虎地秦墓竹簡整理小組. 1978. *Shuihudi Qinmu zhujian* 睡虎地秦墓竹簡. Beijing: Wenwu Press.

Shuowen jiezi 説文解字. 1977. Xu Shen 許慎 (ca. 55–144). Reprinted with expanded commentaries by Dingwen Press, Taibei, as *Shuowen jiezi gulin zhengbu hebian*.

Sichuansheng bowuguan 四川省博物館. 1981. "Sichuan Xindu Zhanguo mu guomu" 四川新都戰國木槨墓. *WW* 1981.6: 1–16.

Sichuansheng wenguanhui 四川省文管會, Ya'an diqu wenhua guan 雅安地區文化館, Yingjingxian wenhua guan 榮經縣文化館. 1984. "Sichuan Yingjingxian Zengjiagou Zhanguo mu qun di yi, er ci fajue" 四川榮經縣曾家沟戰國墓群第一、二次發掘. *KG* 1984.12: 1072–1091.

Sichuansheng wenwu guanli weiyuanhui 四川省文物管理委員會. 1988. "Sichuan Rongjing Tonxincun Ba Shu mu fajue jianbao" 四川榮經同心村巴蜀墓發掘簡報. *KG* 1988.1: 49–54.

Smith, M. G. 1965. *The Plural Society in the British West Indies.* Berkeley: University of California Press.

So, Jenny F. 1983. "*Hu* Vessels from Xinzheng: Toward a Definition of Chu Style." In Kuwayama (ed.) 1983, 64–71.

———. 1995. *Eastern Zhou Ritual Bronzes from the Arthur M. Sackler Collections.* New York and Washington, D.C.: Harry N. Abrams, Arthur M. Sackler Foundation, Arthur M. Sackler Gallery.

So, Jenny F., and Emma C. Bunker. 1995. *Traders and Raiders on China's Northern Frontier.* Seattle: Arthur M. Sackler Gallery, Smithsonian Institution, with the University of Washington Press.

Song Gongwen 宋公文. 1983. "Chunqiu shiqi Chu lingyin xulie bianwu" 春秋時期楚令尹序列辯誤. *JHLT* 1983.1: 70–75.

———. 1988. *Chu shi xintan* 楚史新探. Kaifeng: Henan daxue.

Song Shuhua. 1991. *Bai Yue* 百越. Jilin: Jiaoyu Press.

Stein, Rolf A. 1979. "Religious Taoism and Popular Religion." In H. Welch and A. Seidel, eds., *Facets of Taoism.* Yale University Press, 53–81.

Suixian leigudun yihao mu kaogu fajue dui 隨縣擂鼓墩一號墓考古發掘隊. 1979. "Hubei Suixian Zeng Hou Yi mu fajue jianbao" 湖北隨縣曾侯乙墓發掘簡報. *WW* 1979.7: 1–24.

Sun Chong'en 孫重恩. 1984. "Chu shi shou fengzhe — Yu Xiong" 楚始受封者——鬻熊. *JHLT* 1984.1: 109–112.

Sun Haibo 孫海波. 1937. *Xinzheng yiqi* 新鄭彝器. Kaifeng: Henan Tongzhi Guan.

Sun Kaitai 孫開泰. 1985. "Zhanguo chuqi di zhengzhi junshi gaigejia Wu Qi" 戰國初期的政治軍事改革家吳起. *Lishi jiaoxue* 歷史教學 1985.9: 39–42.

Sun Qikang 孫啓康. 1983. "Chuqi 'Wangsun Yizhe zhong' kaobian" 楚器王孫遺者鐘考辨. *JHKG* 1983.4: 41–46.

Sun Yirang 孫詒讓. c. 1895. *Zhouli zhengyi* 周禮正義. Reprinted in *Sibu beiyao* 四部備要 (SBBY) edition (Shanghai, 1936). Taibei, Commercial Press, 1965.

Suzhou bowuguan kaoguzu 蘇州博物館考古組. 1981. "Suzhou Huqiu Dong Zhou mu" 蘇州虎丘東周墓. *WW* 1981.11: 51–54.

Tambiah, Stanley J. 1968. "The Magical Power of Words." *Man* 3(2): 175–208.

Tan Qixiang 譚其驤, ed. 1982. *Zhongguo lishi dituji* 中國歷史地圖集, vol. 1. Shanghai: Ditu chubanshe.

Tan Qixun 覃啓勛. 1982. "Da niao zhi wu xinjie" 大鳥之鳴新解. *JHLT* 1982.3: 79–81.

Tan Weisi 譚維四. 1980. "Chu du Jinancheng kaogu gaishu" 楚都紀南城考古概述. In Hubeisheng bowuguan 1980b, 1–14.

Tang Bingzheng 湯炳正. 1985. "'Qu Yuan liezhuan' xin tan" "屈原列傳" 新探. In Yu Chongsheng 余崇生, ed., *Chuci yanjiu lunwen xuanji* 楚辭研究論文選集. Taipei, 91–111.

Tang Jiahong 唐嘉弘. 1985. "Shitan Zhou wang he Chu jun di guanxi—du Zhouyuan jiagu 'Chuzi lai gao' zhaji" 試談周王和楚君的關係——讀周原甲骨楚子來告札記. *WW* 1985.7: 8–12.

———. 1988. "Moao he Linyin" 莫傲和令尹. In *XianQin shi xintan* 先秦史新探. Kaifeng: Henan daxue.

———. 1990. "Lun Chu wang di jicheng zhidu" 論楚王的繼承制度. *Zhongzhou xuekan* 中洲學刊 1990.1: 109–114.

Tang Mingli 唐明禮. 1991. "Shilun Chu Lingyin di tedian yiji yu Zhongyuan geguo zhi Xiang di yitong" 試論楚令尹的特點以及與中原各國之相的異同. *Nandu xuetan* 南都學壇 1991.2: 43–51.

Taniguchi Mitsuru 谷口滿. 1984. "Sō to Tanyū tansaku—Kodai Sōkoku seiritsu ron" 楚都丹陽探索——古代楚國成立試論. *Tōyōshi ronshū* 東洋史論集 1: 1–32.

Taylor, Keith. 1983. *The Birth of Vietnam*. Berkeley: University of California Press.

Thatcher, Melvin. 1977–1978. "A Structural Comparison of the Central Governments of Ch'u, Ch'i and Chin." *Monumenta Serica* 6: 140–161.

———. 1985. "Central Government in the State of Ch'in in the Spring and Autumn Period." *JAOS* 23(1): 29–53.

Thorp, Robert L. 1981–1982. "The Sui Xian Tomb: Rethinking the Fifth Century." *Artibus Asiae* 43(1–2): 67–92.

———. 1988. *Son of Heaven*. Seattle: Son of Heaven Press.

Thote, Alain. 1991. "The Double Coffin of Leigudun Tomb No. 1: Iconographic Sources and Related Problems." In Lawton 1991, 23–46.

———. 1993. "Aspects of the Serpent on Eastern Zhou Bronzes and Lacquerware." In Whitfield, 150–160.

Tieshan zhongxue zhenghexian wenwuguan 鐵山中學政和縣文物館. 1979. "Fujian Zhenghe xian faxian Chunqiu shiqi di qingtong bingqi he yinwen taoqi" 福建政和縣發現春秋時期的青銅兵器和印紋陶器. *KG* 1979.6: 565.

Tokyo. 1992. *Sokō Itsu bo* 曾侯乙墓 (The tomb of Marquis Yi of Zeng). Tokyo: Nihon Keizai Sinbunsha.

Tong Enzheng 童恩正. 1979. *Gudai di Ba Shu* 古代的巴蜀. Sichuan: Sichuan Renmin Press.

———. 1986. "Cong chutu wenwu kan Chu wenhua yu nanfang zhu minzu di guanxi" 從出土文物看楚文化與南方諸民族的關係. *HKJ* 1986.3: 168–183.

Tu Shutian 涂書田. 1980. "Anhui Sheng Shouxian chutu yi dapi Chu jin bi" 安徽省壽縣出土一大批楚金幣. *WW* 1980.10: 67–71.

Van Gennep, Arnold. 1908. *The Rites of Passage*. Chicago: University of Chicago Press. Reprinted ed., 1960.

von Falkenhausen, Lothar. 1988. "Ritual Music in Bronze Age China: An Archaeological Perspective". Ph.D. dissertation, Harvard University.

———. 1991. "Chu Ritual Music." In Lawton 1991, 47–106.

Wagner, Donald B. 1988. "Swords and Ploughshares, Ironmasters and Officials. Iron in China in the Third Century B.C." In Leif Littrup, ed., *Analeca Hafniensia* (Scandinavian Institute of Asian Studies Occasional Papers), no. 3. London and Malmö: Curzon Press.

Waley, Arthur. 1938. *The Analects of Confucius*. New York: Vintage Books; Grove Press, 1957.

———. 1953. *The Book of Songs*. New York: Grove Press.

———. 1955. *The Nine Songs*. London: George Allen and Unwin.

Walker, Galal L. 1982. "Toward a Formal History of the 'Chuci'." Ph.D. dissertation, Cornell University.

Wang Congli 王從禮. 1987. "Chuguo mugong gongye chutan" 楚國木工工業初探. *JHKG* 1987.3: 64–70.

Wang Guanghao 王光鎬. 1984. "Shang dai wu Chu" 商代無楚. *JHLT* 1984.1: 74–79.

———. 1985. "Er lun Shang dai wu Chu" 二論商代無楚. *JHLT* 1985.6: 73–78.

———. 1988. *Chu wenhua yuanliu xinzheng* 楚文化源流新証. Wuhan: Hubei University Press.

Wang Gungwu. 1958. "The Nanhai Trade." *Journal of the Malayan Branch of the Royal Asiatic Society* 31(2): 1–135.

Wang Hongxing 王紅星. 1988. "Baoshan Chumu mudi shixi" 包山楚墓墓地試析. *WW* 1988.5: 32–34.

Wang Jiade 王家德. 1991. "Yichang diqu suojian Zhoudai Ba Shu tongqi chuyi" 宜昌地區所見周代巴蜀銅器芻議. *JHKG* 1991.1: 57–58, 94.

Wang Jin 王勁. 1988. "Chu qi yu Chu wenhua" 楚器與楚文化. Paper presented at the International Scholarly Conference on Chu History, Wuhan.

Wang Liutong 王毓彤. 1963. "Jingmen chutu di yijian tongge" 荊門出土的一件銅戈. *WW* 1963.1: 64–65.

Wang Mingge 王明閣. 1988. "Cong jinwen zhong kan Xi Zhou wangchao 'nan zheng' di youguan wenti" 從金文中看西周王朝南征的有關問題. *Beifang luncong* 北方論叢 1988.4: 33–38.

Wang Rulin 王儒林. 1982. "Nanyangshi Xiguan chutu yipi Chunqiu qingtongqi" 南陽市西關出土一批春秋青銅器. *ZYWW* 1982.1: 39–41.

Wang Shancai 王善才 and Zhu Dejun 朱德君. 1991. "Xiangyang, Yicheng jichu Dong Zhou yizhi di diaocha" 襄陽,宜城幾處東周遺址調查. *JHKG* 1980.2: 97–102.

Wang Tao. 1993. "A Textual Investigation of the *Taotie*." In Whitfield, 102–118.

Wang Weiping 王衛平. 1986. "Shilun Wu Zixu yu Wuguo di qiangsheng" 試論吳子胥與吳國的強盛. *Yangzhou shiyuan xuebao* 揚州師院學報 1986.4: 112–117, 121.

Wang, Yu-Ch'üan (Wang Yuchuan). 1951. *Early Chinese Coinage.* New York: American Numismatic Society.

Wang Zhongshu 王仲殊. 1982. *Han Civilization.* Trans. K. C. Chang and collaborators. New Haven: Yale University Press.

Waters, Geoffrey. 1986. *Three Elegies of Ch'u: An Introduction to the Traditional Interpretation of the Ch'u Tz'u.* Madison: University of Wisconsin Press.

Watson, Burton. 1961. *Records of the Historian: Chapters from the Shih chi of Ssu-ma Ch'ien.* Trans. Burton Watson. New York: Columbia University. Rev. ed. 1993.

———. 1963. *Hsun-Tzu: Basic Writings.* New York: Columbia University Press.

Watson, William. 1972. "Traditions of Material Culture in the Territory of Ch'u." In Barnard and Fraser, 53–76.

———. 1973. *The Genius of China: An Exhibition of Archaeological Finds of the People's Republic of China.* London: Times Newspapers.

Watson, William, and R. B. Smith. 1973. *Early South-East Asia: Essays in Archaeology, History, and Historical Geography.* New York: Oxford University Press.

Weber, Charles D. 1968. *Chinese Pictorial Bronze Vessels of the Late Chou Period.* Ascona, Switzerland: Artibus Asiae.

Wei Chang 魏昌. 1988. "Tan Chu Zhuang Wang di li Ba yu geren xingge wanshan di hexie tongyi" 談楚莊王的立霸於個人性格完善的和諧統一. *JZSZXB* 3: 85–92.

———. 1989. "Wu Qi bianfa yu Chuguo guoqing" 吳起變法與楚國國情. *JZSZXB* 4: 62–68, 96.

———. 1990. "Chu Cheng Wang zheng Ba shulun" 楚成王爭霸述論. *JZSZXB* 3: 81–88.

Weld, Susan R. 1997. "The Covenant Texts from Houma and Wenxian." In Shaughnessy 1997, 125–160.

Wen Chongyi 文崇一. 1976. *Chu wenhua yanjiu* 楚文化研究. Taibei: Academia Sinica.

Wen Fong, ed. 1980. *The Great Bronze Age of China.* New York: Metropolitan Museum of Art.

Wenwu bianji weiyuanhui 文物編輯委員會. 1979. *Wenwu kaogu gongzuo sanshi nian* 文物考古工作三十年. Beijing: Wenwu Press.

Whitfield, Roderick, ed. 1993. *The Problem of Meaning in Early Chinese Ritual Bronzes.* Colloquies on Art and Archaeology in Asia, no. 15. London: The Percival David Foundation of Chinese Art, School of Oriental and African Studies, University of London.

Wiens, Harold J. 1954. *China's March toward the Tropics.* Hamden, Conn.: Shoe String Press.

Wile, Douglas. 1992. *Art of the Bedchamber: The Chinese Sexual Yoga Classics Including Women's Solo Meditation Texts.* Albany: State University of New York Press.

Wobst, H. Martin. 1977. "Stylistic Behavior and Information Exchange." In *For the Director: Research Essays in Honor of James B. Griffin.* Ann Arbor: University of Michigan Museum of Anthropology, Anthropology Papers 61, 317–341.

Wu Hung 巫鴻. 1995. *Monumentality in Early Chinese Art and Architecture.* Stanford: Stanford University Press.

Wu Mingsheng 吳銘生. 1982. "Zixing Jiushi Zhanguo mu fanying di Chu, Yue wenhua guanxi tantao" 資興舊市戰國墓反映的楚,越文化關係探討. *HKJ* 1982.1: 105–110.

———. 1983. "Cong kaogu faxian tan Hunan gu Yuezu di gaimao" 從考古發現談湖南古越族的概貌. *JHKG* 1983.9: 52–57.

Wu Shanqing 吳山謙. 1977. "Jiangsu Liuhexian Heren Dong Zhou mu" 江蘇六和縣和仁東周墓. *KG* 1977.5: 298–301.

Wu Shiqian 伍仕謙. 1984. "Wangzi Wu ding Wangsun Gao zhong mingwen kaoshi" 王子午鼎, 王孫告鐘銘文考釋. *Guwenzi yanjiu* 1984.9: 275–294.

Wu Shunqing 吳順青, Xu Menglin 徐夢林, and Wang Hongxing 王紅星. 1988. "Jingmen Baoshan Erhao mu bufen yiwu di qingli yu fuyuan" 荊門包山二號墓部分遺物的清理與復原. *WW* 1988.5: 15–24.

Wu Xinghan 吳興漢. 1991. "Anhui Chu mu yanjiu" 安徽楚墓研究. In Chu wenhua yanjiuhui 楚文化研究會 1991, 101–111.

Wu Yongzhang 吳永章. 1990. "Liang Hu diqu gudai Yue ren yizong tongshu" 兩湖地區古代越人遺蹤通述. *JHKG* 1990.1: 181–187.

Wu Yufang 吳鬱芳. 1992a. "Chu Xiangshi yu Chu san lu" 楚項氏與楚三閭. *JHLT* 1992.1: 79–81.

———. 1992b. "Baoshan erhao muzhu Zhao Tuo jiapu kao" 包山二號墓主昭佗家譜考. *JHLT* 1986.5: 60–65.

Wuhan daxue Jing-Chu shidi yu kaogu yanjiushi 武漢大學荊楚史地與考古研究所. 1984. "Suizhou Anju yizhi chuci diaocha jianbao" 隨州安居遺址初次調查簡報. *JHKG* 1984.4: 1–7.

Xia Nai 夏鼐. 1972. "Wuchan jieji wenhua dageming qijian chutu wenwu jianjie—Anhui gedi faxian Chu guo jin bi—yingyuan" 無產階級文化大革命期間出土文物間接——安徽各地發現楚國金幣——郢爰. *KG* 1972.1: 29–42.

Xia Nai and Yin Weizhang 殷瑋璋. 1982. "Hubei Tonglushan gu tongkuang" 湖北銅綠山古銅礦. *KGXB* 1982.1: 1–14.

Xi'an Banpo bowuguan 西安半坡博物館. 1963. *Xi'an Banpo* 西安半坡. Beijing: Wenwu Press.

———. 1975. "Shanxi Lintong Jiangzhai yizhi di er, san ci fajue de zhuyao shouhuo" 陝西臨潼姜寨遺址第二, 三次發掘的主要收獲. *KG* 1975.5: 280–284, 263.

Xiang Xucheng 向緒成. 1985. "Qujialing yizhi xiaceng ji tonglei yicun wenhua xingzhi taolun" 屈家嶺遺址下層及同類遺存文化性質討論. *KG* 1985.7: 627–632.

Xianyangshi bowuguan 咸陽市博物館. 1973. "Xianyangshi jinnian faxian di yipi Qin Han yiwu" 咸陽市近年發現的一批秦漢遺物. *KG* 1973.3: 167–170.

Xiao Hanming 蕭漢明. 1986. "Guan Shefu—Chunqiu moqi Chuguo zongjiaojia" 觀射父——春秋末期楚國宗教家. *JHLT* 1986.5: 60–65.

Xiaogan diqu bowuguan 孝感地區博物館. 1985. "Dawu Luwang cheng zhong dian diaocha jianbao" 大悟呂王城重點調查簡報. *JHKG* 1985.2: 5–16.

———. 1990. "Hubei Dawu Luwang cheng yizhi" 湖北大悟呂王城遺址. *JHKG* 1990.2: 31.

———. 1991. "Hubei Xiaogan diqu liang chu gucheng yizhi diaocha jianbao" 湖北孝感地區兩處古城遺址調查簡報. *KG* 1991.1: 8–15.

Xiong Chuanxin 熊傳新. 1979. "Tan Mawangdui sanhao Xi Han mu chutu di liubo" 談馬王堆三號西漢墓出土的六博. *WW* 1979.4: 35–39.

———. 1981. "Duizhao xinjiu moben tan Chuguo renwu longfeng bohua" 對照新舊摹本談楚國人物龍鳳帛畫. *JHLT* 1981.1: 90–94.

Xiong Yayun 熊亞云. 1956. "Wuda tielu xiujian zhong faxian dapi gu muzang he gu yizhi" 武大鐵路修建中發現大批古墓葬和古遺址. *WW* 1956.11: 78.

Xiao Tong 蕭統. 1983 ed. *Wen xuan* 文選 (Literary selections). 3 vols. Beijing: Zhonghua shuju.

Xu Huanbin 徐恒彬. 1982. "Shilun Chu wenhua dui Guangdong lishi fazhan di zuoyong" 試論楚文化對廣東歷史發展的作用. *Zhongguo kaogu xuehui* 1982, 74–79.

Xu Jun 徐俊. 1982. "'Yu Xiong zhi shou Zhou feng' chuyi" 鬻熊始受封芻議. *JHLT* 1982.4: 69–71.

———. 1986. "Shi 'Jici zhi dian'" 釋 "雞次之典." *JHLT* 1986.3: 66–67.

Xu Shaohua 徐少華. 1991. "Fuguo lishi dili tanyi—jianlun Baoshan Chu mu di niandi he shishi" 鄘國歷史地理探疑——兼論包山, 望山楚墓的年代和史實. *Huaxia kaogu* 1991.3: 89–95.

———. 1994. *Zhoudai nanwang lishi dili yu wenhua* 周代南望歷史地理與文化. Wuhan: Wuhan University Press.

———. 1996. "Zhu Rong baxing zhi yunxing, caoxing zhuzu lishi dili fenxi" 祝融八姓之妘姓, 曹姓諸族歷史地理分析. *Hubei daxue xuebao* 湖北大學學報 1996.2: 15–20.

Bibliography

Xu Xiangdong. 1992. "Hubei Sheng Honghushi xiao cheng hao, da cheng hao, wanputa yizhi diaocha" 湖北省洪湖市小城濠, 大城濠, 萬鋪塌遺址調查. *JHKG* 1992.4: 1–9.

Xu Zhongshu 徐中舒. 1936. "Jinwen guci shili" 金文嘏辭釋例. *Bulletin of the Institute of History and Philology* 6: 1–44.

———. 1977. "Shilun Minshan Zhuang Wang yu Dian Wang Zhuang Qiao di guanxi" 試論岷山莊王與滇王莊喬的關係. *Sixiang zhanxian* 思想戰線 1977.4: 75–82.

Xu Zhongshu and Tang Jiahong 唐嘉弘. 1981. "Gudai Chu Shu di guanxi" 古代楚叔的關係. *WW* 1981.6: 17–25.

Yan Dunjie 嚴敦杰. 1978. "Guanyu Xi Han chuqi di shipan he zhanpan" 關於西漢初期的式盤和占盤. *KG* 1978.5: 334–337.

Yang Fanzhong 楊范中 and Zhu Maxin 祝馬鑫. 1981. "Chunqiu shiqi Chuguo jiquan zhengzhi chutan" 春秋時期楚國集權政治初探. *JHLT* 1981.4: 104–108.

Yang Hao 楊豪. 1961. "Jieshao Guangdong jinnian faxian di jijian qingtong qi" 介紹廣東近年發現的幾件青銅器. *KG* 1961.11: 599–600.

Yang Jiuxia 楊鳩霞. 1988. "Changfeng Zhanguo wanqi Chu mu" 長豐戰國晚期楚墓. *WY* 1988.4: 89–98.

Yang Kuan 楊寬. 1963. "'Xiangyin jiuli' yu 'xiangli' xintan" 鄉飲酒禮與饗禮新探. *Zhonghua wenshi luncong* 中華文史論叢 4: 1–31.

———. 1981a. *Zhangguoshi* 戰國史. Shanghai: Shanghai Renmin Press.

———. 1981b. "Xi Zhou shidai de Chuguo" 西周時代的楚國. *JHLT* 1981.5: 101–108.

Yang Lüxuan 楊履選. 1986. "Chunqiu Huangguo gucheng" 春秋黃國古城. *ZYWW* 1986.1: 54–57.

Yang Minghong 楊明洪. 1986. "Jiangling Yinxiangcheng yizhi di diaocha yu tansuo" 江陵陰湘城遺址的調查與探索. *JHKG* 1986.1: 1–7.

Yang Quanxi 楊權喜. 1980a. "Chu du Jinancheng xiyuan beibian men di fajue" 楚都紀南城西垣北邊門的發掘. In Hubeisheng bowuguan 1980b, 22–35.

———. 1980b. "Dangyang Jijiahu Chu cheng yizhi" 當陽季家湖楚城遺址. *WW* 1980.10: 31–42.

———. 1980c. "Dangyang Jijiahu gucheng shijue di zhuyao shouhuo" 當陽季家湖古城試掘的主要收獲. *JHKG* 1980.2: 87–90.

Yang Xiaoneng 楊曉能. n.d. *Sculpture of Prehistoric China.* Hong Kong.

Yang Yaolin 楊耀林 and Xu Huanbin 徐煥彬. 1985. "Zhuhai gongbei xin shiqi yu qingtongqi yizhi di diaocha yu shijue" 珠海拱北新石器與青銅器遺址的調查與試掘. *KG* 1985.8: 686–689.

Yang Zifan. 1956. "Shandong Taian faxian di Zhanguo tongqi" 山東泰安發現的戰國銅器. *WWZLCK* 1956.6: 65.

Yichang diqu bowuguan 宜昌地區博物館. 1984. "Dangyang Mopanshan Xi Zhou yizhi shijue jianbao" 當陽磨盤山西周遺址試掘簡報. *JHKG* 1984.2: 7–12.

Yin Difei 殷滌非. 1978. "Xi Han Ruyinhou mu di zhanpan he tianwen yiqi" 西漢汝陰侯墓的占盤和天文儀器. *KG* 1978.5: 338–343.

Yin Difei and Luo Changming. 1958. "Shouxian chutu di E Jun qi jie" 壽縣出土的鄂君啓節. *WWZLCK* 1958.4: 8–11.

Yu, Pauline. 1987. *The Reading of Imagery in the Chinese Poetic Tradition.* Princeton: Princeton University Press.

Yu Weichao 俞偉超. 1963. "'Da Wu Kai Bing' tongqi yu Baren di 'Da Wu' wu" "大武開兵" 銅戚與巴人的 "大武" 舞. *KG* 1963.3: 153–155.

———. 1964. "'Da Wu' wu qi xuji" "大武" 舞戚續記. *KG* 1964.1: 54–57.

———. 1980. "Guanyu Chu wenhua fazhan di xin tansuo" 關於楚文化發展的新探索. *JHKG* 1980.1: 17–30.

———. 1981. "Guanyu Chu wenhua di fazhan yu tansuo" 關於楚文化的發展與探索. In Hubeisheng shehui kexueyuan lishi yanjiusuo 1981, 1–27.

Yu Ying-shih. 1965. "Life and Immortality in the Mind of Han China." *HJAS* 25: 80–122.

———. 1967. *Trade and Expansion in Han China.* Berkeley: University of California Press.

———. 1987. "'Oh Soul, Come Back': A Study of the Changing Conception of the Soul and Afterlife in Pre-Buddhist China." *HJAS* 47(2): 363–395.

Yunnansheng wenwu gongzuodui et al. 雲南省文物工作隊. 1978. "Yunnan Chuxiongxian Wanjiaba gu muqun fajue jianbao" 雲南楚雄縣萬家壩古墓群發掘簡報. *WW* 1978.10: 1–18.

———. 1983. "Chuxiong Wanjiaba gumu qun fajue baogao" 楚雄萬家壩古墓群發掘報告. *KGXB* 1983.3: 347–382.

Zhan Hanqing 詹漢清. 1983. "Gushixian Beishankou Chunqiu Zhanguo guchengzhi diaocha baogao" 固始縣北山口春秋戰國古城址調查報告. *ZYWW.* Special issue : 61–62.

Zhang Chao 張潮. 1984. "Gu Yue zu wenhua chutan" 古越族文化初探. *JHKG* 1984.4: 80–83.

Zhang Guangyu 張光宇. 1992. *Baoshan Chujian wenzi bian* 包山楚簡文字辯. Taibei: Yiwen Press.

Zhang Jian 張謇, Pan Linggao 潘齡皋, Kang Youwei 康有為, and Yu Youren 于有任. 1973. *Jinshi dazidian* 金石大字典. Taibei: reprint ed.

Zhang Jun 張君. 1984a. "Shilun Chuguo di zongzuzhi ji qi tedian" 試論楚國的宗族制及其特點. *Wuhan shifan xueyuan xuebao* 武漢師範學院學報 1984.4: 91–99.

———. 1984b. "Shang dai wu Chu xi" 商代無楚析. *JHLT* 1984.8: 77–81.

———. 1986. "Chu guo Dou, Cheng, Wei, Qu sizu xianshi kao" 楚國鬥成為屈四族先世考. In *Chu wenhua mizong* 楚文化覓蹤. Zhengzhou: Zhongzhou guji chubanshe, 175–179.

Zhang Pusheng 張浦生. 1959. "Jiangsu yingyuan" 江蘇郢爰. *WW* 1959.4: 11–12.

Zhang Shenglin 張勝琳. 1984. "Chunqiu shiqi Chuguo yizuren di laiyuan ji qi chujing" 春秋時期楚國翼族人的來源及其處境. *JHLT* 1984.6: 75–79.

Zhang Xixian 張西顯. 1983. "Qianshuo Chu du Danyang zai Xichuan" 淺說楚都丹陽在淅川. *ZYWW* special issue 1983: 55–58.

Zhang Xuqiu 張緒球. 1991. "Shijiahe wenhua di fenqi fenbu he leixing" 石家河文化的分期分布和類型. *KGXB* 1991.4: 389–414.

———. 1992. "Shijiahe wenhua di yuqi" 石家河文化的玉器. *JHKG* 1992.1: 56–60.

Zhang Yinwu 張吟午 and Li Fuxin 李福新. 1983. "Hubei Yicheng Luojiashan yihao mu chutu di jijian qingtongqi" 湖北宜城駱家山一號墓出土的几件青銅器. *JHKG* 1983.1: 84.

Zhang Zedong 張澤棟. 1983. "Yunmeng Chu Wangcheng yizhi" 云夢楚王城遺址. *JHKG* 1983.2: 94.

Zhang Zhengming 張正明. 1984. *Chu shi luncong* 楚史論叢. Hubei: Hubei renmin chubanshe.

———. 1987. *Chu wenhua shi* 楚文化史. Shanghai: renmin chubanshe.

———. 1988. *Chu wenhua zhi* 楚文化志. Hubei: Hubei renmin chubanshe.

Zhang Zhengming and Zhang Shenglin 張勝琳. 1983. "Chu jun xing shi bian" 楚君姓氏辯. *JHLT* 1983.6: 80–81.

Zhang Zhenze 張震澤. 1946. "Chu Moao kao" 楚莫傲考. *Dongfang zazhi* 東方雜誌 42(15): 47–54.

Zhang Zhiheng 張之恒. 1982. "Shilun Daxi wenhua" 試論大溪文化. *JHKG* 1982.1: 66–71.

Zhang Zhixin. 1980. "Wuxian Heshan Chu mu chutu wenwu ji qi yiyi" 吳縣何山楚墓出土文物及其意義. *Jiangsu wenbo tongxun* 江蘇文博通訊 1980.6: 2.

Zhang Zhongyi 張中一 and Peng Qingye 彭青野. 1984. "Lun Churen ru Xiang di niandai" 論楚人入湘的年代. *JHKG* 1984.4: 84–90.

Zhao Hua 趙樺. 1987. "Chu Zhuang Wang qi ren" 楚莊王其人. In Hunansheng Chushi yanjiuhui 湖南省楚史研究會, *Chu shi yu Chu wenhua yanjiu* 楚史與楚文化研究. Changsha: Qiusuo zazhi she, 28–43.

Zhao Shigang 趙世綱 and Liu Xiaochun 劉笑春. 1980. "Wangzi Wu ding mingwen shishi" 王子午鼎銘文試釋. *Wenwu* 文物 1980.10: 27–30.

Zhao Zhongwen 趙忠文. 1990. "Jiu ding kaolue" 九鼎考略. *Renwen zazhi* 人文雜誌 1990.2: 89–91.

Zhejiangsheng wenwu guanli weiyuanhui 浙江省文物管理委員會 et al. 1984. "Shaoxing 306 hao Zhanguo mu fajue jianbao" 紹興306號戰國墓發掘簡報. *WW* 1984.1: 10–26.

Zheng, Chantal. 1992. "Le Mythe de l'archer et des soleils." In Charles Le Blanc and Rémi Mathieu, eds., *Mythe et philosophie à l'aube de la Chine impériale: Études sur le Huainan zi*. Montréal: Les Presses de l'Université de Montréal; Paris: Boccard, 27–47.

Zheng Jiaxiang 鄭家相. 1959. "Gudai di beihua" 古代的貝化. *WW* 1959.3: 65–66.

Zhenjiang shi bowuguan 鎮江市博物館. 1984. "Jiangsu Wujin Menghe Zhanguo mu" 江蘇武進孟河戰國墓. *KG* 1984.2: 135–137.

Bibliography

Zhongguo kaoguxue nianjian 中國考古學年鑑 (Annual review of Chinese archaeology). Beijing: Wenwu Press, annual.

Zhongguo kaogu xuehui 中國考古學會. 1980. *Kaogu xuehui diyici nianhui lunwenji* 考古學會第一次年會論文集. Beijing: Wenwu Press.

———. 1982. *Kaogu xuehui, dierci nianhui lunwenji* 考古學會第二次年會論文集. Beijing: Wenwu Press.

Zhongguo Kexueyuan kaogu yanjiusuo 中國科學院考古研究所. 1957. *Changsha fajue baogao* 長沙發掘報告. Beijing: Science Press.

———. 1959. *Luoyang Zhongzhou lu* 洛陽中州路. Beijing: Science Press.

Zhongguo shehui kexueyuan kaogu yanjiusuo 中國社會科學院考古研究所. 1984. *Xin Zhongguo di kaogu faxian he yanjiu* 新中國的考古發現和研究. Beijing: Wenwu Press.

Zhongguo shehui kexue yuan kaogu yanjiu suo Tonglushan gongzuodui 中國社會科學院考古研究所銅綠山工作隊. 1981. "Hubei Tonglushan Dong Zhou tong kuang yizhi fajue" 湖北銅綠山東周銅礦遺址發掘. *KG* 1981.1: 19–23.

Zhou Dejun 周德鈞. 1988. "Shilun Chuguo di shehui jiegou" 試論楚國的社會結構. *Hubei daxue xuebao* 湖北大學學報 1988.4: 62–64.

Zhou Houqiang 周厚強. 1991. "Hubei Xiaogan diqu liang chu gucheng yizhi diaocha jianbao" 湖北孝感地區兩處古城遺址調查簡報. *KG* 1991.1: 8–15.

Zhou Zizong. See Chow Tse-tsung.

Zhu Dexi 朱得熙. 1954. "Shouxian chutu Chuqi mingwen yanjiu" 壽縣出土楚器銘文研究. *Lishi yanjiu* 歷史研究 1: 99–118.

Zhu Dexi and Qiu Xigui 裘錫圭. 1973. "Zhanguo tongqi mingwen zhong de shiguan" 戰國銅器銘文中的食官. *Wenwu* 文物 1973.12: 59–61.

Zhu Junming 朱俊明. 1987. "Cong jia-, jinwenzi kaocha Chu ren xing shi ji qi xiangguan wenti" 從甲-金文字考察考察楚人姓氏及其相關問題. *Guizhou shehui kexue* 貴州社會科學 1987.12: 50–55, 44.

Zhu Xia 朱夏. 1953. *Zhongguo di jin* 中國的金. Beijing: Shangwu Press.

Zhu Zhi. 1958. "Henan Wuyang Beiwudu gucheng diaocha" 河南舞陽北舞渡古城調查. *KGTX* 1958.2: 49–50.

Zhumadian diqu wenhuaju 駐馬店地區文化局. 1988. "Henan Zhengyang Suzhuang Chu mu fajue baogao" 河南正陽蘇庄楚墓發掘報告. *HXKG* 1988.2: 21–41.

Zhushu jinian 竹書紀年 (The bamboo annals). SBBY ed. *Sibu beiyao* ed. Reprinted, Taipei: Chung-hua, 1966.

Zuo Yandong 左言東. 1986. *Zhongguo zhengzhi zhidu shi* 中國政治制度史. Hangzhou.

Zuozhuan 左轉 (Mr. Zuo's commentary to the Chunqiu). Compilation attributed to Zuo Qiuming during the Chunqiu period. Probably compiled about 300 B.C.

———. 1872 ed. *The Chinese Classics*. Trans. James Legge. Vol. 5, parts 1 and 2. 2d ed. Oxford: Oxford University Press. Contains text and translation.

———. 1907 ed. *Saden kaisen* 左轉會箋, ed. Takezoe Shin'ichirō 竹添光鴻. Tokyo. Reprinted, Taipei: Fenghuang, 1977.

———. 1983 ed. *Chunqiu jingzhuan yinde* 春秋經傳引得, ed. Hong Ye et al. 2 vols. Harvard-Yenching Sinological Index Series no. 11. Reprinted, Shanghai: Guji.

Contributors

Barry B. Blakeley is emeritus professor of Asian studies at Seton Hall University. He is the author of numerous articles on Chu studies, including "King, Clan and Courtier in Ch'u Court Politics" (*Asia Major* 1992).

Constance A. Cook, who received her Chinese language and literature Ph.D. from the University of California, Berkeley, has published a number of articles dealing with ancient Chinese inscriptions, society, and religion, including "Three High Gods of Chu" (*Journal of Chinese Religions* 1994). She is currently associate professor of Chinese at Lehigh University.

Li Ling is the author of many articles and books on Chu culture, including a book on the Chu Silk Manuscript (published in Chinese 1985) and an ongoing multivolume work on Chinese divination techniques. He is currently professor of Chinese at Beijing University.

John S. Major, who received his Ph.D. in history and East Asian languages from Harvard University, is the author of numerous journal articles and several books on China, including *Heaven and Earth in Early Han Thought* (SUNY Press, 1993). Formerly associate professor of history at Dartmouth College and later director of the China Council of the Asia Society, he is an editor and independent scholar based in New York.

Heather A. Peters received her Ph.D. from Yale University. She is currently an independent museum consultant, in which capacity she advised on the new Sackler Museum in Beijing and the UNESCO rescue and restoration project at Angkor Wat. She has written extensively on the links among history, ethnography, and art in the study of south China, including "Tattooed Faces and Stilt Houses: Who Were the Ancient Yue?" (*Sino-Platonic Papers* 1990).

Jenny F. So is senior curator of ancient Chinese art at the Freer/Sackler Galleries of the Smithsonian Institution. Her work at the Freer/Sackler has included reinstallation of the ancient Chinese art collection and a special exhibition of "The Art of Chu." Among her publications is "Bells of Bronze Age China" (*Archaeology* 1994).

Gopal Sukhu received his Ph.D. from Columbia University in 1994 and is now associate professor of Chinese at Queens College, City University of New York. He is at work on a new translation and interpretive commentary of the classic work of Chu literature, the *Chuci*, or *Elegies of the Chu*.

Susan Weld, who received her Ph.D. from Harvard University in 1990, is a research associate at the East Asian Legal Studies Program of Harvard Law School. She is currently preparing a book-length study of the legal documents on bamboo strips from Baoshan.

Xu Shaohua is professor of ancient Chinese history at Wuhan University, Hubei Province, China. He is a specialist on the archaeology of ancient Chu and author of articles on the Baoshan bamboo strips and other topics. His book, *Zhoudai nanwang lishi dili yu wenhua* (History, geography, and culture of the southern kingdoms of the Zhou Dynasty), was published by Wuhan University Press in 1994.

Index

Index

Manchuria, 152

Manshi, state of, 182n. 65

manyi (southern barbarians), 2, 3

mao men zhi fa (Law of the Reed Gate), 79, 80

Maoping (Xichuan, Henan), 27

markets, 103, 110

marriage alliances, 109, 112

Mashan (Jiangling, Hubei), *33*, 36, 41, 137, *167*, pl. 6

masks, 133, 135, 208n. 16, 209n. 44; Matianping, 127, 128

Maspero, Henri, 88

Matianping (Hunan), 127, 128

Mawangdui (Changsha, Hunan), viii, *134*, 169; coffins from, *130*, 135, 137; funerary banners from, 32, 42, 126, 128, 129, 130–131, pl. 8; *liubo* game from, 127, pl. 9; texts from, 124, 128, 140, 171; Tomb 3, *141*, 178n. 19

Mayang (Hunan), 28, 32, 113

medicine, 96, 115

mediumism, 138, 139

Mei Shui (river), 113

meng (oath), 72–73, 94

Menggu (Chu hero), 79, 86

Menghe (Wujin, Jiangdong region), 28

merchant class, 103, 106, 111

metals, 10, 116; copper, 30, 103, 113–114; iron, 25, 26, 34, 100; steel, 34; tin, 113. *See also* bronze

Mi *xing* (Chu ruling house), 53, 54

military expansion, 67, 69, 72, 75; Chu, 1, 10, 13–17, 25, 26, 57, 62, 99, 110, 113, 115, 168

ming (luminous), 68, 69, 72–73

mining sites, 30, 103, 114, 187n. 105, 197n. 28

mirrors, 141, pl. 10; TLV, 127, 142, 143, 208n. 13

moao (title), 56, 58, 191n. 21

Modernists (Han), 152–153

Mongolia, 137

"Monthly Ordinances" ("Yueling;" *Lüshi chunqiu*), 125, 135

months, 128, 142; in Chu Silk Manuscript, 172, 173, 175–176

"Moon of Pejeng" (drum), 138

Mopanshan (Dangyang, Hubei), 26

Mu, king of Chu, 55, 58, 61, 62, 179n. 11

music: Chu, 122, 131, 151, 156; and inscriptions, 74, 197n. 37; and ritual, 68, 69, 71, 73, 148, 156, 184n. 4; and shamanism, 137, 153

Music Bureau (Han), 152

musical instruments, 171, 209n. 49; Chu, 26, 35, 37,

103, 107; and shamanism, 45, *131*, 137, pl. 1; in Zeng Hou Yi tomb, 38, 188n. 25

myths, 47, 81, 123, 129, 130–131, 196n. 8

Nanchang Basin, 4

Nang lineage, 55, 58

Nang Wa, 65, 66

Nanjun (Qin prefecture), 87

Nanling Mountains, 115, 116

Nanyang Basin, *12*, 14, 15, 17, 18, 20; Chu sites in, 27, 28–29

Nanyang County (Nanyang Basin), 27, 28

Neixiang County (Nanyang Basin), 27, 28

Neolithic period, 40, 99–100, 125, 129; shamanism in, 136, 137

nine, significance of number, 63, 174

Nine Caldrons, 63, 67, 69, 195n. 110

Nine Heavens, 212n. 6

"Nine Songs" ("Jiu ge;" *Chuci*), 136, 139, 145, 151, 164, 165

Ningxiang (Changsha, Hunan), 125

Niuxingshan (Hunan), 28, 107

northern bias, 1–2, 51, 191n. 20

Northern Dipper (Beidou), 172, 210n. 56

Northern School, 10–11, 12, 181n. 45, 185n. 45

Nügua, 3, 43, 130, 131

oaths, 94, 96–97

officials: Chu, 52–53, 55, 56, 106, 107; increasing power of ritual, 67–68, 75, 76, 150; nonroyal, 64–66; reluctant, 61; righteous, 66, 146; shamans as, 161; titles of, 53–54, 56

"100 Yue," 108, 116, 183nn. 84, 86

ornamentation: animal, 35, 36; on bronze vessels, 23, 25, 26, 35, 168; Huai style, 116, 133, 134; naturalistic, 40–43

painting, 47; lacquer, 41, 42, 43, *134*, 135, 137, pl. 1; on silk, 26, 42, *145*

Pan Cheng, 185n. 16

Pan Chong, 193n. 67

pan vessels, 22, 25

Panlongcheng (Hubei), *24*

Panyu (Guangzhou), 114, 115, 116, 117

Paper, Jordan, 138

Pazyryk (Siberia), 137, 209n. 33

Pei (home of Liu Bang), 146–147

Peng Hao, 86, 87, 88, 89

Watson, Burton, 80

weapons, 31, 38, 99, 100, 106; Ba, 109; from Baoshan, 82, 107; inscriptions on, 74, 76; lacquerware handles for, 105; and trade, 112, 115; Yue, 108, 109. *See also* axes

Wei, Empress, 161

Wei, state of, 17, 19, 64, 73

Wei Ao (Sunshu Ao), 60, 61, 78, 196n. 18, 197n. 21

Wei lineage, 29, 55, 58, 70, 71, 75

Wei Zipeng, 29

Weigang (Yicheng, Hubei), 27

weiyi (awe-inspiring decorum), 68, 69, 72

Weizi Ping, 70–71, 197n. 25

Weld, Susan, 77–97

wen (ritual/literary merit), 71, 74–75, 76

Wen, Duke of, 155

Wen, Emperor (Han), 158

Wen, king of Chu, 59, 62, 74–75, 80, 179n. 14

Wen, king of Zhou, 9, 10, 69, 74–75, 200n. 8

Wen Chongyi, 177n. 3

weng vessels, 104

Wey, state of, 17, 64

wooden tomb furnishings, 25, 26, 31, 37

wu (female shamans), 68, 209n. 42

wu (martial), 71, 72, 74–75, 76

Wu, city of, 178n. 13

Wu, Emperor (Han), 140, 143, 151, 158; and shamanism, 152, 153–154, 156, 157, 160–161

Wu, king of Chu, 55, 74–75, 179n. 14

Wu, king of Zhou, 9, 69, 71, 74–75, 80, 159

Wu, Prince (Wangzi Wu), 70–72. *See also* Wangzi Wu bronzes

Wu, state of, 75, 180n. 35, 198nn. 47, 49; Chu relations with, 13, 14, 16, 17, 19, 20, 56, 59, 65–66, 79, 180nn. 22, 36, 182nn. 60, 63; culture of, 31, 105, 123, 187n. 113, 205n. 42

Wu Qi, 56, 64–65, 183n. 84

Wu Rui, 4

Wu She, 65

Wu Xian (Shaman Xian), 136

Wu Yu, 79–80, 86, 95, 203n. 89

Wu Zixu, 61, 65–66, 162

Wuxi City (Qianzhou, Jiangsu), 28, 31

Wuxingzhan text (Mawangdui), 128

Wuyang County (Fangcheng Wai region), 27

Xi, state of, 15, 181n. 51

Xi Wan, 65

Xi Yuan, 199n. 4

Xia dynasty, 2, 142

xian (male shamans), 68

Xiang, Duke, 103

Xiang, state of, 181n. 50

"Xiang Jun" (one of the "Nine Songs"), 164

Xiang River, 115, 116, 158

Xiang Yu, 1, 146, 147, 148

Xiangling, battle at, 83

Xiangxiang (Hunan), 32

Xiangyang County (Hubei), 27, 28

Xiangyin (Hunan), 28

Xiao, state of, 16

Xiao Zhu, state of, 19

Xiaojiawuji (Hubei), *100*

Xiasi (Xichuan, Henan), 27, 29, 34, 106, 184nn. 5, 8; bronze artifacts from, 22, 23, 24, *33, 34*, 35, 36, 37, 39, 40, 184n. 7; human sacrifice at, 38, 188n. 24; inscriptions from, 70–71; and location of Chu, 11, 179n. 20

Xichuan County (Henan), 27, 28, 34, 75, 184n. 12. *See also* Xiasi

Xiguan (Nanyang County), 27

xing (kinship term), 53–54, 190nn. 14, 15, 17, 193n. 68, 203n. 68

Xinjian (Jiangxi), 28, 32

Xinjiang Province, 138

Xinyang (Henan), 26, 27, *131*, 133, 137, 184n. 13, pls. 1, 10

Xinzheng (Henan), 45

xiong (title), 53–54, 190n. 17, 192n. 44

Xiong Li, 179n. 7

Xiong Qu, 2, 179n. 11, 180n. 28

Xiong Shen *zhan*, 23

Xiong Yi, 2, 10

Xishuangbanna Autonomous Region (Yunnan), 110, 205n. 40, 206n. 75

Xiwangmu (Queen Mother of the West), 139, 142–143, 208n. 20

Xixia County (Henan), 27, 28

Xiyang (ancient city), 74

Xiyi (Xixia, Henan), 27

Xu, state of, 13, 56, 180n. 33; inscriptions from, 73, 197n. 29

Xu Huanbin, 116

Xu Shaohua, 21–32, 168

Xu Wangzi Tong *zhong*, 197n. 29

Xuan, state of, 16

Index

DATE DUE

			Printed in USA

HIGHSMITH #45230